As Deep as It Gets

Other Books by Randall E. Auxier

Philosophy of Culture as Theory, Method, and Way of Life: Contemporary Reflections and Applications (co-edited with Eli Kramer, Przemyslaw Burztyka, and Marcin Rychter, 2022)

Logic: From Images to Digits (2021)

Rorty and Beyond (co-edited with Eli Kramer and Krzysztof Piotr Skowroński, 2020)

Tom Petty and Philosophy: We Need to Know (co-edited with Megan Volpert, 2019)

The Philosophy of Umberto Eco (co-edited with Sara G. Beardsworth, 2017)

Metaphysical Graffiti: Deep Cuts in the Philosophy of Rock (2017)

The Quantum of Explanation: Whitehead's Radical Empiricism (with Gary Herstein, 2017)

The Philosophy of Hilary Putnam (co-edited with Douglas R. Anderson and Lewis E. Hahn, 2015)

Pussycat Blackie's Travels: There's No Place Like Home by Josiah Royce (co-edited with Robin Wallace, 2014)

The Philosophy of Arthur C. Danto (co-edited with Lewis E. Hahn, 2013)

Time, Will, and Purpose: Living Ideas from the Philosophy of Josiah Royce (2013)

The Philosophy of Richard Rorty (co-edited with Lewis E. Hahn, 2010)

The Wizard of Oz and Philosophy: Wicked Wisdom of the West (co-edited with Phillip S. Seng, 2008)

Bruce Springsteen and Philosophy: Darkness on the Edge of Truth (co-edited with Douglas R. Anderson, 2008)

The Philosophy of Michael Dummett (co-edited with Lewis E. Hahn, 2007)

The Philosophy of Jaakko Hintikka (co-edited with Lewis E. Hahn, 2006)

The Philosophy of Marjorie Grene (co-edited with Lewis E. Hahn, 2003)

Hartshorne and Brightman on God, Process, and Persons: The Correspondence, 1922–1945 (co-edited with Mark Y.A. Davies, 2001)

The Philosophy of Seyyed Hossein Nasr (co-edited with Lewis E. Hahn and Lucian W. Stone Jr., 2001)

Responses to Royce: 1885–1916, three volumes (edited, 2000)

As Deep as It Gets

Movies and Metaphysics

RANDALL E. AUXIER

OPEN UNIVERSE
Chicago

To find out more about Open Universe and Carus Books, visit our website at
www.carusbooks.com.

As Deep as It Gets: Movies and Metaphysics

ISBN: 978-1-63770-008-2

This book is also available as an e-book (978-1-63770-009-9).

Library of Congress Control Number 20219411780

*This book is dedicated
to my spouse, Gaye,
with whom I watched and
discussed every single one
of these shows, and
many thousands more.*

About the Author

RANDALL AUXIER went to his first movie while *in utero*, which was *West Side Story*. He heard it without actually seeing it, of course. But he was born singing "So nice to be in America, everything free in America . . ." The doctors sent the bill anyway. Lousy bastards. That was somewhere in Kentucky, but he will find them anyway.

He grew up in Memphis, watching Elvis movies and *Bambi*. His first R-rated movie was *Serpico*, which his father regretted choosing, but it was due to Al Paccino's leftist politics, not because of the lasting scars it left on his son. Randy was well on his way to not being a movie critic, asking his father "Why did he call that man a 'fuck'? What's that Dad?" Randy learned not to ask too many questions about movies as a result. He saw *Invasion of the Mole People* on TV one Saturday afternoon and decided to study ancient civilizations that *might* invade America from underground, such as the Russian Empire, the Prussian Empire, and the British Moptops. All this led him to philosophy in about the way that all roads lead to Rome, Georgia. He teaches philosophy and rhetoric, and whatever else they let him teach, at Southern Illinois University, Carbondale.

BRUCE CHANDLER did the pictures for this book. He lives in Austin, Texas, with a spouse and a daughter and a cat named Caledonia (who will only appear from hiding when someone plays bagpipe music on an iPhone). Bruce has a degree in photography from Murray State University and his former professors have not been made aware of what he is doing with all that fine education.

Contents

Note to the Reader

To get the most out of this book, it is best to watch the movie being talked about right before reading each chapter. Having the movie or show freshly in your mind will enhance your enjoyment of these discussions. I don't bother with summarizing the plots or characters. In a number of cases, watching the movie or series again just after reading the chapter(s) will be a lot of fun too, since the discussions point out many things to watch for, to listen for, to check your responses and feelings against. If some of the chapters make you want to watch movies, then success is at hand.

But this book actually makes a fair introduction to philosophy as well as a rollicking good time. It is sufficient as a self-guided introduction, especially if you collect and peruse the "Suggested Readings" listed at the end of the book. These readings are the principal sources used in this book and provide a more serious accompaniment to this fairly light-hearted adventure through the movies. Yet, the number of chapters (fifteen) and the range of subjects is also adapted to the needs of college instructors who will have fifteen weeks of active teaching and then a week of tests. In cases where TV series are suggested, such as six seasons of *House of Cards*, or ten seasons of *South Park*, some selecting has to be done.

The approach to philosophy is decidedly Continental, with some American idealism and process philosophy in support. The emphasis of this book is on the primacy of time as a key to interpreting human experience. In that regard, existentialism, phenomenology, and process philosophy are the better guides to thinking about time in my view than the more popular approaches that depend on language analysis. Analytic philosophers might enjoy reading this book, but I doubt many would want to teach it.

The figures discussed belong to the more humanistic strains of the history of philosophy, and the favorite sources of analytic philosophy (especially the Moderns) do not make an appearance. In their place, apart from Socrates/Plato, is the Continental tradition descending from Kant, and this generally includes the American figures chosen, all of whom might loosely be described as Kantian humanists. There is no effort in this book to balance the sources (one cannot cover everything), but the traditional branches of philosophy are all treated in their turn and clearly defined.

A student who goes through this book will be introduced to ethics, aesthetics, political philosophy, metaphysics, and the theory of knowledge. There is only a light treatment of logic as is needed for metaphysics (and the logic is Kant's, not the extensional logics in the Frege-Russell tradition). Still, students will learn what Kant called "intellectual imagination," how it works in the creation of stories, from mythic to modern. The narrative aspect of this book permeates every chapter— that philosophizing involves telling stories about life that are art, and making up stories that aren't life but provide a contrast to it.

If one were to think of a single philosopher whose theories are closest to what is in this book, it would be Hayden White (who is not even mentioned in the book, but whose humanism is a point of reference, for those who know his work), that would work well as a suggested collection of texts for such an introductory course. A number of other late twentieth-century humanists would also be useful traveling companions, such as Isaiah Berlin, Francis Yates, Owen Barfield, Hans Georg Gadamer, Umberto Eco, Claes Ryn, and Donald Phillip Verene. Of these, only Eco really shows up in this book as a source, but they all hover in the background.

There are a few "bad guys" in the tradition, such as the followers of Leo Strauss, the followers of Heidegger, the followers of Freud, and others who have allowed themselves to become cultish, but I hope I have shown sufficient respect for the philosophers with whom I disagree, if not for their followers. It is certainly not my intention to discourage anyone from reading these masters, only from falling into slavish devotion to any single thinker. I hope to help readers learn to see and value things in the movies that reinforce the philosophical moments that everyone experiences, to value their own insights into the shows they watch, to reflect on stories, characters, and ideas that appear in the movies. And I want readers to add to what I see, and, if they are inclined, to take up interpretations contrary to mine. A healthy discussion is good for everybody.

From the Alamo Draft House to the Livingroom Couch (Or There and Back Again)

Don't be a slyboots. No one likes a shyboots.

—STEVE MARTIN, *Cruel Shoes*

First things first. I don't claim to be a sophisticated film critic. I'm just like you (unless you are a sophisticated film critic, in which case, bully for you). I watch movies because I like movies. I think about movies because I think about everything. It's a problem. I'm a problem thinker, maybe an addict. Be that as it may, I figured out a way to make a living from my problem, so, from the jaws of pathology comes . . . what? Does pathology have jaws? Maybe it has *Jaws*. Shit that movie scared me. I was fourteen when I saw it at the theater. Still thinking about it. See what I mean?

So I admire sophisticated film critics. They know all sorts of fancy things I don't know. They actually study movies and stuff. I mainly watch and think. I know a little bit. I was the main character in a student movie once (like, in 1983), may my friend who made it rest in peace. He was not a happy person but I liked him. I hope he destroyed the movie, which was inspired by *A Clockwork Orange*. My university had a well-known film department and people came from all over to major in film-making.

The guy who lived across the hall from me in the dorm became a famous Hollywood director. We talked about movies all the time. He took our group of friends to the art cinema to see this great young pair of brothers who had made a student film called *Blood Simple*. He said they would be famous. He was right. He also took us all to see *Mystery Train*, the Jim Jarmusch movie. We were all in Memphis where the film was set, so it was a lesson in how to use a city as a set. That now famous director explained many things to us. He doesn't answer my e-mails. So I won't name him.

Ironically, I had a bit part in another movie last year. I played an irritable and demanding Hollywood director, modeled roughly on Jim Jarmusch. I think he's a great director, but I'm a terrible actor. In one scene I lose my temper and smash a cell phone to bits. We had to do about twenty takes (very complicated scene with many moving parts), so I got to smash that phone twenty times (the props people had one that would fly into pieces but could be re-assembled). It was out of doors and started to rain before the director really got what he wanted, but he later said he made it work with what he had.

How? I have no idea how something like that is done. Fortunately, the movie is in Polish (my parts are in English, but the rest isn't), so that should discourage my friends from wanting to see it. I still have no idea how movies are really made. That's my point. Seems like magic to me. I am fascinated by movies in about the way a gorilla is fascinated by a big red ball. If I seem to know what I'm talking about regarding movies at any point in this book, I assure you it's an illusion.

So, I do know some things, but I don't know shit about the movies. This book is for people who don't know shit about the movies. People who do know shit will be disappointed, so they should stop reading. Or not. But it's on you. If you keep reading and you find yourself saying "This idiot doesn't know what he's talking about," just remember, I said it first. Na-na-na-na-na. I hope this is out of the way. I am thinking of one of my colleagues at the university who is a professor of film studies, and I hope he doesn't read this. I admire him, but I don't wish to bear his opinion.

The Slow Death of My Imagination (and Yours)

What I *do* know about is what it's like to love movies. And so much so that they really do and always have been the images that fill my head and accompany both my waking and dreaming with narrative, shots and angles, continuities and discontinuities that make me wonder whether people who lived before movies existed didn't have a completely different sort of consciousness than we have.

Let me give an example. I read Tolkien's hobbit books long before anyone had tried to bring them to any kind of screen. I had a mental image of Bilbo and Frodo and Golem and Smaug. I know I did. But now I can only see Peter Jackson's versions of them. I am stuck with Elijah Wood. You probably are too. I can't even remember how I once imagined these characters that were so close to my heart. It's just gone. Same for the Harry Potter characters. Once I've seen a movie, it's like I can't unsee it and return to the power of images that was *mine*. My autonomy of imagination has been seized by some casting director or art director and becomes his/her permanent captive. There is a part of me that hates this, doesn't *want* to see the movie after I read the book. But I always do it anyway.

My lifetime coincides with the rise of "TV consciousness." By contrast, "movie consciousness" already existed when I appeared on the scene. My mother had read *Gone with the Wind* before it was a movie. They had no movie house where she grew up in rural Alabama. And the one that was closest was well beyond her family's reach and means—not a good use of money when having shoes to wear was a genuine luxury. I never asked her whether Clark Gable, et al., had replaced her imagined characters. But I know she loved the movie when she finally saw it. I have never read that book. I don't intend to, now that I realize it glorifies and sentimentalizes things I hate. But for people of my mother's generation, movies were magic beyond *my* imagining. They only knew the big screen.

If you grow up with TV, it can even be confusing to grasp the difference. You know it's different, but TV is not some johnny-come-lately for people my age, like it was for my parents; it's the visual record of our lives. I can't easily imagine the world without it. Sort of like my students today try to imagine the world without cell phones –and fail. For my parents' generation, the movies played that role, that and the radio, especially radio theater. By the time I was cognizant, radio was for cool music and news, and that was about it. Movies were for family outings, and TV was for everyday entertainment. That's just how the world *is*, I grew up believing.

I now understand the story of TV and the movies better. Yet, none of us knew where it was *going*. I now had two lethal instruments to kill my imagination. By the time video games, computers, and cell phones arrived on the scene, I had little left to destroy. But you young people? How will your imaginations survive this barrage of images? If I do have some young readers, buckle-up kiddies, I'm taking you on a tour of the past so you can learn some things about how we arrived in the glorious present (and I grant it is pretty good to be alive right now, since I still am and so many others aren't).

A Little History (Very Little)

When television appeared on the mass market (late 1940s—and that is before my time, if you're wondering), people said it would kill the movies. People were wrong. If anything, the movies got more popular. The movie experience was different from TV, and—my point—so were the shows. Early television was more indebted to the theater than the movies. If TV killed anything, it was radio theater. I love watching those old TV shows, but they have no kinship to the movies of the same time. By the time I can remember any new movies they were *very* sophisticated. TV was simple and stupid: game shows, soap operas, situation comedies, cowboy serials, an occasional baseball game (man, I *lived* for the Saturday Game of the Week).

But soon enough, TV decided to try to compete. They were tired of paying exorbitant prices for the rights to air Hollywood movies. They said "fuck it, we'll make our own." In 1966, NBC started its *World Premier Movie* series, and ABC followed in 1969 with its *Movie of the Week* series. Most of these were B-quality movies, but people ate 'em up, sorta like they ate up B-movies from Hollywood. We like bad movies. We always liked bad movies. Quentin Tarantino taught us how *good* bad movies really are. I have a bit to say about him in what follows.

Once in a while something among the dull made-for-TV movies shined, like Stephen Spielberg's first feature film ever, *Duel* (1971), starring Dennis Weaver. *That* one even had a *theatrical* release *in Europe* in 1973. Christ on a cracker! The lines began to blur. There used to be a real distinction between TV stars and movie stars, and it wasn't easy to make the transition –Clint Eastwood managed it by taking risky roles in Spaghetti Westerns, but it paid off for him. The spell of the movie house's superiority was broken gradually as more and more movie stars began to realize that they needed to do TV. It took thirty years. The path is still rougher from TV to movies than from movies to TV. But the path into the movies *as a starting place* is no cakewalk either. You're an actor, you're waiting tables, someone says, "Hey, I got a commercial for you, pays $350." You take it.

Over time, there was a greater convergence of TV and the movies. As HBO and Cinemax emerged, the made-for-TV movies got better and better. Hollywood began releasing some of its (unpromising) movies straight to video so they could compete in the growing video rental market. People finally *were* staying home, preferring that to the arduous (not) trip to the multi-plex cinema at the mall. They could have a beer at home, after all, and popcorn, for a lot less money. The cinema owners had to get creative. The seats got more comfortable, the beer became available (still highway robbery), and eventually they had to start selling total experiences.

Remember the Alamo

It was 1997. Enter the Alamo Draft House. The clever people in Austin realized that the experience of going-to-the-movies was actually what they needed to sell, and that the movie was important but not the *only* important thing. People would get a group of friends together and go see a movie they could easily watch on their increasingly large TVs at home, but do the Alamo for a night out. A classic movie was just as good (indeed, better) than a first run movie. Who doesn't want to see *Casablanca* on the big screen, again? Hell, *I* do. Here's looking at *you* Humphrey. They made a shit-ton of money and now they have, like, forty cities all over North America.

So, the wait staff seats us, takes our order (and the food is going to be good, too), brings it to us just as the main feature starts, comes by to refill our beer every half hour, and they will kill anyone who talks or pulls out a cell phone, and it costs about the same as dinner out. Everyone here has seen this movie before. There are occasional comments. From the screen we hear: "It seems the Colonel has been shot," and we hear in our minds, as everyone thinks "Round up the usual suspects." The audience shares a public laugh. The *experience* is different from the living room couch, and we *will* pay for it.

Is the first-run movie in trouble? Yes and no. The Alamo doesn't need it, can take it or leave it. Still, the opportunities for high-end writers, directors, crews, and actors have never been better. A new type of TV series is appearing at about this same time—*The Sopranos* leads the way. No one grasps yet that this is going to change everything. These series offered ambitious directors, writers, and eventually actors, a path around what little was left of the Hollywood studio system. The HBO movies were often good enough to compete with the Hollywood films, so the Golden Globes (RIP) starts to offer an important series of awards for these films, and the recipients *don't* want to "thank the Academy and all the little people." You wanna talk about biting the hand that feeds you? Jesus.

Down but Not Out in Hollywood

At this moment in history, the idea of a bigger canvas to paint on—the story arc of a seven-season series—began to become a clear path to the sort of stardom that only the Hollywood block-buster could have produced in earlier decades. The new Richard Burton is the unlikely Brian Cranston, straight from *Malcolm in the Middle* to Heisenberg and show-biz immortal-ity. And shortly thereafter, the subscription services start to kill the video stores, and eventually Netflix and Hulu become as important in movie-making as any major studio ever was. That was where the energy, the risk-taking, and the big budgets set-tled in. The talent followed the money. They have a way of doing that. You would too.

Hollywood was down but not out. They had to learn a few licks from their more adventurous new competitors, but they were still selling tickets. To give one example, Stephen King's epic coming-of-age horror novel *It* was released in 1986. By then, a number of King stories and novels had been made into successful shows of numerous sorts. *Stand By Me*, was break-ing records at that very moment, critically acclaimed, taken seriously. This is not to mention *The Shining* (the critics hated it, the public loved it), *The Dead Zone*, and of course *Carrie*. *Salem's Lot* was a made-for-TV mini-series that worked (nomi-nated for three Emmys and with European theater releases in a cut-down version).

But there was a problem with *It*. *It* was over 1100 pages long and featured seven main characters, none of whom could be consolidated or cut. And scene after scene was simply writ-ten as if for the screen. And *everybody* read the book. You just couldn't get *It* into a movie *intact*. So they tried a TV miniseries (1990). Not very satisfying, even with the creepy and oh-so-excellent Tim Curry as Pennywise the evil clown. Everyone who ever read the book wanted to see, well, *every* scene, except-ing perhaps the orgy scene featuring eleven-year-old children. I couldn't even *read* that part. Geez Louise, Steve! Is nothing sacred? Could you just *not* do that, *please*? I'm going to leave that aside, and I wish Mr. King had done the same. Still, this novel is an astonishing organic whole and needed to be *pre-sented* whole. Definite exception of an orgy among children.

It still hasn't been done as a whole, so let me play the prophet. To show, in passing, that Hollywood is down but not out: Hollywood's establishment center, from New Line Cinema to Warner Brothers, collaborated on a huge new production, in two parts, released in 2017 and 2019, of *It*. Part one became the fifth highest grossing R-rated film of all time (even adjusted for infla-tion) and the highest grossing horror film of all time. People wanted *It*. And they went to the big screen to get *It*. Part two did-n't do as well, but it grossed $473 million as of this writing.

Anyone can see the next thing that will happen. So maybe I'm not a prophet. There will be a Netflix or Hulu or HBO *series*—after all, that's how Hulu did, with fair success, the equally long King novel *11/22/63*. I personally subscribed to Hulu just to see it, and we still have Hulu, so I guess that worked for them. They had the time, the space and the budget, so *11/22/63* was pretty well done. They spread it over eight two-hour episodes. But now my picture of the main character, Jake Epping, will always be James Franco, dammit. Couldn't they have gotten Tom Hanks?

The Disaster

And then, to bring this story to its ugly end, COVID. Great for Netflix and Hulu and HBO. A bummer for the cinemas. Who could have imagined the whole damn world locked in their living rooms for a fucking year? (Pardon my French. You will have much to pardon in this book.) There we were. With nothing to please us but . . . HBO, Netflix, Hulu, and their lesser cousins. You want a conspiracy theory? How about HBO created COVID? But even the lucky (if luck it was) streaming services had to halt production on their new content. I have been waiting a very long time for the next season of *Outlander* . . .

Will the cinemas ever bounce back? Hard to say, but in my little town, they just re-opened the multi-plex cinema at the mall, and it had been closed for five years. I think *some* people are betting that there is likely a real itch in the pants of the public to get back out and into their comfy new stadium-style cinema seats. The pandemic keeps sucking, in waves, but beyond it? Probably movies. The movies and TV have merged and then re-emerged as new and better beasts than they were apart. The lines have been effectively erased and we still have both and better, if you ask me.

Like a lot of people, then, I have also spent a lot more time with movies of all kinds since the disaster. I took the time to see a bunch of movies for the first time that I had "always been meaning to see," and binged a bunch of series too, and I re-watched some of my favorites, including pretty much everything in this book. It is amazing to me how different things seem on the far side of this disaster—if we are on the far side, which is unclear as of spring 2022. A young friend of mine wrote an article recently in which he argued, convincingly, that the movies have lost the power they once had to bind us together, socially, culturally.[1] But he was talking about the old way of seeing the cinema and movies, pre-pandemic. I think something else is afoot now, something we couldn't have foreseen, something culturally and socially powerful.

I did not have that criterion specifically in mind when I chose the movies and series that are discussed in this book, but as I now survey the whole, I see that one thing all these shows have in common is tremendous social and cultural impact—some were mainly important at some time in history, like *Lifeboat*, while others have perpetual power, like *Oz*. Some are yet to exercise their full power, like *His Dark Materials*, but I am pretty confident people will say that all of these shows are "important" in some sense.

These movies and TV series end up covering, somewhat unevenly, pretty much the whole history of the movies, with representatives from about every decade since the advent of the talkies (with a cluster from the 1990s, admittedly). I wasn't trying to do that either, but I now appreciate the span that ended up getting covered. There was also an unintended predilection for American-made shows. The Brits will get some serious creds when I discuss Monty Python and *House of Cards*, but pretty much it's a New World affair. In my view, the US has contributed very little to the world that is of lasting significance, but our movies and our music are exceptions. It's not that Americans are better at this than other places and peoples, it's that Americans are not good, in the scope of history, at very many things (making money is an exception, too), and in movies and music, we actually do have something permanent to contribute.

The criteria I *actually* used in selecting the shows were opportunity and preference. In terms of opportunity, often someone was doing a book and I was invited to contribute. Or in the case of *Oz*, I was (co-)doing the book and contributed. Many of the chapters in this book appeared, in a different form, in other books. They have been updated and rewritten into a single narrative here. In terms of preference, all of these shows made me think, as I said, and I liked that and liked something (or many things) about these shows, and all of them led me to trace my reflections on the action, dialogue, photography, etc., into what I know about philosophy. So, that's what every chapter does, in some way. The shows are platforms for thinking philosophically. And that brings me to this next (and final) topic.

---

[1] See Federico Giorgi, "The Role of Phantasy in Relation to the Socially Innovative Potential of Filmic Experience."

Movies and Metaphysics: Better Together

This book is going to take cinema and TV together under the name "the movies." There are a few things I will talk about that never made it to the big screen. I will talk about *South Park*, for example, but after all, there was a very successful movie (war with Canada!). Even the most movie-ish of movies eventually shows up on our increasingly huge home theater screens. I don't see any point in treating these shows as fundamentally different. Even if they once were, they aren't for us today. It's all the movies.

But, as I said, what does any of this really have to do with philosophy? A lot, actually. I think that most people find themselves thinking about the philosophical ideas they see depicted in the movies –they're everywhere. But more important is the thinking we do *on our own* as a result of the movies. Most movies, even bad ones, have themes and moral dilemmas and existential struggles that we understand and identify with.

I watched *Forbidden Planet* for the first time recently. It is awful, in an excellent way. I had meant to see it ever since I was an undergraduate and was seeing *The Rocky Horror Picture Show* every week—they sing about that movie in the wonderful opening number. It took over thirty-five years and COVID to provide the opportunity. But there you are: the well-meaning Mad Scientist has externalized his own ego-id complex and now it's trying to have sex with his daughter, Anne Francis.

You think I could write an essay on *that*? Hell, anybody could. As if that macho astronaut-hero doesn't have in mind to do the same thing to Anne. (And as if the male half, and some of the females in the audience aren't following that same naughty path of unconscious desire from their seats.) The distance between Stephen King's actual gangbang of Beverly Marsh in *It* and the imminent situation of Anne Francis in that movie is, well, the distance is not great. And it's icky, and we don't want to see it, but we sort of do want to *think* it, unconsciously, from a safe and condemning distance.

And that's only the beginning of the boundaries that movies allow us to transgress in our minds, while feeling shocked in our senses and sensibilities. In this book I will connect some of the movies to some of the issues. Nobody could get at all the issues. But I'll cover a pretty big spread here. I hope it confirms some of what you already thought about. I also hope it gives you new things to think about and guides you to some of the philosophers in our history who explored those thoughts.

But why metaphysics and not, say, epistemology or ethics? The first reason is personal. Everything I touch turns to metaphysics anyway, and I can't help it. I'm like Joyce Taylor in "Rappaccini's Daughter" (from *Twice Told Tales*, 1963, one of Vincent Price's best performances, in my opinion). I have been slowly poisoned by a life of metaphysics and now am unable to touch anything without killing it ontologically. I note that the first vignette in that movie is "Dr. Heidegger's Experiment," and it seems almost impossible to me that Nathaniel Hawthorne could have, in 1837, understood what Heidegger would write in 1927, but seeing is believing. "Time takes its toll," as Riff Raff famously said. I'll take on that Heidegger problem in Chapter 5.

So, in my weird brain (and I have the scans to prove it is in fact weird), ethics and politics and logic and aesthetics all just become types of metaphysics. Whether I was born that way or got that way by drip-drops is immaterial. Second, metaphysics is, they say, the Queen of the Sciences. I looked around and found there was no King of the Sciences, which suits me just fine, so I settled for the highest ranking royal available, and I assume it commands all the others. About like the venerable Elizabeth II so successfully controls her own family . . . (and who among us didn't watch *The Crown*? Fess up). So in the end, this is both metaphysics *in* the movies and a metaphysics *of* the movies. You'll see.

In my opinion, you can justify the time spent here, to yourself and others, by feeling like you're learning something. Or you can just have fun with it. I'm doing some of both. I watch these movies and I think. Having thought I want to discuss. Having discussed I want to write. Having written I want someone to read it. That's your job. I hope you enjoy your work.

Part I

Rated G:
General Audiences

1
I Know Something You Don't Know

THE PRINCESS BRIDE

The Spaniard apologizes and says that Westley is too good; he is obliged to fight with his dominant hand. The scene pushes on for another minute or two and, sure enough, the Spaniard is going to win unless Westley makes a similar admission: "I'm not left handed either."

I have spoken with my friends who fence. I have spoken with a couple of thirty-something men who learned fencing *because* of this scene. (Is that pathetic? I don't know.) They all assure me that the difference between fencing with the left hand, and *against* the left hand, is as great a difference as one is likely to find in any sport—whether it descends from forms of combat or not. Aaron Rodgers throwing passes with his left hand would be about as easy as switching hands in fencing. Clayton Kershaw launching fastballs with his right hand would be about as easy as switch-fencing.

And yet, as all fans know, Mandy Patinkin and Cary Elwes actually performed every frame of the film and it is good enough to make real fencers go "Wow!" The actors were trained by Bob Anderson, the legendary British Olympic fencer and fight chore-ographer, who has many grand fight scenes to his credit, but probably nothing to equal the scene in *The Princess Bride*.

An analogy for those who better understand other sports: Kevin Costner in *Bull Durham* vs. Robert Redford in *The Natural*. I'll come back to this later in this book. I'm sorry folks, but Costner is an actual ballplayer and Redford, well, as a base-ball player, he's a good movie director. Yet, Patinkin and Elwes knew nothing, I repeat, nothing, about fencing going into the pro-duction of *The Princess Bride*. I'm told that you can't really *teach*

3

what they did with those swords to most people, with one hand, let alone both. I assume that Patinkin and Elwes harbored natural talent that they probably knew nothing about.

It was difficult not to smile as I recently re-watched Elwes flash the saber at Battery Wagner as the executive officer of the 54th Massachusetts Regiment in the 1989 film *Glory*—he was rather more convincing with that piece of hardware than was Matthew Broderick (Ferris Bueller, in charge of a whole regiment? I would like to talk to that casting director). I confess that I envy these actors their latent talent. If someone out there should contradict my fencing friends, I will have to challenge them to a duel—a test of wits, since I am clearly not anyone's physical match. But that brings me to a point.

In the classic three challenges that Westley must overcome to gain possession of his princess (anyone ever heard of Eros and Psyche? Theseus and Ariadne?), this particular tale places a strange, even uncanny, emphasis upon fair play. But the case is not simple.

Let me remind you:

1. The Spaniard announces *in advance* (before Westley made it up the Cliffs of Insanity) that he would fight lefthanded to make things interesting.

2. The Spaniard then helps Westley up to the level ground and allows him to rest before engaging in the fight.

3. Westley, having gained the advantage, decides he could sooner break a stained-glass window than kill such an able swordsman (and this is on top of the significant exchanges of genuine admiration that punctuate the sword battle).

4. When Fezzik throws his first boulder at Westley, he misses on purpose and declares himself to have done so in order to make the encounter a sporting encounter.

5. When Fezzick and Westley are differentially armed and able, they decide upon the oldest form of struggle (hand-to-hand wrestling).

6. When Vizzini is confronted with the clear physical superiority of our hero, he assumes that the hero will accept an (honorable?) exchange of wits, albeit to the death, in exchange for a physical contest that would be unequal.

The three tasks completed, only he who has, by his inordinate pride, secured his own death is in fact dead. On the other hand (and that would be the left hand), there was nothing fair in this contest of wits between Westley and Vizzini, since both cups were poisoned and our hero had immunity. Should he have been trusted? That was the act of a fool? Well, . . . let's return to this question later. Perhaps Vizzini was foully murdered, perhaps not. Let's make that our test case in this . . . shall we call it a test of wits? All's Fair . . . in love and war. You've heard that saying. Who said that? You're thinking "hmmm, maybe Shakespeare." You are wrong! (in my best Vizzini voice). It was Francis Smedley. "Inconceivable," you say. Yes, the Immortal Smedley said that. I hope I didn't ruin your day. What you need to know is whether I'm the kind of person who poisons the cup in front of himself or the one in front of you. Or both. But here are a few thoughts you might not have considered.

First, consider that both The Spaniard and Fezzick would have killed Our Hero if they had won their fights. Of course, then there would be no story, so at one level it's impossible, but at another, there's every reason to believe that both were intent upon killing Our Hero, which was, after all, their job, and no reason not to believe it. Had either succeeded, they would have been murderers, and there is at least some evidence to believe that both had killed before. They are, at best ne'er-do-wells, and at worst, simply terrible people.

Second, Our Hero has been, for some years, The Dread Pirate Roberts, who leaves no one alive. Surely he has been doing some pirating in these years, at the beginning as the First Mate of the former Dread Pirate Roberts, then as Dread Pirate Roberts with the former Dread Pirate Roberts as his First Mate, then alone. Not leaving anyone alive involves murder. Piracy is stealing, and this is not *Men in Tights*, so there's no suggestion of giving the booty to the poor. Our Hero is, therefore, an exceedingly dangerous and wicked individual.

Third, while it's true that the Prince, Vizzini, and the Six-Fingered Man are wicked, are they really any worse than Our Hero and Montoya and Fizzick? I'm not trying to get all literal and factual about a fairytale. I understand how fairytales work (although I want to say something about that in a minute). All I want to do is "level the playing field," morally speaking, to give the bad guys a sporting chance in what follows.

So just remember, everyone is a wanton murderer in this comparison, and while we know very little about how many people they have killed, the evidence points to the clear, likelihood that Westley is the worst of the lot.

An Odd Little Man

Here's a fairytale for you. There was an odd little boy born in California not far from Sutter's Mill during the last days of the

California Gold Rush. His parents had crossed the prairies and the mountains in 1849, real forty-niners, not the kind who play football. As I said, the boy was odd. He looked a bit like an insect (according to his own wife, in a later comment), with an enormous head and flaming red hair. He was a solitary, bookish boy, with a vivid imagination. His cat ran away when he was eight and he wrote an entire book (*Pussycat Blackie's Travels*) imagining the cat's adventures, though that book wasn't published until much later.

The boy's name was Josie, which was short for Josiah. Josie's family was very poor and he was often hungry as he grew up. They had to move to a big city when he was eleven, where his father could look for work, but he still went to bed hungry and with nothing but straw to sleep on for years. But he was smart and good at school, and even though the other boys picked on him, because he was funny-looking and quiet, he never caved in to their jeers and name-calling. He stood up for himself and that led to frequent fights, in which he was always whipped but never humbled.

In time, Josie grew up and got married to a very smart and beautiful and wealthy woman (who didn't mind that he looked like an insect) and they had three sons. He became one of the most famous and creative philosophers in the world, teaching at Harvard University and lecturing all over the world. From rags to riches—well, not riches in gold, but in fame and achievement—he went. He was an odd little man, but he was very widely loved and universally admired.

I wish I could say the story had a happy ending, but he died relatively young and suffered many tragedies in his life. One son was mentally ill and died at twenty-seven. He lost his closest friend at the same time. But he kept writing beautiful and profound books. When a Great War broke out in 1914, it broke his heart and his spirit because he had loved Germany, where he had learned so much and had so many friends. By the end he was very sad. Some people said that the War really killed him from sadness.

But Josiah Royce helped a lot of people with his creative ideas, and there were many, many such ideas, things no one had ever thought of before. One was the idea that we could understand the meaning of life, and its purpose, by cultivating our loyalties in just the right way. And that's the idea I want to bring back to our story about fighting left-handed.

Philosophers have always talked about the meaning of life, and about what is the best life for a human being. Since they are philosophers, they never agree—Bertrand Russell once said that the only thing two philosophers can ever agree upon is the incompetence of a third. But Royce's idea about loyalty was a new suggestion about the best life. Here is what he thought:

> Our lives get meaning from the service we give to causes that are bigger than ourselves. When we willingly pledge our devotion and make daily sacrifices and deeds of service to a cause we have freely chosen, the result is that a "self," an "individual," gradually comes into existence—the person who has done all these deeds and whose life is dedicated to the furthering of this freely chosen cause. We come to be part of a community through this service, we come to have friends, camaraderie, belonging, and most importantly a life plan that provides a purpose for our lives.
>
> The best life for a human being, then, is a life of loyal service, with others who share the cause and whose purpose is the same. Through service we overcome our selfishness, our egocentricity, our isolation from others.

Sounds like something Peter Falk might have said.

A lot of people didn't like what Royce was saying because they were worried that people can serve *evil* causes and might still become, well, relatively fulfilled in their lives while doing very wicked things—there could be honor among thieves, and pirates, for example, but that doesn't mean that the best life is one of thievery, or piracy, right? It may be pretty clear by now why I want to talk about the ideas of that odd little man, since he has some interesting answers to the complaints about honor among thieves.

Honor among Thieves

The argument about whether there really can be honor among people who are doing bad things together, or separately, is at least as old as the Common Era. Cicero talked about it in 45 B.C., and he had ample reason to worry about it. It wasn't clear whether the new dictator of Rome, Gaius Julius Caesar, was or wasn't a rogue. The world still hasn't decided that question, but it ultimately cost Cicero his life. It's a fair thing to wonder about. Can people just keep doing bad things (although they may believe them to be permissible or even good) indefinitely, without the wickedness or wrongness of the deeds eventually catching up to the evil-doers? Is there no justice in the universe?

Here we really have to make a space for fairytale logic and hold it apart from the way life really is. Not many philosophers talk about fairytales, but Susanne Langer (1895–1985), a very accomplished American philosopher, did. She says: The fairytale is irresponsible; it is frankly imaginary, and its purpose is to gratify wishes, "as a dream doth flatter." Its heroes and heroines, though of delightfully high station, wealth, beauty, etc., are simply individuals; "a certain prince," "a lovely princess."

> The end of the story is always satisfying, though by no means always moral; the hero's heroism may be by slyness or luck quite as readily as integrity or valor. The theme is generally the triumph of an unfortunate one—an enchanted maiden, a youngest son, a poor Cinderella, an alleged fool—over his or her superiors, whether these be kings, bad fairies, strong animals . . . stepmothers, or elder brothers. (*Philosophy in a New Key*, p. 175)

This all sounds pretty familiar, doesn't it, right down to the Rodents of Unusual Size? We all know the logic of fairytales, but sometimes we forget that morality has little to do with it. Moral of the story my ass. More like the immoral of the story. We just ignore it. How can that be? It gets me to thinking. Why don't I worry about showing children Westley and his dirty deeds? He's a cad. A murderer, on a wide and lengthy scale. And here they make him a hero.

The Story of the Moral

Doesn't every story have a moral? Not in the case of fairytales, as Langer says. Maybe *fables* do, and that is their purpose, to convey a moral lesson. But fairytales are about wishes, not about lessons. And satisfied human wishing is, well, shall we say, somewhat different from what satisfies our moral demands. Our younger minds want their wishes and do not much pause over the morals.

Yet, Royce's philosophy of loyalty cuts through this veil between the real world and Neverland. I think it throws a lot of light on Our Hero and on why we find his conduct satisfying, if not precisely moral. I know you wanted Westley to get his Princess. It had to happen. By hook or crook.

The reason Royce can do this bit of left-handed ethics, where other philosophers cannot, is that he takes account of our process of maturing. When we're young and we have to make a life plan, we're never really ready to do it. We're too naive to grasp what life is really like—the compromises we will have to make, the mistakes, the human weaknesses and frailties, the unforeseen tragedies and occasions of fortune, and so on. Yet, we have to make decisions that will affect everything.

A young person making a life plan is not so very different from a character in a fairytale. We are trapped in a world we never made. So, for example: Young people can easily believe that war is glorious, if older people they trust tell them so. Or they can believe that they will not themselves make the mistakes their parents made. Young people often believe they see clearly and that they choose their causes with open eyes. They do not yet understand all of the unconscious forces that move within their own depths and they usually don't realize how resistant the world is to being changed, or even bent a little, in the direction they desire. They don't know the hardness. They also don't know what lies within the depths of other people.

Yet, and here's the rub, they are capable of loyalty and they are able to serve. Young people make the best soldiers, mainly because they don't really understand what they are doing. You can convince someone eighteen years old that war is glorious; you can't convince someone who is twenty-two of that. That difference in years and experience is very real and it changes both the community and the individual who serves.

It isn't surprising that young people choose to serve conflicting causes—some that bring them into conflict with others, some that are in conflict with others they simultaneously serve, says the devout Christian, age nineteen, who kills civilians in a war. Who would Jesus slaughter? Not many of these young people are envisioning world peace and universal tolerance. To a kid that age, there is only a difference of degree between competitive high school sports and war.

Getting Your Ass Handed to You

Royce wrote an interesting essay on football in 1908, when football was in poor repute and there was widespread talk of banning the game. There he says:

> I know some public servants, men now devoted to the noblest and hardest social tasks, who assert that they personally first learned unselfish devotion, the spirit of "team work" (that is, of social service) on the football field; and who say that the "roughness' and perhaps their own broken bones, first gave them the needed moral lessons in what have since proved to be the most delicately tender and the most earnestly devoted forms of loyalty. ("Football and Ideals," p. 216)

So, a process of maturation that passes through such teamwork is a part of developing into a better servant. But it is only

a part. Losing the game with one's teammates, is more instruc-
tive than winning it. Finding a way to "pick up" a teammate
who has disappointed the team, and turning the mistake into
a gain somehow—this and dozens of other lessons of loyalty are
crucial to later life.

As I write this, a pitcher on my favorite major league baseball teams gave up ten runs in the first inning, including four
walks. He was pulled from the game while still in the first
inning. How will his teammates treat him tomorrow? Being
grown men, one assumes they will "shake it off," slap him on
the back and say "You'll get 'em next time." But in high school,
that same performance might cause permanent damage to a
person and his team. Even a grown man might not recover
from that.

I can certainly attest that I have professional colleagues
who could have benefited from being repeatedly put on their
asses, back when they were young, by a physically superior
opponent. A lot of my colleagues never suffered that kind of
defeat, and man, they needed the experience. They needed to
find themselves in a situation where no application of their
wits would save them from having the same happen again on
the next play, until the game mercifully ended. They would be
a lot less ego-centric now if they had faced this kind of hopelessness. It's the beginning of the game, the quarterback says
"Hike," and you become quickly aware that the kid on the other
side of the line, whom you will face every play for the next four
quarters, is going to kick your ass.

Don't bother looking to the coach for help. It's your job to
take that licking. I have been there myself. I once pitched a
game where I walked the bases loaded and hit the next batter,
giving up the winning run to the other team. That was when
I was about thirteen. I never pitched again. Couldn't face it.
Couldn't be that guy who loses the game for his whole team.
Makes me think about what kind of strength it takes to be a
professional athlete, or a loyal soldier. So, remember your own
youth. Remember the moment when you were most irrepara-
bly humiliated. I know you remember it. It's fucking hard to
grow up.

Let us invoke the cliché: it builds character (to have your
ass handed to you, repeatedly). One assumes that Westley and
Fizzick and the Spaniard all endured these humiliations in
the process of becoming good enough at what they do
to prevail over those who have not been so humiliated. Yet,
this is only the beginning of what Royce calls "training for
loyalty."

Training for Loyalty

The first phase of life can become an obsession, a purpose that does not open the way to anything further. In considering the Spaniard and the memory of his father, we also see that he has given his life, his all, to the relentless and cruel pursuit of the father's killer. "My name is Inigo Montoya. You killed my father. Prepare to die." He is loyal to the cause of revenge, in a highly particular sense, and it is a great motivator in learning swordsmanship, but it doesn't do much to prepare a person for anything beyond that (unlikely) goal.

That is part of the reason the Spaniard is in no position to be anything except the next Dread Pirate Roberts by the end— to steal and leave none alive. But this training also prepares him to appreciate excellence in swordsmanship for its own sake. He makes an aesthetics out of the form his revenge will take. This borders on psychosis. Yet, there is something he learns, almost incidentally, which is how to recognize and appreciate anyone else who has given such devotion to the perfecting of combat with a sword.

And yet, in doing so, Montoya becomes not a person but a stained-glass window; he is a thing of beauty, and that is impressive because there is nothing easy about it, but he is lost without a commission, without a direction given by a guiding hand. He becomes a sword for hire, even though it is beneath his artistry, and thus is prone to serving the shifting ends of a no-good weasel like Vizzini.

Seeing this, Westley spares him for the sake of art, not for the sake of goodness. A similar tale may be told about Fezzick. But Westley is different; he belongs to no other man, and that is interesting.

Songs of Innocence, Songs of Experience

When young people imagine their lives, they haven't got much more to work with than Fred Savage had when Peter Falk read him *The Princess Bride*. One of the best parts of the movie is enjoying that contrast between innocence and experience we get with those two, and the benevolence of grandfather as *he* sees one story while his grandson sees quite another.

But Rob Reiner captures a point of contact, a poignant sense that the youngster knows his grandfather knows what the youth cannot know, and senses the difference between them. But they tacitly agree to pretend it doesn't matter, at least for the time they have together—story time, and they are in it together. By conspiring so, they give the audience permission to love fairytales, too.

Still there is a lot more. Westley is the one who sees the limitations of Fezzick and the Spaniard, and he grasps how they have come to where they are. For them, struggling against him is a sporting proposition, but only because they have gotten the benefit of their own process of maturation: they have outgrown the cause they serve (currently Vizzini's business deal with the Prince), and they know how causes come and causes go. They have become artists of a high grade by following the paths they were on, and what was once mere utility has become, for them, an exercise that brings its own inherent (if temporary) reward. They have come to the point that what is serious for others is merely play for them. Westley sees this and understands it. These artists do not have to be killed, they need to be directed into causes worthy of their achievements, and they have some understanding of the emptiness in their lives. They are suitable for higher service, in their innocence.

This situation does not hold for the Six-Fingered Man, who has sunk into a debauched enjoyment of physical power over others, and is now a sadist. This artistry of Fezzick and the Spaniard also does not describe the Prince, who is locked in a Machiavellian Game of Thrones and cares nothing for anything in which the stakes are lower. And this does not describe Vizzini who has become an arrogant mercenary who will sell his unusual services to anyone who can pay his price. These are pathologies of sex, power, and gain.

That is not Fezzick and the Spaniard. With interventions at earlier stages, these loyalists might have been saved, but by the time Our Hero encounters them, all innocence is lost. They have chosen their own ends, as the fairytale makes perfectly plain. Our test case, then, is complete. Vizzini got what he had chosen. So did the others.

Lost Causes

Westley and Buttercup are a different story altogether. Royce says that you don't advance beyond the fairytale version of your own life-plan until you've failed, and that can happen in a lot of different ways. There are two important ones.

The first happens to people who rise higher and higher within the service of their cause, until they can no longer distinguish themselves from the causes they serve. These people always eventually betray their own causes, and they do it semideliberately. At some unconscious level, they want to be free of their cause. The cause doesn't fail, but the individual does. Having done so, such individuals occupy a position of ignominy and humiliation. Nothing can be done for them until, gradually, the community that remains in the ruins of their betrayal begins to pick up the pieces and to do the work of atonement, rebuilding the community.

Such is ever the fate of the powerful, and this is the fate of the Prince in our (favorite?) movie. We don't see what happens, but our Grandfather points out that it is better if he has to live through the repairing of the damage he has done, although the grandson expresses his disdain for this outcome. Still, you know and I know that it is more satisfying that the Prince should live with his ignominy and wait to see whether anyone will reach into the abyss he inhabits and remind him, "You are our prince, after all, worthless as you are." Thus does the traitor to his own cause rejoin his community, and we know the repair work is never entirely successful.

But that is not what happens with Westley and Buttercup. Both have failed, but neither one has really betrayed the "cause," which is their love. Still, each lives in the abyss of loss. They assume it is permanent. That love, that union, *was* their cause. They serve not one another, but their union, as an ideal. And their union cannot be. And that's how life goes sometimes.

When Westley leaves to make his fortune, it is for the sake of the cause; and when news filters back to Buttercup (and it is not false news) that his voyage has fallen prey to the DPR, their union becomes, as far as she knows, a lost cause. Westley is in limbo, not knowing whether he can ever reclaim the cause, but unlike her, he actually knows there is a slim hope. That hope inhibits his moral development in a way that hers is not inhibited. *She* serves a lost cause. Royce says:

> The lesson of the history of lost causes . . . has deep importance for our individual training. We do not always learn the lesson aright. . . . Defeat and sorrow, when they are incurred in the service of a cause, ought to be a positive aid to loyalty. . . . they enable us to see whether we have really given ourselves to the cause, or whether what we took for our loyalty was a mere flare of sanguine emotion. When sorrow over a defeat in the service of our cause reverberates through us, it can be made to reveal whatever loyalty we have. (*The Philosophy of Loyalty*, p. 136)

In the permanent loss of our cause, we face ourselves in the raw, so to speak, and know what we have been. The structural weakness in *The Princess Bride* is that the person who suffers this loss most fully, Buttercup, is passive. She doesn't *do* anything except wait and, ultimately, in despair, gives up on serving the lost cause. That isn't good storytelling. And it's totally sexist. Claire Underwood wouldn't stand for it (I'll have something to say about her later in the book) –and neither would the mature Robin Wright, but hey, she needed the part.

The person who suffers defeat, Westley, is unable (or unwilling?) to return to serving the cause until it is (truly) on the brink of being lost—the impending death of Buttercup, or her marriage to the Prince, either of which will transform Westley's cause into a lost one. Thus, he never really travels through the abyss of the lost cause, as she does.

This moral differential may explain why Westley does not emerge from his experience of confronting the Dread Pirate Roberts (and then *becoming* the Dread Pirate Roberts), as a morally purified symbol. Why, after all, did he wait so long to return? Was he just too busy *being* the Dread Pirate Roberts until news reached him that Buttercup was actually going to be obliged to move on with her life? Couldn't take a holiday? Really? Just couldn't send word?

I will now make an inference:

I do not think Westley grew up. He didn't mature. He was off playing pirate. I think he learned some valuable things and became the cleverest but not the wisest of the boyz. That is one reason he needed to die—well, mostly. He actually hadn't come back from the lost cause until Billy Crystal raised him from the dead. Then and only then is he fit to lead his band in the triumphal reclamation of his cause.

Build Me Up, Buttercup

Seriously? That's supposed to be a woman's name? No. It is the name of a placeholder, not a woman. But geez, is Robin Wright ever a total babe—then and now? Still, I need a real princess for the bride in this story, a three-dimensional woman. There really is something to be said for seeing Buttercup as Jenny in *Forrest Gump* and as Claire Underwood in *House of Cards*. I need all of that complexification in *my* Bittercup (yes, that's not a typo), supplied by the amazing actress, in order to imagine the character of Buttercup in something more than cartoon terms.

Buttercup is the only character in the story who's really in a position to grow from the arrangement of her external circumstances. So . . . Claire Underwood is the one who would *really* understand the meaning of "As you wish." And Jenny needed to find a way to escape the abuse of her childhood and never could see love for what it was, or appreciate it. Together, these three women, with Robin Wright's help, become something of a full-blooded woman.

And now I have a question for you to consider: what use would Claire Underwood have for Westley? She might do better working with the talents of the Prince, or, better yet, the Six-Fingered Man, don't you think? Now *there* was a fellow with some prospects. Just needed to find his match and helpmeet. But Buttercup, even as the helpmeet, is something less than a fully developed moral person. It's not just that Claire Underwood and Jenny are a mess, it's that all of us must learn to idealize our lost causes. Buttercup had more to gain, morally speaking, from Westley's permanent demise than from his return. When we serve a lost cause, we idealize the cause and it becomes for us something we could never have served with the same devotion when it was still an achievable goal. The memory of what *might have been* is more powerful, morally, than the striving for what might be, Royce says. That may not seem very cheery, but remember, the man looked like an insect. That's an interesting way to go through life. But there is something to what he says.

If you want to grow up, *really* grow up, you learn to respond to what is best in others, which is the earnestness with which they pursue their causes (even when their causes conflict with your own). Royce calls this being loyal *to loyalty itself*. I see you serve your cause, and you see me serve mine. What is best in me, my loyalty, hails what is best in you, your loyalty, and even if both of our ships are sinking, we are friends in a deeper sense; we are the legion of the loyal, of those who have fallen in love with the world, and whose service has been in earnest.

Revisiting our amazing swordfight, we can see that what's best in Westley hails what's best in Montoya, and there is genuine joy and admiration in their combat. And, if Royce is right, that would not be spoiled even if one did kill the other. There's such a thing as loyal killing. Westley spared Montoya not for moral reasons but for aesthetic reasons. And there was recognition across conflicting causes—neither cause being particularly exalted, but one commands our sentiment while the other does not, in that moment.

When we're allowed to see Montoya in service of his true cause (revenge), we're inspired to sympathy. I notice that Montoya does *not* fight with his left hand against the Six-Fingered Man. Sometimes we *don't* need to give people a sporting chance. That happens when they serve only themselves and their twisted egos. In cases like that, it is more merciful to put them out of their misery, which is, after all, what they have chosen. It isn't revenge, it's mercy, which is one form loyalty to loyalty can take.

Or at least, that's how the story goes, as fairytales become life-plans and life-plans become legends. Whether Westley and Buttercup lived happily ever after, well, maybe you know something I don't know, but if I had to choose Westley, or Forrest Gump, or Frank Underwood, I would think the one who knows the most about lost causes and loyalty is in the middle. As he once said to his Buttercup, "I'm not a smart man, but I know what love is." Besides, I'm pretty sure Westley died bravely at Battery Wagner, two years later, serving a very fine cause indeed.

2
Lions and Tigers and Bears

SCARY STUFF IN *THE WIZARD OF OZ*

Delightful little girls. Sadie is seven and Vega is four. They were visiting my home with their parents recently, and they come from Kansas. Hmmm, little girls from Kansas. I should have known better, but I suggested that we watch the *The Wizard of Oz* while we were babysitting the girls.

"No," said their mother, "the monkeys scare them."

Well, yeah. They scared me too when I was a kid, gave me awful dreams. But some of us sort of like the feeling of being frightened, you know? I think I might have been touching on this in the last chapter. We sort of do and don't want to see, you know? There's something alluring about it. But *why* does such stuff chill a child? And especially, *why* do things like flying monkeys give children "bad dreams."

Songs of Innocence, Songs of . . . Ignorance

We visited this theme in the last chapter, but since this is rated G, supposedly, let's continue to probe into the forbidden regions of childhood. It sort of *isn't* rated G. but it sort of *never was*, you know? Revisit Grimm's fairytales, I mean the real ones, if you dare.

There was a gloomy Dane by the name of Søren Kierkegaard (1813–1855). He thought too much. He thought so much that eventually he even thought about the question I just asked (though he never watched *The Wizard of Oz*). He said:

> Innocence is ignorance. In innocence, man is not qualified as spirit but is psychically qualified in immediate unity with his natural condition. The spirit of man is dreaming. . . . In this state there is peace and repose, but there is simultaneously something else that is not con-

tention and strife, for there is nothing against which to strive. What, then, is it? Nothing. But what effect does nothing have? It begets anxiety. This is the profound secret of innocence, that it is at the same time anxiety. Dreamily the spirit projects its own actuality, but this actuality is nothing, and innocence always sees this nothing outside itself. (*The Concept of Anxiety*, p. 41)

Whew. I warned you about Kierkegaard, right? Let me see if I can translate, and you'll have to strain your memory back to your own childhood to get a feel for this (I realize that's more of a stretch for some of you than for others).

When you're a kid, you sort of live *in* your body and that's all there is to you, apparently, just a little collection of physical functions you basically ignore, preferring instead to just experience things *innocently*. You'll become obsessed with the physical functions when you're old, and you won't talk about much else, but as a kid the world is more like a big picture show and you don't worry too much about the projector, the film, the price of a ticket, and suchlike.

But no, Kierkegaard says, even when you're a kid, there is something inside you already dreaming, your "spirit," the man calls it. What's it dreaming of? Well, basically it's your adult self, but you don't know that's what it is. So you innocently take that dream of what you *will* be, or *might* be, and you see it outside yourself, but you don't recognize it *as you*. That's because you're innocent, and you don't realize that what *the adult you* will become has done some ugly and unbearable things. Your childhood dream of you just doesn't include the shitty you that you now are. What shitty you? You already know, so get real.

You will have broken people's hearts, lied, cheated, screwed up royally, perhaps even killed. But it's all already *there*, in your dreaming spirit. Kierkegaard even says this dream of the innocent (ignorant) spirit *is* "original sin." Geez, man, give the kids a break, huh? Already dreadful sinners dreaming of their sins? Holy cod.

Fucked Up Shit

Sorry, this was supposed to be rated G. But you should know better. My point is that people didn't invite Kierkegaard to dinner, and they certainly didn't let him babysit. Maybe Pennywise the clown would have been less cruel to children. After all, he only wants to eat children. By comparison, Kierkegaard is scarier, if you ask me (and I know you didn't).

So I don't know whether any of this stuff Kierkegaard says is true. I hope not, but I admit that it makes some sense to me.

Poor Sadie and Vega, frightened by the flying monkeys, and if Kierkegaard is right, those monkeys are pretty much just external projections of what they will be and will do, or at least some part of their own hideous future deeds, a symbol in a spirit dream of their own ugly and unworthy souls.

Kierkegaard needed to lighten up. Everyone thinks so. But he's right; things that scare us are probably, at least over time, things that come to symbolize something within ourselves. We scare ourselves far more than the world scares us. That's why the scariest movies have a human "monster."

Kierkegaard also says that the "something" inside us is, apparently, nothing at all, and *that's* actually the problem. It's not that we're afraid of "nothing," it's that the nothing *inside us*, our own ignorance, our own freedom to be evil, makes us anxious, and being anxious (as children often are), we readily see in the world things (like flying monkeys) that somehow manifest physically some hint or shade of ourselves, and we fasten onto it, and then we feel afraid of *it*, instead of ourselves.

Anxiety has no special object, but fear always does. This idea is provocative, and perhaps a bit dubious. You may be inclined to dismiss it. That's what Kierkegaard expects you to do, but not because you're right. He thinks you'll be uncomfortable with this suggestion about the dream of your innocent spirit—or not so much uncomfortable as, well, actually a bit anxious. And that's a reason to think he may be right, your own discomfort.

This is subtle stuff, so let's back away from it and come back to it later, see if it's any more plausible then.

So all this set me to thinking (but then again, what doesn't? I'm not as bad about it as Kierkegaard, at least). I remember being frightened or disturbed by a lot of things in *The Wizard of Oz*, and as I got older, different things worried me, and in different ways. As I grew, it wasn't the flying monkeys anymore so much as the idea of the Wizard's demanding that a child commit murder to earn a reward he hasn't even got the power to bestow. That's one of the worst things I could ever imagine. I mean, just think of what a scary movie you could build on such a premise.

But it looks to me like that's the very essence of this story, and it's awful. Who invents such a twisted idea? I think that now I may be afraid of L. Frank Baum. So I'm still not entirely free of it, fear I mean, and my guess is that lots of people are like me in this regard. It's like the realization of how evil Westley has to be in order to stitch together the pieces of the Princess Bride. I sort of *don't want to know.*

So, I began to wonder whether a more systematic description of what was scary, and how so, might reveal a pattern. Lo
and behold, it does.

A Method in the Madness

Philosophers have a number of tricks they can use to sort out
experiences, but I think the right one for this question is a
method called "phenomenology." Now that's an imposing
word. It's really two words: "phenomenon," that is, anything
that appears in our experience, and "logos," which means a lot
of things, but one of them is "logic," or in this case, the structure and principles of the ways that things appear in our
experience.

If we can do a phenomenology of scary things in *The Wizard
of Oz*, we may find some common ground. We may ask what
things create a tension in our common anxiety in such a way as
to catapult us out of the dream of spirit and into the world of
our sense experience. I'm sure that *The Wizard of Oz*, the 1939
movie I mean, does this very well because it scares lots of kids,
most kids, and it's the same things that do it. In this case, the
experience I'm after, the "phenomenon" in this phenomenology,
is "fear," but that's just a word. It covers millions of different
experiences, just like the words "love" or "hope" do.

The philosopher Alfred North Whitehead (1862–1947)
once observed that human understanding is greatly inhibited
by the poverty of our language about subjective feelings. I
mean, one word for all the experiences that are involved in
"love"? If Eskimos can come up with thirty words for "snow,"
you would think we could all have at least a few dozen for
"love." In a sense we *do* have lots of words, for both love and
fear, but the connection of such words to all those feelings is
vague, indistinct.

Phenomenology sort of specializes in creating more distinct
connections between our inner lives, including both our feelings and our thought processes, and our descriptions of those
processes in language. It's an important part of philosophy, but
it requires a talent: the power to bring inner experience of
images to language. Some folks just don't have the talent for
isolating and holding images as they process through our
minds and imaginations; others can isolate and hold the
images, but don't have the language or the insight to describe
them for others in a valuable way.

I'm okay at this, not as good as some people I know, but good
enough that I think you'll get the hang of how this method

works. Maybe you'll start doing your own phenomenologies. But before we do any phenomenology, let's look at something a little more familiar.

Primal Stuff

There are some things that seem universally scary to pretty much *all* human beings, immediately, involuntarily, instinctively. The list of such things is not long: sudden loud noises, falling, sudden bright light, the dark, Ozzy Osbourne, and that's about it. Okay, I'm kidding. I know that not everyone is afraid of bright light. But since Kierkegaard says that in our innocence we are at one with our bodies (the "immediate unity with our natural condition"), it makes some sense to look at what happens in our bodies, our physiology, when we experience fear. It explains a lot about what happens to us, although it doesn't even begin to explain what it comes to mean to our lives (which is what Kierkegaard is more on about).

There are a lot of ways to think about our bodies. For example, we could "know our bodies" the way that athletes or dancers "know" their bodies, knowing what the body will and won't do, mastering and refining its motions. Or we can know our bodies in the sense of knowing how they look and feel. When my clothes get too tight, I "know" it's time to lay off the rich foods, and when I haven't had enough sleep, my body lets me "know." I also "know" when I'm getting angry, feeling impatient, hungry (or hangry, which combines all three of those). You get the picture.

One familiar way to think of our bodies is as objects of science, using concepts of anatomy and physiology. From that point of view, you have a little part of your brain called the amygdalae (that's two amygdalas, one on each side of your brain). Brain scientists say that these little guys process and retain emotional memories, and they sort of take quick snapshots of stuff you see or hear. Then sometimes, if the stuff happening to your senses is severe enough, your amygdalae short circuit the rest of your brain processes and send a message straight to your adrenal gland to release some epinephrine into your blood stream. The result is what's called the "fight or flight" response.

I know you've been there. You'll be minding your own business, and all of a sudden "Crazy Train" starts playing on the sound system, there is an adrenaline rush, and you know you either have to smash the radio or get out of there. You can recognize this condition easily: your heart starts beating faster, you feel like you want to run or you can't listen to another excruciating note. Bluto Blutarsky has this reaction to folk music in *Animal House*, smashes the guitar and says "Sorry." Lt. Commander Whorf re-enacts this scene in *Star Trek: The Next Generation*, smashing Giordy LaForge's mandolin. Sometimes you just have to.

The amygdalae are powerful provokers of action. This is the onset of primal fear, accompanied by disgust. Do we find this in *The Wizard of Oz*, stuff that sets off the amygdalae? Sure, there are several things. I'll just look at three. But one thing that makes a big difference to the overall experience is its duration, how long it lasts, because the duration affects the amount of "reflection," conscious thought, that accompanies the experience. Bluto Blutarsky really pauses over what he is hearing to make certain that he really has no choice but to smash the guitar.

Some experiences happen too fast for any thinking to occur, but the ones that are most interesting, in my opinion, are the ones that take just a bit of time to unfold. But we'll look at three from the movie, increasingly spread out in duration, and see how the effects are different.

Your Brain and You

Now phenomenologists are not so much interested in brain chemistry. They are interested in the you that has a brain, not the brain that has a you. They know the brain is important, but a question they like better is how those emotional memories, the sort of thing scientists say are registered in the amygdalae, come to be saturated with certain kinds of meanings. I mean, if you think about it, you'll notice that the same memories can have different meanings and carry different emotions from one person to the next. For instance, not everyone likes *The Wizard of Oz*, even when they're remembering the same movie. They have different emotive triggers and associations. Even for a single person, the same image can be experienced differently, take on different qualities, in different situations, and change over time. *The Wizard of Oz* just doesn't mean the same thing to me now that it did when I was eight, even though I do remember, sort of, what it meant back then. Yes, my brain is different now, but I don't think that's the whole reason.

So how do the images we perceive come to be experienced in such varied ways, with such varied meanings? Phenomenology is sort of an art (or some say it's sort of a science) of describing that process. And one way that we can get at it is by introducing variations in the experience to see what remains constant and what changes. It's called "imaginative variation." Let's do some of that varying with the scary stuff and see what we can see.

Naughty Glinda?

Everyone gets how scary the cyclone is, and it just goes on and on—Dorothy stomping her foot on the doors to the root cellar, running desperately, the twister getting closer and closer. Geez I hated that. But that is a long, long scare. The fact that it is in sepia tones makes it all the more ominous. But let's start with something a little quicker.

There actually is a good moment in the movie that is quite fleeting, a shock to the old amygdalae that we feel first, all over our bodies, and have to sort out later because it happens so fast. We've been dancing and singing all around Munchkinland and then without warning the Wicked Witch of the West shows up in a puff of red smoke, scattering the little people to and fro; that sets us on edge to be sure, activates our "fight" response.

But the moment that sticks in the amygdalae is when, after confronting Dorothy and Glinda (and since Glinda isn't afraid, we aren't so much either), the Witch goes to fetch the ruby slippers from her dead sister's feet. Naughty Glinda apparently waves her wand (it's off-screen) to put the slippers on Dorothy's feet instead. But of course, the image that stays with us is those legs shriveling up and withdrawing under the house.

I know you can see it right now. We all cringe. Makes you wonder who came up with that, right?

Well, in a sense, it's in L. Frank Baum's original book, but the variations make a difference. In the original book, the Wicked Witch of the West makes no appearance at all in this scene, Dorothy is all distracted with the Munchkins, and with the good Witch of the North, who is not Glinda, but rather a little old woman (and a far cry from the glamorous Billie Burke!). In Baum's tale, Glinda is the Good Witch of the South (a detail that was restored to the plot when it became a Broadway musical in *The Wiz*, along with the magic shoes being silver rather than ruby).

In the book, Dorothy has to make an extra journey to see Glinda after the Wizard fails to get her back home. But in the scene we're examining, this is what Baum says:

> Dorothy was going to ask another question [of the Witch of the North], but just then the Munchkins, who had been standing silently by, gave a loud shout and pointed to the corner of the house where the Wicked Witch had been lying.

"What is it?" asked the little old woman; and looked, and began to laugh. The feet of the dead Witch had disappeared entirely and nothing was left but the silver shoes.

"She was so old," explained the Witch of the North, "that she dried up quickly in the sun. That is the end of her. But the silver shoes are yours, and you shall have them to wear." She reached down and picked up the shoes, and after shaking the dust out of them handed them to Dorothy. (*The Wonderful Wizard of Oz*, pp. 24–25)

Yuck. Shoes filled with dead witch-dust. I wouldn't want those shoes on my feet until they'd had a bit of scrubbing, if even then. So, sort of the same thing happened in the book as in the movie, but we don't "see" it in our imaginations because it is described as having happened just the moment before our attention was drawn to the spot.

The feeling of having just missed something is very different from seeing it happen (as any moviemaker knows). That moment's respite is like arriving at the scene of a car accident while the wheels are still spinning—scary enough, but not as hard on the amygdalae as actually seeing it happen. Among the images we can't erase from our emotional memories is the stuff we see in an instant, before we can even grasp what is happening, that imprints the amygdalae. A strong link has been demonstrated by neuroscientists between these sorts of moments and Post-Traumatic Stress Disorder.

The decision to show this shriveling moment in the movie is, physiologically speaking, a recipe for PTSD, especially among kids. It lasts only a second, and in the film the Munchkins don't see it because they are cowering some distance away. The main characters do see it, as do we, but they sort of proceed as if it weren't scary. The Wicked Witch of the West, who is only a foot or two away when the shriveling occurs, only reacts to the slippers' disappearance, not to the horrendous shriveling.

No one discusses it, and we get no reassurance that we have even seen what we thought we saw. As we search our minds for the cause of this awful sight (and this happens only after we've seen it), the inference we all make is that Glinda did it with her wand, or maybe Glinda just took the slippers and the shriveling was a result of the magic in the shoes being taken away from the witch. But it's the *image* on the screen that imprints in the amygdalae, and our *reflection* (which is where phenomenology comes from, reflection) on the cause feels quite secondary. Why? And what is its phenomenological meaning?

The Men behind the Curtain

As we move from physiology to phenomenology, let's start by noticing something about the moment: the music. The moment we are discussing is accompanied by a sudden jump in volume and a highly dissonant blast of brass (this sudden loud noise signals us to be afraid, while the dissonance presses us toward disgust), then in a second or two the music is fading off into the bass instruments, a little like the music from *Jaws* when the shark has done his worst and is swimming away. If you ever doubted that this moment was intended to shock, the music will confirm that it was all well contrived by the filmmakers. As the moment fades, the music recedes again into the background and the visual images come back to the foreground of our perception, and we are being prepared for more dialogue.

I'll say more about what music does in a moment, but for now, just notice how the shocking image is reinforced by a sudden sound. Makes you wonder what your daily life would be like if it were accompanied by a movie score. It can be fun to imagine it: you walk in the door alone and your spouse says, "You forgot to pick up the kids?!?" Is that serious? A sudden dissonant chord. Or is it no big deal, just old forgetful you, backing out the door to get them . . . with a little playful clarinet flourish as in a Dick van Dyke episode . . . "whoops."

Similar sorts of effects can be achieved with shadows and light. The same event takes on a different meaning in the shadows than in bright light. Every quality of your perception can be varied to reinforce one effect or another. It's a play of the senses that is fairly delicate and thus, particular effects can be difficult to achieve. Getting something to be scary in a movie is one of the hardest effects to achieve, along with getting something to be funny. (Hitchcock was brilliant enough to do both at the same time; see *Frenzy*.)

For instance, sometimes, depending on context and set-up, showing something in bright light so that you see every detail can be scarier than showing it in shadow. The shriveling shot we are discussing is an example of that. So the reason the moviemakers show you the feet only for a second, and in bright light, is that any more time or any less light wouldn't be scary, any less time and it wouldn't register in your conscious mind what you just saw. The duration has to be just right.

So much for the physical and perceptual aspect, what about the phenomenological side?

If I Only Had a Brain

There are many things we could say, but I'm drawn to some observations that were made by a phenomenologist named Maurice Merleau-Ponty (1908–1961). He said that scientific explanations of what happens in the body are actually very different from our *experience* of our own bodies. After all, we may be terminally ill and feel just fine. The *experience* is far more basic and more important than the science, even if the science tells us stuff we wouldn't have known based on our experience. It isn't so much the body science studies that we are trying to cure; rather, the effort to cure a body is a mean of prolonging our *experience*. If you can still have all your experiences without your body, you'd be less dedicated to preserving and maintaining your body.

This seems pretty obvious, but people fall in love with science and forget that it isn't the be-all and end-all of their own experience. You don't need any science to have a good experience, *or* a bad one. You have no direct experience of your amygdalae, and you may not have even known you had any such thing. The amygdalae aren't really "things," they are clusters of neurons in the center of the brain that have a separate name because they have specialized functions.

That's a handy concept for a brain scientist, but not much use to most of us. Even the concept of a "neuron" is less than a hundred years old, so billions of people have lived and died (and still do) without the least clue that they even *have* "neurons," let alone amygdalae. Science gives us very abstract causal explanations of the body, but there's far more to the body than science can even describe, let alone explain.

So Merleau-Ponty reminds us that people had ways of perceiving their bodies that were rich and highly functional long before science ever told us anything about how it all works. The same is true for kids. They don't even know they have something called a brain until you teach it to them, but that doesn't keep them from perceiving and thinking and experiencing.

Take the Scarecrow. *Why* does he think he has no brain? His problem may be that he got some very narrow ideas about what a "brain" is: just the physical mass of, well, I hate to tell you this, but the brain is pretty close to being just fat. So the Scarecrow started getting all worried that he couldn't think without one. He wasn't willing so much as to trust his own experience of thinking, which he was obviously good at, because somehow he heard that you can't think without a brain.

Phenomenologists like Merleau-Ponty tell us that with or without science, we still have experience of our bodies, so there is a broader and richer perception of the body from which our science derives. Science is a genre of meaning, a sub-field of meaning we created with our language, and it's a bad idea to mistake one part of meaning for the whole of it. Don't be a Scarecrow.

Your Body, Your World

So what is a frightened body, to a phenomenologist? Well, Merleau-Ponty says that basically your living body, as experienced, is your whole world:

> The body is the vehicle of being in the world, and having a body is, for a living creature, to be intervolved in a definite environment, to identify oneself with certain projects and to be continually committed to them. (*The Phenomenology of Perception*, p. 82)

That comes down to saying that what we *do* in the world (not what we *think* we are doing, what we are actually doing) forms our perceptions of our bodies. Athletes and dancers live in a different world than I live in, because the things they do with their bodies are so different from what I do with mine. But our bodies won't do just anything and everything, won't reveal to us everything about the situation or environment they inhabit. There are limits and gaps, deficiencies.

Yet even the deficiencies are concealed, "silent," Merleau-Ponty says, especially to children. They don't grasp what's missing from their experience, because the world seems more or less complete to them, relative to what they do with their bodies. He continues:

> . . . in concealing [the] deficiency from [us], the world cannot fail simultaneously to reveal it to [us]: for if it is true that I am conscious of my body via the world, that it is the unperceived term in the center of the world towards which all objects turn their face, it is true for the same reason that my body is the pivot of the world: I know that objects have several facets because I could make a tour of inspection of them, and in that sense, I am conscious of the world through the medium of my body. (p. 82)

If I'm getting his point, he's saying that the world can teach me that my experience has something missing in very simple ways. For instance, you're reading this book (thanks for that, by the way). But you aren't looking at every page right this second, so the book is not all before you. You can make a tour of inspection of the pages, but the only reason that makes sense is because the book *isn't* all there right now, even though you're holding the whole book in your hands. Your experience is incomplete.

But here we come to an interesting point about movies. They show us "objects" (or pictures of objects) in motion, the sort of stuff we would normally be able to wander around and inspect, but they do so in such a way as to make that "tour of inspection" impossible.

When watching a movie, my body is no longer the "pivot of the world." Instead, I'm glued to my seat and at the mercy of what the camera shows me. I'm arrested, unable to act on my usual habits of perceiving. The camera has become a substitute for my living body, and presents itself to me as a total world, but one that is in someone else's control. I'm already helpless, and then, as I settle in to watch the movie, I sort of forget how much control I have given away—until the feet shrivel, and I don't want to see it, but it's too late. And I can't move around the scene to see what happened, to reassure myself that there is a benign explanation.

So *part* of the reason I'm afraid has to do with the fact that I'm helpless, and until that moment, I had forgotten it. I trusted Victor Fleming, and he took advantage of me, using his wicked camera to shove images into my world that I didn't want.

Now we see something about the men behind the curtain, the concealed portion of our living world. In the same way that you're careful about what food you put into your mouth, you have to be careful about the images and sounds your body consumes from the wider perceptual world. It's really the same thing to see and hear as to eat. It all becomes *you*. You *are* what you see and hear as truly as you are what you eat.

Think about that next time Ozzy comes on the sound system, and ask yourself, if this were food, what sort of food would it be? Would it be like eating a live bat (or whatever live beast he supposedly ate)? And would I really bite its head off? To quote Dorothy: "Oh, my." So those shriveling legs are scary because you just ate them with your eyes and ears, and now it's too late. That's the chance you take when you trust a moviemaker.

A Great Gig in the Sky

Now, the cyclone surely sets off our amygdalae too, but, as I said, because the events occupy a longer duration, about five minutes, we do not register the same adrenal reaction, as viewers, that we do when the shriveling occurs. Dorothy, on the other hand, is getting some serious "flight" signals (you don't stand to fight a cyclone) when she's stomping on the door of the storm cellar with her foot, as I mentioned—you're helpless too, and now you know why.

Notice, by the way, her foot makes no noise when she stomps, even though you can hear other sounds that wouldn't be as loud. This is the work of the men behind the curtain again, controlling everything you hear. Anyway, I think you'll agree she engaged in adrenaline-assisted behavior, and watching her act out the flight response fills *us* with some of the same stuff. But there's more. The noiseless stomping actually makes us feel more desperate, ineffectual, and powerless, and that isn't just amygdalae stuff. Your "mirror neurons, "the ones that lead you to imitate what you see and hear, these little bastards have *you* stomping your own mental foot, and maybe your physical one, a little bit. You're getting signals to flee but you can't. So you try to *think* and you can't. Your thinking has been bypassed.

Over the course of a minute or two, you start to feel desperate. The tornado sequence contains just about everything you need to fire up your amygdalae: especially loud noise, falling, impending darkness. If you've never actually heard a tornado (I've heard one, and I can tell you there's nothing like it) it is so loud that it cancels out the other senses. That's part of why you can't think. I've heard this noise described as sounding like a freight train, but that doesn't do it justice. It's more like sticking your head in a jet engine powering up, or maybe gluing your ear to a speaker at a Black Sabbath concert back when Ozzy used to be able to screech the high notes.

Here's a little thought experiment. This isn't actually imaginative variation, this will be perceptual variation, but it'll help you get a handle on imaginative variation. Some of you will have seen *The Dark Side of the Rainbow*, which is the synching of Pink Floyd's recording *The Dark Side of the Moon* with the 1939 *The Wizard of Oz*. When this is done, the whole tornado sequence lines up with the song "The Great Gig in the Sky," and I suspect that the near-perfection of the timing of this synchronization is what has led some people to think it just possible that Pink Floyd *intended* this synchronicity. It is, after all, *Dorothy's* great gig in the sky (if ever there was one), and here is this woman wailing like a Les Paul guitar, and since that song has no lyrics, why did the band entitle the song so? With no lyrics, they could have called it anything at all.

But I'm sure the whole thing is a happy accident. Very happy, for us, as you'll see. Now, I want you to watch the tornado sequence with the Pink Floyd music. Then watch the sequence with no sound at all. (You can find this on YouTube.)

It's very different, isn't it? In 1939, sound technology in theaters was not advanced enough to create quite the experience of sudden loudness that activates the amygdalae, although today it could be done well enough. The famous "Voice of the Theater" speaker was created by Altec Lansing in 1947. Before that, theater sound was fairly pinched into the mid-range (and of course, Dolby came much later than that, first used in the movies in 1971).

But people don't like the experience of sudden loud noises, and they go to the movies to enjoy themselves. So filmmakers more often use music to suggest the experience of sudden noise rather than to actually create it (that, and, unlike Ozzy and his crew, they worry about being sued for damaging people's hearing).

For most people, the music in movies is a part of what phenomenologists call the "passive synthesis" (Husserl, *Analyses Concerning Passive and Active Synthesis*). This idea is complicated, but basically when you pay specific attention to something, you process *that* actively, but you don't pay attention to everything in your perceptual field, just a small part of it. The stuff you aren't actively noticing is still there, as a sort of background awareness. You're "synthesizing" it passively.

The relationship between the active and passive aspects of the perceptual field is slippery and delicate, but *manipulating* that relationship is where all the action is. Filmmakers can alter your emotions about anything and everything not only by altering loud and soft, shadow and light, but more essentially, they are altering what you're noticing and what you're not, what you synthesize actively and passively. They do all this by first controlling what you actively notice, and then screwing around with the background stuff, and moving your attention around with sound and light and action. Magicians do the same thing. I suppose Wizards do too. But filmmakers have much better tools.

When you alter the background stuff, you alter the total experience a person has. So, if you watch the tornado sequence with the original soundtrack (now that I have called your attention to it), you'll see that there is no music at all until the moment when Dorothy is hit on the head by the dislodged window. The music at that moment is at first characterized by descending tones as she falls unconscious, then by ascending tones as the house is lifted, and then it turns into a sort of overture of themes, both playful and threatening, as various things pass by the window. Then there's more descending orchestration as the house falls into Oz. At the moment the house lands, dead silence.

The visual images are such that you really can't give your active attention to anything else but the images (especially on the big screen), because the human eye is drawn by motion and flickering light (as any moviemaker knows), so the music is perceived passively by most people. If you're a filmmaker and you want the music to rise toward active consciousness, you need to hold the visual scene still; when you want the sound to recede into the background, you move the images.

The *absence* of music during the first part of the cyclone sequence makes the music more powerful and meaningful when it comes in. You probably never actively noticed all this, just "synthesized" it passively. But put in the Pink Floyd as a substitute and the whole sequence becomes ethereal, actually sort of calming; you are far more aware of the sequence as a whole, there is no real danger (since you know how it comes out), and you feel like floating with Dorothy to Oz. So the same images take on a different overall quality, and thus, a different meaning.

I wonder what would happen if you showed the tornado sequence to children before they had ever seen the movie, and used the Pink Floyd music. Or what if you just showed them the images with no sound? Would their amygdalae register different primal emotions?

Anyway, the point is that the process by which some scary things come to scare us is dependent on the way we "synthesize" the background stuff, passively, and every moviemaker (and every writer of horror stories) knows this. Do you like to read scary books at night, alone? Why? Is part of the reason that they're not scary enough to be fun when the sun is shining and others are around? And why is that?

I think the cyclone images themselves do carry some primal stuff, but it's one thing to see the whirlwind on a screen, and another thing to reap one in 3-D, with sound effects worse than Ozzy's flattest note. So remember this when we get to flying monkeys later on, and when you want to calm down, *Dark Side of the Moon* may be better for that than *The Blizzard of Ozz*. . . . But I'd love to hear Ozzy's rendition of "The wind began to switch, the house to pitch. . . ."

Okay, maybe not. For now, I do want to point out that you can't easily sustain a "fight or flight reaction" for very long. Your body begins to adjust and equalize itself in just a few seconds, and your reflective powers begin to operate, on high alert. This is no instantaneous reaction, it becomes a heightened response, one that "intervolves" the whole body and its surroundings, and this response is more exhausting than enlivening.

As you remain in the situation, you accept more and more responsibility for continuing to watch or wait. You come to be aware that the experience can change you, and you choose to endure the change. It isn't like the shriveling feet.

Damnable Monkeys

So we come to what scared the little girls, Sadie and Vega, and what frightened me the most too, as a child. Actually, the worst recurring nightmare I ever had was of the Tin Man, of all things, but in watching the movie, it was the monkeys I couldn't bear. So what's the deal with the monkeys? I remembered they bared their teeth, and Charles Darwin (who should know about monkeys if anyone should) says we all have a primal reaction to that.

But watching the movie again, I see there isn't any gnashing of teeth until later. The littlest monkey who has Toto, in the witch's castle, bares his teeth at Dorothy when she reaches for the basket Toto is in. I had imagined teeth earlier, to make things worse than they are. But there might still be something to thinking of these beasties in Darwinian terms. I have later noticed that the monkeys are played by some of the Munchkins, the same little people all suited up, with blue Mohawk hairdos (perhaps subliminally reminding Anglocentric viewers of "savage" Indians), and in the days before you could get this "do" for yourself at Sportcuts in the local shopping center. Shocking blue hair, really.

I didn't notice, as a child, that the monkeys were transmogrified Munchkins, but perhaps I was dreaming of distorted little people in my innocent spirit, to return to what Kierkegaard said. Instead of little people with monkey suits on, was I grasping the monkeys as something that lurked within the Munchkins? Am I afraid of little people? And there I was, sort of a Munchkin myself, a little person, fearing the monkey in *me*? Maybe the human being is the suit, and the flying monkey is the essence of a person.

There may be something to all this, but I have come to think it isn't the key to the castle. Following what we have discovered so far, I see that the duration and placement of the monkey scenes probably make a difference. By the time the monkeys show up, which is over an hour and fifteen minutes into the film, the attention and natural defenses of a child (or an adult) have been greatly weakened, the sense of self-control much diminished, and the moviemakers take possession of more and more of our psychological space, penetrating more deeply into our consciousness and perception. We have forgotten who we are.

And at just this moment, Victor Fleming and his diabolical cronies do something they haven't done before; they've been saving it, but it's also a reprise, a repetition of sorts. They prepare us by dimming the lights. The monkey scene is preceded first by the frightening encounter with the Wizard (nice special effects for 1939). The lights dim as the companions proceed down the endless hallway toward the Wizard's throne room, or whatever it is, where the companions are utterly dwarfed by the scale of the place (which makes *us* feel small, since we have been taught by now to identify with the companions).

Then Oz (not Ozzy) speaks in a painfully loud voice and the intermittent music is highly dissonant. Without a break or bright moment, this scene is followed with the companions treading warily through the Haunted Forest, and here everything is shot in shadows. There had been a bit of contrast in the Wizard's throne room, with isolated lights we could see that were casting the shadows. Now it's all in shadow.

This effect is more powerful and invasive precisely because we can't see any source of light. We had grown accustomed to the brightness of Oz and this would have been even truer for our parents and grandparents in 1939, since *The Wizard of Oz* was the first major motion picture made with Technicolor processing. On the big screen it was stunning to them, I'm sure, so that the contrast of the Haunted Forest in shadows would have had an even greater effect, I suppose.

The shadows had been used before, in an earlier forest where Dorothy, the Tin Man, and the Scarecrow first encounter the Lion, as a sort of self-fulfilling prophecy coming in answer to their chant of "Lions and Tigers and Bears, oh my!" The encounter with the Lion is followed immediately by our first glimpse of the Witch in her castle, and just one small flying monkey, conjuring the poppies for the companions. This is foreshadowing, but also your passive side is being trained to place the Witch and the monkeys after the forest.

In a sense, then, you know what's coming when the companions enter another, even darker, forest. You're being taught to project it, and to take responsibility for projecting it, to become active in the face of the future and be terrified at what you yourself are doing. The slide from passivity to active projection is a central gear in the filmmaker's machinery.

These Things Must Be Done . . . Delicately . . .

Now we come to a point about passive synthesis, and I have suggested how delicate the balance is between active and passive synthesis. I will tell you something that may surprise you, even shock you. When Dorothy and the companions are treading through the Haunted Forest, the Tin Man, Lion, and Scarecrow are armed to the teeth. Did you ever actively notice that the Lion now has a giant mallet and a butterfly net? The Tin Man has not only his trusty axe, but also a giant pipe-wrench. And the Scarecrow, my friends, has not only a big stick, he's actually packing heat. That's right, the Scarecrow has a .45 pistol. It isn't concealed at all in several shots. But for some reason you just don't see it, actively at least. Still, you *perceive* it anyway, and all the other oversized weapons too.

By the time the monkeys show up, all these fine weapons are somehow gone, except the Tin Man's axe (which the monkeys take easily as they swarm around him). So, if you're one of the rare people who noticed all these weapons, congratulations. Most people don't. The weapons tell us, passively, that this situation is more threatening than any other we've yet encountered, and the dim lighting reinforces the message.

But Fleming isn't finished with us. When the monkeys first appear, he uses a well framed shot of the Witch and her crystal ball in the center, her long boney fingers hovering threateningly, greedily, just above the image of the Lion repeating "I do believe in spooks . . ." and there are the monkeys with their hideous wings framing all corners of the shot. We are much too close and we can't get away, monkeys everywhere we look, and one stone raven floating in the upper left taking in the whole wicked scene. No escape.

Then, as if we hadn't had enough, the witch sweeps around a velvet cushioned chair and the camera follows her—the camera movement is too fast and so it's disorienting—and then it closes on her still further, framed by the large window overlooking a precipitous fall. If we were too close before, we are *way* too close now. She barks orders to the monkeys and soon they fill the skies on an awful sortie like Messerschmidts headed for London. They are so numerous as to darken the skies to near blackness.

Nightmares

In the monkey air-raid, our devilish filmmakers employ a number of common nightmare images: things swarming around us, being chased through a forest, being unable to move one's leaden body, being scattered and separated from one's companions, fear of heights, in short, complete chaos. And all of this havoc made by those monkeys. Then it all subsides, but the damage is done.

"Nightmares for you, my pretty, a lifetime of them . . . and your little dog too!"

It has been too much, and we're exhausted. Sure, the director draws us back in and scares us some more, but it's suspense rather than shock from here.

Why is this scene so effective, especially in frightening children? I think I know, or at least here's part of the answer. Obviously, a number of things are at work in us, but this is not the effect of our amygdalae secreting epinephrine. This is much more complicated and involves the training and manipulation of the processes of active and passive synthesis, exchanging background for foreground, just as in our earlier examples. Merleau-Ponty makes the point that really we have two bodies, a "habit body" and a "lived body." The lived body is the one you can move easily, but the habit body has coalesced into a less flexible sort of image you carry around with you. He gives the example of a person who has lost a limb, but can't quite remember it isn't there. The habit of feeling it and expecting it to be there is very strong in us, and becomes inflexible.

The same thing happens with our entire body, which is to say that in our perception it becomes overlaid and coated with a whole armor of habit and expectation. We all become Tin Men living inside a habit body. And here is the scary part: Merleau-Ponty says, and he's right, that our habit body is an "impersonal being," not *us* at all, but a sort of trap we're caught in, and one of our own making.

This is one reason, for instance, that people suffering from anorexia nervosa can't see themselves as too thin. No matter how thin they may be, they are at the mercy of a habit body they have created, a hard-shell image, unalterable by living perception, and that body, while only an image, is too fat. You know how tragic this is, but you have a habit body too, and it probably isn't nearly as beautiful as your lived body. This relationship is not easy to control.

Now, the habit bodies of children are less well-formed, and in fact, they are so malleable that children can make for themselves a new one in the course of a single movie, if the filmmaker is sly enough to manipulate the active and passive syntheses well enough to get a child to form and project a habit body from which he or she cannot later escape.

And that's what happens in *The Wizard of Oz*. Children build for themselves an image-world while their living bodies are immobile before the screen. They become quickly habituated to what they have projected, and before they know it, they can't get out and can't get away. And then there are the monkeys, inside the space they have projected, too close, uninvited. You bet they want to go home. I am pleased to report that *The Princess Bride* does no such manipulation.

The effect of this situation on adults is smaller because our habit bodies, impersonal and uncomfortable as they may be, are less easily manipulated by our present perceptions. The active and passive syntheses are familiar, routine, patterned for adults. It takes a better moviemaker than Victor Fleming and his crew to penetrate *that* habit body. But still there are the nightmares, aren't there? The memories abide of when we first encountered the impersonal being, the habit body, we would become.

That brings us back to Kierkegaard, I suppose. He spoke of innocence as a dream of the spirit that is moved into existence by nothing at all, a nothing *in us*. That nothing isn't just the projection of the bad things we will eventually do, it is the spiritual torpor from which we will allow ourselves to become a mere habit of existing, impersonal, a shell that cannot remember its own living self.

That is living death, which is a fair way of understanding original sin, as far as I can see. To live and allow your projections and habits to dull and blunt all that your living body could bring you—the bright joy and wonder of the world. We build our prisons and then can't find a way out of them.

It wouldn't be so bad except for the monkeys. We never counted on the monkeys. That's the stuff of nightmares, far more than any lions or tigers of bears. In a word, it's the Ozzy in us more than the Oz beyond us.

3
The Monster and the Mensch

A Child's Eye View of *Super 8*

You're starting to think I'm obsessed with scary movies. Okay, think that. Monsters bring out the metaphysics in us better than singing and dancing and baseball.

Well, maybe not baseball. That's metaphysics too. But monsters *teach* us things, in my opinion. We get to learn from the relatively safe distance of the stadium seat or the living room couch. Not everyone is so lucky. Some folks learned about the scary stuff with no buffer between themselves and the monsters, whoever and whatever they were. Count your blessings if you didn't, eat your popcorn, and keep reading.

The Climax of the Film

Why save the best bits? J.J. Abrams's movie *Super 8* reaches its climax when the young hero, Joe Lamb, and heroine, Alice Dainard, are being chased through the subterranean nest of an escaped alien being—a being something like a giant spider.

We've had the grand moment set up for well over an hour with various characters indicating that the "monster" is empathic, and it communicates by touch. We've also been prepared to assume that Joe really understands monsters. He spends his free time building models of them, and when it's time for Alice to play a zombie in the kids' own *Super 8* film, she asks Joe how to do it. His description, while still kid-like, is on the money and Alice turns out to be a natural.

We also have the information that our monster is 1. hungry, 2. terrified, and 3. wants to go home. I felt that way when I saw the first *Alien*, the Ridley Scott movie. Only Sigourney Weaver in her underwear would have persuaded me to stay, especially after the alien bursts from that poor guy's chest. But my point is that hungry, terrified, and wanting to go home (while unable to do so) isn't a good combination for anyone, least of all an intelligent being that has been imprisoned for over twenty years and held among aliens it regards as hideous insects (i.e., we humans).

And our *Super 8* monster has every reason to see us this way. After all, we never touch the creature except with probes and prods, and for it, touching is the basis of communication. Hence the primary evidence of the existence of a moral conscience in us is unavailable to the "monster." As far as the monster can discern, humans have no such capabilities. To analogize, at best we seem like reptiles to this being, and at worst, yes, cockroaches. In twenty years of imprisonment, the alien has never had the opportunity to discover that we have any moral feeling at all.

Thus, in the key moment, the alien catches Joe, scoops him up and starts to eat him, but feels (and thereby notices) that Joe, while perhaps afraid, is trying to *see* the monster, to study the monster's face. Studying faces is another thing Joe does, as is made abundantly evident in his work as a make-up artist. In that crucial instant, the monster pauses, ponders, *feels* Joe seeing him, offers his own eyes for Joe to look into, and then suddenly grasps that human beings do with their eyes what the alien beings do by touching. The alien realizes that Joe is "touching" *with* his eyes, and while it is a strange thing, and hard to understand, the alien is, after all, far more intelligent than a human being, so the matter is puzzled out. The alien is able to grasp, in that moment, *why* all the humans have responded as they have. To them, the visual appearance of such a spiderly alien is terrifying, while to the alien, the withholding of touch is barbaric, a kind of unimaginable torture. But now the alien knows that humans did not understand, *could not understand*, its own moral frame of reference.

In that climactic realization, the alien becomes aware that it is wrong to feed on these beings and that its first and only imperative is to *get off this planet and go home*. And what is more, the alien being now knows *how* to do it—how to build a ship that will take it home. It may not be obvious to those who haven't reflected on the matter, but the motive force that creates the alien's spacecraft is a kind of *love*, in the form of desire to touch to hold, to be near, to possess. The parts are drawn together by empathy. That is why the sad little piece of the alien spaceship that Joe takes home from the site of the trainwreck "wants" to be with the other pieces. The ship is made of and powered by something like *longing*.

Looking for Love in All the Wrong Places

When the alien becomes aware that humans actually do have love, or more precisely, *longing* within themselves, it also realizes that it can use *anything* that *anyone* loves (in the relevant sense) to rebuild its craft. That is why, in the denouement, only *some things* are drawn upward into the water tower and fused into the ship. The things being drawn up are things that someone *loves*. That gun the soldier won't relinquish, that cool car, and yes, the necklace that Joe's departed mother wore, and which he has invested with every ounce of his personal longing.

Giving the locket to the alien is, as we know, a "Spielberg moment," but I think the philosophy transcends Spielberg's typical (and unhappily simplistic) moral messages. In Abrams's hand, it isn't actually unselfishness or *agapic* love that is relevant, nor is it *eros* of any kind. He has thought this through more carefully. The operative kind of desire is, as I said, *longing*. But what is that?

Abrams tells us, by way of Alice Dainard who, *unlike Joe* (who depends on his eyes for understanding), is an empath. It does not occur to Alice that not everyone who is touched by the monster comes to understand the monster. Only some people do, like Alice and Dr. Woodward. Alice gets it and reports it to Joe, just before he is scooped up. It is crucial for the story that Joe *believes* Alice completely, even if he can't feel it himself. He has *seen* what she can do. She says longing is a mix of 1. hunger, 2. terror, and 3. wanting to go home.

The thematic suggestion made by the movie is, therefore, that when it comes to making the monster into a Mensch (that favored trope of the movies endowed to us by Mary Shelley's *Frankenstein*), the trick is to grasp that *longing* is the connection we have with the monster. And beyond Abrams's insight about longing, there looms a really tough philosophical question. So I will ask you.

A Few Questions

Is this "longing" what empathy really means? Can we, as humans (or even including other species) share, at any equally profound level, any *other* form of desire? Or is the bottom line that we can all be afraid, hungry, and far from home, together, and *that's* about the long and short of who we are? Can *agapic* love, or friendship, or erotic attraction go deep enough to contribute *anything* to empathy? Or is empathy really just a power to *develop* that moment of longing within ourselves *by sharing it with others*? In my view, that is what *Super 8* is about, and it's a little more far-reaching than the usual Steven Spielberg questions. I say without hesitation that Abrams is a lot more philosophical than Spielberg, but there are many philosophical directors in Hollywood history, so it's nothing unusual.

Now that you know *what* this chapter is about (longing/fear/hunger/home and empathy), let me take a few steps back to examine *how* Abrams accomplishes his aims. There are many monsters in Abrams's head, as everybody knows, and not all follow the patterns established in *Super 8*. I will privilege this movie and this monster as a clue for understanding Abrams, and I believe this movie and this monster are special for him. I think they show something about the man that he hasn't put into his other projects, at least not so fully as this one.

Hunger: The Peculiar Appetite of Film

"Quotationalism" is a word culture critics created to describe the (apparently infinite) capacity of mass culture to digest and regurgitate itself in allusions of allusions, parodies of parodies, and tributes of tributes.[1] Perhaps television is most gluttonous among the various media, but long before the advent of television, or even commercial movies, books were already about other books. What has changed in the last hundred years is that a new *feast* of morsels for quotation has been cooked up in appetizing visual images, and delicious lines that make memorable sound bites (rather than high-brow fare, where people show off their stale Shakespeare or their crusty Byron). And for desert, there is recorded music in general, which, please recall, didn't exist until a little over a century ago (so, yes, it's a processed food, but who can resist Twinkies and Ding-Dongs?).

Yet, the appetite isn't limited to the *content* of mass culture. Everyone knows, I think, that movie-making has the advantage of consuming every other artistic *form* and commercial medium, using them to their fullest as dependent art forms. All the other arts show up in movies, and since movies pay artists, all types of artists gravitate to the movies. In the same way that sculpture was absorbed into architecture during the Middle Ages but then broke free again in the Renaissance, many art forms are simply absorbed by other art forms for a time, and no art form ever existed that is more voracious than the movies.

---

[1] See the informative essay by Carl Matheson, "*The Simpsons*, Hyper-Irony, and the Meaning of Life," which is all about quotationalism.

We talked about the use of music in the last chapter. Lots of great musicians ended up in Hollywood. And others, like Gustav Mahler, became the unwitting composers of music for horror movies by being absorbed in a day before copyright enforcement was on everybody's minds. Obviously, a symphony, created independently, and aimed only at its own musical target, can accomplish artistic ends that a film cannot.

So can a book. And that is also why we often comment that a movie "wasn't as good as the book," and so on. What we mean is that a book can tell a story in a way the movies cannot equal. No major medium of artistic expression is at its very best when it becomes a mere ingredient in another, but it has to be admitted that feature-length movies can preserve *more* of what makes another artistic medium valuable in its own right than any other art form. What a canvas of space, time, image, word and sound! Makes me sort of hungry. For images, soundtracks, and popcorn.

And in a way, we go to the movies *because* we're hungry for something—not just images and stories, but the sequence of feelings these evoke when we eat them with our eyes and ears. (Remember Merleau-Ponty from the last chapter?) We want to devour all the forms at once. A feature film can bring to the table an orchestral piece or song, for example, as the music it *really is*—there's enough time for that in a full-length feature. I savor, emotionally speaking, the scores of John Williams—especially the only two scores that ever actually brought me to tears, which were *Goodbye Mr. Chips* and *Amistad*—and I wonder, would these amazing works of orchestral music exist *without* the movies? No, I don't think so; although it's true that the music is subordinated to the film, it's also the case that sometimes the music swells and overtakes the film and seems to drive the whole flavor. Think of the forgettable *Last of the Mohicans* (Daniel Day Lewis is not always a great actor) compared with the amazing score for that movie that it definitely didn't deserve.

The genre of "the Musical" adds in so much music that it becomes the main course. When we consider a smorgasbord like the long scene in *An American in Paris*, in which Leslie Caron and Gene Kelly dance their way through a dozen styles of French painting to the strains of Gershwin, well, I don't need to say more about this phenomenon. My point is that emotional and aesthetic desire fall within the limits of our sensuous hunger, humanly understood. There is, as Kant insisted, a subjective universality that connects at this level any being worthy of the name "human" to all the others (*Critique of Judgment*, pp. 89–90).

And the fact is that because the movie industry has been able to spend hundreds of billions of dollars *on art* during its great commercial century, artists who wanted to make a living have been drawn thus and were willing to develop their gifts and expend their creativity in service of the meta-artform of movie-making. People who would have gone into different arts, or who wouldn't have had artistic careers at all, were drawn into the movies. The simple fact that people were willing to pay handsomely to dine on the results of all that artsy cooking did most of the work.

When we consider the *auteur* director, of the J.J. Abrams type, in this light, a sort of magnificent chef of images and emotions, it is tempting to wonder what any one of our famous directors might have done for a living in the centuries before the invention of movies. I think Steven Spielberg, for instance, belongs to the Hans Christian Andersen and Brothers Grimm line of writer/story-collectors. For all his imagistic prowess, Spielberg is no painter. He really is a storyteller, first, but he might also have found work as an illustrator. The kinds of stories he tells are fairytales, very self-serious ones, so, not like *The Princess Bride*. Rob Reiner would have been a stand-up comedian. He is a very silly person. I think it is pretty clear that Hitchcock would have directed plays and run a theater. I think Tarantino would have been a playwright (I'll get to Tarantino and Hitchcock in their turns). And J.J. Abrams? What of him? I will answer that question at the end of this chapter. If I say it now, it invites controversy. Yes, all this is just my opinion, but, as with the three opinions I expressed about those other directors, there is a *case* for the opinion.

But where it concerns quotationalism, every art form consumes every other in the feeding frenzy of global mass culture. Abrams seems to understand this and has indeed undertaken the process of perfecting it, but his use of the "film within a film" device as the B-story in this movie shows that he wants to be light-hearted about this part of the structure of the movie and its narrative. Like Tarantino, Abrams understands that what you quote become part and parcel of the Warholian identity you beget in the public mind. Abrams is crafting his own image in his choices. It's a kind of artistic styling made from lots of little squeals that say "I like this!" I think of the moment in *Super 8* when a *Starsky and Hutch* 1974 Gran Torino crosses a distant intersection just as the camera fades away from a scene. That is playful. The movie is literally made of such quotations.

So it's an artistic styling made in little squeals, sideways whispers, and elbows nudging at your ribs. In the same way that Kid Rock can assert his redneck credentials, his love of redneck Michigan, and his redneck conservatism by combining, of all things, a groove from Warren Zevon, a guitar lick from Lynyrd Skynyrd, and a piano tinkle from Bob Seeger into a musical manifesto . . . well, let's just say that if a dim bulb like Kid Rock can pull that off, even if it makes me want to barf, someone with J.J. Abrams's cultural background has plenty to choose from. But when you're hungry for a series of feelings, there's nothing quite like going to the movies—or making one.

Fear Itself: 1979

As we know, Abrams wrote, directed, and produced *Super 8*, but he took his Baby Boomer adoptive Uncle Steven along for the ride. Abrams's penchant for quoting Spielberg in images, in cinematic style, in script-style, and in theme, has been commented on by, well, just about everyone. Some people can't stomach this level of hero worship. To be honest, if I personally believed that was the real story, I wouldn't be writing this. I like Spielberg's movies just fine, and I never miss one, but he annoys me enough to discourage any writing from my end (I'm sure he's devastated . . .). Spielberg's simplistic moralizing, his inability to recognize when he's said enough, the out-and-out obviousness of his symbol choices, the total absence of subtlety, and most of all the self-serious self-indulgence . . . well, *I* have said enough, but he insults the intelligence of his audience and leaves nothing to *their* imaginations. Yet, I prefer him to most of his generational cohort, since it doesn't look like he sold out.

On the other hand, I like J.J. Abrams version of Spielberg better than Spielberg. There is a deconstruction of Spielberg in Abrams (I am far from the first to say this, of course). Part of the reason I like Abrams is that, in a way, the Goonies are *better* the second time around. The setting of *Super 8* is exactly calibrated with Abrams's own childhood (more on that shortly)—it was a weird in-between time to grow up in. Abrams is too young to be a Baby Boomer, but as the oldest of the Gen X'ers, he really isn't a quite child of the Eighties either. 1979, when this movie is set, was a cultural void. Disco and Southern rock had gone rancid, Zeppelin was moribund, Springsteen was on hiatus, and we were still listening to *Hotel California*. Stirrings of the 1980s were underway, for sure, but Abrams chose not to bring in the music of 1979. That was a conscious decision, I'm sure. He must have judged that it would detract from the mood he wanted to create. This was not primarily about nostalgia for that year. It was more about what was *scary* that year.

The Iranian Revolution was underway (but no one understood what it meant). Carter was still President, but the country wasn't going to be recovering from Vietnam, Watergate, and the Oil Crisis. The President had given a speech, now dubbed "the Malaise Speech" in which he told us that we were living beyond our means, and that if we didn't make sacrifices now, consume less, and pay down our debts, that our economic future was very uncertain. That displaced feeling of being betwixt and between, a sort of aimlessness as the nation's industrial base disintegrates, pervades *Super 8*. We hardly know what to think, today, as the movie opens with a scene of a still-functioning steel mill, something that would be almost extinct before too many more years elapsed. Abrams said in an interview that the whole film grew from the idea of having someone change the safety sign at a steel mill. If that writing decision doesn't give us a clue that this movie is about *truly* scary stuff, then we're pretty slow.

But fear isn't the same as terror. They're related, but it isn't easy to understand how vague fears grow into total terror, especially for kids who haven't got enough life experience to have their fear generalized into existential angst. As every storyteller knows, things have to come apart gradually and build into an apocalyptic moment. You can't escalate fear into terror by having things jump out from behind trees. Terror takes time.

Abrams wanted to capture that transitional time in our history, a time almost no one takes the trouble to remember—post-Seventies, pre-Eighties, and to make it vaguely scary. Not much was going on, but there was one thing good about 1979: the box office. Abrams grew up in LA, in a movie-making family. It was a big year out in LA. There was *Apocalypse Now*, and the (very) first *Star Trek* movie (ironically), and *Kramer vs. Kramer*, and most importantly, this was the year *Alien* came out.

Our monster in *Super 8* is modeled on the monster from *Alien*, and the camera technique of Ridley Scott and Derek Vanlint, showing parts of the alien without allowing the audience to get a sense of the monster as a whole, is repeated in *Super 8*. Obviously they weren't the first to come up with the idea, but the technique had become a cliché by 1979. Scott and Vanlint resurrected it with powerful effect.

Many writers and critics have remarked that *Alien* signaled a real change in Hollywood. It had been foreshadowed with *Jaws* (1975) and *Dawn of the Dead* (1978), but with the release of *Alien*, no longer would movie-goers be bothered with the complexity of needing to empathize with the monster. In 1979, the requirement of conscience that marked the Sixties and

Seventies, in which Mary Shelley's softer sensibilities about monsters would dominate, suddenly retrogressed to the Fifties (taking Sigourney Weaver's pants along with it—so, not *everything* would be like the Fifties . . .).

Back in the duck-and-cover Fifties, you were allowed, nay, *expected* simply to be horrified at the alien invaders, at their shear otherness. You weren't expecting the Frankenstein scenario, the misunderstood monster-is-the-Mensch moment. Sigourney's nemesis in *Alien* wasn't misunderstood, it was evil, violent, and planning to eat us all. But the monsters Joe builds models of are the old-style, misunderstood creatures for whom we find some feeling. It's not an accident. It's foreshadowing and a signal: Old School Monster Ahead.

The residents of 1979 live on the cusp of Reagan's cruel world, and they don't know it. The slow creepiness of the Eighties hasn't yet poked its way out of their bellies and into their consciousness. These characters still think it's the Seventies, and in a way it *is*. But the struggle for the souls of movie-*goers* was well underway (after all, one last monster-Mensch needed to phone home, in 1982, before the good guys lost and evil was evil again). The main change was that the public was given permission to refuse the moral chore of seeking the monster's point of view.

J.J. Abrams remembers all this. In retrospect he has also been able to see something of its meaning, so the writing, set decoration, art direction and even the acting in *Super 8* captures that time and its insensibility of the future. It's a world with no war-mongering neo-conservatives, or war-mongering neo-liberals, a world in which airlines and utilities and the telephone company are regulated by the government in the public interest, and a time when steel mills still made steel. No Walmart, no internet, no stadium seating at the movies, no MTV, and, by the way, no Rubik's cubes (Abrams missed that detail—but the geek squad on imdb.com has several dozen other anachronisms you might want to note; none of them hurts the movie). The more you study the details of the movie, the more you'll be able to grasp the comparative innocence of the moment.

(What's So Funny 'bout) Peace, Love, and Understanding?

There really was some extremely cool music in 1979—Elvis Costello, Blondie, Talking Heads, The Clash—are you kidding me? Great stuff. All missing from this movie, partly because that music really heralds the 1980s. So, if that's 1979, then *why*

1979? The movie is autobiographical in many ways, and J.J. Abrams came from a movie-making family and started making *Super 8* movies when he was about eight years old, so by the time he was thirteen, he was probably pretty far into what he would do for a living. He did enter film contests when he was a kid, and I wouldn't be shocked if there was a *Super 8* zombie movie in a can somewhere from, oh, about 1979. But nothing depends on that hypothesis.

Instead, I stake my case on this: we all have to concede that age thirteen is the paradigm for the last year of innocence. Many critics have remarked how good this movie is at making them feel like kids again, and there is the *gotcha* device that the movie uses to make you care, to evoke not just your sympathy but your empathy, your identification with the characters. Not all of us lost our mothers or had drunk fathers, but we all were thirteen once. If I were a writer-director and I wanted to capture thirteen, I would use my memory rather than just my imagination. Setting this film in 1979 enables Abrams simply to *remember* his way through a million decisions.

But I think there is more. I see the middle-aged man Abrams, at the height of his artistic powers, reflectively at work here too. There is a retrospective understanding that intensifies this particular year, this time, and it isn't nostalgia. These kids are the first Gen X'ers, but of course, they also don't know *that* yet. Capturing this variable innocence and ignorance in his characters, as well as his setting, was, in my view, important to the message Abrams wanted to convey, and it is the retrospective understanding that is crucial to building the terror. I think most thirteen-year-old kids in America during that year heard Elvis Costello ring out the death knell of the Seventies with the following repeated lament:

> So where are the strong?
> And who are the trusted?
> And where is the harmony?[2]

The Baby Boomers were selling out. I suppose we could say that 1979 was the year that we collectively ceased pretending

---

[2] These are lyrics from the Nick Lowe song "(What's so Funny 'bout) Peace, Love and Understanding," written in 1974, but recorded by Elvis Costello and the Attractions and released as the B-side of a Nick Lowe single in 1978. Recognizing the song was going to be popular, it was added to the American release of Elvis Costello's 1979 album *Armed Forces*, where it proceeded to end up in the record collections of a high percentage of 13 year-old kids in that year (including, unless I miss my guess, J.J. Abrams).

to care about the absurd Age of Aquarius and the ridiculous promise of Woodstock. It was the year the Baby Boomers became honest with themselves about wanting a lot of money. Not everyone went along, of course. Spielberg didn't, for example. But for Abrams, the experience of Gen X was beginning. The Baby Boomers were too self-absorbed to notice the path of cultural and political destruction they were leaving in their wake, and Jesus, it got a lot worse (thank you Donald Trump). There was nothing but scraps and hair bands for a boy like Abrams born in 1966. But my, oh my, there *were* scraps. *Super 8* doesn't just quote them, it is *made of* them.

Tom Wolfe famously described the 1970s as the "me decade," in contrast with the 1960s, and with some justice. But if that was true of the 1970s, then the 1980s must have been the "not you" decade, for then, in our boredom, we took the opportunity not only to ignore interests beyond our own narrowest ones, deregulating everything and everyone, declaring war on labor, taxes, public support for education. Our free-market fundamentalists opened the gates to global exploitation of the poorest of the poor so that we could send domestic, working-class jobs to places with no laws or unions protecting the men, women and children—often suffering on the brink of starvation, but conveniently out of sight. We decided to arm any group of thugs who would do our bidding in tiny countries too poor to resist their tyranny, and unsatisfied with doing this sort of thing passively, we organized coups to take down independent-minded democracies.

Yes, all was done with the co-operation and full approval of the Baby Boomers. They didn't want jobs in the steel mills, they wanted executive salaries, and they didn't want to think about what some child was doing for food in Bangladesh or Indonesia. Gordon Gecko says "Greed is good. Greed works." By 1989 it was over—both the Cold War and the transformation of the Third World into the unseen, unheard, and underfed sweatshop to sate our consumerist appetites (not that they ever *can* be sated, really).

Pure Evil Incarnate: Baby Boomers

In short, in 1979 we were about to take our selfishness global in a neo-imperialism the aim of which was to make others pay for our party back here at home. That was the alternative Carter failed to mention in his malaise speech. Use the military to compel others to make the US prosperous without ever having to pay for it. There may have been *better* parties had on the backs of oppressed and starving people, under the reign of

Caligula, for example, but I doubt there has ever been a *bigger* one. Culminating with NAFTA in which we gave ourselves permission to rape Canada, exploit Mexico, and assfuck working class America. Thanks Baby Boomers. Thank you slick Willie, W. and the Bone Spur in Chief. Puffed up cowards bombing anything that moved.

I give you genuine human terror. We have met the enemy. We looked in the mirror and failed to recognize that Ridley Scott's alien was looking back at us. It was a Baby Boomer's reflection, a selfish, violent, inhuman, consumption machine. It was the USA, in the hands of 78.3 million spoiled fools who have yet to turn loose and probably never will. Last I checked, the oldest imaginable Baby Boomer is President in 2022. Still doing what Baby Boomers do. If I weren't a Baby Boomer myself, I'd be pretty cynical. But there you are.

Generation X watched helplessly and tried to understand. They still do. This younger group collected a reputation for cynicism, for being without ambition and without distinct achievement. Still, it isn't easy to imagine what they could have done, and many have not been slow to wag a finger at the Boomers and say "Look at the mess you made of everything, you unfeeling murderers of all hope." And the children of the X'ers, those pesky millennials, hate the Boomers with a passion. I guess they saw the situation for what it was. I don't blame them. I have started claiming to be a Gen X'er to evade their ire.

And here, *here* I believe we reach the heart of the matter. The problem that constitutes the moral backdrop for *Super 8* just *is* the problem of empathy. The Baby Boomers lack it, in *Super 8*—although the only examples we're given would be chubby Charles Kaznyk's sexpot older sister Jen and her drugged-out lusty admirer Donny. These fine citizens will soon be in charge of everything. There are over seventy million of them and they all vote for each other.

The adults in *Super 8* are people born during the Depression or during the Second World War itself. They have lost their power of empathy, not due to hunger for the pleasures of the flesh and pure consumption, but from fear itself. The Depression, the War and the Cold War have done them in. They were the officers in the Vietnam era, taking their orders from veterans of the Second World War and carrying them out without asking too many questions. After all, their elders won the big war and they know what is best. Not one of the depression babies will ever serve as US President.

They are a silent and lost generation, and the movie captures this, but also provides one exception: the science teacher,

Dr. Woodward, who essentially sacrifices his life to help an alien creature. His last words, to the evil Air Force Colonel Nelec, is an assertion of the primacy of empathy, which comes down to saying that the alien is *in* him and he is *in* it. Nelec is unmoved and orders another black soldier to execute Woodward. That's pretty much how you kill conscience.[3]

The Exception Proves the Rule

If Dr. Woodward had a PhD in some sort of biological science in 1958, when he was among the scientists the Air Force chose to study the alien, he was something of a pioneer. There were precious few black PhD's in that day, and those who were around had *reason* to understand the alien's predicament. Being surrounded by white people who are completely unconscious of their privilege and in deep denial about their racism must bear some analogy to the predicament of the alien. Woodward is transformed by the alien's touch, but we are not told whether the alien is aware of it—an important detail.

In any case, Dr. Woodward understood that the basic moral requirement in this situation, for any intelligent being, was that the creature must be set free, at any personal cost. That alien's treatment was thus a symbol of what fear does to us over time. In short, Dr. Woodward became conscious of the *genuine* terror, and that was the idea of a world full of pod people, Baby Boomers and their unfeeling older Silent cousins, people who refused to feel the longing of others, who would defend their own physical safety, and their power and privilege, at the cost of their souls. Being robbed of peace and love, for two generations, we lost our capacity for understanding. It isn't funny.

Thus, the terror relevant to *longing* is the way in which we can come to fear losing ourselves, our very souls, to any set of social protocols that requires us to be, well, zombies. The kids in *Super 8* are *surrounded* by zombies—hunger zombies and fear zombies, like those in the military. What are they? As Joe says to Alice: "Pretty much be a lifeless ghoul, with no soul. Dead eyes. Scary. Did you ever have Mrs. Mullin?" All the adults they know are terrifying and terrified, even though no one knows it, because that is what fear will do over time.

The Cold War is so old, by 1979, that no one could even remember what it was like *not* to live on the brink of apoca-

---

[3] There is an outstanding analysis of this time, and especially Carter's malaise speech, in Andrew Bacevich, *The Limits of Power*.

lypse, and so in Abrams's script, the zombie apocalypse *did* happen. But it was gradual, so no one knew when to declare it openly. The effect of two generations of Cold War was that no one noticed it when our souls were gone and we just became hungry, frightened, consumerist pod people. We were ready for Walmart. And so Abrams did actually make a zombie movie, in the scariest sense of the word.

So Far from Home: Empathic Longing

The problem of empathy doesn't have a long history in philosophy—at least, not when compared to other long-standing problems in Western thought. For most of our history in the West, the prevailing view was that the power of reason is the distinguishing trait of humanity. In all fairness, people in the Eastern world were talking about whether the power of sympathy might be the distinguishing trait of humanity for over two thousand years. And there were certainly wise ones in the West who placed great value on fellow feeling. But in the West, somehow these commonsense observations never became a central part of the *philosophical* conversation.

Philosophers, from Plato onwards, were critical of anyone who deployed human intelligence or persuasive speech for the purpose of stirring up the emotions of those who heard or read such rhetoric, and over time, the general opinion came to hold that emotion in general degrades and distorts our powers of reason. One could say we chose to philosophize like zombies, and having developed the habit of doing so, we came to be unfamiliar with the very real (and positive, constructive) relations between feeling and reasoning. It's kind of scary, actually, but we got used to it.

So it came as something of a radical suggestion in 1755, when Jean-Jacques Rousseau asserted that our power of sympathy (along with our power of healthy self-love) is essential to our humanity.[4] Obviously there's a very great difference between sympathy—the pity we feel when we witness suffering—and empathy, which is feeling *exactly* what another person (or being) feels. But the question of empathy doesn't arise philosophically, in the West, until the questions of sympathy and *healthy* self-love are under discussion.

Most of the attention of the philosophers in the nineteenth century, insofar as they addressed this question at all, was

---

[4] These assertions were part of the argument in Rousseau's famous "Discourse on the Origin of Inequality," also known as his "Second Discourse." I prefer the translation by Roger and Judith Masters.

devoted either to justifying or attacking self-love, and sorting out the good from the bad kinds of love. There was significant discussion of sympathy, but the prevailing opinion among those Europeans who had colonized the world, and who intended to exploit and oppress it further—almost like alien invaders— was that sympathy makes human beings weak and unable to do what is necessary for the advancement of the race. (Granting that the British, French, Spanish, Portuguese, Dutch, Italians, and Germans had very different ideas of what *would* advance the human race, they seemed to agree that sympathy was a luxury no powerful nation could afford.)

The colonizers had philosophers like Herbert Spencer and August Comte and Charles Darwin and T.H. Huxley and Arthur Schopenhauer to gird up their colonizing loins and assure them that all the invasion and murder of "less civilized" people was absolutely necessary, or at least not morally significant. The Marxist reaction to all this slaughter and misery wasn't exactly characterized by an emphasis on compassion. Thus, after Rousseau's assertion, it took another 150 years before any major Western philosopher took up *empathy* as a subject for constructive discussion. There were some literary heroes like Charles Dickens who defended the dignity of the poor and Mark Twain, who attacked colonialism without mercy. But the philosophers stood mute or piled on with the colonizers.

Phenomenology Again

The group of thinkers who finally examined the question were phenomenologists. (Remember them from the last chapter?) They were committed to giving reflective descriptions of subjective experience. They took for granted that, as a matter of necessity, *my* experience is *mine* and *yours* is *yours*, so the issue of whether *we* could have "the same feeling" posed a number of formal problems. Since your feeling is *in* you and mine is *in* me, so the story goes, they can't be "identical," and so if they are somehow the "same" feeling, they must have either the same *form* or the same *content*, or both, but they are different instances—in sort of the way that two sisters can belong to the "same family" or the "same parents." But obviously siblings are also different.

By analogy, wouldn't there be differences between *my* version of say, feeling *your* suffering and your version of it; or of *your* version of feeling *my* suffering and *my* version of the same? And would the difference be greater still if someone steps on your toe and I say "ouch" and reach for my own toe in empathy? At what point do we simply just admit they are

different, or different enough that empathy is not real, just a
story we tell ourselves? Is empathy real? Or is it something we
wish for but actually lack? A lot of our behavior would be easier
to explain if empathy is only a wish.

Questions such as these are addressed in the writings of
Max Scheler (1874–1928) and Edith Stein (1891–1942). They
were phenomenologists. In 1913, Scheler criticized in detail
those thinkers after Rousseau, from Adam Smith to Sigmund
Freud, who collapsed sympathy into self-love and insisted that
the roots of sympathy lie in self-interest. That, Scheler
believed, was a very great mistake. In *The Nature of Sympathy*,
Scheler sorted out the various modes and types of sympathy,
including fellow feeling, identification, egoism, love, hate, emotional infection, and (most important for us) empathy.

In 1916, Stein (who subsequently was canonized in the
Roman Catholic Church) framed and published her theory of
empathy—the word in German is revealing: *Einfühlung*, or
"single-feeling"). Stein believed that the questions associated
with the experience of empathy were among the most revealing
philosophical questions we can ask. The very structure of *all*
human experience is bound up with feeling what others feel,
she says. Without belaboring the subtle story, Stein claims that
what *I* experience, what is truly *mine* in an experience, is the
act of experiencing. The content of my experience, whether it is
a memory, a fantasy, and anticipation, or a feeling, is not exclusively mine—even if it is *my* memory, the immediate mine-ness
is in *the act*, not in *the content*. The content, whatever it may
be, "announces" itself to the act of experiencing. So even my
own memories must be announced and re-lived to be experienced at all.

If this is right, then there is no requirement that any content of experience must be the private possession of the experiencer. When we empathize, then, we do not *infer* what another
is feeling (by interpreting bodily responses or facial expressions), and we do not *project* our so-called "private" feelings
onto others, and we do not *make conjectures* or guesses. Rather,
the content of the experience "announces" itself *to* the *act* of
experiencing.

Hence, we really could *share* a memory, an anticipation, or
a fantasy as well as a *feeling*, if the same feeling announced
itself to both your act and my act of experiencing –and that
need not be at the same moment; we could be separated by
decades or centuries. In empathizing, we actually share the
"same *feeling*" in two different acts, yours and mine (which
need not even be simultaneous). Stein does not claim that the

feeling content is identical in every respect, but she does claim that ideally it *could* be ("On the Problem of Empathy").

What Empathy Isn't

This brings us back to J.J. Abrams's exhibition of empathy in *Super 8*. What is it, for him? It isn't the self-sacrificing love Christians call *agape*. *Agapic* love is not a *kind* of understanding, it *passes* understanding. It is self-sacrifice for those who cannot understand, either what they are doing or what is being done *for* them by a being that is morally superior. I don't see this in *Super 8*. Neither our Goonies nor our alien is in any such frame of mind. Dr. Woodward might be, but he dies vowing revenge, which isn't very Jesusy, and Abrams makes sure he gets it, so I don't think this is *agape*.

Is it friendship? Friendship (*philia* in Greek) in the highest sense is based on equality, Aristotle says; one discovers a sort of "second self," and the two souls are alike not just coincidentally, but in their moral achievements and judgments. They are alike in virtue, and that is the basis of such friendship (*Nicomachean Ethics*, Books VIII–IX). One would expect an ideal empathy in such friends, and I think that is what happens. But the interesting thing about empathy is that it can exist across great distances and differences –in time, place, virtue, even species. Whatever it is that enables us to *share the same feeling*, it does not require very much sameness of circumstance, or of past experience, or even of physiology. Empathy is not a kind of friendship.

Is it erotic attraction? Not in Abrams's view. First of all, Abrams is very, very careful not to objectify or sexualize any characters in the movie except Jen Kaznyk and lusty Donny. The relationship between Joe and Alice is basically non-erotic—yes, he thinks she's sad and beautiful, but he is awestruck, not enamored. Abrams is very careful in how he frames the shots Alice is in so as never to do with her what male directors always do with pretty young girls, which is to make sure we lecherous men can gawk at their bodies. And even set with an entire passel of young boys, Abrams steers away from having them even so much as notice how attractive she is; they are amazed by her acting ability and that she has the guts to take off in her father's car. It's sort of the opposite in Stephen King's Goonies in *It* where Beverly Marsh is continually objectified.

No, Abrams refuses the standard moves and that is because he wants to show us the *person*, not the *thing* that Alice is. So she sneaks out to see Joe, knocks on his window, and the romantic possibilities become an empathy-fest. That, friends and neighbors, is *deliberate* on Abrams's part. It blocks our voyeuristic efforts to sexualize Alice. He is saying: "Hey, you, zombie pervert in the tenth row, yeah you with your mind in the gutter, I'm talking to you. Would you give your lizard brain a rest and think about something else for the balance of this movie?"

And this shows, pretty clearly, that Abrams is aware that erotic feeling really isn't empathic at all; it takes us beyond ourselves, projects us into a realm of desire that *seems* to be shared with another for a time, but that relation turns out to be unsustainable. Yes, the soul grows wings under the sway of *eros*, but the wings get tired and the soul descends into debauchery. We do not know whether the alien is male or female, or whether gender applies to it at all. The reason is simple. This isn't about *eros*.

And empathy is *not* self-transcendence and it is *not* ecstatic or mystical. There is just no religion or spirituality in this film. No preachers, no prophets, and no churches. The funeral scene at the beginning of the movie would have been the obvious moment for at least a shot of a church, whether interior or exterior. Abrams explicitly avoids this. It's a conscious decision. There will be no revelations in Lillian, Ohio, in 1979. The people will have to solve their problems without that kind of help.

What Empathy Is

For Abrams, empathy is centered in the body, not the soul, and it does not, by itself, cause action. Yet, empathy is also not strictly passive or a passion of any kind. It is not something we suffer. What the devil is it, then? It is clear rather than cloudy, a clear moment of understanding of some sort. It doesn't lift us up and it doesn't bring us back down, so it isn't levity or gravity. It's a moment of presence. I think J.J. Abrams thinks that we come to recognize empathy when *together* we find that we are, together, hungry, afraid, and homesick. The solidarity of the friends in *The Wizard of Oz* provides a paradigm. See the previous chapter.

Note that Dorothy is not sexualized in the 1939 movie—by anyone, Professor Marvel/Wizard, the hired hands/Oz companions, nobody. As thoroughly Freud/Jung as the whole thing is, no eros. Imagine how scary that movie would have been if anyone was pedophilic *as well as* predatory. Glad I didn't have to consider *that* in Chapter 2. Something to be said about the chastity (one assumes?) of Buttercup in *The Princess Bride*.

Stephen King could take a lesson. Are you listening Steve? Never mind, I know you can't hear me over the screaming of your characters.

We recognize that combination of fear, hunger, and home-sickness in others, across the most varied of circumstances, but it is difficult to do so when we are *sated, secure,* and *home.* In fact, the great killers of our empathy are just those three things, which is why Americans of the almost endless Second Gulf War/Afghan War era didn't give a tinker's damn about their own troops, either when they were fighting or when they come home ruined. There is something cloudy and grave about satiety and security, especially when we think that home is something we can possess and defend. I, for one, would sooner be homeless than call the United States the "Homeland." I do hate that rhetoric. Who cannot see that this view of "home" is the essential ingredient in fascism? *Der Vaterland, nein?* No, we shall have no homeland, if I can stop it, and here I am pretty sure that I simply state Abrams's (and Spielberg's) view of the matter as well—and they can do more to stop it.

It's good to be aware that the hunger *without* the terror is just as dangerous as the terror without the hunger. I think I just described the two American political parties, but they seem to agree on the Homeland idea. What have we become? Yet, at the very bottom of the well of *longing* is the *absence* of home. The truth is that humans are vagrants on the doorstep of being; we are frail, stupid, dying, creatures with nothing to guide us back to our cosmic Kansas except our own pathetic cries and yelps of pain. That is why we can feel each other's feelings. It isn't our intelligence, it's our emptiness, our ontological homelessness, that we can share.

You Can't . . .

. . . go home again? But we *have* no homes, at least not after about age thirteen. Woodie Guthrie said so. It was something he knew about. I guess 1979 was the thirteen of US history. Or one of our thirteens. Maybe every two or three generations our culture is thirteen again, probably after war and economic disaster. Then comes a generation that didn't live those traumas but understands it has come of age under a shadow. I feel that way. Too young to go to Vietnam, a child of the Cold War, on the edge of nuclear destruction I never made and could not comprehend, and so on (I am five years older than J.J. Abrams.) It seems to me that the older kids are ontologically homeless and don't know it, and the younger ones know it but can't do anything to help because the older kids won't listen. And none of us could be called kids any more. No wonder the Millennials are so disgusted.

Yet, sometimes we do feel, together, that there is no home, no place where the steel mills are still open, no way back to our own Lillian, Ohios. We were dying before we saw it clearly. The only aftermath of the zombie-alien apocalypse we get in *Super 8* is the kids' movie itself, the one they are making as the B-story line. It lacks much in the way of "production values," but it's innocent. We notice our homelessness when we reflect on lost innocence. And we wouldn't want to have known then what we know now.

We are in the frame of mind to make this leap into the emotional arms of others mostly when we are hungry and frightened and far from home, in some sense of those words. I think this is why we still like to leave home and go to the movies, with strangers, and munch on overpriced popcorn, and get the shit scared out of us by monsters, and feel the same things everyone else is feeling, alone, in the dark, immobile, but with our friends, and with others—possible friends.

The longing that brings us out of our homes is what we really share, it is our civic bond, a resoluteness to come clear about our weaknesses, and *that* is what makes us human. I thought you were a monster until I really saw you. Now I see it was me all along, us. Rod Serling wrote a famous *Twilight Zone* episode once called "The Monsters Are Due on Maple Street," showing how little it takes to bring out the fear, the hunger, and the homelessness in our lonely souls. I'll finish this book with a look at what that insightful man said with his writing.

Obviously the twist in *Super 8* is that the alien's moral decency is never really in question; *ours is*. Any being, whether divine or alien, that can *see* the longing in us can also know that our weaknesses are understandable. As the alien said to Ellie Arroway in *Contact*, "humans are an interesting mixture, such dreams, such nightmares." And that *being-seen-by-the-alien* isn't redemption, exactly, but it isn't damnation either. Once the *alien* understands that the monsters are the Menschen, it's time to go home, and that's true whether you're *in* the movie, or you just went to *see* it.

And, as promised early on, here is the opinion: I think J.J. Abrams would have been a healer of some kind, perhaps a veterinarian, if there were no movies. I leave it to you to puzzle out why I might think that, but I will offer this much of a hint. Abrams has a whole stable of monsters, and he seems to be responsible for their care and feeding, and when they get sick, monsters can't *tell* you what's wrong with them. They don't know. But remember, as you consider this opinion, who the monsters are in *Super 8*.

4
Chef, Socrates, and the Sage of Love

FINDING LOVE IN *SOUTH PARK*

L et's be clear about one thing from the start: by "love," in this chapter, I do mean *eros*.

I just got finished dissing *eros* and praising three movies for leaving it out. And part of the reason I wanted to steer clear is that children, or as Chef would say "chilrens," were involved. And chilrens, rather than children, will be involved for the rest of Part One. I turn to the smaller screen, but they don't put *South Park* during children's viewing hours. Get those kiddies to bed! This isn't really rated G, whatever that means.

I find the MPAA designation "G" for "General Audiences" to be offensively vague. What on Earth are they talking about? Movies for military generals, perhaps also admirals? Movies for people who don't exist particularly, only in general? I couldn't be a general audience if I tried. Every time I show up at the movies, I'm quite specifically just me. Bringing my particular friends doesn't change that. Maybe it means "anyone with ten dollars." That is hardly "general." That is pretty exclusive company in this cruel world. Go to the Mississippi Delta and see who has ten bucks to burn. How about Bangladesh? You got ten bucks over there and you spend it on a movie you're a heartless bastard. Anyway, that bad old Hays tradition has my knickers in a twist.

This part of the book is going to make a statement about such standards. Fuck 'em. Let's have some *eros*, and if not real children (I strongly insist they not be real children), then irreverent cartoons of chilrens, the nastiest lot of them you ever dreamed of are on the table. One is reminded of Parker and Stone's view of this in the weekly disclaimer:

> The following program contains coarse language and due to its content, it should not be viewed by anyone.

59

I'm doing what might be called "classic *South Park*" here. They did twenty-three seasons and continue to do specials, but this chapter focuses on Chef, who was killed off at the beginning of Season Ten, as a result of a conflict between the Parker-Stone duumvirate and Isaac Hayes, Chef's voice—no relation to Wil Hays of the Hays Code, except that some of Hays's very distant cousins may have owned Hayes's great great grandparents. I have watched enough *South Park* since the tenth season to know that the show is just as funny as it ever was and has never lost its delightful edge (I will look at that edge in the next chapter).

But after Chef left, there was a missing element for me. The chilrens *trusted* Chef. After he was gone, they never had a real mentor. I seriously missed that. But I grant that the world must move on. Still, Chef had the nads, the salty chocolate balls, to go with the voice and the soul. The kids knew he was a different kind of guide in the world. I also admit that I'm going to have revenge in this chapter on some philosophers I detest. I'm giving in to my baser urges here. Why should I argue with these people when it's more fun to mock them? That's pretty much what Parker and Stone did every week anyway. My turn.

Of Gods and Infinite Desire

Eros. The god of erotic love. Yes, yes, long before his name came to be the marketing label for the porn industry,[1] Eros was indeed a Greek god, the son of Aphrodite, goddess of beauty—and so many other delectable things. I'm guessing I have your attention so far. And in singling out eros, I am obviously leaving aside for now *philia* (the love of friends like Kyle, Stan, Cartman, and Kenny, but not Butters), and *agape*, the self-sacrificing love of humble service, of which there is precious little to be found in *South Park*, or Colorado, or anywhere else in the present age.

Now it's common to complain that the English language is impoverished, having only one word, "love," to do the work of all three ideas, but I come to praise English, not to bury it. I think it's a great advantage to have deeply ambiguous words with which to weasel out of uncomfortable situations (ask Lemmiwinks). I couldn't write a letter of recommendation without such words. I write:

---

[1] The word "industry" is interesting to consider too, since its Latin root means "to pile things up," so I guess these folks are nothing if not industrious.

I am pleased to say Professor A. is a former colleague, and I can honestly say that no one would be better for this position. I cannot recommend him too highly, yours sincerely, etc.

So, to illustrate the case of "love," I can say, without fear of contradiction, Cartman loves his mother, and so does everyone
else.[2] And I can say I'm writing this because I want you to love
me, and I'm not embarrassed about it at all, since you haven't
a clue what I mean (or whether my intent is even legal in
Mississippi, and I confess it is not, but that doesn't narrow
things down overmuch).

See how easy it is? Yes, English is God's own language (I am
going to prove that in my chapter on *The Life of Brian*), which
is why so many Baptists think Jesus spoke it, in red ink and
King James idiom. Ah, but Jesus and Baptists aside, Chef
exceeds us all. Chef loves everybody and everybody loves Chef.

But here's an interesting thing to think about (otherwise I
would be finished now, but they wouldn't pay me for just three
chapters, although I did try that): Chef seems to have something we all want, maybe a kind of practical understanding
about human nature, or female nature, or just an infallible
map to the clitoris,[3] and either way, it would be nice to possess
something like that, even if only to keep it on the shelf (not).

So, is love a kind of "knowledge," a way of knowing something? And would having the knowledge lead to any sort of, oh,
let's not say "prowess," right now, let's keep this in the living
room for the moment, on the couch, with soda and Cheesy
Poofs—let's call it "virtue"? Yes, would the acquisition of "love's
knowledge"[4] lead to a virtue? I'm sort of hoping this is true,

---

[2]   Look, I think I was pretty clear that *South Park* is not for the squeamish,
and there's no virtue in sanitizing this discussion. There's going to be some very
juvenile stuff coming up. Go buy the book on *Mel Gibson's Passion and Philosophy*
if you want to avoid references to the clitoris—as I recall, it doesn't get mentioned
there, but I was too squeamish to see his movie, so maybe the clitoris made an
appearance, for all I know. I did see *Apocalypto* and wished I hadn't. Even *I* needed
a trigger warning.

[3]   I can resist noting the Oedipal undertones here, although I suppose I didn't,
but I cannot resist observing that Eros the Greek god, became Cupid in Latin, and
that there is just something so utterly undeniable in Cartman's cupidity—if Venus
were my mother, and I were Cupid, I can hardly imagine that I wouldn't be just
like Cartman.

[4]   If you were really serious about learning something on this subject, which I
doubt (after all you probably watch *South Park*), there actually is a good bit to
know. I recommend, first that you cease reading this chapter immediately, and second that you get your hands on two books by Martha C. Nussbaum, *Love's
Knowledge* (Oxford: Oxford University Press, 1990), which has a half dozen awe-
some essays on the topic, and *The Therapy of Desire* (Princeton: Princeton
University Press, 1994), if you are unusually patient or obsessive. These are very

since Aristotle says that the way to acquire any virtue is to practice it.

That sounds appealing. That was certainly Alfred Kinsey's method (I mean, who knew that the residents of Indiana were so much in love?).

A Man, a Plan, a Canal, Panama

But this is a philosophy book, and we can't just keep casting about for clever thoughts. There has to be a plan and method, and a point.

So here's the plan: I think Chef just is Socrates, writ in suburban American English. I am going to convince you of that truth by choosing the bits that confirm my notion, and mainly ignoring, dismissing, or twisting those bits that suggest otherwise. This is my method.[5] No serious philosophy can be done without the ability to do this sort of verbal two-step—that's what they teach in graduate school.

And here is the point: since South Park is to Denver what the Piraeus was to ancient Athens (I am using my method here), anything that Plato says about his city and suburbs, I can say about South Park and Denver. This will lead to astonishing insights, and then you will love me—and that is the point.

It should be clear enough that I want to be Chef (at least up until South Park's ninth season). But so do you. The difference is that I'm the one with a plan, a method and a point. You, on the other hand, dropped twenty bucks on this book because you have no life and watch cartoons and movies instead of going to singles bars (where people have a life). I would feel better if I could say "I have your twenty bucks," but it's embarrassing to confess how little of that I actually get, so that information is

---

respectable books to have on your shelf, but they will not make people think you are hip. If you want that, you need to get the three-volume *History of Sexuality* by Michel Foucault and anything by Julia Kristeva and/or or Hélène Cixous. You will not be able to read these books, but don't worry, nobody else can either. You can make up shit and say it's in the book. No one will dispute it if you say it with conviction. If someone does, double down and claim they don't know what they're talking about.

5   Before my colleagues in philosophy set about crucifying me (some more), I will point out that Socrates himself sanctions my method, at least regarding this subject: "I saw what a fool I'd been to agree to take part in this eulogy [of love], and, what was worse, to claim a special knowledge of the subject, when, as it turned out, I had not the least idea how this or any other eulogy should be conducted. I had imagined in my innocence that one began by stating facts about the matter in hand, and then proceed to pick out the most attractive points and display them to the best advantage" (*Symposium*, line 198d). Let my essay be a eulogy and let this defense be my own. I had imagined similarly.

excluded by my method. Not just philosophers, but well-paid scientists follow this method of excluding the inconvenient.

In Praise of Love

Love was a pretty big deal in Ancient Greece. Actually it's a pretty big deal anywhere—which is one reason it's hard to understand why contemporary philosophers spend their time thinking about language or mind or Being or breakfast. Of course, one could actually *sell* a book about breakfast, at least. (Do I seem obsessed by this money thing?)

But Plato, now there was a guy who knew how to sell books. His books are just filled with sex, love, war, death, taxes, and other certainties of life (the Bible sells well for similar reasons), serialized in the Adventures of Socrates and His Pals. It was cancelled after about ten seasons, and Plato sold into slavery. I hope Parker and Stone are getting the point, packing for Canada. Well, maybe not Canada. Lithuania is nice this time of year. Granted, reading Plato is something more akin to reading the *Atlantic Monthly* than watching *South Park*, but a close examination shows that there's little difference in these media apart from what their audiences think of themselves.

In one particular dialogue, called *Symposium*, Socrates and his pals take turns trying to outdo one another in speeches praising the god Eros. And here Socrates, who is always claiming he knows nothing, only *seeks* to know, makes a startling and singular claim—the only such claim he ever makes: "Love is the one thing in the world I understand" (*Symposium*, line 177d). Socrates later had reason to regret having said this, but it was too late.

As I said, it seems like Chef, the Socrates of the South Park suburbs, may also know something we do not, definitely about love. He is so very Socratic, If we are to learn it, and to trace his destiny in South Park, we need to know what he knows, and Socrates knows what he knows.

What does Socrates know, then? It seems that it comes down to this:

> If it were given to man to gaze upon Beauty's very self—unsullied, unalloyed, and freed from the mortal taint that haunts the frailer loveliness of flesh and blood—if, I say, it were given to man to see the heavenly beauty face to face, would you call his an unenviable life, whose eyes had been opened to the vision, and who had gazed upon it in true contemplation until it had become his own forever?" (*Symposium*, 212a)

Here, then, is how to find the clitoris. We must see Beauty itself, and that is not quite the same as looking at pictures of Susan Sarandon, although I'm thinking that a date with her might be closer. (Showing my age, I guess, but you have to admit, she's held up well.) I want *her* to love me too, and I might be able to make that worth her while, if she reads this and calls me.

The Secret Spice

We're now confronting the daunting task of glimpsing the Beautiful. Not to fear. There is a way. This may sound difficult to believe, but there are some Plato scholars, something bordering on a cult of them, who have explained how to see the Beautiful. Unfortunately, they have explained it only to each other, not really to us because, well, we're not worthy.

These Plato scholars are called "Straussians," and while they do have names (and code names), I am not going to call them here, except for their founding leader, a scholar named Leo Strauss, who fled the Nazis in the 1930s, and set up shop on the South Side of Chicago, where things were somewhat more peaceable, and proceeded to disseminate the truths of Plato for another forty years or so. And he got himself some disciples, a bunch of them actually, and they are still pretty noisy, very quirky and very smart. They like to organize secretly and take over departments of philosophy and political science, and then hire only their like-minded friends.

Thank God our government isn't like that.

You can easily learn about as much as you care to know about Straussians by typing the name into any search engine. Here I will recommend something to balance out whatever praise for them you may find. Some of the most dedicated and able critics of the Straussians have published their work in the journal *Humanitas*, it is available online. Go to http://www.nhinet.org/hum.htm and have a read. What you will discover is that Straussians would probably be harmless enough if they weren't bent upon infiltrating the highest levels of political influence in the United States, but since they are bent on this and since they have had some success in doing so (influencing, for example the notorious Project for a New American Century), they may not be altogether harmless—depending upon what you think of their ideas.

Straussians are not as much unlike Scientologists as we might wish either, except they are somewhat less famous and wealthy and way smarter. But the analogy is a good one because, well, I am going to have to admit that not only do I like the movies of Tom Cruise, John Travolta, and other Scientologists, I confess to being a long-time admirer of the music of Isaac Hayes. He's the bee's knees. I consume the products of Scientologists with a more or less clear conscience because, well, because they're good. Fess up. You loved *Risky Business*. Let's not be coy. You saw it more than once, and I know you've done the underwear dance.

By the same token, I like the books the Straussians write on Plato and Socrates not because I believe them, but because their ideas about Plato are just spicier than dry, careful and more sober scholarship.[6] It's sort of like discovering that a bunch of people you really don't like make the very best bar-b-que, and trying to decide whether to endure their company in order to get some. I have been to this Straussian bar-b-que, and I can report that they found me harder to endure than I found them, and they do know how to roast that beast.

Yes, they have all these secret stories about the recipe for the sauce, but who cares? The stories are part of the fun, so if it tastes good, have a bite. Just be sure to take a crap when it's all digested. Otherwise, you'll become a Straussian and it will come out of your mouth instead.

Real Philosophers (That Is, Cultish People)

Alright, so what do these Straussian-scientology people say about Socrates? A great deal, actually, but to put it in a nut-sack: Socrates spoke truly and the teeming ignorant mass of Athens killed him for it. Those bastards! And from this the Straussians take the lesson that any time a True Philosopher (sometimes they say a Real Philosopher—you can hear the capital letters when they say it) appears in the city (Athens, Denver, or wherever), he (and it *will* be a "he" although it's okay if "he" is gay, so long as "he" is a Zionist as well, although "he" need not be Jewish) is likely to appear daft and outlandish, and if he doesn't watch his step, he ends up dead. Women and non-Zionists are unsuitable for this stature of Real Philosophers. Some try, but they never get the thirty-third degree secrets.

Socrates and Chef didn't figure it out in time, and hence fell short of being Real Philosophers. From the need simultaneously to protect himself from the ignorant mass and to pursue the philosophical life, a slightly-smarter-than-Socrates-Real-

---

[6] For careful, dry, sensible scholarship on Socrates, you cannot do better than *The Philosophy of Socrates* by Thomas C. Brickhouse and Nicholas D. Smith. This book will never make the six o'clock news, but things with the ring of truth about them usually aren't too exciting.

Philosopher (like Plato, or Strauss, or his sycophants) must develop *two* teachings, which the Straussians call the "exoteric" teaching—this is what the philosopher says to the mass of ignorant people—and an "esoteric" teaching—which is what he says to the secret initiates. This "esoteric" teaching is "between the lines" of the exoteric words, and available for anyone smart enough to decipher it. But I'm not smart enough and neither are you.

A Bar-b-que

Straussians and wannabe Straussians don't read books about *South Park*, let alone write for them. So this esoteric teaching is not intended for us. But I have been to just enough of their bar-b-ques to get an idea how the sauce is made. Besides, I know what the secret spice is. It's Sage. They put Sage in the sauce. The Sage isn't hard to find, if you know where to look. So you put a little in your bar-b-que and suddenly you can read between the lines and get the esoteric teaching for yourself, because, well, you are what you eat.[7] Eat more Sage(s). I will make some of that sauce for you, right now; it won't be as good as theirs, but I belong with the white trash, not the initiates, and those of us down at the trailer park know how to have a good time too.

"Know thyself," said the Oracle at Delphi, and who am I to argue with those women? So this is how to find the clitoris, get a date with Susan Sarandon, and see the Beautiful, head-on, so to speak. I can do this. You watch. You will love me for this.

You Killed Socrates! You Bastards!

I *know* that Chef is Socrates, and that was what Parker and Stone *intended* from the outset. This is because like me, Parker and Stone are really white trash don'twannabe Straussians too, which is to say, they're my kind of people. I will reveal *their* esoteric teaching. White trash don't wannabe's prefer irony to posturing bullshit, but not the irony of hipsters. That is too cool for us. This is just homecooked irony.

So, we can see that Parker and Stone were going to kill Chef all along, but not because they didn't love him. They were the best friends Chef had. And the whole Scientology to-do was an

---

[7] This may be difficult to believe, but a German philosopher named Ludwig Feuerbach (1804–1872) actually made a career (albeit not a good one) arguing that you are what you eat. It sounds even better in German: "Man ist was man isst." At least his book was about breakfast, so people still read it.

exoteric cover story. They needed to kill Chef because Socrates got himself killed and Chef *is* Socrates. They had to teach us, the chosen, the Sage-eaters, what happens to a wise man like Chef in a place like South Park, and they leave no doubt whatsoever that Chef is the only adult in South Park who is anywhere near sane, let alone wise.

And now that both Socrates and Chef are dead, we have to rely on whatever evidence they left behind. Unfortunately, they left to us no writings of their own, except that Chef may have written one song. And in spite of heartfelt testimonials from Elton John, Ozzy Osbourne, and other equally credible people who were inspired by Chef, whether he really wrote the Alanis Morissette classic "Stinky Britches" has been, and remains, in serious dispute.

We shall have to proceed on the basis of testimony and what others have said about both Chef and Socrates. Parker and Stone actually based the character of Chef on their extensive study of Socrates. They haven't said as much, but here is how I know: There are hundreds of parallels between the two, but the master key to the secret lies in Salisbury steak.

According to Wikipedia, Salisbury steak is "mystery meat." <http://en.wikipedia.org/wiki/Mystery_meat>. Thus, when the character of Chef is introduced in the first season, he is repeatedly insistent upon serving the children Salisbury steak. Here's the indication, for those like us who are smart enough to follow it, that there is a subtext here. Chef is recruiting the boys into an esoteric wisdom.

Now "Salisbury" is a town in England which was called by the Romans "Sorviodunum," but get this: as Stone and Parker knew, neither "sorvio" nor "dunum" is in the huge Latin dictionary in my office, and I mean it's a big one. It has lots of words. So now I suppose you're following my drift.

Romans spoke Latin didn't they? Here, I have to think, is the secret link between Socrates and Chef that Parker and Stone so cleverly concealed. No Sorviodunum in the Latin dictionary. I mean, it's just not there. Can you believe that?

And here is what clinches it: neither is "Chef." Both terms are entirely absent. But "Socrates" is right there in the dictionary, and he wasn't even a Roman, just like Chef *who also wasn't a Roman*. See? We can only conclude that Sorviodunum and Chef were left out of the dictionary *intentionally*, and that Parker and Stone noticed it—perhaps they were the first to notice it—and they employed this startling omission to point us toward the *inclusion* of Socrates in the Latin dictionary, even though Socrates was *dead*.

Why else would they associate Chef with Salisbury steak?

Now you're closer to seeing the Beautiful than you have ever been. As you'll note, it's fun to be a Straussian, although sometimes they do have trouble getting tenure. They can be hard to follow for those of us not smart enough to be Straussians. They sort of need a lot of evidence to be missing to give them room to work, and in the case of Socrates, history has fondly seen to their deepest needs. All sorts of interesting stuff is missing from history, in fact, most of what actually happened is entirely unrecorded.

So if I found incontrovertible evidence today that Socrates wrote a treatise, I would have to destroy it as a matter of principle, and not just out of gratitude to the Straussians. The last thing philosophers need is someone spoiling the party, which is part of the reason I am fairly certain that most Christians also actually don't want Jesus coming back, especially those who have convinced themselves they want to see him face-to-face. Won't they be surprised when Parker and Stone are raptured and they are left behind, with Kirk Cameron, but without Jesus and his pals?[8] Philosophy, like Christianity, really depends on having plenty of space to make things up. It isn't a bad thing.

For the Challenged

Okay, so let's say you just couldn't follow my argument in the last section. I shouldn't really care, and I don't, except I'm worried that Susan Sarandon didn't follow it. And that would

---

[8] Since I'm not saying very much about *agape* in this essay, the kind of love Jesus favored, I want to make one point on the side. I don't claim to know exactly what *agape* is or requires of a person, but if we take the actions of Jesus as a guide, it would seem that *agape* can include being altogether merciless toward hypocrites. In this instance, I have to think that Parker and Stone have certainly found the "tough love" part of *agape*, and do much to redeem the, er, umm, less elevated aspects of *South Park* by rendering the service of roasting hypocrites every week. And I would point out an example. Some people say Parker and Stone are anti-religious, but I don't think that's right at all—they are anti-*hypocrisy*. When they decided to take on the Mormons in an episode, they did some investigation, discovered that the Mormons are, for the most part, not hypocrites (in contrast to most Christians, they make an honest effort to live what they believe and don't condemn those who believe differently), and darned if the Mormons don't come out smelling like a rose in that episode. I don't have to remind you that they made a successful musical from *The Book of Mormon* somewhat later. It was surprisingly respectful. Parker and Stone don't become hypocrites themselves because honesty requires the presentation of things in their true light. That light, when cast upon most people, is a bit unflattering, but not always. But if *South Park* didn't ring true, people wouldn't watch it. I would point out that I think it not an altogether ironic decision to name their production company "Avenging Conscience, Inc."

pretty well sacrifice the point of this chapter. It seems best to cover all the bases.

So how are you to see the Beautiful?

Alright. If I have to hold your hand, I'll do it. Socrates was convicted of corrupting the youth and worshipping false gods. That's why they killed him. And if you think about it, that's pretty much what led Chef to his demise too. But what is far, far more important is that Chef and Socrates see Eros in the same way. By the bye, the Straussians are very keen on eros—they've been known to call for "erosophy" instead of philosophy, since when it comes to wisdom, they would sooner take her to bed than shake her hand. I mean, when Athena, goddess of wisdom, sits down at the bar Straussians buy her a friggin' drink and say "Do you come here often?"

See what you're missing staying home, watching movies and cartoons? I told you people at the singles bar have a life; I mean they're hooking up with Athena and shit. Somebody is going to take Athena home tonight and be very, very bad, and if not you, it will be some Straussian in tight pants and platform shoes, with a medallion. Surely if he has a shot with her, *you* do, dweeb that you are, with your underwear dance. Hell, just get her number if you can't handle "Your place or mine?"—take it slow, maybe you get lucky.

So anyway, an erotic attraction to wisdom is in fact the substance of Socrates's very speech in the *Symposium*. Eros he says, is a way of getting outside of yourself; philosophers call it "transcendence," and it's significantly better than taking the bus. When you think of it, we all need to get outside of ourselves once in a while, and there are several ways to do that. Some people meditate, some astrally project, some sky-dive, and, in our test case, some take the eros express.

The question how you get outside of yourself affects what you find when you arrive on the other side. Socrates describes the path of eros in detail in a dialogue called *Phaedrus*, named after the handsome fellow he is talking to. Indeed, it is this same comely fellow to whom all the speeches in the *Symposium* are addressed. But it turns out that the bloom is just a bit off the rose in his case, and he isn't the fairest of them all, as we will see (he's no Athena, to be sure; she's very hot, like Susan Sarandon).[9]

---

[1] Phaedrus is a dude and Socrates is a dude. If you get uptight about the idea of two dudes together, you didn't make it through the first season of *South Park*. You certainly won't make it through Part Three of this book. There was nothing weird about all of this in Socrates's day and age because they were, like, civilized.

In the *Phaedrus*, Socrates pulls off an act of transcendence right in front of Phaedrus (they have wandered off into the countryside, so no one is watching, and the question before them is whether to get it on or talk about it). Socrates invokes the Muse and she brings to him a divine madness—he declares himself "possessed" and breaks into song.

Is any of this sounding familiar yet, you Chef fans? So what about the song? It is, of course a song about love. I could give you the text of it, but frankly, this is the essence of it:

> CHEF: Sometimes you fall in love! And you think you'll feel that way forever!
>
> You change your life and ignore your friends 'cause you think it can't get any better!
>
> But then love goes away, no matter what, it doesn't stay as strong!
>
> And then you're left with nothin' cause you're thinking with your dong!
>
> So watch out for that lover! It can destroy like a typhoon wind!
>
> Just play it cool and don't be a fool!
>
> MR. GARRISON: And never let poontang come between you and your friend!
>
> CHEF: Damn Right, Garrison!

Stone and Parker have a great economy of language. They took Socrates's song[10] and cut it by about ninety-five percent. If you don't think this is really what they did, I invite you to read it for yourself.[11] Chef was just about to marry a Succubus, but then his true friends, the boys, revealed that she was a psychobitch from hell (literally in this case), and he was saved and heart-broken all at once.

But Socrates and Chef both know this isn't the whole story about eros. If love is both a madness and a virtue (a sort of knowledge), then we really have to grasp the *sort* of madness it is, first, and *then* see whether we know anything new. Obviously neither Chef nor Socrates, being mortal, is wholly immune to the madness. After all, Socrates actually married a

---

[10] Just like "Stinky Britches," the authorship of the song is in question; there was an Athenian bluesman named Lysias who wrote a song Socrates sang earlier in the dialogue, and as for this song, well, its source is unclear, except that Socrates said "You made me do it, Phaedrus, I didn't wanna do it" (this is my translation of line 242e). But as Mick Jagger said, "the singer not the song"—at least I think it was Jagger; it may have been Richards.

[11] See *Phaedrus* 238d–241d. I'm not making this up, although I am twisting it a little and ignoring some parts.

Succubus named Xanthippe (where the heck was Plato when he was needed?—I mean if Kyle, Stan, and Cartman can reveal a Succubus, surely the greatest philosopher in history would notice the situation and give his old teacher a head's up on it).[12] And any time a mortal transcends himself he gets a little crazy.

So after Socrates sings the blues to Phaedrus about how love is no damn good, he tries to leave, but Phaedrus says, oh so seductively, "Don't leave now, the sun is so hot, stay here where it is cool, while I slip into something more comfortable" (*Phaedrus*, line 242a, my own somewhat free translation). Then Socrates tells Phaedrus about his own "divine sign," which is a little voice inside his head that tells him when he should definitely *not* do something. And of course, as we learn in Season Six, Chef is like Socrates:

> CHEF: Hello there, children!
>
> STAN: Chef! What would a priest want to stick up my butt?
>
> CHEF: Good-bye!

And he really leaves. This is intentional. Parker and Stone are telling us that Chef has the same divine sign as Socrates. Of course, the little voice doesn't *always* say something when it's needed. For example, when Socrates was on trial for his life, instead of defending himself, he suggested that the city of Athens should give him a friggin' pension for pointing out their hypocrisies and improving the place. That might have been a nice moment for the "divine sign" to say "Put a lid on it, you idiot!"

But in this case, with Phaedrus, Socrates has offended the god Eros with his songs about how love stinks, and now he must atone (and besides Phaedrus is still a looker, and Socrates is afraid he'll go blind if he doesn't take it all back), so the little voice inside his head tells him not to leave the spot. Then we get a speech about the types of madness love brings.

She Drives Me Crazy, Woo, Woo

Fine Young Cannibals understand this much about the madness of eros. I know, that's ancient history. But so is Socrates. So Socrates says the madness of love is not a curse; it comes from heaven, not from hell, or in his words, a mad lover is not manic, he is "mantic," and that little "t" is what saves him

---

[12]   I had a friend who married a Succubus once, and he wouldn't listen to me. So what I'm saying is maybe Plato did his best and Socrates was just an idiot.

(Phaedrus, line 244c). With a "t," love is like speaking prophecy, not like superstitiously reading omens. We should certainly prefer "heaven-sent madness over man-made sanity" (244d).

Madness with a "t" not only comes from heaven and gives us prophecy, it gives us poetry—love songs: it "seizes a tender, virgin soul and stimulates it to rapt passionate expression" (245a), which is to say, the madness sort of gives the soul a woody. You wouldn't want to go through your life without a single woody, so even if you're worried about, in Chef's inimitable words, "thinking with your dong," remember, your *soul* has a dong too. Yes, this includes women, even if Socrates would be surprised. I warned you it might get weird.

And there is nothing like the woody of a virginal soul. It's pretty "mantic." As you can see, the "t" sticks up above the line and is shaped like a dong.[13] It's an erection of the soul, and in this case, size *definitely* matters. So, for instance, when his soul was virginal, Bob Dylan had a very big "t," maybe even a "T," but as you can see, it's more of a "y" these days.[14]

Madness isn't all bad, then. And Socrates tells us it feels like having the soul grow wings and fly. That's the transcendence part. That's why Cupid is always pictured with wings. But he's about as angelic as Cartman. No, those wings are for something else than praising God. If they grew from his chin, at least he could get on Maury Povich.[15] If we have established that under the sway of eros, the soul gets excited and grows wings (and a "t"), then the question is, where the heck does it fly to? Or if you don't care for my grammar, "to where the heck does it fly?" Socrates does tell us that.

Finding the Clitoris

If you imagine that the "t" is like a little charioteer, and the wings are like two little flying horses, you can find out what Socrates and Chef know. One of the steeds is good and the other is quite naughty, and believe me, that's how your little "t" wants it. Socrates describes these beasts that pull the Eros Express: one "is upright and clean-limbed, carrying his neck high, with something of a hooked nose"; he "consorts with gen-

---

[13] Yes, smart-aleck, it does that in Greek too. Go join fraternity Tau Tau Tau.

[14] This note is just for Susan Sarandon, so it's probably none of your business. Sue, I consider the early Dylan to be among my most important songwriting influences—the *early* Dylan, okay? I'm no Dylan, but I think I can hold my own against Slim Tim Robbins.

[15] And if you wish to know why Cupid's penis is so small, well, consult the Chinpokomon episode and consider that Cupid is not an American.

uine renown, and needs no whip, being driven by the word of command alone" (253d). Yes, you do want that; this is you at home, when the big head is in charge.

But you want something else too: "The other is crooked of frame, a massive jumble of a creature, with a thick short neck, snub-nose . . . consorting with wantonness and vainglory, shaggy of ear, deaf, and hard to control with whip and goad" (253e). This is you slumming it, and the little head is calling the shots. Now, the "t" is caught in the middle of this argument, once the soul has grown wings; it wants what is good, and it wants what is bad, and how does a "t" make out which head to follow?

It isn't a pretty picture, I'm afraid. You may not like this part, but it's going to hurt me (and Susan, maybe) a lot more than it hurts you. The charioteer has to beat the poor crooked beast into utter submission, and it's a god-awful bloody mess, and that has to be repeated often, until "the evil steed casts off his wantonness; humbled in the end, he obeys the counsel of his driver" (254e).

That sucks ass. Frankly. But it isn't gay at all. Socrates is saying to Phaedrus, in *South Park* parlance: "Don't be so gay, let's just talk." And Socrates apparently said that to everyone, male and female, who wanted to jump his bones, except (presumably, Xanthippe, but I think she wasn't exactly Susan Sarandon). He even said the same thing to his favorite boy, the most desirable dude in Athens, Alcibiades (I know, but what's in a name?). Alcibiades did everything short of the Dance of Seven Veils for Socrates, and Socrates wouldn't do him.[16] And it wasn't because he was a dude, it's because it isn't wise to do your friends. Better to beat the little head to a bloody pulp.

Chef has done this in the relevant sense (it is the source of his wisdom—knowing whom to do, whom not to do, and when), and through mortification of the little head you can be like Chef. Cartman's mom didn't manage it, but she has her punishment (I mean, she has Cartman, right? Not to mention the genital warts). I have a cat who is a lot like Cartman, but I didn't deserve that. Honest.

---

[16] This all comes out and embarrasses Socrates at the end of the *Symposium* when Alcibiades breaks in on things about the time Socrates is pontificating about how no mortal can look Beauty right in the eye and control himself. Alcibiades says, in effect, "You looked at me and wouldn't do me, so am I not the fairest of all?" This is sort of like when your girlfriend says "Does this outfit make me look fat?" or your boyfriend says "Am I the best you ever had?" There's no way to answer the question: I recommend ambiguity: try "I love it," and if that doesn't work, you're on your own. If it does work, be sure to thank God you speak English instead of Greek.

So where does the chariot go once the bad horse is all sweetness and light? Up to the roof of the heavens, silly. Where else would it go? There it looks upon Beauty, itself, and not just TikTok videos of it. It's like God's own porno up there, but instead of gyrating, grinding hips and taut bodies from La Jolla and Van Nuys, it's purified of all that unnecessary bodily stuff. I know I told you that Plato knew how to sell books, but maybe I didn't mention he was considering a long-term market more than a quick cash-infusion.

So the outcome of all this is that there is, well, Socrates favors a chaste sort of love that is content to lie beside the beloved and just enjoy the company. This, by the way, is the source of the saying that a non-sexual friendly love is "purely Platonic"—Socrates is saying, "Don't do the nasty with your friends, you'll never see Beauty that way; and you don't want to find the clitoris, you want to find The Clitoris." And it turns out that The Clitoris really is a divine being, and when you find it, it speaks instead of doing whatever else you were imagining.

If your memory is failing you, here is the relevant exchange (and Chef has just offered the children Salisbury steak, with Sage):

STAN: Chef, do you know anything about women?

CHEF: Ha! Is the Pope Catholic?

KYLE: I don't know.

CHEF: I know ALL there is to know about women.

STAN: What's the secret to making a woman happy?

CHEF: [*dishing out the Salisbury steak*] Oh that's easy. You just gotta find the clitoris.

STAN: Huh?

CHEF: Oops, I guess you haven't gotten that far in your anatomy class, huh?

STAN: No, what does that mean, "find The Clitoris"?

CARTMAN: Is that anything like finding Jesus?[17]

---

[17] Some will say that I have the dialogue wrong, that the conversation really went:

STAN: Chef, how do you get a woman to like you more than any other guy?

CHEF: Well, that's easy; you've got to find the clitoris.

STAN: Huh?

CHEF: Oops.

Then Chef's divine sign says "Don't go there" and he shuts up. Of course, Cartman has it right. It's very much like finding Jesus, since the following advice from The Clitoris is really a paraphrase from the Gospels. This bit of wisdom is for Stan, whose soul has grown wings for Wendy Testaburger, and it sets Stan off on a quest for The Clitoris. When he finally finds it, here is what it says:

BIG THING: Be not afraid . . . [Stan trembles]

STAN: [*weakly*] Oh my God!

BIG THING: Behold my glory.

STAN: What . . . are you?

BIG THING: I am The Clitoris. [*Stan's eyes grow wide, MUSIC starts to swell up*]

STAN: The Clitoris?! I DID IT! I FOUND THE CLITORIS!!

BIG THING: Stan, your friends need you. They are in trouble and you must help them.

STAN: Wait, you're supposed to tell me how to get Wendy to like me.

BIG THING: There are more important matters right now . . .

STAN: NO WAY, DUDE! I'VE LOOKED ALL OVER FOR YOU, AND NOW YOU HAVE TO TELL ME HOW TO GET WENDY TO LIKE ME!!

BIG THING: Dude, she's eight years old. Just give her some ice cream or something.

STAN: Of COURSE! Ice cream!

BIG THING: Now go, your friends are in danger . . . The USO show is a mile east of here, just over that ridge. The Clitoris has spoken [18]

STAN: No, what does that mean, "find The Clitoris"?

CHEF: Forget I said anything. . . .

But if this is what you heard, you have experienced only the exoteric teaching. The esoteric teaching, which includes the *real* conversation, for the sacred initiates, is at https://southpark.fandom.com/wiki/South_Park_Archives.spoken.[18]

[18] The exoteric conversation in the movie went:

BIG THING: Be not afraid . . . [*Stan trembles*]

STAN: [*weakly*] Oh my God!

BIG THING: Behold my glory.

STAN: What . . . are you?

BIG THING: I am The Clitoris. [*Stan's eyes grow wide, MUSIC starts to swell up*]

STAN: The Clitoris?! I DID IT! I FOUND THE CLITORIS!!

As is obvious, this is the inferior, or "lower" teaching as white trash Straussians call it. It is the teaching without the Sage.

This may seem like a bit of a let down, but not really. The Clitoris says, in effect, "Stop worrying about the little head and start using the big one." This is Plato's whole theory of the soul, in a nut-sack (Plato could be wrong of course).

The point is that Chef and Socrates both claim that love is the one thing they truly understand, and they really mean something like "philia trumps eros every time." The virtue of "love's knowledge" is knowing who your friends are. So if you were to gaze upon Beauty unsullied and unalloyed, you might sing it a song, have a conversation, go to the movies, but you wouldn't want to mess things up by using your "t" on it.

And that is why you want to study philosophy and not erosophy. Just be a friend to wisdom, okay? There are enough people screwing Athena, so don't be like them. And the Straussians don't know anything you really need to know; buy them some ice cream or something. Go talk with your real friends. And now that I've slipped some Sage into your bar-b-que, you have to love me . . . Susan.

BIG THING: You must not let Terrance and Phillip's blood be spilled on the ground.

STAN: Wait, you're supposed to tell me how to get Wendy to like me.

BIG THING: There are more important matters right now.

STAN: NO WAY, DUDE! I'VE LOOKED ALL OVER FOR YOU, AND NOW YOU HAVE TO TELL ME HOW TO GET WENDY TO LIKE ME!!

BIG THING: Dude, you just have to have confidence in yourself; believe in yourself and others will believe in you. Chicks love confidence. Now go, the Clitoris has spoken.

5
Killing Kenny

DEATH THERAPY IN *SOUTH PARK*

You'd think that one look at *South Park* would be enough for any decent book. But who said this was gonna be decent? I think you gotta hand it to Parker and Stone, seriously. They have passed through most of their adulthood without any sign of maturing beyond what they found funny as junior high boys. And they got rich doing that. I just got sent to the Principal. Until I was too old. Then I got sent to the Dean's office. That will probably happen again when this book comes out. Besides, there's something pretty profound in repetition. Kids get that. Adults have forgotten it.

Messkirch Meets South Park

We're going to try to understand what Martin Heidegger (1889–1976) can teach us about death, especially Kenny McCormick's death(s). Since Heidegger has been dead for quite some time now, he may be a good person to ask—maybe not so much because he is dead (I mean, a lot of people are dead, like Francisco Franco, and probably Elvis), but because he was obsessed with death from about the time he was Kenny's age, and as you can see, he had a long time to think about it.

Before we get to the fun stuff, a couple of words about Heidegger are in order. His name isn't exactly a household word, and I am certainly not saying you should read his writings—the word "writings" just isn't quite the right word for the voluminous pile he left to the world. Writings can be read. Heidegger never wrote anything that could actually be read by untroubled humans.[1]

Part of this was because he was German and didn't have the decency to write in English. Part of it was because he was German and the German language proceeds without the benefit of a comprehensible grammar.[1] Part of it was because he was German and the Germans encourage their philosophers to be incomprehensible by rewarding them with lots of servants and perquisites, and more of this the more incomprehensible they are.[2] The rest, as far as I can tell, was just because he was German.[3]

If we have established that Heidegger's writings are unreadable, we can now say a word about his character. Heidegger was an asshole.[4] No. A flaming asshole. No, wait. A flaming Nazi asshole.[5] So why would you or anyone else care about what a flaming Nazi asshole whose writings are unreadable has to say about death (granting of course that Nazis do know a good bit about death)?

---

[1]   Some of you don't believe me and think you may want to try your hand at it. Let me save you some effort. Here is a passage—not atypical, randomly selected, I just opened his most important work, *Being and Time*, to any page and typed what was there (I swear to God, that's all I did):

> Now that resoluteness has been worked out as Being-guilty, a self-projection in which one is reticent and ready for anxiety, our investigation has been put in a position for defining the ontological meaning of that potentiality which we have been seeking—Dasein's authentic potentiality-for-for-Being-as-a-whole. By now the authenticity of Dasein is neither an empty term nor an idea which someone has fabricated. But even so, as an authentic potentiality-for-Being-as-a-whole, the authentic Being-towards-death which we have deduced existentially still remains a purely existential project for which Dasein's attestation is missing.

This is from p. 348 of the Macquarrie and Robinson translation (New York: Harper and Row, 1962). In context and with requisite painful study, this passage makes perfect sense. But do you really want it that bad? Life is short. Somebody else can do it; why don't you have a beer instead?

[2]   See Mark Twain's 1897 speech "The Awful German Language," at: https://drive.google,com/file/d/0B4xHZbr3ygOmYm5teGIsSzQ4a28/view

[3]   You think I'm exaggerating. Alright, think what you will. But before you decide the case of Heidegger in your mind, please consult Victor Farías's book *Heidegger and Nazism* (Philadelphia: Temple University Press, 1989), pp. 73–74. I'm no fan of Heidegger, and even less a fan of his cultish following in academia, barely closeted quasi-Nazis, except for the few who are not like that but cannot seem to leave this miserable person alone. Picking up from the last chapter, even the cultish Straussians find the Heideggerians to be too cultish. They all say "Heidegger was the greatest philosopher of the twentieth century; so much the worse for the twentieth century . . ." and go back to their Plato.

[4]   Some of my best friends were once German (now they all have the decency to speak English), so don't take this the wrong way, okay? I love Germany, when it isn't in the mood of world domination. It's funny. They thought they wanted to rule Europe, and now, since Brexit, they actually do, and they realize they should have been careful what they wished for.

[5]   This is not the actual word used by any biographer I have read, but it sums up a lot of their other words, and no one, even his greatest fans, makes him out to be all sweetness and light. There are several biographies. My advice is don't fully believe any of them. Everyone who takes the time to write a biography of Heidegger either hates him with a vengeance, or worships him like an idiot. Like Trump. It's hard to get the truth about a guy like that.

Well, you may not care, but as much as I hate to admit it, Heidegger is probably the only philosopher of the twentieth century whose unreadable writings will still be studied five hundred years from now. That isn't fair at all, but it might be justice. The twentieth century was a pretty bloody affair, all things considered, and it might as well be *remembered* that way. And we (I can't excuse myself, my first thirty-nine years were spent in that century) certainly left some butt-ugly architecture for future people to wonder about, and I can't say much for the art either.

The philosophy of Heidegger goes pretty well with the building I inhabit on a daily basis, and most of you are no better off. This building is definitely about death. I feel like a gerbil in a Habitrail. (I know Lemmiwinks. Mr. Slave. Don't go there.) So, we are sort of stuck with the twentieth century and with the Bad Boy of Baden-Wurttemberg, whether we like it or not.

It is sort of like imagining, what if Eric Cartman became an adult and actually attained immortality as a thinker? I'm afraid that's Heidegger. He came from a little town in the mountains called Messkirch, and it has more in common with South Park than is comfortable. And if, in Heidegger's childhood, there was an equivalent of Kyle, *he* went to the camps, and if there was a Stan, he probably died fighting in the resistance, and if there was a Kenny, well, you know what happens to Kenny. For the first six seasons it was death every week. That got old, but not old enough to disappear entirely. Alexa killed Kenny at Jeff Bezos's command in Season 22. Still a trope of the series, no doubt it always will be.

You and the Boys

Before we can really get our cerebral endowments around Kenny's deaths (126 times, if Wikipedia is to be trusted), we have to pause for a bit of quick psychology. The reason for it will be clear later. Anyone can see, and you have probably noticed, that *this* collection of boys—Kyle, Stan, Cartman, and Kenny—really works well. If you have a psychological turn of mind, you may have also noticed that Freud's standard schema, the one we all had to learn, applies pretty well: Cartman is the Id, Kyle is the Superego, and Stan is the Ego. If you got that far on your own, you may have also said to yourself: "What the hell is Kenny?" Advanced students of Freud will smile in a self-satisfied way, finger their cigars, and say (in a markedly Austrian accent), "Ja, ja, Kenny, he ist der Death Impulse."

Freud decided, after observing the behavior of the humans in the First World War, that he just couldn't explain it all with "libido," that delicious sexual energy that he previously thought was doing all the work in the world.[6] He decided that there was a second fundamental principle at work in the human psyche which he pretentiously labeled "thanatos"—everything sounds more convincing in a dead language, especially words for death.

However that may be, it is hardly satisfying. Kenny dies all over the place, so he represents the Death Impulse. That's about as informative as saying that Homer Simpson represents the "stupid impulse," or as the Latins would have said, "stupiditas." We can do better.[7]

If we entertain the idea that the reason the four boys work so well for everybody is that together they form one complete psyche, we are still a ways from grasping what Kenny is up to. He is definitely lurking around in your psyche doing something, and he does a lot more than just die and rot there. For some initial help, we need to move beyond Freud and into the strange world of his least favorite student, Carl Gustav Jung (1875–1961).[8] Jung, in spite of some flakey followers, has a pretty interesting take on the activity of the human psyche. His theory is complicated, detailed, somewhat German, and helps with Kenny.

---

[6]   For more on this topic, and I know you want more, I can hardly think of a better source than the well-written and extremely entertaining previous chapter in this volume.

[7]   This is utterly and completely unfair to Freud. His theory of thanatos is in fact subtle and interesting. Feel free to look it up. Being unfair to Freud has become a popular sport in intellectual life, and I confess to "piling on." This is my favorite penalty in football—I loved to do it when I played, I love the referee's signal for it, and I wish they would make greater use of it these days; I would start watching football again if they would just call players for piling on. Now, Freud would have a great explanation for why people like to pile on, and he would need one given that he's at the bottom of the pile these days. I also like "unnecessary roughness," with its invocation of "necessity" as defined by "the minimum required to put a guy on the ground, plus just a little more" and anything beyond that is a "personal foul"—another great term. The suggestion of guilt and culpability here is fascinating. But nowadays they usually just call "personal foul" and leave out the sub-category, which is frankly too abstract for me. It is like saying "Bless me father for I have sinned," and the priest says "what have you done?" and you say "Oh, it was just a sin." It would hardly be worth the vow of celibacy to get that sort of confession. Next time I go to confession, I shall say, "well, piling on and unnecessary roughness." If the priest says "And whom did you so treat, my son?" I will say "Freud, but not Heidegger, since Heidegger had it coming . . ." See how many Hail Marys that gets me.

[8]   The relationship between Freud and Jung is complicated, and people argue about why they had such an awful falling out. My favored explanation is that Jung actually challenged Freud on the appropriateness of Freud's relations with the sister of his own wife. The "official story" is that Jung became dissatisfied with Freud's reduction of everything to sex, but if you think about it, that is sort of the same objection in different words.

I will not trouble you with the details, but let us keep the Freudian assumption that Cartman, Kyle, and Stan are pretty much Id, Superego, and Ego. Kenny is what Jung calls the "transcendent function." Now this is a fancy term, and it names an equally fancy idea: "The psychological transcendent function arises from the union of conscious and unconscious contents . . . the unconscious behaves in a compensatory or complementary manner towards the conscious."[9] Wherever the unconscious and conscious meet, you get this conflict and mutual completion.

So you each have a "Stan" mediating between your "Kyle" and your "Cartman," and your Stan is under a lot of pressure to keep your Kyle and your Cartman from killing each other. It is from this very stress that your Kenny springs into action— and action it is. This is his Mysterion function. Kenny *solves problems*, all kinds of problems. Jung says (somewhat Germanically) "Man needs difficulties; they are necessary for health" ("The Transcendent Function," p. 278). My difficulty is "What the hell is Kenny about?" Let us look at how Kenny compensates and complements. Our health depends on this.

What Did He Say?

Let's go at this problem by a slightly indirect path. Why is it that Kyle, Stan, and Cartman can all understand what Kenny says, and we get hardly a word of it? Well, Kenny is not there to communicate with *us*, he is there to communicate with the boys. Sure, the activities of the transcendent function are evident to others (even if they don't exactly stand up and say "I'm Kenny McCormick, by God"), through our behavior, attitudes, and choices, our little Kennys are communicative, but what they say is clear only within the psyche. And all of our Kennys are daring, but they are not all equally successful.

For example, I know this is a dated example, but it's irresistible under the circumstances. You can imagine, say, Bill Clinton's Kyle telling him not to mess with Monica, his Cartman saying "just do her, dude" and his Stan saying "Well, how about the cigar?" In light of this conflict, Bill's Kenny leaves a tell-tale stain; I guess the French would say Bill's Kenny did a "petite mort." This really cannot be called a fully successful Kenny. He created far worse problems than he solved, although it's hard to deny he solved a certain transient

---

[9]   C.G. Jung, "The Transcendent Function," in Joseph Campbell, ed., *The Portable Jung* (New York: Penguin, 1976), p. 273.

problem. A trained Jungian therapist works with your Kenny, encouraging it to compensate and complement differently, since its present ways of mediating are not working out so well for you (otherwise you would be a Jungian therapist instead of paying one $150 an hour, minimum).

To put it in the vernacular, you try to zig and your unconscious just zags, and then there's your transcendent function with its ass just flapping in the wind for anybody to see, but it doesn't say a word, just does crazy things to try to keep you from looking like the idiot you really are. Sometimes it saves the day; sometimes, well, it gets gunned down by the Transportation Security Administration, or some other bastards. The solution to this problem, as Jung puts it "obviously consists in getting rid of the separation between conscious and unconscious" (p. 279). But he continues, "this cannot be done by condemning the contents of the unconscious in a one-sided way" (you'll all recall that Cartman was grounded for forming a Nazi party in South Park, but it wasn't permanent), "but rather by recognizing their significance in compensating the one-sidedness of consciousness . . ." (p. 279).

And here Jung gives us our marching orders:

> The tendencies of the conscious and the unconscious are the two factors that together make up the transcendent function. It is called "transcendent" because it makes the transition from one attitude to the other organically possible, without the loss of the unconscious [which is why Kenny does not speak to you; we can't bring the unconscious to full consciousness without losing its, well, "unconsciousness"]. . . [the] method of treatment presupposes insights which are at least potentially present in the patient [that's you, or Bill Clinton, or all four of the boys taken together] and can therefore be made conscious [that's Kenny solving the problem by some kind of action]. If the therapist [that's me and Jung] knows nothing of these potentialities, he cannot help the patient to develop them either. (p. 279)

We can now understand one reason why it just didn't work when Parker and Stone actually killed Kenny for a couple of Seasons Six and Seven—Kenny was written out of the show. It's easy to understand how they grew bored with killing him nearly every week (more about that shortly). But something has to do the work of uniting the boys. Thus, whether it is Butters (recall they made him wear Kenny's coat) or the contest for the fourth friend (won by Tweak—now there's a nervous transcendent function for you), no one could really do the job except Kenny himself. The boys said it, and Parker and Stone knew it.

Kenny's return was inevitable for a healthy show. So Kenny is the transcendental glue that holds South Park (and you) together, and indeed, you don't want to face life without your transcendent function—you can't. This helps us get a grip on what Kenny's constructive contribution is to South Park, but in some ways, it just makes it harder to understand why we have to kill the little dude every week, or at least once in a while. And Jung won't take us there. He just isn't German enough.[10] And Freud was even less German.[11] I'm afraid we need Heidegger now.

Falling to Your Death

The most basic thing to understand about Heidegger is a distinction between what he calls "ontic" and "ontological" levels of human experience and existence. This is a pretty tall order, and I need to put you on notice now that you cannot go off to the coffee house after reading this chapter and expect to impress any of Heidegger's devotees with what you learned here. Part of this is because Heidegger's followers cannot be impressed by anyone except Heidegger, but part of it is because I'm only going to give you some of the juiciest bits.

I will put this in my own words (and believe me, that's what you want), but my summary is a paraphrase of Heidegger's story in *Being and Time* (call it *Sein und Zeit* for the best effect in a coffee house, but be sure to pronounce it correctly—"zine unt tzite"—so that your Kenny doesn't leave a stain).[12] Suppose you walk up to the edge of a cliff and look over. You will experience two things at the same time: first is fear, and you will want to step back; the second is a desire to keep looking, to linger over it.

According to Heidegger, in this second desire you are encountering something quite a bit deeper and more puzzling. You're pondering your freedom to jump, and in so doing, you are confronting your own death, your limit, your "ownmost possibility" as he calls it. The response to this is not fear, it is

---

[10] Jung was Swiss, which is German lite. The Swiss have the trains running on time (so they obviously aren't French or Italian), but they aren't sure why. They think the answer may lie in the structure of the watch

[11] Freud was Austrian, and Jewish, which is almost the opposite of being Heidegger.

[12] The account I am summarizing is in the Macquarrie and Robinson translation, beginning on p. 226, and continuing farther than you will be willing to read. And also notice that in Ethan Hawke's first appearance in *Reality Bites*, he is reading this translation of *Being and Time*, in a coffeehouse, and, unless I miss my guess, the very pages I am summarizing.

"Angst" (or "anxiety," or even "dread," but keep it in German for better effect).

Fear is merely "ontic," which is to say that fear is associated with your everyday self and its bundle of survival instincts and social skills (and the things you repress as socially unaccept able[13]), but Angst is "ontological." Angst brings you into an awareness of your total-self, your self-as-a-whole, by bringing into your vague awareness the limits of it (and death can be oh-so-limiting).[14] So there you are, staring over the precipice, pre-ferring your (apparently idle) curiosity to your safety, and now I want you to take stock of what you are experiencing.

The reason you like this isn't just because you are danger-ously curious. You like it because it gives you a sense of your-self-as-a-whole, and that is what happens every time you consider yourself ontologically instead of just ontically. Angst is the response to this way of doing it, because you feel your freedom to jump over the side, and that freedom "totalizes" you in the face of your decision not to do it (or to do it, but the people who make that decision are not reading this, I think)—I mean your decision not to jump sort of crystallizes you into one unified act of willing: "I-shall-not-jump-(although-I-can)." And you sort of like that; it makes you feel powerful and free.

Of course, you really haven't accomplished very much in practical terms, so don't expect a medal. But there is something practical in this: you are practicing "anticipatory resoluteness," in Heidegger's terms. Eventually this will make dying easier for you, which you only have to do once, but you should try to do it well (since no one else can do it for you, except maybe Jesus, and that may count ontologically, but it won't get you out

---

13   The reason why Freud won't get us to an adequate understanding of Kenny is that Freud thinks anxiety is pressure on the ego from the accumulated repression of socially unacceptable impulses: anxiety is just fear without a specific object. This overlooks the specific character of each and every fear, and Kenny actually isn't afraid of anything in that sense, and hence represses nothing. No, Freud won't do the trick.

14   To speak of Heidegger in either English or German, one has to hyphenate all sorts of words. The reason is that the hyphens are supposed to help us remember that even when we are using several words, they all designate just one phenome-non, taken together. So for instance, a normal person would speak of his or her "state of mind," but that would be merely ontic. In order to make it ontological, you should speak of your "state-of-mind," or if it is really, really deep, put it in italics too, your *state-of-mind* (see *Being and Time*, p. 227). Now, *now* my friends, you're doing *fundamental ontology*. And isn't it *nice*? This is useful to know, and to master, because it can be used in lots of other settings. So if you want to share a meal with someone, but you want him to know that your interest in doing so is existential, not just social, you can say "let's-do-lunch," or even *let's-do-lunch*. Such a lunch is not only gabbing and chewing, it is a resolute decision not to die from starvation . . . just yet. But you *could*, after all.

of going through it ontically). You have a lifetime to think about this, so don't screw up your own death. Be resolute. Don't die like a wimp. Kenny never, ever dies like a wimp.

Ennui and Other Childhood Ailments

We have lots of experiences that are like the cliff, in that they sort of show-us-ourselves-as-a-whole, and there are other responses to the experiences than Angst. For example, one I like is what Heidegger calls "ontological boredom." This one actually sounds better in Frech: *ennui ontologique*. In German it is *ontologische Langweiligkeit*. That's pretty hard to say. This means that you are so very bored that nothing interests you or *can* interest you. All is tedious and wearisome *in principle*. This is actually what happens to you if you read Heidegger.

It is a mood, or "Stimmung," which is a very interesting word. This ain't about your transitory feelings, it's about the way a mood sort of takes hold of you and you can't do much about it. Our moods, Heidegger suggests, reveal to us something of our ontological "modes" (so moods are really modes). They reveal our orientation to our deaths, our ultimate finitude. When you consider yourself-as-a-whole, you have to include your beginning and your *end*. Obviously there is something about joy, and hope, and love, and so on, that shows-us-ourselves-as-a-whole. But Heidegger is not a real cheery guy, so we get Angst and ennui and despair and the like.

Why You Should Care

Things are about to become a little bit sticky, but stay with me. The reason you should care about any of this (according to Heidegger at least) is because you already *do* (or as he says, you "always already" care). As long as you're alive, every single one of your ways of dealing with the future is some way of caring about it. Even hopelessness is a kind of caring.

Let's say you love someone who not only doesn't love you, but never will. Now that sucks ass. Bad. How bad? Well, not that bad, because it still makes a difference to you, and that's sort of good. It means you're not dead yet, and your future might be bleak, but it's better than *no* future. In fact, try as you might, you'll *never* be able to have no future at all. When you try to have no future, you just hit a brick wall, because you are trying to pretend you are dead, but dead people don't try to pretend. They don't care.

You *do*—at least enough to pretend you don't. And you aren't fooling anybody, especially not Heidegger. You do sort of experience yourself-as-a-whole, but not really, because it isn't over for you. You can jump off a cliff, sure. But you aren't doing it *now*, right? Or maybe some ferocious animal is "coming right for you." But it hasn't got you *yet*. Your death is a possibility, but not an actuality. And it has *always* been like that.

And yet, you want to experience your own life-as-a-whole, even though that brings up the matter of your death. It's built-in-to-the-way-you-are. You want to know how the episode ("The Life and Times of You") comes out. So how is it that you understand your own death? And here's the rub. You watch other people die. And they do. Dropping like flies all over the damn place, especially the last couple of years. I think you may be getting the picture now.

Kenny certainly dies a lot. Spectacularly. Nearly every week for six years he was taking a fall so you can do-vicarious-death. That's healthy for you, believe it or not. Here is how Heidgger describes it (keep reading, it will be worth it, I will translate as we go):

When Dasein[15] reaches its wholeness in death, it simultaneously loses the Being of its "there." [That is, you die, so you aren't "there" anymore.] By its transition to no-longer-Dasein, it gets lifted right out of the possibility of experiencing this transition and of understanding it as something experienced. Surely this sort of thing is denied to any particular Dasein in relation to itself. [This is you failing to grasp your own death, because you aren't "there" to grasp it.] But this makes the death of Others more impressive. [That's why you like watching Kenny's demise.] In this way the termination of Dasein becomes 'Objectively' accessible. [This is you saying "geez" at the creative spectacle of Kenny getting killed this way and that.] Dasein can thus gain an experience of death, all the more so because Dasein is essentially Being with Others [That is, Kyle, Stan, Cartman and Kenny are all in it together] . . . Even the Dasein of Others, when it has reached its wholeness in death, is no-longer-Dasein, in the sense of Being-no-longer-in-the-world . . . Yet, when someone has died, his

---

[15] This ugly German word "Dasein" is one you'll have to live with, literally. Its ordinary meaning is "existence," but it literally means "being-there," and Heidegger uses it to describe the peculiarly human way of existing in the world, "ontologically." The translators leave it untranslated, and Heidegger's disciples talk about "Dasein this" and "Dasein that" all over the place. I have a lot of opinions about this that I will spare you. Just remember when you see it that "Dasein" is "you-in-a-bad-mood," or in any-mood-at-all for that matter.

[16] This is from *Being and Time*. I warned you about reading Heidegger. Maybe now you believe me.

Being-no-longer-in-the-world (if we understand it in an extreme way) is still a Being, but in the sense of Being-just-present-at-hand-and-no-more of a corporeal Thing which we encounter. [This is the rats eating Kenny's dead body.][16]

Kenny is a cartoon. That may seem obvious to you. But what is handy about it, is that he is about three or four times removed from actual people in your life. If someone you love dies, it isn't funny, but there is therapy in the grief—hard, hard therapy. Even if someone you don't know dies, that isn't funny, but we learn compassion toward those who have lost someone, a hard therapy. If someone pretends to die, say, in a play or on TV, but doesn't, that *can* be funny, but one needs to be careful about it. To make it too graphic raises ambivalent feelings in us, and curtails the therapeutic value. If a cartoon dies, it just doesn't matter very much in the grand scheme of things, no matter how graphic the death is.

The deaths of children are the most challenging and griev-ous kinds of deaths. And here is eight-year-old Kenny dying and it's a riot. It may seem callous to treat one's friends as per-sons whose deaths don't even require burial, and who are ade-quately mourned by yelling "You bastards!" and going on like nothing happened. But something did happen. Kenny was "there" all along so that we (and the boys) would feel complete, which requires "being-toward-death" in Heidegger's words.

We don't become aware of how important this is to compen-sation and completion (in Jung's terms) until Kenny is "really dead" for a couple of seasons. How can we laugh at death if nobody dies? Where will our therapy come from? When death took a holiday for a couple of seasons, we all had a problem, and so Parker and Stone were continually referencing Kenny's absence in order to remind us. But having Butters or Tweak or even Timmy die spectacular deaths just will not do the trick. Kenny must die so that we can all live better, and so that our unconscious awareness of our ultimate end can communicate with our conscious lives. It really is death therapy.

Healing a Neurosis

So we conclude with a question of sorts. You know you will die. Why doesn't that, in and of itself, make you crazy? Human beings live their entire lives in at least a vague, but sometimes very clear awareness that they will die. Now imagine for a moment that this awareness was never really clear to us. What would life be like? I am sure that many animals are at least vaguely aware that they will die, some even mourn the deaths of others. What do *we* who are Dasein-ing along gain by being sharply aware?

In this generation, we have Kenny, and Kenny is not just the death of another, he dies for me and is me, that is, the part of me that dies every time I experience-myself-as-a-whole. Kenny is my ontological ground and limit –and yours too. *South Park* would just be silly without him. Well, it's just silly anyway, but silliness is ontological, I think, not merely ontic. We are silly to the core (see the chapter on Monty Python).

And life would be a lot less precious if we were never clear about its limits. We symbolize those limits to ourselves by "practicing for death"—Socrates said that that's what philosophy *is*, practicing for death. No one gets as much practice as Kenny, and so Kenny becomes very good at dying, at showing us how. Socrates also insisted his own death was a sort of healing, and I think that those who die well do teach us something, and perhaps they learn something themselves: Death does not cancel out all meaning in life.

How many times do we have to repeat this to ourselves before we really believe it—at least believe it enough to keep death from driving us crazy? Well, the answer is "every day." We need a daily dose of death to remind us of the value of life. Or maybe not. I mean, that sounds right, but I really don't know what I'm talking about. Ask Heidegger.

Part II

Parental Guidance Suggested

6

The Good, the Bad, and the Beautiful

Sergio Leone's Animals, Actors, and Aesthetics

> There's two kinds of people in the world, those with loaded guns, and those who dig.
>
> —Blondie

There are actually *three* kinds of people, but one kind just bit the dust when Blondie offered this memorable piece of philosophy to Tuco. Picture, if you will, the famous Mexican Stand-Off in the Sad Hill Cemetery in Sergio Leone's *The Good, The Bad, and the Ugly*. God knows Tarantino has re-staged it enough times to drive us all bananas, but we have come to expect, no, to *demand* it from him. I'll get to that in a later chapter.

Philosophers like to say "I'm playing Plato to my own Socrates," when they ask a question they intend to answer themselves. But now, playing Quentin to my own Tarantino, imagine this: instead of Blondie, Tuco, and Angel Eyes, you've got a dog person, a cat person, and a horse person. Who draws first, and who is left standing? We'll get to the bottom of it before all is said and done. But it's good to remember that the stand-off occurs in the film *not* because the three antagonists don't *like* each other. They have a grudging respect, even admiration of one another. But that is irrelevant. They don't *trust* each other, and *that* is the problem.

Horse People

Cats are the choice of thinking people. Over dogs, I mean. Horse people are another story altogether. Something primal is going on there that I will never quite grasp. When I first saw *Equus*, I had a hard time following it, the idea of horse worship being so far beyond my teenage imagination. Richard Burton was also, well, a bit too subtle for me. But as time passed and I met some horse people, I began to sense something quite human but also strange to me in this. And then I read about Catherine the Great, and then I got to know some more horse people (especially of the feminine bent), and, well, I still really don't get it. I know what it is only by its profound contrast with my sense of the world.

But I still have to say a few words about horse people. As far as I can see, horse people are all about *eros*. This is about sex. I think that's fine, and I'm sure that horse people have the very best sex of *all* people. Horses are very big. They run really fast, and that's what they *like* to do. You can draw the analogies. I don't envy horse people, except for a vague feeling that I might be missing something—the thing they all seem to know that evades the rest of us. That's why I don't trust them, I confess. They know something I don't know, and are perfectly alright with the idea of being kicked in the head once in a while, and with suffering horrible injuries and even death just to go nowhere in particular *faster*. That changed for the first time in human history when trains appeared. Now it's very far from the truth that I would need a horse go nowhere in particular faster. But there is still something primal in *this* kind of fast. It's a living beast of some sort for Pete's sake. Jesus on a donkey! The world needs them, but they aren't my friends.

Dog People

I get dogs and dog people. They are people of action, and that's a good thing. The world needs people like that. Dog people aren't *always* dull-witted, but they aren't thinkers. They fetch and sit and stay and shake hands. All very necessary to social order. Cat people probably understand dog people better than dog people understand themselves; just as cats understand dogs better than dogs understand themselves. This arrangement is fine with dog people and with dogs. I mean, how much does anyone really *need* to know? Life isn't about knowing things, it's about *doing* things, from their point of view. Like going for a walk; or another walk, or how 'bout sniffing that butt?

And it's easy to see the attraction of an animal that adores everything you do and everything you are, whose sense of self-worth depends entirely upon your next act. I have to think that dog people want to be admired almost as much as they want to go play Frisbee, which is apparently quite a lot. If I want to be admired for no good reason, I'll certainly get a dog. They are virtuous beasts, and their owners are usually dutiful people. But I don't trust them. There is a slight hint of the totalitarian mindset in them. They can be our friends, but don't go into business with one—unless you're also a dog person, in which case, I don't know why you are reading this chapter (gathering intelligence on the loyal opposition?).

Cat People

Cats don't admire us and yet, they don't really need us. Oddly, they like us (after all, we constantly do their bidding, so maybe it isn't terribly odd). But cats are what they are with or without us, which is part of what we like about them. They choose us, for reasons of their own. Like many of you, I have spent decades trying to descry the feline and grasp their choice to live with us. Because they choose me, they are my life companions. I like people well enough to live with one of them—another cat person of course—but our several cats currently outnumber us. That happens with cat people. One cat just leads to another, as Hemingway said.

I trust cat people, and I get them. Cats are more reliable than cat people, but neither is very reliable. Cat people will make promises they cannot keep, but at least it's predictable, so we cat people forgive each other. Dog and horse people cannot understand this, and they never forget, and they don't trust us. Cat people rarely have a strong sense that they need to go to the protest or the march against assholes. They can be activists, but normally they'll be stuffing envelopes, making lists of contacts, taking minutes, that sort of thing. They aren't entirely domesticated (cat people and cats), they are easily offended and they hiss at you if you linger too long or stroke them the wrong way.

Now, trust me, if you are the sort who can trust a cat person—perhaps it's beginning to dawn on you that this whole thing is about trust, just like I said about the Mexican Standoff, and trust is delicate and hard to find in a hard world. But I swear, this chapter *is* about *The Good, the Bad, and the Ugly*. You currently have no idea why I am talking about horses, dogs, and cats. But if you followed the advice at the beginning of this book, perhaps you just watched that movie. You may not have noticed it, but horses, dogs, and cats play a very great part in Sergio Leone's message to you, as *auteur*. This is going to require some set-up. So indulge me for a few pages while I talk about animals and aesthetics, and we'll come to the movie, and it'll be worth it.

I've figured some things out, I think. And some of those things are philosophical. I will present them in vignettes, but there is an overall point in this. I want to know why cats are the choice of *thinking* people, and I have some suggestions that are not, I hope, simply partisan generalizations proffered by a cat person. I aim to say things that even dog people would have to concede. Horse people aren't reading this, or any other philosophy book, so we will never know what they think or why. They have other things to do with their horses and with each other.[1]

I also want to add that I think it is interesting that one thing cat, dog, and horse people agree on is that they like the movies. But I wonder, rather pointedly, whether we see and experience the same things at the movies and with the movies, and in the movies. I have this sneaking suspicion that the catharsis we all get is different among the three types.

By the way, there are actually four kinds of people, because bird people are very real and just as common as horse people. (Cat people and dog people are more common than either of the other types.) But I just don't have room for the bird people here. Maybe in a future book. Burt Lancaster did a great job in the Alcatraz movie. I loved that. But there are no bird people in *The Good, the Bad, and the Ugly*.

Feline Phenomenology

We did some phenomenology in Part I of this book, but now I want to give you some background on that method. About a hundred and twenty years ago, some German and Austrian philosophers first described this method of doing philosophy called "phenomenology." People have been doing this as long as there have been people, but it hadn't congealed into a method. And as I said before, it's a fancy word for a fairly simple activity. How does it work?

Most of the time, when you're thinking, you're thinking *about* something, some object of your thought, say, breakfast, or a nap. Now, if you pause for a moment and consider not breakfast itself, but *how* you're thinking about it, you become aware that you can think about breakfast in a lot of different ways. You can remember past breakfasts, or you can be estimating

---

[1]   I know thousands of people who read philosophy. I know precisely one (1) horse person who reads philosophy. She is a writer. I am still trying to figure her out. I think she does have a cat, at least. The world allows for degrees and hybridity. I mean, she's a *horse* person, but maybe she *acquired* a taste for cats and philosophy? I mean, that *could* happen, right?

whether you have time to cook this morning, or you can be rearranging the anticipated parts of the meal while sifting the contents of the refrigerator and cabinets in your memory. There is no limit to the variations in *how* you can think about breakfast, and yet, it's all still breakfast.

When you consider the variations themselves, and how you feel and think differently depending on how breakfast is "given" to your thinking, well, you are doing a phenomenology of breakfast. To give one example, thinking about breakfast feels very different when you're really hungry compared to when you aren't.

Phenomenologists love to discover patterns in these differences and describe the general features of the patterns in long, boring treatises. I will explain more about phenomenology as I go, but I am reminding you from earlier in the book that there is a method to the madness in what follows, and this particular madness flows from wondering *how* cats experience their world(s), meanwhile the method licenses us to pretend we actually understand what we're talking about when we offer answers. That movie taught me something very interesting about this question.

To Will One Thing

I chose breakfast for a reason. The ways in which cats consider breakfast is astonishingly unified, by which I mean that the variations among them are not great. Cats never approach breakfast with studied indifference. It is the one time of day when they can be counted on to lose their natural detachment. With effort, a cat can be nonchalant about almost anything—a mouse scurrying across the floor, even a mid-day bowl of tuna juice (I have seen this with my own eyes)—but when it comes to breakfast, there is a noticeable unanimity of engaged concern. So I started thinking, because that's what I do, what is breakfast to a cat? How is it experienced?

Some (dog people) may say "well, their hungry, and thats controling them" (dog people can't spell and have poor grammar). That isn't right. Cats behave this way about breakfast even when they intend to take only a bite or two and wander away. This isn't about over-weaning hunger. It's something else. It has the power to unify cat consciousness into a single aim, just one possible course of action to the exclusion of all others. Breakfast takes a cat whole, possesses it, drives it into an anticipated future that simply cannot fail to happen.

Breakfast is like an object of religious fervor and devotion for a cat. In the morning, cats are like the little band of true believers waiting on a remote hillside for the Second Coming of Christ, and for them, *you* get to be Christ. (Don't get too excited, it's a temporary office.) But if you wait too long, you'll be the devil, but simply arrive within the appointed hour (actually, you have about fifteen minutes) and you're the savior. It's not that the cats are hungry (they may be, but it isn't relevant), it is that cats are better at worship than their humans are, more faithful, more ardent believers. The ritual is simple, but it is of infinite significance. The act of feeding/being fed is sacred, the connection between the feline believer and the higher power, which they experience with a fervor that would shame any dog-loving Pentecostal.

Now, you will say dogs are like this about when it's time to go for a walk, or, better yet, a ride in the car. But that's just the problem. Dogs are too promiscuous in their religiosity. You're not just Jesus, but God, all the time, no matter what you do. That isn't religion, that's slavery. You want to whip a dog into a religious lather? Do anything, anything *at all* that includes them. This includes even mistreating them. (God, I hate people who mistreat animals. Or helpless humans. It is the only thing I know of that could move me toward violence.) But the point is that it isn't breakfast that unifies dog consciousness, it's the presence of the Master. Man, I can't handle that sort of self-abasement. With cats, it is dignified. It's about breakfast, not so much about you. You or *anyone* else bringing breakfast will suffice, at that moment of the day.

Humans (even horse people) have nothing in their experience to compare with this perfect bliss. As I have contemplated what in my own life might approach a cat's level of unified consciousness in the presence of the breakfast communion, I can only imagine what beatific vision might be like—but I am not so pure in heart as to have seen God, and not so other-worldly as to wish to.

The Danish philosopher Søren Kierkegaard (1813–1855), you remember him from the Oz chapter, taught, following the Apostle James: that purity of heart is to "will one thing."[2] This is to say, that if a human being could ever succeed in drawing all of his/her disparate desires to be focused only upon one end, one idea, one object, that would be "to will the Good" in the purity of heart—to see God. I don't think Kierkegaard was

---

[2] *Purity of Heart is to Will One Thing.* The scriptural passage is the Epistle of James 4:8.

likely to have been a cat person; if he had been, he would have realized that his thinking implies that, from a certain point of view, breakfast is God.

Stages on Life's Way

Kierkegaard thought that life can be divided into three stages: an aesthetic stage, an ethical stage, and a religious stage. A person's development has to move through these three before the heart can ever be pure, but it is easy to get stuck at one of the earlier stages. Most people do get stuck, and *no one* was religious enough to suit Kierkegaard, *including* Kierkegaard. Instead of growing spiritually, when we get stuck, we might instead commence *refinements* of the stage we're at, either the aesthetic or the (merely) ethical. Such refinement is the work of pride. And of course, *that* is Satan's own sin.

So, for example, some people live their whole lives as though the edification of the senses, and the continual refinement of the pleasures they crave, can appropriately consume a whole life. You become a wine connoisseur, or an art aficionado, or even a porn junkie. This doesn't necessarily mean that such people are *always* debauched addicts of some sort, although Kierkegaard thought it was about the same thing, wine, art, porn—everything was a stark either/or for him.

But he wasn't quite right, because people who remain in the aesthetic stage may spend their energies perfecting, for example, their pallets for the tasting of the subtlest differences in wines or chocolates, *without* becoming alcoholics or gluttons. They may accumulate books and read for edification rather than for, say, moral instruction. They may watch thousands of movies and other shows without becoming mindless consumers of images, pornographic or otherwise.[3] They may acquire three or four cats without needing twenty or thirty. Yes, I think you

---

[3]   This is one issue Kierkegaard did write about explicitly. He never went to the shows (that was the theater in his day and age), but he would put on his theater-going clothes and stand around outside the theater before the show, and then go home. Then he would come back as the show ended to *be seen* loitering outside, so everyone would *think* he had been to the show. You're saying: "Why?" Because he was worried that if he *stayed away* from the theater, people would come to think that he held himself above and apart from others. He wanted to cultivate the reputation of being a debauched man of leisure so he could be certain he wasn't pridefully seeking to have a good reputation among his fellows. If everyone *says* you're a lazy good-for-nothing, and you cultivate that as well as suffer it, I guess you could keep you pride in check, unless, of course, there is pride in *knowing* privately that your bad reputation is utterly false. He struggled with that. It's like reverse narcissism. I feel pretty sure he would hate our narcissistic age. He hated his own age and it was pretty reserved, in Copenhagen at least.

see where this is going. There is virtue in moderation, self-control, balance. But not in Kierkegaard's world.

Kierkegaard was, by anyone *else's* standards, a religious guy. So he didn't think it was a good thing to get yourself trapped in the aesthetic stage of life. But cat people, and movie people who have cats, might take issue. It is true that we aren't driven by ethical concerns, like dog people are, but we do admire the *beauty* of morality, which is something even dog people can appreciate from a safe ethical distance. And cat people *want* to be good, just not at the expense of pleasures, especially refined pleasures. We can point to the horse people and say "well, now those are hedonists, pleasure addicts, at least we aren't like *them* . . ."

Cat people do something similar with the religious side of life, which they are prone to aestheticize. A good liturgy, a well-formed sermon, rhetorically perfect, a Bach chorale sung with exquisite precision, and some nice stained-glass windows—*these* make for a properly fulfilling worship experience. Let the dog people go to the praise and worship service in the aluminum building on the edge of town, singing the same bad songs over and over. Kierkegaard would be horrified either way.

And yet, our cats teach something about the purity of heart that cat people can learn in no other way. We cat people never "will one thing," we will *many* things, all of them pleasing, and refined, and long-lasting. But with spiritual matters, we like paradoxes and puzzles, questions and doubts, and go to our various meditations and prayers (well meditations; only dog people actually pray) with our manifold sins and perhaps just a little wickedness, not knowing quite how or what to confess (they are such minor infractions in the grand scheme of things) and not feeling any special need of forgiveness. We leave the deep feelings of moral inadequacy before God to the dog people, who approach their God as if He were a scolding Master with a newspaper for their noses. (See the excellent prayer and hymn led by Michael Palin in Monty Python's *The Meaning of Life*.)

But our feline companions? They have pure hearts, precisely once per day, and we minister to their desires as bearers of the only kind of grace we can receive ourselves—the undeserved dispensation from above, the unmerited, unearned sort, but desired with as much ardor as we can gather, on set occasions. Our cats show us how to gather it, how to skip straight past the ethical stage of development and into, if not the Goodness of God, then the *beauty* of the Goodness of God, *if* He shows up on time. If God expects more from us than this, He should have withheld the wine, the chocolate, the books, and the cats when He was thinking up ways to compensate us for the sufferings of mortal life. I will have more to say about this in the chapter on Monty Python's *The Life of Brian*.

If I must choose between a pure heart and my cats, I choose the cats. But surely God is at least as merciful as I am, in the morning when nothing matters except breakfast—or at death, which is when I plan to worry about salvation (and not before). If God strikes me dead for saying this, then I hope he will also feed me breakfast as I go (and punish those horse people for my spiritual education).

The Kitty Sublime

I admit I have gotten distracted. We have a movie to discuss. I warned you I'm doing it backwards. Hang with me just a little longer. Roger Karas, the great cat-commentator, among others, has suggested that part of the reason we are able to co-habit with cats so easily is that our social instincts and theirs are *accidentally* compatible (so much for providence). That is, cats are not so much domesticated and brought into our social order, as they are able to interpret *our* social order as being some version of *their own*. In short, cats experience us and interact with us *as if* we were simply larger cats. With thumbs. There is something to be said for this suggestion.

I took Karas's idea seriously and began interacting with my own companions in ways I recognized from their social behaviors—growling to assert dominance, butting heads as a greeting, stuff like that (no one has made a video of me doing this, I hope), and I find confirmation of Karas's idea. My cats do seem to think I am a bigger cat. I am very glad they don't have thumbs, though. Holy cod, what if they did?[4]

But this seems inconsistent with the results of the last section, in which I was allowed to be a god. Perhaps it isn't, though. From an aesthetic point of view, one thing that makes God god-like is, well, God is very *big*, to quote Michael Palin.[5] Philosophers use the word "sublime" to describe an aesthetic experience of something so big that we can quite take it all in, such as when we look at the Grand Canyon, or the stars, or

---

[4]   I am not the first to ponder this nightmare, of course. I recommend this frightening commercial: <www.youtube.com/watch?v=_GSuH6LYMho>.

[5]   If you haven't seen this, you really must
: <www.youtube.com/watch?v=fINh4SsOyBw>.

Mount Fuji, or yes, perhaps when we consider God. The German philosopher Immanuel Kant (1724–1804) pointed out that when we experience something as beautiful, we consider its *form* (nevermind what he means by that, trust me, it's a long boring story), but the *experience* of something as sublime, while also pleasing to us, is *formless*, because it is too big for our senses to take in a form.

This brings me back to cats. Cats have fine senses, but their sensory limits are different from ours. For example, a moving automobile makes fair sense to us, and we can adjudge not only its speed and color, but also whether it is or is not a "nice" car, perhaps even a beautiful car (if it happens to be the sort from the early 1960s with big tail-fins). But to a cat, a moving automobile is simply incomprehensible. It moves too fast, makes too much noise, and is too large to be considered as anything except something to be avoided (and sadly, our kitties often fail to avoid them). Except for the small yip-yip dogs,[6] dogs are just big enough and just fast enough to be able to take in a car as an *object*, but a Greyhound bus is a little beyond them.

Now, Kant also says that whereas the judgment that something is "beautiful" comes from a *restful* state of mind and a consideration of its form, saying something is "sublime" involves the *movement* of a restless mind in trying to take in the formlessness of something, well, big enough to be awe-inspiring. An IMAX movie screen is well on the way to this experience. You can't take in the whole screen at once, and that is the point. And of course, someone is always trying to do bigger and bigger.

So think about this. Human beings are about ten times taller and weigh about ten times more than their cats. We are pretty big. When I imagine what it would be like to share intimate space with something *that* much bigger than I am, I imagine having, say, a Clydesdale draft-horse in my living room, and with a living room that was scaled to his proportions rather than mine. And here I am, this tiny thing, in the midst of all that clopping and neighing. Horse people *like* this sort of thing, which is why they spend so much time in barns. But it horrifies cat people.

---

6   These are not *really* dogs, and their owners are not *really* dog people; these are inferior cats with slightly perverse owners—I mean if you want a dog, get a *dog*, if you want a cat, get a *cat*, and if you can't make up your mind, let someone more stable choose for you . . . I don't know *what* a chi-hua-hua is, but it's closer to a rat than a dog.

Yet, domestic cats are not only *not* afraid of their people, they fearlessly wind around our legs as we walk, and they even look upon us as potential sources of amusement. I cannot easily imagine finding the courage to wind around the legs of a Clydesdale while it walks, or hopping between the horse and its food to see if I might want some. Even horse people know better than to try that. Horses *bite*. Whence this astonishing boldness among the cats? Cats are *not* cowards. They choose their battles.

Cats at the Threshold

It's impossible not to have noticed that cats pause at the threshold, between indoors and out-of-doors, especially. It takes them a moment to undergo the transition, to gird themselves up for the larger world outside or the smaller one inside. Sometimes they pause for maddeningly long stretches: "Hmmm, shall I go in, or stay out? I just don't know . . . on the one paw, there is food in there, but on the other paw, there are birds out here . . . hmmm." This is a third aesthetic experience, not the beautiful, not the sublime, but it is "liminal," which comes from "limen," the Latin word for threshold or boundary. It is part of the word "subliminal," and "sublimation," as well as "sublime."

Cats are mistresses of the liminal, the borderland between the beautiful and the sublime; this region of experience is populated with things that have *some* form and *some* formlessness. This power of the threshold among cats comes from cultivating the parts of experience that are *almost* too big to handle, but not quite—like humans, but not moving automobiles—along with the parts that are *almost* too small to be significant, but not quite—like a cricket, but not an ant.

The secret of feline detachment, and their forms of engagement with life, derives from their power of noticing and interacting with the liminal aspects of it. And so it is with their people, even if the scale is different. The *idea* of a horse is fascinating to a cat person. The horse itself is just too big, but the idea of such a beast, well, it is not something we cat people would have conjured up, but it's not bad to imagine. *That* idea is on the edges. Horses. What a concept! Great big beautiful beasts you could ride at amazing speeds. What an experience that would be, for someone *else*. . . .

Dogs and their people are uninteresting precisely because there is nothing liminal about them. They both exist in a middle-sized world filled with middle-sized objects and middle-sized ideas. Dog people don't do metaphysics or mysticism, and they are content with Budweiser, Hershey's chocolate, and the television shows selected for them by Fox or CBS, and Will Ferrell movies. By analogy, their dogs are content with rolling in putrified dead things, and searching the cat box for treats, followed by licking their masters' faces in a most undignified display of affection.

A dog person's idea of a big aesthetic decision is whether to put the gun cabinet in the den or the living room. If they start imagining anything bigger, they become fundamentalists and neo-conservatives and Trump supporters and the like. And that only happens when no one rubs their bellies. It is a good idea to rub the belly of your favorite dog person. Cat people are bad at that. But you should create some middle-sized problem for him to solve and watch him fetch the solution like a nice middle-sized stick. Keep them all busy with that sort of thing and they will leave everyone else alone. When dog people don't get their middle-sized belly rubs for solving middle-sized problems, they do things like watch Fox News and storm the US Capitol. It's easy to understand and completely preventable.

But horse people are downright scary. They want the dynamical sublime, way past the threshold, not just the idea of it. I hate to admit it, I mean I *hate* this, but horse people make the best leaders—dog people are more trustworthy on the whole, but they will not take your institution or business into new and daring frontiers. Dog people make good bureaucrats (and the world needs dutiful bureaucrats), but poor chief executives and presidents. No vision, little imagination, need too much belly-rubbing. Horse people, by contrast, may wreck your life, your health, and your business by trying foolish things, but they won't sit still and accept the status quo, and they will not busy themselves in *pointless* re-organizations of the staff—like cat people will. If they re-organize it's to re-balance power. They *invent* Fox News and the 1776 Project and that sort of thing. So horse people also make the worst leaders, but only because they could have been the best.

It almost makes me cry to give first rank to horse people. They scare me. I don't understand them. They do things I wouldn't do—couldn't do. And why don't they ever give *me* a shot at carrying out a task? I mean, surely if a mere dog person can do it, *I* can. How much can there be *to it*? But I guess, when I think about it, I don't even always answer when my name is called, and then I pretend I didn't hear it when forced to answer. Perhaps it would be unwise to trust me with something that requires a kind of loyalty I cannot find inside myself. Take it from an honest expert at sifting the liminal options, you horse people and dog people, you don't want to be in a fox-hole with me. I may have the courage it takes to *think* sublime thoughts, but my reality definitely should not include enemy soldiers charging my position.

And in this light, aren't horses and dogs, for all their insensitivities to the very finest things, astonishing in their bravery and fortitude? They can send horses and dogs into battle, you know, with full expectation of service to the death. Try *that* with a cat. Try it with a cat person. I think the wise general on horseback knows well enough that the cat people will do better at breaking enemy codes. But cat people are not cowards, I'm not suggesting that. It takes a kind of courage that both horse and dog people lack to, well, tolerate and work creatively with *profound* ambiguity. This is the threshold, the liminal part of life. Cat people have tremendous, nay *infinite*, patience with ambiguity –both emotional and intellectual. That ability, and the kind of courage (and aesthetic understanding) that goes with it, astonishes dog and horse people. And it is on this account that they don't trust us.

High Noon in the Sad Hill Cemetery

I have promised, and I think, *delivered* an answer to the question why cats are the choice of "thinking" people. You may not agree. Write me an angry e-mail. I'll ignore it. Faced with a choice between beautiful and sublime, cat people will press everything in the direction of thinking, and then live at the liminal edges available there. There is both virtue and vice in it, both courage and cowardice. But these failings are mainly aesthetic preferences, not really moral principles.

In Plato's *Republic*, Socrates says that in order to understand justice fully, we also have to understand *in*justice. I think Socrates is right. We have looked at some to the virtues of cats, dogs, and horses, and the aesthetic virtues and failings of their people. But what happens when cat and dog and horse people go *bad*? I don't mean aesthetically ugly, I mean morally *bad*.

When cat people go bad, it's just as bad as when dog or horse people turn vicious. And when they are good, they are as good as the best people. Cat people make fine advisers, faithful companions, even fine teachers of, if not the purity of heart and the seeing of God, at least the *ideas* associated with these matters. And when any situation requires a high tolerance of ambiguity, well, the dog needs to ride the horse to the nearest cat house. But what of badness?

I promised a solution to the Mexican Stand-Off, didn't I? You know, cat people don't always keep their promises. But I suppose I will, *this* time. All this work has been about how different people experience that scene: the *waiting*. It dawns on the observant moviegoer that the entire movie was setting up this one scene, written for the sake of this scene, the characters developed *for* this scene. I defy you to say it was otherwise. (I'll take you through the movie, and you'll see.)

The first thing to bear in mind is that all three of our principal characters in that movie are *bad*, very, very bad. We don't notice it much since there are no good guys to hold in contrast. We saw this earlier in *The Princess Bride*. Withhold the good guys, and we start elevating the least bad guys. We'll see this again when I talk about *House of Cards*. But these bad guys, Blondie, Tuco, and Angel Eyes, are all devilishly smart, and utterly ruthless, and quite fearless in their own ways. Even among the very, very bad there are important differences.

I haven't studied the facts of the matter (that would be boring), but I think Sergio Leone was, almost certainly, a cat person. In the famous stand-off, Tuco's gun wasn't even *loaded* and Blondie *knew* it wasn't, since he took the bullets the night before. Some would say that this is cheating the audience of the "real" Mexican Stand-Off. "We were tricked!" The people protesting are dog people, I assure you, and they should go watch Tarantino movies instead; there's plenty of other resolutions for them there (coming in Part III!).

The cat people, on the other paw, just *love* this contrived Sergio Leone stuff. It's like he's given us a ball of yarn to unwind. Sure there's nothing in the center, but who cares? Meow, you know? The horse people simply could not sit through five minutes of surf-punk theme music waiting for someone to draw a gun, no matter how great the music is. But the cat people could wait longer than anyone, like a cat outside the mouse-hole. The waiting is liminal. It is the perfect joining of the beautiful and the sublime. There *might* be a mouse—we certainly aren't waiting for enemy soldiers here. Maybe no mouse, ah, but the *idea* of the mouse, now that is enough to hold us in the moment, indefinitely. Leone gets this. The dog people are complaining, bitterly, that they were cheated; sure, but he gives them a bone. You'll see.

If you watch the stand-off in the film closely, you will see in Eli Wallach's eyes—what a beautiful performance he gave— that Tuco knows he has no business *whatsoever* in this god-forsaken stand-off, and no desire whatsoever to do anything but run. This stand-off is not liminal, this is the real thing. Tuco is a cat person. (Actually, he is a cat.) Not a very nice one. He cannot prevail in such a confrontation, and he would do well not to try, as he knows very well. He's not going to draw first, no way. He wants out, but he can wait. Ever watch cats in a stare-down? They are *made* for this.

A Liminal Threshold

Tuco faces two others. After having so flattered the horse people above, I must now report, and they will have to accept, that Angel Eyes, Lee Van Cleef's character, is a horse person who has gone very, very bad. We could spend many pages on how horse people go bad, but suffice to say that there is no possibility of reprieve or repentance when it happens. When a horse person goes bad, the kindest thing to do is, well, shoot him— unlike dog people, who will sometimes beg forgiveness holding nothing back, and cat people who will at least grudgingly admit a mistake, if they *must*. It isn't *legal* to shoot horse people when they go bad, I'm just saying it would be *kinder* than watching Trump-like people flounder in their loss and ignominy, but no cat person is going to put them out of their misery. Our guns aren't even loaded.

Cat people are very bad at admitting mistakes, and moral failings they will admit least of all—they invent all sorts of aesthetic excuses, some quite convincing. Horse people not only don't admit mistakes, they don't even *believe* in them. You'll get no justifications from a horse person, especially a very, very bad one. And Angel Eyes has crossed the line, has no conscience, no fear, and no limits. He's off the map. Leone wrote him this way. He seemed bad but benign at first, but watch the movie again, keeping in mind he's a horse gone bad. Maybe somebody mistreated him, way back when, but he's way far gone by the time we meet him.

Is There Really a Dog?

Perhaps we'll never know. But Blondie, Clint Eastwood, knows very well who *is* dangerous and who *is not*, standing in that cemetery. Perhaps he took Tuco's bullets so that he wouldn't have to kill Tuco later (since saving Tuco's life is actually what Blondie does for a living in this story). And Blondie is counting on Angel Eyes to make the mistake of thinking Tuco is *just as* dangerous and unpredictable as any of them is. Holy cod is Blondie cool under pressure. You do know that dogs are smarter than horses and cats? Not all dogs, but at the upper end, there can't be any doubt about it.

You may now be thinking Blondie is the dog person, and I think that is right, although you may be vaguely remembering a scene in which he spits on a dog rather than petting it—something *no* dog person would *ever* do, nor ever *forgive*. Even to imagine it is the work of a liminal imagination—but that was a different movie. Blondie most definitely is a survivor dog, I imagine a Heinz 57 (always the smartest dogs are mixed) mutt, a little mangey and ragged, but still in his prime and not interested in growing very old or being very comfortable.

The dog people win the stand-off, then, precisely because they live in a middle-sized world; they're restrained, capable of self-restraint, indulging neither their imaginations nor their desires, neither fears nor hopes, and *nothing* liminal. Dogs are not vexed by mere possibilities. The situation just is what it *is*, and nothing else. The horse person draws first and is certain he is faster. But he is wrong, if for no other reason than because Blondie already knows who he does and doesn't have to shoot. If Angel Eyes moves *at all*, Blondie shoots him. And he doesn't even have to wait, remember. He *chooses* to wait. You may not believe me about all this now, but you will in a moment.

Naughty Sergio

In the scene just before the stand-off, Tuco is running through the Sad Hill Cemetery, looking for the grave of one "Arch Stanton," where Tuco believes there is buried gold. The cemetery is round and has hundreds of graves. Now, Sergio knows very well, good Catholic boy that he was raised to be, that *no* Christian cemetery is round. Believers are buried so that if they were to sit up in their coffins, they would be facing east, to see Jesus coming from the heavens. That is why Christians orient all their graveyards in rows, like old theater seats, waiting for one helluva movie to start. Sergio made up the circular cemetery for the sake of the stand-off. He doesn't care about the theology, he wants the *scene*. It just doesn't work unless it's in a circle. As Tuco runs through the cemetery, the scene swirls into a dizzying sublimity—where is the grave, where is the gold?

Sergio Leone *did not* tell Eli Wallach what he intended to do, but as the scene began, Leone released a *dog*, yes a *dog*, into the cemetery set, so that when Wallach *saw* the dog, he would be *genuinely* surprised. The cinematographer, Tonino Delli Colli was instructed to capture the liminal moment when Tuco sees the dog. When it happens, Wallach's whole body seizes up for just a moment, and, professional that he is, he stays in character. Only a cat person would have imagined such a foreshadowing of the impending stand-off.[7] The dog is going to get you, Tuco. No, he already got you. Your gun is already empty.

Now, Blondie is a dog person; no matter how smart you are, he can best you if you get too far away from the practical world yourself, failing, for example, to make sure your gun has bullets when you wake up in the morning. And, yes, as I insisted, dogs are smarter than cats as surely as Blondie is smarter than Tuco (who is no idiot, but he wakes up with gold on his mind, and *only* gold, like a cat at breakfast time). And so Blondie will win the stand-off *because* he is a dog person, and Tuco will be surprised when he shouldn't have been. But he's a cat gone bad, and greed is his unifying principle. It blinds him to anything else. He can wait, yes, but not when breakfast is close at hand.

Seriously, a Kitten?

The cat just never takes the dog's intelligence seriously enough. It is a fatal weakness in both cats and their people. The one appearance made by a cat in the film is when Blondie is sitting in a war-scarred town and hears a gunshot across the way. He is petting a *kitten*, yes, a *kitten* (a very cute one), and this is completely gratuitous and out of place *unless* Leone means it as a symbol. As Blondie sets the kitten down, he tells his momentary companions that he has recognized the sound of Tuco's gun. *Tuco is the kitten.*

It takes a pretty keen ear to discern individual gun sounds—something well beyond the abilities of cats or horses, and cat people and horse people would never attach significance to learning such a thing. Dogs have ears like that, though. Dogs know the master's voice, the sound of the master's car, the master's footfalls, the master's rattle of the leash. But Blondie *has* no master. He's a stray, and his ears (and nose) are trained on whatever leads to the next episode in the adventure of his life. It's pretty tough to surprise a stray dog.

The final proof comes when Angel Eyes is (mercifully) dead from the stand-off, and Tuco has, at gunpoint, dug all the gold from the *right* grave. After all, there's only two kinds of people (left) in the world. Blondie has fashioned a noose (leash? Cats *hate* leashes) for Tuco in the meantime, and orders him to climb atop a rickety cross, put the noose around his own neck (this is payback for something similar Tuco did earlier in the story). If Tuco slips, it will cause his (well-deserved) hanging—

---

[7]   It is worth noticing that the second shot of the entire movie (shot, not scene), is a dog sauntering across a dusty, deserted street. Talk about foreshadowing . . .

at which point, being a cat person, it will finally occur to him to worry about salvation.

And then—now pay close attention—*Blondie leaves half the gold for Tuco.* That has always been their arrangement, to split things fifty-fifty. And it is atonement for Blondie's having taken all the money and left Tuco in the desert earlier. Then, as the movie ends, Blondie shows Tuco a kind a loyalty that Tuco hasn't earned by shooting the rope from a distance and freeing Tuco from his predicament. As Blondie rides away, the last line is Tuco screaming after Blondie that he is . . . what? Do you remember? Tuco screams that Blondie is a son of a . . . . Leone cuts off the last word. Think about it. The movie ends as it begins, with a dog. But *you* have to fill in the symbols. He's given you enough clues.

There's your bone, you dog people, so stop bitching. You win, okay? I know that's very important to you. And Tuco, instead of being grateful to Blondie for the reprieve, screams hateful canine epithets. If there is one thing dog people can't abide, it's ingratitude. Recall my saying that you cat people shouldn't go into business with a dog person? Well, they won't cheat you, but don't be surprised when they leave you with your half of the business because you were ungrateful and whiny just one time too many.

Now, a dog might rescue a cat, or a horse, but it would be the rare horse or cat that would rescue a dog—or another cat or horse for that matter. Dogs and dog people just dig beneath the ambiguities and find reasons to be loyal and good that the rest of us can't even smell. I still don't trust them, but I guess I should. But what can I say? It's not in my nature.

7

Democracy Adrift

HITCHCOCK'S *LIFEBOAT*

Just about every textbook for introductory ethics courses contains a provocative essay by Garrett Hardin (1915–2003) entitled "Lifeboat Ethics: The Case against Helping the Poor."[1] Hardin was not a "professional" philosopher (whatever that really is), he was rather a professor of "human ecology" (whatever that really is) who became notorious by arguing for extreme positions no one could really stomach.

In this case he pictured poor nations as swimmers around a lifeboat, and lifeboats as inhabited by rich nations with their resources and economies and institutions. Hardin argued that rich nations could not help poor nations without swamping their own boats. The best solution was, he claimed, to let the all the swimmers drown.

Arguing in such unpalatable ways is a good method of baiting professional philosophers—seriously try to defend an utterly indefensible position, then wait for their feeding frenzy to begin. Plenty of people wrote articles attacking Hardin, and he became prominent by being so often, so vehemently, and so completely refuted. One reason Hardin's essays are still fed to freshman and sophomore small fry in college is that his arguments are so thin and simplistic that even intellectual *shrimp* can reasonably expect to dismember the bait without biting the hook. It is thought by many ethics teachers that this sort of thing is good practice for young minds before they have to confront any serious reasoning about ethics.

---

[1] Hardin's reasoning has been nicely handled by Michael Patton in "Game Preserve Ethics: The Case for Hunting the Poor," which demonstrates light-heartedly that by Hardin's reasoning one could not consistently stop with not helping the poor, but would in fact be morally obliged actually to *hunt* the poor.

I have my doubts about this pedagogical notion. Thought experiments are of dubious value when ethical problems are real, not conceptual puzzles. But movies can be less simplistic teachers. Hitchcock fans know the lifeboat scenario by other and older means, and indeed, Hitchcock's handling of the scenario is neither simplistic nor extreme.[2] It is challenging to hold in one's power of thinking the vertiginous complexities of his presentation, but we shall do our best in what follows, using the best binoculars that moral philosophy has to offer.

Ethics and Politics

Let's do some boring stuff first, sort of Philosophy 101. I have been doing mainly phenomenology, existentialism, and aesthetics so far. Let's do a little ethics and political philosophy, expand our range a bit. Here are the basics.

Ethics asks the perennial question "what is the best life?" Even in ancient times people knew it is impossible to address that question without including politics as a part of the answer—since the best life always includes other people and some sort of governance. The companionship of others is essential to living a truly human life, let alone a good one. Hitchcock loved to explore what happens on the outskirts of that need, the pathologies of companionship, if you will. But separating the political and ethical aspects of such difficult questions is tricky, perhaps impossible.

In the history of Western philosophy, the three concepts with which moral philosophers have been most occupied are the "Good," the "Right," and the "Just." The Good is connected to whatever makes a goal or course of action more desirable than some other. The Right concerns what is lawful (whether natural or human or divine law) and how to create or live by such law. The Just concerns the development of character and virtues, socially and individually, that can distinguish the best answers as they relate to and balance the Good and the Right. We have justice when our aims are truly good and our laws are truly right, and we're morally developed enough to recognize that and understand why. Here we have a general way of approaching "the best life" that is strongly dependent

---

[2]   The script for *Lifeboat* was committee work. Built from a play called "Lifeboat 13" that Twentieth Century Fox had rights to, the script was crafted by John Steinbeck, Jo Swerling, Darryl Zanuck (mainly by complaining about it), Ben Hecht, and throughout the process Hitchcock himself contributed to writing and revising it. Since Hitchcock was responsible for its final form and the dramatization, I will treat the script as his work.

upon the political arrangements of communities. The principles of ethics are crucial to understanding a good, right and just political order.

There, I'm glad that's over. Back to the movies.

Being Better than, or Not as Good as, Your Fellows

The political ordering of a community sets the context and limits for the moral development of most people who live in it (there are always a few who rise above the standards of their time and circumstances, saints, if you will, and these will not be found in Hitchcock movies).

Wherever people desire things which only *seem* good to them, but really are not, disorder and unhappiness follow, while wherever the laws are bad, justice is not possible and people are stunted in their moral development. Many such people appear in Hitchcock films, one is tempted to say that *only* such people appear—people who beyond a shadow of a doubt, will mistake what seems good for what really is good, who will not know what is right, and who will have skewed notions of justice and strange character flaws. This is Hitchcock's home turf.

Why? Even John Milton himself admitted that the Devil is more interesting than God in *Paradise Lost* (do they still make kids read that in high school or has it fallen victim to the separation of church and state? Or to the limits of the new shortened attention span—I mean, when is the movie coming out? Oh, that's right, it *did* come out, sort of. See the next two chapters on *His Dark Materials*). The intrigue of the Devil may also explain why Hitchcock is more interesting than Stephen Spielberg. In any case, there are no saints in Hitchcock's lifeboat, and plenty of sinners. Interesting sinners.

It Was 1942, Way Scarier than Any Movie

Hitchcock's explicit intention in making the movie *Lifeboat* was apparently political, not primarily ethical. The concept for the script presented itself to Hitchcock in 1942, after France had fallen, his native Britain had been daily besieged by merciless Nazi bombers, the allied forces were getting their collective derriere kicked by Rommel in North Africa, and Russia was in hard retreat before the Panzer columns. In short, things looked bad for the Allies, and the outcome of the conflict was very far from assured. As Hitchcock put it:

We wanted to show that at that moment there were two world forces confronting each other, the democracies and the Nazis, and while the democracies were completely disorganized, all the Germans were clearly headed in the same direction. So here was a statement telling the democracies to put their differences aside temporarily and to gather their forces to concentrate on the common enemy, whose strength was precisely derived from a spirit of unity and of determination. (Truffaut, *Hitchcock*, p. 155)

Thus, we see that a group of survivors in a lifeboat from a US Merchant Marine vessel, sunk by a German U-Boat, contains a hodge-podge of political viewpoints such as one might find in a democracy. Hitchcock says, "the seaman [Kovac], played by John Hodiak, was practically a Communist, and on the other extreme you had the businessman [Rittenhouse, played by Henry Hull] who was more or less a Fascist" (pp. 155–56).

The German U-Boat has gone so far as to fire upon the American *lifeboats*. The Americans in the main vessel have returned fire on their way to the bottom and sunk the German submarine. It is tempting to see the struggle as the snake biting the foot that crushes it, and everyone loses everything, except for an enduring sense of vengeance fully realized.

The political plot thickens when the survivors from the ship drag aboard a survivor from the German U-Boat, known only as "Willy" (perhaps a demeaning and not too subtle allusion to Kaiser Wilhelm II), and must decide what to do with him. To symbolize the political situation, Hitchcock uses as the movie's McGuffin a compass. The Nazi sailor secretly has a compass, so he knows where the boat is going, while the others (even the sailors) have no sense of the boat's direction. But the compass is as much a moral as a political direction-finder. Initially it makes a difference to the survivors whether they are rescued by the Nazis or the Allies, but this concern begins to fade as they become more desperate and would welcome rescue from any quarter.

Politics and Ethics

It would be a great task to sort out the political meaning and ethical aspects of this voyage, and such a task would need to consider Hitchcock's other two wartime movies, *Saboteur* and *Foreign Correspondent*, not to mention his subsequent Cold War films. A fine study already exists in Ina Rae Hark's work, so I will not pursue this concern further. To understate it, people have written about Hitchcock. But I have a point to make about *Lifeboat* that might be overlooked in the political complexities of its plot and conception. No sooner have the survivors dragged aboard the Nazi sailor than a dispute breaks out:

KOVAC: Throw the Nazi buzzard overboard.

RITTENHOUSE: That's out of the question and it's against the law.

KOVAC: Whose law? We're on our own here. We can make our own law.[3]

And that is my point. This sabotages the "Right" in our schema of ethics, the place where politics mainly resides, the domain of law. The lifeboat setting reduces (without eliminating) the relevance of political loyalties in light of pressing ethical dilemmas—the reason for tossing Willy overboard is on account of what he has done and what he will do, regardless of whether his political loyalties or his personal judgment were to blame. As the movie unfolds, we discover that Willy is in fact the captain of the U-Boat, and had *ordered* the shelling of the American lifeboats upon his own authority, removing the question still further from politics and making it a war crime for which he would be held morally responsible in the aftermath of war. This scenario is not about politics, primarily, and the lifeboat *situation* is what eliminates it from serious consideration.

And I would suppose that this is part of the reason Garrett Hardin uses the same metaphor to focus his own question about helping the poor. He isn't examining the political convictions and systems of wealthy nations at all, simply pointing to a moral fact about them, uncomfortable as it may be. A lifeboat scenario effectively turns political questions *into* ethical questions by isolating the actors from what would normally be the legal and political consequences of their actions. As James Agee observed at the time of Hitchcock's film, "the initial idea—a derelict boat and its passengers as microcosm—is itself so artificial that . . . it sets the whole pride and brain too sharply to work on a *tour de force* for its own sake." But what may be a limitation from a filmatic standpoint is an attractive device for a philosophical thought experiment, or, one critic's trash is another philosopher's treasure. Among the many things a philosopher might praise in the lifeboat scenario, I will use only two to illustrate my point about the division of political from ethical loyalties.

---

[3]   Quotations from the script for *Lifeboat* are based upon a transcription of the movie by Gaye Chandler Auxier and myself. If the script itself is commercially available, I am not aware of the source.

Equality?

First, in the lifeboat there is an equality of condition that would be hard to achieve in a complex political world, a world in which a manual laborer like Kovac could have no serious or meaningful argument with a wealthy mogul like Rittenhouse: the power differential between them determines the outcome of any argument. But in the lifeboat, they can have a real dialogue. Second, since rescue itself is uncertain, since only the *survivors* will tell the story about what was done and how decisions were made, and since everyone knows that juries will consider their extreme circumstances in determining justice for their actions, even the *idea* of political and legal consequences is largely neutralized in their thinking and deciding. The lifeboat may be artificial, but such situations can and do occur, might happen to any of us, and when they do, it will be our moral rather than political principles that are tested.

As if making this point intentionally, Hitchcock has the survivors try a hand at organizing themselves politically right from the start. The businessman Rittenhouse makes this point: "Now, now, now, we are all sort of fellow travelers in a mighty small boat on a mighty big ocean. And the more we quarrel and criticize and misunderstand each other, the bigger the ocean gets and the smaller the boat." After assuming command of the boat, Rittenhouse begins to issue orders (and he is clearly accustomed to being obeyed). Here is how the scene plays out:

KOVAC: Who elected you skipper?

RITTENHOUSE: Well . . . I . . . of course if there's anybody else you'd prefer . . .

KOVAC: What do you know about a ship?

CONSTANCE: Among other things, he just happens to own a shipyard, that's all.

KOVAC: Has he ever been in it?

CONSTANCE: He has thousands of employees. Of course he knows how to handle men.

KOVAC: Not in a lifeboat. What we need is an able seaman and we've got one.

GUS: Who me? I'm a DISabled seaman. Anyhow, I never did have no executive ability. I . . . I think maybe Sparks there . . .

SPARKS: No, not me. I know a bit about navigation, but . . . when it comes to taking charge of a boat . . . well . . . What about Kovac?

CONSTANCE: That klunk? Run this boat? With what? An oilcan? If you're talking about a skipper, we have a skipper right on this boat [*indicates the German, Willy, who isn't listening*].

RITTENHOUSE: He wasn't the captain.

CONSTANCE: Wasn't he? [*tricks him*] Herr Capitain?

WILLY: Ja?

GUS: Well, I'm a monkey's uncle!

CONSTANCE: There. You have a man who's familiar with these waters. He knows seamanship and he knows navigation. What about it?

KOVAC: Do you mean you want to turn the boat over to the man who sunk our ship and shelled our lifeboats?

CONSTANCE: I mean I want YOU to turn the boat over to the man obviously best qualified to run it.

KOVAC: You're crazy.

RITTENHOUSE: Now wait a minute. There are two sides to everything. Let's look at this thing straight, calmly, and reasonably. The German is just as anxious to get to safety as we are. And if he's a trained skipper, why shouldn't he take charge?

KOVAC: Because I'm taking charge.

CONSTANCE: Since when?

KOVAC: As of now, I'm skipper. And anybody who don't like it can get out and swim to Bermuda. What about that?

GUS: I'll buy it.

SPARKS: Suits me. What about you, Miss?

MACKENZIE: I'm for it.

JOE: Yes sir.

RITTENHOUSE: Well, if the rest agree . . .

CONSTANCE: Alright, Commissar, what's the course?

So much for democratic politics. Faced with the issue of leadership, the democratic method is here turned on its head, and the survivors respond not to leadership experience (Rittenhouse), not to skill (Willy), but to a threat.[4] It is worth noting that Kovac's objection to putting the German in charge was not that

---

[4]   I have no reason to think Hitchcock was aware of it, but Plato describes an uncannily similar scene in *Republic*, 488a–489d. Hitchcock was a highly literate person. I'm sure he read this at some point. But remembering it? Well, you tell me.

he was a Nazi, but that he sank the American ship and then shelled the lifeboats. This was an objection to his moral fitness, not his political loyalties.

Without necessarily intending to do so, Hitchcock rendered the political issues largely symbolic and allegorical. He motivates the actions and words of the players in accord with their most basic moral and ethical loyalties, not primarily their political loyalties—even Kovac finally accedes to giving control of the boat to Willy when he recognizes that their survival depends on it. This dynamic allows us to examine the action from an ethical point of view without worrying overmuch about the politics. But I should point out that I am not taking Hitchcock's "intentions" blithely. The "Trouble with Alfred" is that it is not really possible to determine what his true intentions were at any given time. One of his biographers pointed out, "Alfred Hitchcock was a master of the red herring, and he told interviewers just what they wanted to hear—a neat psychological explanation, connected to a facile anecdote, to justify a frequent plot device."[5] And Hitchcock was not one to spoil a good story by encumbering it with the truth, either.

Ethical Pluralism

One of the first things a person should notice is that any political system can be served for a variety of ethical reasons. One may become a Nazi because one is afraid of the consequences of refusing, or because one approves of the goals of the Nazis and thinks they have admissible means of achieving them. One may become a Nazi because of a sense of duty to one's nation or race, and the consequences do not really matter. One may become a Nazi because one believes that they are superior people, people who should be imitated, trusted, and looked upon as models of efficiency, intelligence, insight. One might become a Nazi out of pure self-interest, or for profit, or fame, or power, or simple survival.

The last of these, survival, is Willy's ethical motive, as far as we can ever learn. If he has ethical principles that rise above the intention to survive, we never see them. Each and every act, from saving Gus's life by amputating his gangrenous leg, to murdering him later, and everything in between, is calculated as means to personal survival. But people also became Nazis on the weight of all of these different ethical judgments and many more. People subscribe to democracies for exactly the

---

[5]   Spoto, *The Dark Side of Genius*, p. 15.

same various formal and practical reasons—because they believe a democracy offers the better or best ways of obtaining whatever they value most. Both totalitarian and democratic states can accommodate the variety.

"Ethical pluralism" means recognizing that, as a matter of indisputable fact, in the world we actually inhabit, people embrace the same goals, laws and balance between them (Good, Right, Justice) for different and often conflicting reasons. Our anti-heroes in the last chapter illustrate the point. Some degree of consensus can be attained even among damaged and dangerous people. So, even among the bad, the lawless, and the unjust, there is some kind of social functionality. Ethical pluralism isn't just a good idea, it's the way of the world. You can't do anything about it.

On Hitchcock's lifeboat, among the citizens of democracies, we find: a person who thinks that the best life is that of making money (Rittenhouse); one who thinks that fame is the best life (Constance Porter, the reporter); one who thinks that the best life is equality in community (Kovac); one who thinks the best life is to serve God (Joe Spencer, the ship's steward); one who thinks the best life is to help and care for others (Alice MacKenzie, the nurse); one who thinks that romantic love is most worthy of human pursuit (Stanley Garrett, the radio operator); and one who lives for pleasure—the metaphor is dancing, but Hitchcock makes it clear enough that this is about sex (Gus Smith, the ship's helmsman).

Along with this dizzying array of ideas about the best life comes an equally complex set of reasons for choosing them and ways of pursuing them. These survivors are all more or less committed to democratic principles, more or less patriotic citizens, more or less agreed that Nazism is morally and politically bankrupt. But their problem is that they have spent such a long time pursuing their own ideas about the Good, within the broad limits of Right and Justice that democracy allows, that they are slow to recognize the gravity of their situation and more inclined to have philosophical arguments about what they should do, and why, than to act decisively.

As a result, Willy is able to manipulate all of them, not because they lack ethical principles, but precisely because they hold their personal versions of those principles so dearly. Each of the principal characters, apart from Willy, is willing to consider the idea of dying rather than releasing those personal principles. They can always come up with individual reasons satisfactory to themselves (even if in conflict with one another) to allow the German to have his way. And so the German is able to sink their ship, shell their lifeboats, conceal his true identity as Captain, pretend not to speak English, withhold the compass, lie, dissimulate, deceive, and finally even commit murder, all with impunity while the others debate the Good, the Right and the Just. Sounds like some presidents we've had, with just a couple of revisions. This is the challenge to ethical pluralism. What do you do with the monster among you?

A Voyage Down the Hierarchy of Needs

As annoyingly simplistic as it is, the psychologist Abraham Maslow truly put his finger upon some facts about human beings and their capacity for moral reasoning. His paper "A Theory of Human Motivation" appeared at the auspicious moment for a pluralistic world, that is, in 1943, just as everyone was beginning to wonder anew "What is humanity?" I have no reason to think that Hitchcock would have been aware of Maslow's "hierarchy of needs" when he made *Lifeboat*, but in many ways the hierarchy is common sense anyway, and Hitchcock didn't need a psychologist to help him grasp human motives—which is not to say Hitchcock didn't need a psychologist.

As time passes on the lifeboat, the survivors descend the hierarchy of needs, and Hitchcock demonstrates to us just how tenacious are those values we seek at the highest and most luxurious perch of self-actualization—and here Maslow lists creativity, problem-solving, spontaneity, lack of prejudice, acceptance of facts, and most importantly, *morality*. Maslow claims that people ultimately seek to be moral as a luxury (which is not to say it isn't a genuine need), when all the more basic needs are satisfied. In the levels below self-actualization we find, in descending order, needs associated with esteem, love and belonging, safety, and basic physiological functioning. In the lifeboat, only Willy recognizes from the outset that their situation must be decided on the basis of the lowest level, that of physiological functioning, and so he gets water for himself, extra food, conceals energy pills and the compass, and knowing he is not safe, feels no compunction about still higher needs of love or esteem or least of all morality. Some people live every day by these notions. Some even become leaders of whole nations.

It is a lot of fun to quibble with Maslow about where to place various needs in his famous hierarchy, but what is difficult to deny is that they do all tend to disappear, for most people, as we are reduced to meeting the merest survival needs. And in this domain, well, ethics seems to take a serious holiday. Or does it?

If Hitchcock has a single theme in this movie, it is that survival can be, and sometimes must be the spring for action and decision. He does not deny that different people will act from different motives, and he does not suggest that they ought to have the same motives, only that they must learn to recognize that survival is a defensible value. Thus, the climactic scene comes when Willy is exposed as having water while the rest are dying of thirst. Let us see what sets them off, finally brings them to kill Willy:

> **Willy:** [*smugly*] I took the precaution of filling the flask from the water breakers before the storm, just in case of emergency. And I had food tablets. And energy pills too. Everybody on the U-boat has them. You should be grateful to me for having the foresight to think ahead. To survive, one must have a plan. But there's nothing to worry about. Soon we'll reach the [German] supply ship and then we'll all have food and water. Too bad Schmidt couldn't have waited.

In referring to "Schmidt," Willy is speaking of Gus Smith, whose family has changed the spelling of its name to conceal German heritage. It is clear that, although he "had to" murder Gus, Willy admires only Gus among the passengers, feels a certain solidarity with him, but not enough to alter the uncompromising hierarchy of needs—and after all, Willy has given orders that led to the deaths of many of his countrymen without hesitation, since he views their collective survival as requiring the noble sacrifice of some, a sacrifice he is himself clearly willing to make.

Immediately following the speech above, our democratic individualists suddenly abandon their endless debates and mob Willy, beating him and throwing him overboard. Perhaps the hierarchy of needs has had the last word, but I do not think so. Not only does each "kill Willy" for his or her own reasons, what has actually motivated their action is not a desire to survive but in fact it is moral outrage. Somehow Willy has, in this speech, managed to trigger the moral outrage of the critical mass, and in doing so he badly miscalculated, for the first time. To put it in the vernacular, you actually can piss off a group of pluralists to the point of collective action, but it isn't easy. Apparently inciting fanatics to lay siege to the Capitol isn't enough.

But are these lifeboaters *really* at the mercy of the hierarchy of needs? It's clear that Hitchcock is saying they are not. In fact, Hitch is saying the opposite. When they killed Willy, as Rittenhouse points out, they actually doomed themselves:

RITTENHOUSE: [*in bemused resignation*] Till my dying day, I'll never understand Willy and what he did. First he tried to kill us all with his torpedoes. Nevertheless, we fished him out of the sea, took him aboard, shared everything we had with him. You'd have thought he'd have been grateful. All he could do was to plot against us. Then he . . . he let poor ol' Gus die of thirst. What do you do with people like that? Maybe one of us ought to try to row. Where to? What for? Nah, when we killed the German, we killed our motor.

This sparks a "quitters never win" and "never give up that ship" speech from Constance, but the point is made. The collective action came at the expense of hope for survival, not on account of it. Maslow loses the card game: some people would rather die than curb their personal moral outrage. It makes one wonder about present day geopolitics in light of available analogies here.

E Pluribus Unum?

The motto of the United States means "from many, one," but I think Hitchcock has been careful to preserve that "many" in this ethical situation. He has partly done this by showing the possibility of decisive collective action, simultaneously but for many different reasons, and also by showing that our German antagonist has taken the wrong turn by imagining that *survival* will be the moral bottom line for his boat-mates. This leaves the Good, the Right and the Just intact, and even in charge, in Hitch's pluralism. But there are three other altogether crucial features of the film and script that reinforce this pluralistic standpoint.

The first is that Joe, the pious, God-fearing steward, simply refuses to participate in killing Willy. He interprets this as mob behavior, bent upon violence, for which there is *never* a justification. But he does not stand idly by while the others kill Willy—rather, he makes a sincere effort, even in the heat of the mob, to dissuade Nurse MacKenzie from participating. Yes, Willy will now be killed. But Joe recognizes in MacKenzie's commitment to helping others a kindred soul, someone whose principles, while they are different from his own (being humanitarian rather than theistic) nevertheless overlap.

Joe knows she will always regret having taken a life, will not be able to reconcile it with herself, and tragically, she has no God to approach for forgiveness. But he fails to dissuade her. Humanitarian moral outrage trumps humanitarian impulses to nurture, in Hitchcock's ethical worldview. The others don't actually need MacKenzie to dispose of Willy. She chooses to participate anyway, freely and without necessity (again Maslow takes a hit).

Yet Joe not only maintains his peaceable disposition, he will not even look upon the violence, bows his head and turns away. Hitchcock neither presents him as a coward nor as a hero. Joe embodies a worldview, that of pacifism and genuine piety, which is a permanent fixture of ethical pluralism—he pleads his case only to the one who has a reason to listen, and leaves the others to their own consciences. And note that Rittenhouse's conscience is not troubled in what he says after he has killed. He is troubled by ingratitude and irrationality, not by his own actions. No one else has a serious bout of conscience, and Joe does not judge them for doing what they have done.

Hitchcock's ethical pluralism can not only allow this pacifism, but he can present it as a crucial presence in the moral mix. Yet, when the conscientious objectors have made their decisions (and there were certainly still these voices in the US and Britain, even in 1944), still the collective "coalition of the willing" (and I do despise that phrase, coined by George W. Bush) will have to act, not for the survival of the democracy, but for the sake of the principles each holds dearly enough to die or kill for their sake.

The More Things Change . . .

Second, and more important, is that no character in *Lifeboat* demonstrates any significant moral growth, no basic change of attitude or outlook, no expectation of making a fundamental movement from the principles with which he or she began. We have some serious *candidates* for moral growth. Constance has every opportunity, as her treasured symbols of success and fame disappear one-by-one, to come to a new understanding of the best life, but upon realizing that they will be rescued, her first concern is for her appearance, and her second is to make certain that her new love, Kovac, does indeed take charge of the factory he has won from Rittenhouse in a card game—she wants a man of means, even if he is a socialist.

Kovac has every opportunity to learn how his collectivism is ideological and how he really *isn't* a socialist but a disempowered capitalist. Rittenhouse teaches him as much, but Kovac goes along his merry way, collecting a new lover whose grasping worldly values he presumes to despise, and becoming a factory owner himself, with notions of empowering his own workers with weekly meetings and joint decision-making. We'll see how well and for how long *that* works. In short, he learns nothing.

Rittenhouse is another well-developed character who does not need to survive and does not fear death, but if he is to live, he will live for the joy of making money. In some ways, the ironic reversal is embodied in the responses of Kovac and Rittenhouse to the circumstances of the group's ultimate rescue.

A Dish Served Cold

And the third (and most important) point arises here. The group of survivors is resigned to being rescued by a German supply ship—this has been Willy's plan all along. As the supply ship approaches and sends out a boat to pick them up, a Hitchcock-esque twist follows. An American ship appears and begins to fire on the German supply ship, payback one assumes, and hits the would-be rescue boat and then sinks the supply ship itself. Hence, our many-faceted survivors have a moment of well-earned vengeance, to be followed by a rescue by a friendly vessel. But then two hands appear from the sea and a young German sailor is dragged aboard. Examine closely the dialogue that follows:

CONSTANCE: And a . . . Look!

SAILOR: Danke Schön.

MACKENZIE: Let's get his coat off.

RITTENHOUSE: Hey, wait a minute. Have you forgotten about Willy already?

CONSTANCE: Well, Ritt, this is different. The kid's wounded.

RITTENHOUSE: Throw him back!

CONSTANCE: Don't be silly, darling. He's . . . he's helpless. He's only a baby.

[*The German sailor pulls a gun and points it at the survivors; they are completely unafraid.*]

The baby has a toy.

JOE: I should have frisked him.

RITTENHOUSE: See? You can't treat them as human beings. You've got to exterminate them.

[*Joe grabs the sailor's wrist; the sailor drops the gun, Constance throws it overboard. Rittenhouse makes a move to throw the sailor overboard.*]

KOVAC: Easy Ritt. He'll be taken care of.

[*German speaks*]

CONSTANCE: [*translating*] He says, "Aren't you going to kill me?"

MACKENZIE: [*looking at the wound*] We'll have to tie this up until the ship's doctor takes care of it.

KOVAC: Aren't you going to kill me? What are you going to do with people like that?

Herkunft Ist Zukunft

We are cued that this is a recurrence of their first argument among themselves by the German's saying "Danke schön," Willy's first words after he was pulled aboard. What goes around comes around. Here is an opportunity to see what our survivors have learned. The answer is "nothing" or "not much." But there is a nice role reversal. In the first occurrence, Kovac is the one who argued for throwing Willy overboard, and Rittenhouse resisted. Now Rittenhouse wants the German thrown out and Kovac resists. This is emblematic of the way in which a socialist and a capitalist are really, for democratic purposes, two sides of the same coin: but for luck and circumstance, one would have been the other, as Hitchcock nicely symbolizes in having Kovac and Rittenhouse play poker all the way through the episode. Only chance and circumstance separate the two ethical viewpoints, but they are what they are: potent, vital, and different.

So what is Hitchcock saying? One does not want to wait upon Sir Alfred for one's ethics, frankly. He didn't have a reputation for living by any scruples; quite the reverse. But there is a certain wisdom in this, and a surprising theme. It is, if I am correct, that there *are* ethical resources in each of us that demand moral outrage in the presence of those whose only principle is survival. By 1944, that's a pretty timely message.

If democracy as a form of life stands for anything at all, it stands for the idea that we may pursue different versions of Good, Right and Justice, but that we can still act in concert on the basis of moral outrage when we can recognize it. It isn't about survival, it goes beyond that. The question that remains is why are we so slow to recognize it? Why do we not learn from having seen it before? Of course, Hitchcock does not answer that question. If he had, he would be Spielberg. And we wouldn't want that.

8
Cuts Like a Knife

CUTTING TO THE CORE OF *HIS DARK MATERIALS*

I don't like that knife.

—IOREK BYRNISON in *The Amber Spyglass*, p. 160

Wearily Lyra sighed; she had forgotten how roundabout scholars could be. It was difficult to tell them the truth when a lie would have been so much easier for them to understand.

— *The Golden Compass*, p. 85

Methinks Master Pullman has known a scholar or two. Tiresomely roundabout. We ask the most annoyingly precise questions, and we insist that everything make genuine sense, so if you don't want to watch your own story melt away into contradictions and paradoxes, you'd best avoid us.

But in this case, it's too late, Philip. We found you. And not only scholars, but the most tiresome lot of them . . . philosophers. No one has more patience with hair-splitting than we do, and no, we won't settle for lies. Fortunately, I'm only having some fun at the moment, so we I ought to be able to loosen up a little for the space of one chapter. Or two, actually. I couldn't leave it alone. Some shows just have so much going on that one chapter isn't enough. I'm giving you two.

I see you've been at it again with your new *The Book of Dust*. A Prequel and a Sequel. Nice. We wanted more, as you know. I have no doubt that the BBC and HBO will want that story too. I'll write about that when they make it into a movie, Sir Phil. Meantime, let's talk about your latest success on BBC/HBO.

Of Prequels and Sequels

BBC/HBO has completed and aired two seasons of *His Dark Materials*, and has contracted for a "third and final" season, which is supposed to be shooting now. I expect that *The Book of Dust* could be done with the same cast, roughly (a baby and child Lyra, different actress, and a twenty-year-old Lyra played by a grown-up Dafne Keen, who is doing such a great job of being Lyra).

The writers and directors have followed the Pullman books as closely as possible up to now, so those who have read them know what will happen in Season Three, and how it will all end. I seriously doubt that the series will deviate from the third book in the trilogy in its main plot. They changed only a few details in the first two seasons, and that was done in order to get the story told in eight or seven episodes, respectively.

It will be interesting to see how they manage to get *The Amber Spyglass* into that frame, since it is twice as long as *The Golden Compass*. The second book, *The Subtle Knife*, splits the difference, of course. The second season had to do more cutting to fit the allotted window, so to speak. Ha-ha. So pleased with his own cleverness is the present writer. But in the next two chapters we will focus on the original trilogy and what is implicit in that. These essays were originally published in 2009 in *The Golden Compass and Philosophy*, long before the series was envisioned, but after the first movie attempt appeared. They were re-written and updated in 2020 as the BBC/HBO series was appearing. They are rewritten again here, following two seasons and, I think, with a fairly clear idea of how Season Three will follow the books.

In 2017 Pullman's various essays, edited by Simon Mason, were released under the title *Daemon Voices: On Stories and Story Telling*, and the collection includes a good bit of discussion of Milton's *Paradise Lost*, and some more information about how he conceives of the plurality of worlds, about God and Dust and other aspects of these stories that I will discuss in the next two chapters.

Spoiler Alert

A novelist friend of mine, the one who put me onto this trilogy years ago, made an observation I have always remembered. We were in a bookstore in south Texas, browsing, and I was looking for something like *Lord of the Rings* to really get my teeth into. There was the Pullman trilogy on the shelf, and he recommended it highly, knowing me well, and said I would love it. He was right. But picking up the books, I noted how much longer the third book was. He said "Yeah, Pullman didn't have as many ideas, so he had to write more." Whoa. I had never thought about that. Of course, I'm not a novelist. (Yet. Retirement is coming . . .) It never dawned on me that having ideas saves words, when writing fiction, especially fantasy. But that's exactly right, isn't it? Ideas save words. That sets up an interesting challenge for the adaptation people. It is clear HBO's people had some ideas about how to present Lord Boreal's forays into our world that saved a lot of exposition.

Anyway, I know that Season Three will air about the time this book appears, so maybe I won't be spoiling anything by the time you are reading it. But I need to register the caveat that *I* haven't seen Season Three, because no one has, but I am going to write about the whole story. That means using the books. I will mainly be talking about the story in this chapter, and the characters in the next chapter, and on these matters, the series has followed the books very closely, so it doesn't make too much difference which I speak of.

I do want to say some things about how HBO brought the books to life, but I must say from the start that, unlike so many earlier adaptations, this one really is very close to the way I imagined the story and characters, reading it years before it ever became a movie, let alone a series. And I have re-read the books as well, which is quite unusual for me, when it comes to fiction. I don't read very much fiction, let alone *re*-read any. This is a fascinating story, great characters, lots of ideas.

I want to commend HBO and everyone involved for not screwing it up the way Peter Jackson screwed up *The Lord of the Rings*. I realize that may be an unpopular assessment, but frankly, I wish I hadn't even seen those movies. Except for Liv Tyler as Arwin Evenstar. That part was okay. And Cate Blanchette's Galadriel. That worked. You can have the rest.

I didn't experience the same disappointment when they made the first try at *The Golden Compass*. They had a killer cast, I mean A-list, even for just the voice cast. The CG effects were the best of their time (not as good as the HBO series, but the technology has come a long way since 2007). New Line spent 180 million on the thing and really tried to do it right. Although some of the casting didn't fit my imagination (such as Nicole Kidman as Mrs. Coulter, and more about that is in the next chapter), but I could accept it.

Why did the movie fail? After all, they projected two more films if the first succeeded, and it definitely failed, in spite of an Oscar and a BAFTA award, and a bunch of other nominations and some wins. A lot of people blame the script, which departed from the book in a lot of ways. Some people blame New Line for insisting that the movie be under two hours, and for cutting the depictions of the last three chapters of the book so that the movie would have a happy ending. Some people blame the Catholic Church for organizing a ban. All of these things contributed, I'm sure.

But my explanation is simpler and includes all of these things: you can't get the first book into a movie, even three hours long, intact. Even less would it be possible to get the next two books into three-hour movies, and in fact this is what screwed up *Lord of the Rings*. To tell these stories, you really have to tell the whole story. I mentioned Stephen King's *It* in the Introduction to this book. That story still hasn't been told. It won't fit even into six hours of movie time. The Harry Potter movies had the same problem. If you have an epic story to tell, you need the time allotment of a multi-season series.

It really is that simple. To get *His Dark Materials* on film, three seasons minimum. The first movie wasn't good, for the simple reason that what makes the story great didn't survive into the medium of film. The most talented people in Hollywood could not get it to work, and they *tried*. And they knew that the public wanted this story on film. But New Line was pennywise and pound foolish. They shortened the movie to increase revenues, it is reported. Yet, they invested a huge amount in production, the most expensive movie they had made up to that time. The outcome was a loss big enough to require the restructuring of New Line.

So, as I was saying way back in the introduction, this larger canvas of the series arc is going to make possible the presenting of longer and more complex stories, true epics, like this trilogy. It is a great time to be alive, as far as that goes. The HBO people have, so far, managed to capture the story. I think they have their work cut out for them in Season Three, but, as my novelist friend said, there aren't as many ideas in the third book, so it is cumbersome and it drags, and it really is for those who fell in love with the story and are determined to see it through. I was one of those. I think that maybe HBO can pull it off. Book Three will be easier to cut, it seems to me, but what do I know? On to the story, okay?

What in the Worlds Is He Talking About?

*His Dark Materials*is is brimming with philosophical themes and ideas. So my friend is right, not as many ideas as the story wears on, but I have to counter that in terms of philosophical ideas, they get thicker as we get deeper into the story. The third book is almost a philosophy book. Maybe Pullman was more interested in developing the philosophical ideas than he was in moving the plot along. Probably so. But even allowing this, I don't think it's quite right to think of Pullman as a philosopher, even secondarily. He wisely does not even try to solve all of the problems he explores, and indeed, he doesn't make any serious effort to be logically consistent in presenting them.

Trigger warning: Metaphysics on the way. For example, in Book I Pullman has Lord Asriel describe the splitting of worlds this way:

> Now that world [in the Aurora], and every other universe, came about as a result of possibility. Take the example of tossing a coin: it can come down heads or tails, and we don't know before it lands which way it's going to fall. If it comes down heads, that means the possibility of its coming down tails has collapsed. Until that moment the two possibilities were equal. But on another world, it does come down tails. And when that happens, the two worlds split apart. I'm using the example of tossing a coin to make it clearer. In fact, these possibility collapses happen at the level of elementary particles, but they happen in just the same way: one moment, several things are possible, the next moment only one happens, and the rest don't exist. Except that other worlds have sprung into being, on which they did happen. (*The Golden Compass*, pp. 376–77)

This, and most of the metaphysics in the story doesn't make it into the scripts of the HBO series or the first movie. But in the series, they show this idea in the opening credit sequence. If you know the metaphysics of the trilogy, you see it illustrated in the layers depicted as collapsing into threads in the credits. With movies, some metaphysics just can't be explained. But they give it a shot in Christopher Nolan's *Inception,* so a few chapters from now, we'll see how this kind of exposition can be done without being boring.

But this bit of metaphysics from Lord Asriel doesn't hold the full stage. In Book III, narrating a tough decision to be made by Will Parry, Pullman says:

> Will considered what to do. When you choose one way out of many, all the ways you don't take are snuffed out like candles, as if they'd never existed. At the moment, all Will's choices existed at once. But to keep them all in existence meant doing nothing. He had to choose after all. (*The Amber Spyglass*, p. 12)

That's it. No mention of other worlds springing into being in which each alternative was respectively taken. Looking at the two passages, anybody can see that we can't have it both ways. At least sometimes (or maybe even always), making a choice either creates a new parallel world (first quote), or it doesn't (second quote). If our choices only *sometimes* create new worlds, it would be nice to know when that happens and why. Pullman is unhelpfully silent on the matter.

Yet, looking at the second passage, if there really is no other world in which Will's various other choices are acted on, then it undermines the premise of the whole trilogy, because there wouldn't be other worlds for Will to cut into with that cool knife. On the other hand, I'm sure you can see what a mess it would be to try to tell a story where each choice by every character resulted in a new alternative narrative thread, describing the events in which each genuine option really happened in some world. In fact—unless you're Stephen King—telling any story requires that you exclude all the stories that you're not telling at that moment, right?[1]

That's all well and good. We're telling the story we're telling, and not telling the story we aren't telling, and that is both wiser and necessary. We may tell a story about many worlds without trying to tell about every single one. So, actually things don't get too tedious or paradoxical until one supposes that we might *travel* between these contrary worlds that (at least sometimes) get created when we make a choice, or when a coin comes down heads. Lord Asriel says, in the same conversation as above:

> No one thought it would ever be possible to cross from one universe to another. That would violate fundamental laws, we thought. Well, we were wrong; we learned to see the world up there. If light can cross, so can we. . . . And I'm going to that world beyond the Aurora, because I think that's where all the Dust in this universe comes from. (*The Golden Compass*, pp. 376–77)

The issue is really "travel." Such travel, philosophically speaking, requires four ideas:

1. **something that remains identifiable, while**

2. **moving through some arrangement of**

3. **space, in some**

4. **duration of time.**

---

[1] I have written on this in quite a lot of detail in two chapters of *Stephen King and Philosophy*. King worked out a method for telling every single story that was excluded from the story he is telling at the moment.

We can generate all sorts of paradoxes regarding any of these four ideas, once we have that subtle knife. And you've seen plenty of movies where these problems come up.

Just as a teaser, consider this: Whenever Will and Lyra make a bad choice, why don't they just use the knife to cut right over into the nearby world (that recently sprang into being) in which they made a *better* choice? Well, part of the problem is that they would, I assume, encounter the doubles of themselves, and that would get complicated in a hurry. Pretty soon we'd have a whole herd of Wills and Lyras, making better choices for sure but increasingly bothersome to feed and clothe. This paradox calls into question #1 above, since we now do not know how to identify the "thing" (Will or Lyra) that has moved through space and time. Who is the *real* Will or Lyra? The hungriest? The Best dressed?

Pullman briefly considers this prospect in Book II, when he has Lyra contemplate whether there might be "another Lyra" in *Will's* Oxford. "A chill ran down her back, and mouse-shaped Pantalaimon shivered in her pocket. She shook herself; there were mysteries enough without imagining more" (*The Subtle Knife*, p. 74). So Pullman leaves the question open, and proceeds to tell a story in which "transworld identity" is unique— only one Lyra, one Will, one Mrs. Coulter, and so on. He evades the question rather than answering it. That's fine for a novelist. The movie and series scripts just ignore this and most other questions associated with the many-worlds hypothesis.

Similarly, we could wonder why Pullman decides to keep day and night constant across the various worlds—night-time in Cittàgazze corresponds with night-time in both Oxfords, and similarly with the seasons, and so forth. I see no reason why this has to be a constant, but it does avoid troublesome questions. So when I picture the Earth hurtling through space, I suppose that I need to imagine billions more such bodies right on top of it, in other dimensions of possibility, but all of them are in the same "place" as far as their turning and orbiting goes.

So, that is one way of handling number 3 above, space. But if we imagine that there's even just one world that, for some reason, falls a little behind in its rotations or its orbit, could Will still cut into it? How? Does the knife do space travel? And if so, what time would it be when we stepped through there? And why? I have trouble enough understanding what happens when I cross the International Date Line in *this* world.

I would also point out that Pullman likes to keep *spaces* constant, so that whatever world exists "on top" of another world shares the same constant space in a different dimension of possibility. He assumes that when Will and Lyra sit on the "same bench" in their different Oxfords, they remain "close," in some sense. That's how Pullman wants us to imagine it. Even though the movies can create a kind of magic that we can't get in our real world, depicting the many-worlds on top of one another is harder in a movie than in a novel.

But don't think about this too much, even on Pullman's literary terms. It may begin to dawn on you that somehow Lyra walks into the hills above Cittàgazze from the far north of *her* world, over Asriel's bridge, while Will finds a window into the same city from *his* Oxford, which is supposed to be right on top of Lyra's Oxford, which is a thousand miles from where she walked over Lord Asriel's bridge. My advice is not to expect consistency in these matters. It will simply frustrate your mind and spoil your enjoyment of the story, whether on the big screen, the little screen, or the printed page. It's best to evade, as Pullman does, and the screen writers do. There are mysteries enough without imagining more, as he puts it.

The Barnard-Stokes Business

Such evasions may serve a novelist or screenwriter well enough, but they won't do for a physicist or a philosopher. Remember, we scholars are wearisome and roundabout. In Lyra's world, a pair of troublemakers, "renegade experimental theologians" named Barnard and Stokes, suggested a theory that Pullman clearly likes. In the novel he calls it the "Barnard-Stokes business." This didn't make it to the HBO screen. What is Pullman alluding to?

In our world, the physicist Hugh Everett (1930–1982) proposed this same hypothesis of the "plurality of worlds" in 1957. He was no renegade—he actually did top-secret work for the US Department of Defense—but he was trying to provide an interpretation for some unsettling implications about the collapse of wave functions in quantum physics. He wasn't at all interested in the possibility of travel among complementary worlds, or even whether such worlds are "actual places." That is a question for metaphysics, not physics.

And some metaphysician was eventually bound to try to defend the idea that such possible worlds really do exist. Most notoriously, a philosopher named David K. Lewis (1941–2001) tried to argue for it in a book called *On the Plurality of Worlds*. I have no reason to think Pullman read this book or even knows about it, but it was widely discussed by philosophers, and it still is. But Pullman constantly violates Lewis's restrictions on the idea of many worlds, restrictions which avoid paradoxes of just the sort I illustrated above.

And Pullman *makes* arguments of the sort that Lewis happily destroys. In particular, Lewis insists that even though the many worlds actually exist, they are "causally independent" of one another—the very view of which Lord Asriel says "we were wrong." (And that *does* make it to the screen, when he speaks to the scholars about the city in the Aurora Borealis.) What Lewis means is that the worlds have no effect on one another. Thus, travel among them is impossible. Meanwhile Asriel says that if light can travel between the worlds, so can we.

It is unlikely enough to defend the actuality of all (or some) possible worlds, but it is simply crazy to suggest viable travel among them, Lewis thinks. In this instance, I'll have to side with the commonsense of the despised Church in Asriel's world. It's not that Barnard and Stokes are heretics, it's that they aren't talking sense. Anyway, in *our* world, the "Barnard-Stokes business" might be called the "Everett-Lewis business." It's out there (in both senses of the word), and you can learn about it if you want to.

A Shout-Out

Church and Everett-Lewis be damned, for Pullman there are *lots* of ways to get from one world to another, apart from the windows and Lord Asriel's bridge. Consider some. Witches "know" about the other worlds, but do not traditionally visit them, Serafina Pekkala says. How they "know" isn't clarified (I have a theory about that in the next chapter). Yet, even just "knowing" requires that something permits exchange or communication of some sort among the worlds. The Gallivespian lodestone resonator, which you'll learn about in Season Three, also communicates across worlds by quantum entanglement (it is claimed), and the alethiometer somehow *reads* across worlds. Add to that: a single hair of Lyra's remains vitally connected to its owner, even if she's wandering around the world of the Dead (again, Season Three).

Then there's Dust. You knew we were coming to that, and you learn a lot more about it in the final book, the philosophy book. Assuming that Dust:

1. **moves the alethiometer needles,**

2. **interacts with Mary Malone's computer apparatus, and**

3. **moves the sticks of the I Ching (whether in Will's world or in that of the mulefa, which I can't wait to see in Season Three—how will they depict these creatures?),**

Then Dust also somehow communicates across worlds or exists in many at the same time. These happenings indicate that the many worlds may be causally connected.

Whether things like quantum entanglement and the non-localized exchange of information require "causation" remains a hot topic among philosophers and physicists, but it's enough to be aware that some intelligible connection (whether causal or not) is involved in communication. These worlds can affect one another.

A Pause for the Cause

Communication isn't the only effect of one world on another. For Pullman, angels can travel among the worlds, both physically and using imagination, and affect things. And someone can open a huge doorway by harnessing the energy of Dust released in that awful process of intercision (separating a person from his/her daemon). One can also make a bomb so powerful as to detonate it in one world and blow a hole through another world, a hole so big that it opens onto the Abyss, itself. And apparently there are "cracks" everywhere after that explosion, in which all the worlds are bleeding vital force (dust) into the Abyss. I think some of this may be depicted in the CG graphics in the opening sequence for the HBO series. These connections among worlds seem pretty "causal" to me.

And finally, there's the knife—our particular point of interest, if you'll tolerate my pun, in what is coming next. So not only does Pullman allow us to remain who-we-are as we move among worlds, he devises a bunch of different ways that such travel might be carried out. We could spend all our time thinking about any one of these—for example, the use of imagination fortraveling among worlds, described by the Angel Xaphania near the end of Book III, could easily occupy us for a whole chapter. I hope some of that makes it into the script for Season Three.

But now I want to cut to the quick. I want to be the bearer of my own subtle knife (and unlike Will, keep all my fingers), and use it to reveal a "cosmos" in Pullman's ponderings, because I think that his knife helps us see how it all fits together, to the extent that it *does*.

Cosmos

I've already said a few words about physics and metaphysics, but philosophers and physicists also share another word: cosmology. Obviously, physics is concerned with the physical world, and metaphysics includes all the problems of physics and also questions about whether (and how) nonphysical entities or energies might or might not exist, and how they might affect or influence physical things. For example, is an "idea" a physical thing? It's not obvious.

Metaphysics concerns itself with questions such as whether the "mind" is just the same thing as the "brain," with no remainder, on the one hand, or whether I might have an idea in my mind that can be correlated with some sort of physical process in my brain, but the two are *not* the same thing, on the other hand. Physicists sometimes show a vague curiosity about such questions, but they don't make a profession of trying to answer them. Philosophers *do*.

But in addition to all this, philosophers and physicists also discuss cosmology, which is the science (or study) of order (*kosmos* is just the Greek word for order). In modern times, this has meant the study of the order of nature. Most scientists and philosophers believe that "nature" is an ultimate category— nothing beyond nature really exists, is their consensus these days. So, studying the order of nature is the same as studying *all* order. Anyone can see that nature is complex, so the study of cosmology has to do with grasping how the various *forms* of order we find in nature are best explained. Cosmology is neither quite the same as physics or metaphysics, but it uses both, just as far as they reveal patterns of order.

For example, time has a characteristic "order," a "before and after," a sort of durational arrow of cumulative flow. And space has a characteristic order, in which everything must be somewhere, a sort of localizability that can be measured with instruments or modeled with geometries. And perhaps consciousness has an order as well—it's one type of temporal process that is spontaneous and intentional, directed toward objects in space and time other than itself. And so on. These are three examples of types of order, and cosmology tries to say how they fit together into one order.

Our popular Big Bang theory is a bit of cosmology. When we speak of cosmology, then, we're concerned with how all the things that really exist are ordered in relation to each other, how the fundamental forces we discover combine to create all that we see, feel, and experience. Needless to say, it's not rocket science or brain surgery—it's far worse. Rocket science and brain surgery are pretty clear and simple by comparison. At least we know whether and how brains and rockets exist. No such simple facts in cosmology.

And Chaos

The ancients had lots of different cosmologies, so you would find many different answers to questions about what is the sky, where did the earth come from, what is a person, what is a soul, what are the stars, how were people created, and what are the gods. The ancients also usually had an idea like "chaos," which was either an absence of order, or more commonly the power of *dis*order or the destruction of order. These ancient cosmologies are expressed in stories and myths that say what sorts of things exist by telling how they came into being. Sometimes also there are stories about how and when things pass out of being.

In the book of Genesis, when God is intent on whipping up a cosmos, "the Earth is without form and void." That's Hebrew chaos. The Greeks thought of the primal waters around the whole world as chaos—they called these waters *okeanos*. Pretty much everyone seems to agree that chaos is "deep" and very much to be avoided, so it's a relief when God or Cronos tells the Abyss to behave itself and stay over there, where it belongs, away from us and our order.

A Menagerie

Phillip Pullman's cosmology is, frankly, a mish-mash of ancient and modern ideas about what types of things exist and in what order. But let me offer just the simplest list to give you a sense of what we're dealing with. According to Pullman, at least the following types of conscious entities exist:

1. **humans (this may or may not include witches),**

2. **ordinary animals (like Moxie, Will's cat),**

3. **talking Animals (like armored bears and arctic foxes),**

4. **night-ghasts (a type of spirit who haunt Lyra in Book I; may include Nälkäinens, Breathless Ones, the old ghost at Godstow, and the bad spirits pinned to the clockwork of the buzzing spies, or spy flies as they are called in the series),**

5. cliff-ghasts (ancient dragon-like noxious beings),

6. ghosts (such as are found in the world of the Dead, and perhaps what Billy Costa is "like" when he is found intercised),

7. daemons (this may or may not include "souls"),

8. angels (apparently a different kind of spirit than the various ghasts),

9. Dust, or matter (which "loves Dust").

There are also some beings that may be peculiar to the world of the dead (coming in Season Three), such as: 10. harpies, 11. deaths, and 12. the uncooperative Boatman. And there are the mulefa, whom we are told are "people," so one assumes that they are, in the relevant sense, the same sort of thing as humans, but we are not told whether they have daemons inside them, or ghosts, or deaths. Then we have to add 13. the specters (also apparently the same as "Windsuckers").

We learn near the end of the trilogy that specters are little pieces of the Abyss, set loose in the world by the unwise (sinful? forbidden?) act of cutting through from one world to another. The specters are conscious (Pullman calls them "malevolent"— which literally means having a bad will) and they can be commanded (by Mrs. Coulter, who also teaches them they can fly). These remind me of the Dementors in Harry Potter. So here the suggestion is that 14. the Abyss as a whole may also be conscious in some sense, since the parts of it are conscious. As you can see, I've been tiresomely scholarly in listing Pullman's entities. There are probably some I've missed, of course, but this will be enough for a sketch of a cosmology.

Panpsychism

There you have at least fourteen types of conscious beings that can exist more or less independently, or separate conscious modes of existing. It would take a good while to sort them all out. As a list, this is not a cosmology, it's an "ontology," which is to say, it's an account of what exists without much regard for *how* they exist, and their levels of being and their origins and relations and dependencies upon one another. I have listed only the conscious beings because, as far as I can tell, Pullman intends to occupy a position philosophers call "panpsychism," which is the view that everything that really exists *is* conscious. So the idea that "dead matter" exists is an idea Pullman rejects. That is also part of the reason I am inclined to say that the Abyss is in some way conscious (and malevolent).

Panpsychism is not a popular view among philosophers these days, although it is gaining ground. But some very famous ones in the past have defended panpsychism. These days there are simply oceans of philosophers who believe that some things are conscious and some just aren't. This conviction provides them with endless oceans for swimming (and treading and drowning) as they marvel at how *anything* can be conscious, since they think most things aren't, but a few things (like philosophers), clearly are. These ocean swimmers are called dualists. I don't like them. They are silly people who don't *know* they are silly. They take themselves very seriously. Fortunately, no one listens to them.

Pullman skips over these vast and tedious waters and just dives into the small (but much more interesting) pond of current philosophers who think that *everything* is conscious, and who just smile at the idea of "dead matter."

I think we can safely say that all of Pullman's worlds are conscious, and they all rest delicately above the Abyss, and the Abyss doesn't *like* it, which is why all those worlds are in danger of falling back into a sort of chaos. I wonder how much of this they can possibly explain in Season Three. You may need to read the books. In the Abyss these tiny drops of awareness are powerless to connect with one another, communicate, build, create, even though they still "exist." That's what the Abyss likes, isolation, disconnectedness. *This* is chaos for Pullman: a kind of awareness that is isolated and alone, which is to say, awareness trapped and powerless amid the complete absence of beauty.

Lost in Space(time)

So, given the list of conscious beings above, all kinds of questions arise. For example, why do ghosts hold together in the world of the dead (whether they like it or not), but dissolve in the "open air"? Why can some ghosts resist dissolving in Asriel's Republic, and why can they "fight" with specters? What would happen to Lyra if Pantalaimon, accidentally got swatted when he was moth-formed?[2] Where did the night-ghasts come

---

2   They answered this one in the HBO series, as we see Lord Boreal crushed the moth daemon of Adele Starminster. The delicacy (or sturdiness) of daemons is unclear to me from either the books or the adaptations. Sometimes they seem indestructible, sometimes very fragile.

from, the ones that haunted Lyra after she switched the coins betokening their daemons? (This didn't make it into the HBO series; I mean, they had to cut *something*.) If these ghasts had been ghosts, they'd be trapped in the world of the dead, right? Do the mulefa have or need daemons? Are tualapi (those weird swan-things in the mulefa's world in Book III) *animals* (as their "grazers" clearly are)? Or are they some further order of conscious beings, like cliff-ghasts? Why do they obey Father Gomez (some have suggested "domestication" as an answer)? The questions continue.

Mrs. Coulter teaches the specters to fly. How can a specter *learn* something? Do they have individual memories, a social order, rules of behavior, communication skills that can be improved with effort? Are they maybe like the Borg from *Star Trek*? This could go on forever, rather tediously, as we try to compile all the types of beings and all their interactions—who can communicate with whom, who can hurt whom, and so on. We need a method of sorting it all out.

Normally a good way to begin to put things in order in cosmology is to ask two questions: "When does it exist?" and "Where does it exist?" Where and when would a person expect to find whatever it is we're looking for? If you know the space and the time, you can begin to tell a story about how it all fits together, by hypothesizing what caused what. Here we always assume that what comes later is caused by something earlier (time), and we expect to find things that cause one another in close proximity (space). Such is the structure of standard cosmologies. Quantum cosmologies are not as clear.

But this method won't work for sorting out Pullman's cosmology. That's because he has taken a certain delight in messing around with our ordinary ideas about space, time, and causality. He explicitly holds constant a *few* features of space and time and cause, but not reliably. In his naughtiest moment, he actually has Will use the knife to cut through time, by just a few moments, when he and Lyra and the Gallivespians are looking for the world of the dead. Will had been using the knife as a tool to cut across spatial dimensions, or dimensions of possibility, but then Pullman just teases us by having it cut through a few minutes of time. How wicked! What a knife!

In terms of space, it's good to remember that Pullman also has the worlds of dreaming and waking in close spatial relation, as when Serafina Pekkala projects into Mary Malone's dream so as to awaken her without frightening her, and Lee Scoresby accompanies John Parry on the mission to destroy Zeppelins in his dreaming state. (I'm going to confront this problem in my chapters on *Inception* in this book, both of which are about time-bend-ing.) Pullman also has Mary do something akin to astral projec-tion from her platform high among the wheel-pod trees in Book III. These are not the sorts of space-time-cause relations that we can explain with modern physics, so our ordinary assumptions about the relative constancy of space and time and cause will not help us tell the story of Pullman's cosmology.

Mephistopheles Is Not My Name

But I know what you're up to just the same. So Sting claimed. This slippage of space, time and cause is to be expected, how-ever. Pullman is no doctrinaire defender of modern science. If anything, he sees the scientific revolution as a moment when humankind, in many worlds, lost its way. He explicitly dates the time when things start to go "wrong" as being three-hun-dred years ago, when Newton was framing his physics in *our* world, the Guild of the Philosophers was creating the subtle knife in Cittàgazze, the experimental theologians were devis-ing the alethiometer in Lyra's world, and the wheel-pod trees began to fail in the world of the mulefa. This is a critique of sci-ence as well as the Church.

Pullman is toying with the idea that modern science, and its fetish for technology, is a sort of Faustian bargain human beings made with themselves (not the devil) by being overly curious and greedy for knowledge. *Every* world has suffered from their unwise quest for a kind of truth that destroys beauty. This is not even the fault of the Church, in Pullman's tale—it's one of the few things he does *not* blame on the Church. They are actually trying to keep humans "in their place." The point is that trying to use a cosmology of space, time, cause, and nature to grasp *this* cosmology will not work. Writings and movies and other artistic creations in the genre of fantasy take liberties of this kind all the time. That is part of what distinguishes fantasy from sci-ence fiction (see the last chapter of this book—I have a *very* high regard for science fiction).

Another Day in Paradise

Instead, we need to remember that, apart from the obvious fact that this story is in the fantasy genre, there is also a certain "mythic" cast to the trilogy that reminds us of some basic features of mythic consciousness (and of dream consciousness), which need not obey the laws of space, time and causation that we take for granted these days. If I had to name a single cosmology from history that is most akin to Pullman's it would be John Milton's, which has the same odd mix of modern science and mythic beings, and it offers the same judgment of humans when they get too curious about nature. Of course, unlike Pullman, Milton (as far as I can tell) actually believed in all these sorts of mythic beings. That's hard to do these days, but the stories still tug at our feelings. A lot of people still believe in angels, at least.

In Pullman's universe you can't even pin down identity, let alone space and time. People do remain more or less who they are from one world to the next, but identity is plural in Pullman's cosmos. He has a favorite strategy for handling the issue of plural identity, which is to give a separate identity to every layer of the self he can imagine. Every time he catches himself imagining a basic layer of self-experience, he externalizes and personifies it. So, for example, our human souls become daemons, and a bear's armor is an external soul of a different sort, and our "deaths" are outside of us, but always nearby. The insects of the Gallivespians are external manifestations of their nurturing instincts and their clan idenities (Salmakkia feeds hers on her own blood at one point, yuck). I think Gallivespians are sort of Scottish. You'll see, wait for Season Three. I'll bet they have Socttish accents.

But this is Pullman's standard move: externalize, personify. If we had eyes to see every level of conscious existence at once, and we saw Lyra coming down the High Street in Oxford, we would behold a veritable crowd: her regular body, the small amount of Dust she attracts, her death, her daemon, her ghost, and, I assume, the part of her that is spirit or mind (the part that can become an angel, if someone helps her like Balthamos helped Baruch in Book III). Maybe we would also see some witch oil. Who knows?

And then, having externalized and personified all these aspects of the self, Pullman likes to pull the various identities apart—just like the golden monkey does with bats and Gallivespians, and whatever it can get hold of. (More on Mrs. Coulter's daemon in the next chapter.) Pullman uses his imagination to part children from their daemons, and later, Baruch from Balthamos, and in death, he cuts off ghosts from their physical bodies, and finally (spoiler alert), he tears apart Lyra and Will, banishes them forever to different worlds. It seems like a cruel experiment, actually, to spend one's time wondering what a person would be without his spirit, or without his soul, and so on. But that is part of the clue to figuring out how Pullman's cosmology really works, what principle is really behind it. It's about cutting things.

Rock, Paper, Scissors

When you can't quite count on space, time, and causality to give you the order of the universe, you have to start looking around for other ideas that help in grouping things in order. It's like a game of rock, paper, scissors, which is a complete triad of dependency relations. You know the game: rock smashes scissors, scissors cut paper, paper covers rock. There are three ways of *being*: smashing, cutting, covering. And we have three types of entities that do these things, each being limited by one of the others. It's a perfect cosmology.

If you go back before the time when we decided cosmology was about space, time, and cause (before modern physics), you discover that philosophers have been playing rock, paper, scissors for the whole of Western history. Their three favorite entities are the Good (which is sort of a rock), the True (which is like a pair of scissors), and the Beautiful (like the paper), but people don't agree on the rules or the functions or the ways that each limits the other.[3] Plato started the game, and he enjoyed playing around with all three. Ever since then, philosophers have tended to favor one of the three and to try to get it to do the work of both of the others. In the Sergio Leone chapter, it was the Beautiful we were working with, the feline aesthetics of his movie. In the Hitchcock chapter, we were looking at the Good, parsing it into what is desirable, what is lawful, and what is just. We worried about the Good in the *Princess Bride* chapter too. We will get to the True when we examine the movie *Inception*.

In the last hundred years or so, the philosophers who like the True have had all the power in philosophy. The defenders of the Good, after a brief period of disorientation, have been climbing back into the conversation, but the believers in the Beautiful have been both cut and smashed in the last hundred years of philosophy. They had their heyday in the Renaissance, with a flurry of further prominence during the two generations dominated by Romanticism (late eighteenth, early nineteenth centuries). The lovers of the Good simply *owned* the Victorian era. Now we have these boring philosophers who only care about Truth. If I had to guess, I would predict that we are in for another round of dominance by the lovers of Beauty in the near future, when everyone tires of the True (the dominance of sci-

---

[3]   This is not to be confused with the Good, the Right, and the Just, from the last chapter, which was all about ethics, not cosmology. Those divisions, the Good the Right, and the Just, are all just ways of seeing the Good, when we are doing cosmology.

ence in this case). I like science, but I am bored with its exercise of authority. I like movies because they don't have to answer to truth. Or science.

So, I'm tired of Truth myself. I'd rather be lied to, which is part of why I like Pullman and this excellent HBO series. I like *Outlander* for about the same reasons, but we still don't know how that story comes out, since Diana Gabaldon won't give us the next book (Amazon currently says November 23, 2021, but they have moved that back a couple of times already). The Starz series hasn't caught up to the books she has already written, but production was halted by the pandemic, as was everything else. It was weird taking a year off. Gave Diana a free year to write, I guess. That must be nice, except now the next book is going to be *two* thousand pages instead of just a thousand, and from the publisher's description, it doesn't look as if the ninth (!) book will be the last. Geez Louise. The pandemic did at least give our HBO Lyra and Will (Dafne Keen and Amir Wilson) a chance to grow up some more, which happens in the novels, too.

Back to the story: in fact, Pullman is definitely one of the friends of the Beautiful, and quite possibly an enemy of the True and the Good. I have a feeling that's pretty close to where I am too. I have some sympathy for the Good, but not very much. I don't like authority, and that is how I read Pullman too. And that is why his cosmology is difficult to understand by means of either a moral order or a scientific (or logical or epistemological) ordering. And thus, we have our clue: The Pullman cosmology obeys aesthetic principles, the logic of imagination and feeling, not the order of good and evil or of truth and lies (for more about those types of order, see the next chapter). For heaven's sake, his protagonist for the whole story is a pathological *liar*, named Lyra Silvertongue. And she is the one who gets the truth, mediated by aesthetics from the alethiometer—reading it is an aesthetic task, which is why it's so hard for the scholars.

The Beauty in the Beast

Aesthetic cosmologies follow the order of images and possibilities, what images can suggest. Here we are not very interested in arguments and what they logically imply, or in moral principles and what they demand. Cosmologies of the True and the Good are built around *necessary* relations—not what can be, but what *must* be. Cosmologies of the True and the Good are stern and humorless companions. You wouldn't tolerate a novel, or a movie, or even a song that was just one long series of logical implications or moral commands.

People who read the Bible as just one long series of moral requirements are missing a lot about that book—it's interesting literature. People who read the Bible as an explanation of the natural world, like a bit of science that is literally true, are very much to be pitied. Imagine being that unimaginative. I just can't. Here they have like, well, the greatest story ever told, and instead of enjoying it, they are sitting there vexed about whether it's true or whether they are good enough. *Of course* it's "true" (symbolically) and of course they are good enough, if they'd just let themselves *imagine* the God they claim rules the universe. True and good don't have to be all black and white; they can be a whole spectrum of shades of colors. So, next time you see someone vexed over the truth of the Bible, ask them whether God is more purple or more yellow. And whether God smells more like roses or gardenias. Maybe that'll awaken them to their narrowness.

One of the coolest things about aesthetic cosmologies is that they are built around possibility instead of necessity—what can we imagine, and what can we do in imagination? The cosmology of the Beautiful does not want to be told that "You can't really do that, it isn't physically possible," or "You ought not do that, it's morally wrong." Weren't they the ones who said all things are possible with God? And this is really the clue we need, to make sense of Pullman's cosmos. We should ask: what's possible and what's impossible in his story? Doing useful philosophy really depends on finding the right question and asking it in the right way. Simply being aware that cosmologies can proceed in different ways is important background knowledge, but until you have the question firmly before you, you have no direction.

Scholars are roundabout, but they usually get where they're going. I knew what my question was at the outset, but I only now share it with you, dear reader. The question is: what will the subtle knife cut and what *won't* it cut? I put that in the chapter title. Having settled on the idea that Pullman's universe is governed by aesthetic rules, it's easy to see that he's worried about possibility, not necessity. That's why he doesn't care to give us consistent physics or to solve impossible moral dilemmas with some set of clear rules.

Searching through the universe of Pullman's imagination for a key to the kingdom is not difficult. Three powerfully suggestive images jump out immediately:

1. The Golden Compass (the alethiometer);

2. The Subtle Knife;

And, in Season Three,

3. The Amber Spyglass (that is, the idea of learning to see Dust).

I wonder: where might a semi-observant person get the idea that just these three images/objects are important? Duh. Maybe from the titles of the books?[4] In any case, thinking about these three and asking what is possible for them provides us with our rock, paper, and scissors: the aesthetic order of Pullman's universe. We need only ask what is possible for these things and what is impossible, what they'll do and what they won't do. So let's do that.

Dust

Dust is the agent, the active principle, having an interesting relation to all three objects. Obviously, Dust moves the alethiometer. That's one thing it *can* do. If Mary Malone had been kind enough to point her spyglass in the right direction, I'm sure she would have seen the Dust dance on the alethiometer. Maybe she will in Season Three. She doesn't do it in the book. This dance shows up in the opening credits sequence of the series.

But it's also clear that Dust has limits. It can't do just anything. Its main limit is that it can organize itself into something communicative only in the presence of an appropriate *intention*. How this works would be a long story, but controlling one's intentions in that way is like doing phenomenology, and we learned all about that in Part I of this book. But let's affix the agency of Dust to the "science" of the story. Basically, Mary Malone, our hero scientist, thinks that the human brain had just the right sort of sympathy and resonance to permit Dust to organize itself in ways that communicate. We learned all about sympathy and empathy in the chapter on *Super 8*. Let's use that now.

---

[4] The British release of Book I was entitled *Northern Lights*, but the US release, and the movie was *The Golden Compass*. No one calls the alethiometer by that name within the story, but it's a catchy title. I recall also that Book 1 of Harry Potter was *The Philosopher's Stone* in Britain, but *The Sorcerer's Stone* in the US. I don't understand British people very well. I will ask my publisher, who has strong opinions about titles that often contradict my opinions, to explain himself and his kind, since he is British. In no way do I allow that the title he gave this book is better than my idea, "Socratic Cinematics." He did choose *As Deep as It Gets* from a list of several dozen titles I brainstormed. The fact that *all* of my friends agree with him doesn't move me an inch. One of my friends pointed out it sounds like a porn title. I hadn't considered that. Maybe people will buy the book by accident.

Without that sympathetic connection, Dust cannot become *conscious of itself*. This is not science, really, it's an invention of the imagination, Pullman's imagination. But plenty of philosophers have said that humans become conscious of themselves only in the presence of others. Royce, whom we learned about in the very first chapter, said that. Others have too, especially phenomenologists, such as Jean-Paul Sartre. Consciousness needs other consciousness to sort of bounce back and turn upon itself.

So even though Dust can express itself through computers and the *I Ching* and the alethiometer, it is not a powerful force at all. We have to *expect* to see it before we can make use of its benefits. The benefits are: truth, goodness, and most of all, beauty. Dust is beautiful. So when we understand the word "moves" in "Dust moves the alethiometer," I think we mean "moves" in a physical, a moral, *and* an aesthetic sense. Something "moves" us when we experience our whole moral and physical and emotional existence *at the same time*. That is what Dust does, it "moves" things that are susceptible to being moved, and that want to be moved, in short, things that are in sympathy with the living principle in Dust. That includes the alethiometer, *but not the knife*.

The Compass

The relationship between the alethiometer and the knife is a little harder to understand, but properly used, the knife actually *guides* the alethiometer. That's one thing it *can* do. In an important conversation, as Lyra and Will are wandering around in Will's Oxford, he is unsettled at the idea that Lyra can use the alethiometer to know what she shouldn't know, to invade privacy. In the book, Will says: "that's enough. You've got no right to look into my life like that. Don't ever do that again. That's just spying." But Lyra's all important answer is:

> I know when to stop asking. See, the alethiometer's like a person, almost. I sort of know when it's going to be cross or when there's things it doesn't want me to know. I kind of feel it. This en't like a private peep show. If I done nothing but spy on people, it'd stop working. I know that as well as I know my own Oxford. (*The Subtle Knife*, pp. 104–05)

Lyra doesn't explicitly say this to Will in the series, but it is implied. What the alethiometer *can't* do is tell the future, but that isn't as important as what it *won't* do. In the very next moment the question is raised about whether Will's father is still alive, an absolutely crucial question—and Lyra doesn't ask the alethiometer because Will doesn't direct her to do so. Why Will doesn't ask her to consult the device is hard to understand, except that he's consistent in this attitude throughout the whole story. He is struggling with freedom and fate, and he resolutely chooses not to know all sorts of things he could know, because he wants to preserve his sense of freedom (not his freedom itself, just his *sense* of it). So he chooses to preserve an aesthetic feature of his life, the *feeling* of acting freely, instead of knowing morally or scientifically what he "must" do.

The alethiometer, however, works with and through its interpreter, and so long as Lyra accepts Will's guidance, the instrument works to the "best" (meaning the most beautiful) purposes. That purpose is saving Dust, not because it is good or true, but because it is the basis of all that it beautiful in the world, as we are told. This also tells us what's possible and impossible for the alethiometer, and what we mean by saying that the knife "guides" it. We mean that Will, the bearer of the power, tells Lyra when to use it and when not to, for the most part. And Lyra wisely obeys. Thus, the alethiometer submits to the knife.[5]

Cut to the Chase

But the all-important and pivotal cosmological function is that of the knife itself. If you can tolerate an analogy for a moment, I will clarify. If I had been writing this chapter on Tolkien's *Lord of the Rings*, I would have made almost the same argument about aesthetic cosmologies, because I think he and Pullman are kindred spirits (C.S. Lewis is different; his cosmology is clearly moral, as are all its symbols). But if this were about Tolkien, I would have analyzed all the rings—nine for the humans, seven for the dwarves, three for the elves, and then, the One Ring, the Ring of Power—to find them and in the darkness bind them (why in darkness?). Clearly Tolkien's cosmology is symbolized in what becomes of these rings, and one is at the center.

The subtle knife is like that for Pullman. It plays the part of the one ring, which is the reason it (spoiler alert) has to be

---

[5] I won't pursue it here, but it is interesting to ponder whether Pullman's decision to place Will in the active role and Lyra in the passive role is just old-fashioned, or problematically sexist, or symbolic of something (I suspect this is the answer). Clearly Pullman isn't old-fashioned about same sex couplings, and that sort of sexual ethics. But there is something in the pairing of Mrs. Coulter and Lord Asriel that follows a similar pattern. We will look at that in quite some detail in the next chapter.

destroyed, in the end (and that is an old trope in imaginative literature, that the power that tempts us must be destroyed). I am quite certain that Pullman is giving a nod to Tolkien when he has Will destroy the knife, and when he has so many characters say that it "never should have been made," and when he places its origin in a Tower in a land that has fallen into ruin. I think Pullman makes it clear enough that the knife is the center of his cosmology. But an especially revealing passage is worth quoting, since it brings together Pullman's panpsychism and cosmology all at once. Iorek Byrnison is speaking (remembering that these bears know more about metal than any other beings):

> I don't like that knife. I fear what it can do. I have never known anything so dangerous. The harm it can do is unlimited. It would have been infinitely better if it had never been made. With it you can do strange things. What you don't know is what the knife does on its own. Your intentions may be good. The knife has intentions too. . . . The intentions of a tool are what it does. A hammer intends to strike, a vise intends to hold fast, a lever intends to lift. They are what it is made for. But sometimes a tool may have other uses that you don't know. Sometimes in doing what you intend, you also do what the knife intends, without knowing. (*The Amber Spyglass*, p. 161)

Even ordinary tools have intentions. Lyra, with a fairly lame argument, tries to talk the bear into fixing the knife but the bear is moved only by whether the alethiometer recommends fixing it. Thus, there is a sense in which the alethiometer has a power over the knife's continued existence. This completes the circle of rock, paper, scissors, but there is more to be observed. The alethiometer's power is not ultimate because we don't know the knife's intentions, or how to handle them. But, like the alethiometer, the knife needs a human actor to carry out its intentions, and like the alethiometer, only the right sort of human can use it.

That actually makes our quest for the cosmic order of Pullman's universe a lot easier. All we have to do is look at our ontology of conscious beings, all fourteen of them, and ask "what's possible for the knife, and what's impossible?" What beings can it damage, and how, and are there any it *can't* damage? You can have a hell of a lot of fun going back and doing this now. I won't do the whole thing.

I just want to call your attention to some really interesting stuff that tumbles out of this observation. The impossibilities, what the knife *cannot* do, are far more revealing than what it can do. But let's look at what it can do first.

In the right hands, the knife will cut the bear's armor (made of sky metal), it cuts through space and time (and that's a heck of a trick), one assumes that it will kill or damage pretty much anything on the list of beings, with a few interesting exceptions. It wards off specters and harpies but we don't know whether it can kill them. The knife kills cliff-ghasts, and certainly could kill ordinary animals, talking animals, humans, witches, and daemons.

There are a number of interesting open questions, like whether the knife can affect night-ghasts and ghosts. And I want to use that knife on the creepy Boatman on the lake of the dead (coming in Season Three), but Pullman has the old fellow claim he *can't be hurt by it*. I would like to find out for sure. I also don't know whether one could "kill" one's own death with it, but I suppose not. Death is already dead, right?

Since it is called the "god-destroyer," one assumes that the knife can kill angels. And the knife can cut Dust. The energy in Dust is released not only by the knife, but by a blade less fine: the guillotine at Bolvanger can do it, so certainly the subtle knife can. But the ultimate power the knife has is to sever the delicate membrane that protects the many worlds from the Abyss. Again, Season Three, and how in the world are they going to represent the Abyss? There is some connecting and depicting in the opening credits that may give a suggestion. I feel sure that the BBC filmmakers had the whole series arc in mind when assembling the opening credits.

A Matter of Love

Pullman is silent on the issue of whether there was a creator who first set the Abyss (Chaos) and the Cosmos in their separate domains. He allows that perhaps there was a creator, but the Authority was not the Creator. All we can know is that the most powerful thing the knife can do is to rejoin Cosmos to Chaos, such that Chaos comes in (as specters) and Dust (the basis of conscious order) flows out. And if Iorek Byrnison is right, then this is what the knife *intends*: to undo the work of the creator. But we also have a clue as to what is powerful enough to smash the knife: love. Thus, when we know what Pullman means by "love," we know what's stronger than the knife, stronger than the golden compass, and stronger than Dust.

Both times that the knife is broken, it is the power of Will's love that does it: for his mother in the first instance, and for Lyra in the second. It's an ancient cliché to use love as a *Deus ex machina*, but hey, this cosmology is mostly ancient anyway, so why not? But Pullman's ideas about love are not Romantic, they are cosmic, aesthetic ideas, summed up in his statement that "Matter loved Dust. It didn't want to see it go" (*Amber Spyglass*, p. 404). A number of philosophers in history have spoken of "love" in this way, notably St. Augustine and St. Thomas Aquinas. One finds John Milton speaking this way also.

The traditional cosmologies of love are usually Christian. But we all know that Pullman has little sympathy for that. The philosopher whose ideas about love most closely correspond to Pullman's use of "love" are those of the American philosopher Charles Sanders Peirce (1839–1914). The reason Peirce's view is closer to Pullman's than the traditional Christian cosmologies is basically because Peirce, like Pullman, is an evolutionist. I will not weigh you down with a long description of Peirce's cosmology, called Agapasticism (after the Greek word *agape*, love). Suffice it to say that this is an aesthetic cosmology, in which everything that exists is built on mutual feeling. Here is a little sample:

> Three modes of evolution have been brought before us: evolution by fortuitous variation, evolution by mechanical necessity, and evolution by creative love. . . . the mere propositions that absolute chance, mechanical necessity, and the law of love, are severally operative in the cosmos, may receive the names of tychism, anancism, and agapism. (*Philosophical Writings of Peirce*, p. 364)

Peirce believes the universe allows all three types of evolution to exist, but he doesn't think all three modes are equally operative in what exists. Agapism is the more comprehensive proposition. It accounts for "the bestowal of spontaneous energy by the parent upon the offspring, and . . . the disposition of the latter to catch the general idea of those about it and thus to subserve the general purpose. . . In the very nature of things, the line of demarcation between the three modes of evolution is not perfectly sharp. That does not prevent its being quite real" (Ibid.).

Peirce carries on about all this, brilliantly, for quite a few pages. If you now look back to where we began with this chapter, you'll see that Pullman handles evolution by chance and by mechanical necessity as being modes that work at a lower level of explanation than his idea of "love." So, he is consistent; he just isn't interested in *logical* consistency. He plies the trade of the story-teller, which requires aesthetic and imaginative rules, not logical, scientific, or moral ones.

But Peirce is a little further down that same path. He actually reconciles, with logic and science, these different modes of evolution using viable philosophical arguments—although it isn't as much fun to read as to read Pullman. Now, you may never have heard of Peirce, and I have no reason at all to think that Pullman has ever read him. And you might think, "Well, other philosophers and scientists and even theologians must think Peirce is daft, to defend such ideas as 'evolutionary love'." But that would be very far from the case. Peirce's influence has been steadily growing for many years, and even his critics stand in almost perfect awe of his intellect and his learning, which are only recently beginning to come into common understanding. You might want to read a little ways into Peirce's philosophy, since I know you like Pullman's ideas, if you have read this far.

My point is that if you follow Pullman's knife right into the world of contemporary cosmology, you might be surprised to find out how viable his most central ideas are. You don't need to travel to other worlds or believe in them. All you need is an open mind and a fair command of the game of rock, paper, scissors. If you don't believe me, check your own alethiometer.

As Lyra once said, "I'm the best liar there ever was. But I en't lying to you, and I never will" (*The Subtle Knife*, p. 103).

9
Mrs. Coulter—Overwoman?

HER DARK MATERIALS

She's Cleopatra and Mata Hari and Madame Bovary and Joan of Arc all rolled into to one, isn't she? Maybe you should add in your favorite Bond Girl to complete the list.

Back when they tried to make the first novel into a movie (2007), they cast Nicole Kidman as Mrs. Coulter. That was Phillip Pullman's idea. He had described her as dark-haired in the books, but he repented of that when they got Nicole Kidman—who had to be convinced, since she didn't want to play a villain. I guess they needed star power.

Hell, they had Daniel Craig and Sam Elliott. I don't know about you, but I don't really picture Nicole Kidman when I try to imagine Mrs. Coulter from the books. I was talking earlier in the book about how my imagination gets squashed once somebody casts a movie and all my pictures of the character become automatically whoever was cast for the part. But not in this case. I really couldn't accept Nicole Kidman as Mrs. Coulter.

Don't get me wrong, I'm a huge fan of Nicole Kidman, but she just doesn't quite have the right *femme fatale* sort of energy (plenty *femme*, not enough *fatale*). She's also not crazy enough. And in a two-hour movie she had to get evil too quickly. Mrs. Coulter is far beyond *Noir*, anyway, don't you think? Ruth Wilson has a longer arc to develop the character, and through Season Two, I have to admit, she is doing the job almost too well. It's getting pretty creepy, especially when she threatens to kill her own daemon, which isn't in the books.

But there's still a big diff between a three-season series and three substantial novels. That character is hard to capture in a script, no matter how long the arc is. Philip Pullman created this character before Claire Underwood (*House of Cards*) appeared on the scene, and yet, I wonder whether Robin

Wright read the novels and thought "Hmmm, I'll play Claire like *that*." So I guess I want Robin Wright in that part. She's a little bit too old, but she could pull it off. I spent years trying to imagine Mrs. Coulter, and then, like magic, there was Claire Underwood. I am going to spend a good bit of time with Claire Underwood a little later in this book. One thing they'll never say about me is that I neglected the feminine energies in the metaphysics of the movies.

I'm going to have to confess something. I don't really dislike Mrs. Coulter as much as I'm supposed to. Well, maybe I'm actually supposed to *not* dislike her, but for me it goes beyond that. In fact, I have a silly crush on her more wicked side, not her (oh so transient) vulnerable side. Part of it is that I can't quite get her character to "hang together" in my mind, a fact which is intriguing all by itself. That must be part of what makes the role so hard to play. I'll bet I'm not the only person out there who gets her (or fails to get her) this way. She's a deliciously mysterious babe, and quite a dangerous one to have around (spoiler alert: ask Lord Boreal). And part of the attraction is that she's a fictional character, which is the safest sort of dangerous woman to be infatuated with. So, there you have it: she's dangerous *and* she's safely non-existent, and I think about her all the time (well, a lot of the time, more than I should). It could be a problem. Fortunately, that's my job. Good work if you can get it (and keep it).

My Theory

So I came up with a theory. Philosophers like theories quite a lot. Not so much as we like chocolatl, but chocolatl doesn't pay our bills and theories do (oddly enough). They left chocolatl out of the movie and the HBO series. Seems a shame. I started off just wondering whether Mrs. Coulter is really religious at all (it would spoil the attraction if she were; don't ask me why). Her ambiguous religiosity seemed to be at the heart of the puzzle, or so I hypothesized, and since it was *my* puzzle, no one prevented me from thinking so. The HBO series does not do a good job of making her ambiguously religious, like the books do. The series presents her as driven entirely by power in its several forms, like Claire Underwood. The books are subtler. She might actually be religious in the books.

So it's my theory, so I get to decide what counts. I explained all this back in the Oz chapter. It is not easy to tell the difference, by the bye, between good philosophy and people just thinking stuff up. If you are beginning to get the sense that philosophers sit around making stuff up, I would say you're getting the message here. I'm going to do what I can in these next pages to show you a few things about how to make stuff up and call it philosophy (and get away with it). Sociologists and psychologists also make things up, but (from what I can tell) their theories need not have anything to do with reality, so philosophy is more constrained.

Back to my theory. I decided that there are two main ways we might understand Mrs. Coulter's obsessions and motives (this is how philosophical theories usually start: on the one hand . . . on the other hand . . .). First, Philip Pullman offers, on several occasions, the suggestion that Mrs. Coulter is *afraid* of Dust and genuinely wants to use the power of "experimental theology" to spare people from sin in the future. You gotta love the idea that what we call "physics" could have been "experimental theology" had a few things been different in our world (like the hilariously creative notion that John Calvin becomes Pope). And frankly, if Einstein's General Relativity isn't theology, nothing is. (I am far from the first to assert this.) Anyway, we might call this anti-Dust crusader the "religious" version of the Coulter character.

Finishing Off Mrs. Coulter

But on many other occasions, Pullman suggests that Mrs. Coulter is really only interested in power, and she uses all the means available to a woman in her world to gain it. Echoes of *The Handmaid's Tale*, and Serena Waterford, no? Now there's a thought. Give this part to Yvonne Strahovsky. In Mrs. Coulter's quest for power, she doesn't seem to be afraid of *anything*, least of all sin. On the face of it, these seem like two different people. I will get to the bottom of this with my theory, and I hope to get it done before (spoiler alert) Mrs. Coulter gets to the bottom of the Abyss.

I think that there is a sort of genius in the way Pullman finishes off Mrs. Coulter: locked in an eternal struggle with Metatron, who symbolizes the *religious* craving for power, in all its perversity, and Lord Asriel, who symbolizes its contrary, the *worldly* will to power, the Faustian bargain, all falling forever together, kicking, biting, pulling hair. Their plunge is, I think, intended to allude to the fall of the angels banished from heaven in Milton's *Paradise Lost* (I, 44–75; VI, 860–877). Shades of Golem and his Precious at the Cracks of Doom, also, right?

But what would you bet that Mrs. Coulter switches sides whenever either Metatron or Asriel gets the upper hand in that endless struggle? And they all fall into a pit so deep that a physical body would starve before it hits the bottom (to use Pullman's image), and then their ghosts continue falling and fighting forevermore. I think that Pullman was telling us not to expect a final resolution between these contending forces, but Mrs. Coulter seems to hold them in balance by never quite committing herself wholly to one or the other.

My Theory, Redux

There was a good deal to think about here. I had so many questions and so few answers. So I did what anyone with too much free time would have done: I started poking around in likely books to see where Pullman got all this stuff, and to try to figure out his angle on Mrs. Coulter. I really think that the writers who created Claire Underwood and Serena Waterford must surely have read Pullman. The characters are just too close to be accidental. But that was AP (After Pullman). I went looking BP specifically for a model for her character in all this ancient sacred literature and also in John Milton, who were sources for this story. I think I found Mrs. Coulter, but I will save that for near the end (don't peek—just because I'm spoiling everything doesn't mean I want you to spoil *my* fun). So, basically, I'm not going to tell you my theory until I'm ready. I'm just announcing that I have one.

Paradise Re-lost

Lots of people have commented that Pullman sort of rewrote Milton's big ol' poem about the war in Heaven and turned the story on its head. In terms of the *content* of the trilogy, I think there is a pretty good case for seeing it this way. But what's going on *philosophically* with Pullman is really a different story. Let's cover Milton first. I'm assuming they made you read this in high school. They certainly made *me*.

You may recall that in the days before the world was created, a third of the angels took up battle with the Almighty. It didn't turn out well for anybody, really. Maybe Pullman didn't buy the way Milton depicted Adam's attitude toward the tragedy of world history near the end of the big ol' poem, when our common progenitor pretended to be grateful for all the blood, sweat, and tears shed by his many sons and daughters, just so that his heirs could be "saved" by Jesus later on.

Well, did Pullman rewrite Milton? Was that what he set out to do?

Someone had to "take one for the team," so I did it. I went and reread *Paradise Lost* to see what all came from there that later shows up in Pullman's trilogy. The writers of the HBO series surely did the same. It looks to me like they did. I found some stuff that others haven't noticed, mainly because no one really wanted to reread the whole thing. Do they still teach Milton in high school? God, when I was a youngster, *everyone* had to read this blasted thing, which I always wanted to rename "Boredom Gained." But I now know that it's a better read when you get older.

Okay, I'm not quite being truthful. I bought the audio book version and listened to it on a car trip to Kansas City. But I *did* dig out my old high-school textbook version, snickered at my comments in the margins from when I was seventeen, and marked it up anew as I came to things I recognized from Pullman. And I am coming clean about this because I need you to be aware that there is a fantastic audio version of this book, read by Anton Lesser, whose vocal interpretation of the poem is so good that the whole thing became comprehensible to me for the first time. It's published by Naxos audio books and it is worth every cent of the $40 it costs.

Anyway, here is some stuff I found.

Many Worlds

We don't need recent physicists like Hugh Everett (whom I discussed in the last chapter) to find the "many worlds" hypothesis, although Pullman does have Mary Malone mention Everett's hypothesis by name in Book III (*The Amber Spyglass*, p. 77). Milton already had a similar idea: "Space may produce new worlds; whereof so rife / There went a fame in heav'n that He erelong intended to create" (I, 650–51). So, there are many worlds. No big deal. Further, the same idea occurs in the very line that gave our trilogy, and our HBO series, its name, where Milton says that all the several causes of the world would struggle in endless chaos, "Unless th' Almighty Maker them ordain / His dark materials to create more worlds" (II, 915–916).

In fact, it is mildly un-Biblical (as Milton knew) to pretend that God made only one world. Certain passages, especially in Genesis, but also elsewhere, whenever angels are being discussed (such as Psalm 82, or Revelation), only make sense by supposing a vast cosmos of many worlds, and many levels of existence beyond our familiar realm of the senses.

The idea that these many worlds might exist right on top of each other *in dimensions of possibility* is not in Milton, however. So the business in Lyra's world about the "heretical" Barnard-Stokes Hypothesis (which is supposed to correspond to the Everett hypothesis) is only intended to remind us of how the church has been suspicious, historically, of new ideas and science. This "many worlds" idea is not heretical in *our* world, so making it a part of a heresy in Lyra's world is a difference between hers and ours. I can't see that Milton would have had a problem with the plurality of worlds in dimensions of possibility. And the idea is probably not heretical. For him, the other worlds were in other *places*. The Swedish mystic Emanuel Swedenborg (1688–1772) proposed the dimensionality view, and I am betting Pullman consulted his writings too.

Milton was very, very smart, and he was more than just a poet. He wrote some philosophical prose that philosophers still read and teach, especially his defense of the free press. In the big ol' poem, he articulated a fairly subtle theory of knowledge, suggesting a dynamic physical intercourse (Milton loved the word "intercourse") between the worlds of spirit and sense. For example, the inhabitants of these two worlds might eat the same food (V, 475–505), which is probably why the angel Balthamos eats a mint cake when Will offers him one in Book III. It will be interesting to see what the HBO producers do with Angels and in particular Balthamos. But most importantly, the inhabitants of heavenly domains can have sex and reproduce with humans. Yes, that's also in the Bible.

We will get to this point in a bit, but I want to make it clear that Milton vehemently denied that it was *sex* between Adam and Eve that made them "fall." Milton explicitly has Adam and Eve doing the deed in paradise (it isn't dirty yet), and he says they would have had children, eventually, even without falling. The difference is that there was no lust in the pre-fall intercourse of Adam and Eve. There was pleasure, but no lust, which I find a bit difficult to imagine, fallen sinner that I am.

In any case, those who want to attack Pullman for promoting sex as a perfectly sinless thing should examine and compare his presentation of sex between Will and Lyra (sorry to those who aren't reading, only watching, but yes, there is sex in store for Lyra and Will in Season Three, assuming they follow the book) with Milton's description of sex between Adam and Eve *before* the Fall. My point for now is that angels are *physical* beings. The relevance of sex will become clearer in a few moments.

Dust to Dust

The idea of "Dust" is also in Milton, just before the line about "his dark materials." He is speaking of the elements and forces that make up the physical world, and he says that Hot, Cold, Moist, and Dry each have an army of particles contending with one another "unnumbered as the sands" and these atoms are "levied to side with warring winds," and "To whom these [particles] most adhere, / He rules a moment" (see II, 898–908).

That explains a few things, like the dust winds discovered by Mary Malone on her platform high in the crown of the seed-pod trees (again, Season Three). It also explains the relationship between Dust and the *will to power*. Milton has it right here: those who rule a moment. Such individuals as Mrs. Coulter and Lord Asriel are probably very "dusty," but maybe not in quite the same *way*—for example, I think Asriel is probably Hot and Mrs. Coulter is probably Cold (that's my suggestion about why Pullman names her "Coulter" and insists on calling her that throughout the trilogy—Mrs. Colder is a cold customer, colder than Asriel in any case).

The idea of dust occurs in much the same way that Pullman speaks of it near the end of Book I (*The Golden Compass*, pp. 370–74, 376–77), when Lord Asriel is explaining to Lyra, in his comfy prison near Svalbard, where Dust comes from. That does make it into the series; it really has to be included because it's the ontological pivot of the whole tale. Asriel quotes the famous Biblical passage from Genesis "for dust thou art and unto to dust shalt thou return" (p. 373).

Milton has Adam pondering this same admonition and his own "death," and Milton comments about whether our human inability to be satisfied might continue beyond death, but "That were to extend / His sentence beyond dust and Nature's law" (X, 805–06). Milton is saying that desire and dissatisfaction die with physical death and do not extend beyond our dissolution to dust. Dust is an ultimate destiny for us, which is a point Pullman uses freely. It is not heresy unless Milton is a heretic (plenty of people, such as William Blake, have said he was).

So, an aside about Milton and heresy. The more I studied him, the more I realized both that Milton is a heretic and that a bunch of people in his time and his court knew that perfectly well. But he was just too well-positioned with the Lord Protector for anyone to do anything about it. He was "Secretary for Foreign Tongues to the Council of State" for ten years (1649–1659), meaning that he was basically in charge of making sure that all business and political dealings of the government under Cromwell which were to be expressed in two or more languages (especially with those tricky French folk, the clever Dutch, and the still pesky Spaniards) said exactly the same thing, legally speaking, in the other languages as they said in English. It's hard to openly accuse a man who is *that* useful.

Returning to dust, as we always do, it's good to be aware that the tradition of orthodox Christian theology makes a place for this sort of idea, this dissolution to dust. For example, when Macrina (324–379 C.E.) explained her theology to her brother, whom we now know as St. Gregory of Nyssa, he asked her how the final resurrection of the body is possible, given that the bodies of the disciples have (by the fourth century) dissolved into atoms. Macrina said that the atoms have "known" each other in life and will recognize one another when God ordains their rejoining. This is not heresy, it's integral to the Christian tradition, and it also turns out to be the truth about the physical universe. We now call it "quantum entanglement" (see *The Amber Spyglass*, p. 156).

Many of us don't expect God ever to ordain or command a final resurrection, but both Milton and Pullman are well aware that Christianity requires an interpretation of the simplest particles that compose the physical world. Pullman is not making this up and it isn't even an inversion of Christian doctrine, or of Milton. It's orthodoxy. So the church and the Church have been complaining bitterly about Pullman's portrayal of ecclesiastical authority—which sells more books and gets him more viewers, as he has pointed out—but I wonder how much the Church would be willing to allow is orthodox but unfamiliar to most believers. Pullman is quite Biblical, even in his portrayal of the Ancient of Days.

Touched by an Angel

Pullman's description of the huge battle between the forces of Lord Asriel and Metatron in Book III owes a good deal to Milton's description of the first war in Heaven, a war replayed on the Plain of Armageddon in the Christian book of Revelation.

Regarding this battle, Pullman suffers from the same sort of problem as Milton and the writer of Revelation: how do we describe, in *physical* terms, a conflict among angels, none of whom can quite be killed or even go to war in the ordinary sense? (*see* Milton, VI, 345–354). The writer of Revelation gets all symbolic and cryptic and indecipherable. Milton just has Raphael (the archangel who brings all the messages from God to Adam) lament that this is a "Sad task and hard, for how shall I relate / To human sense th' invisible exploits/ Of warring spirits?" (V, 564–66) It all just sounds silly when we bring it down to a level of description we can grasp.

So the Archangel decides to describe it *as if* it were a war among human-like beings, and warns us that this is only an analogy. Something similar is going on at the end, with the fall of Mrs. Coulter, in an endless . . . well, it's a threesome. There. I said it. And not for the last time. It's the threesome to end all threesomes. The Mother of all Threesomes. A trinity, if you will. Sort of the condemned counterpart of that other threesome, the Holy Spirit, God the Father, and the Holy Virgin. (Am I getting too imaginative?) Jesus. I'll quit.

This narrative strategy of Rafael is reminiscent of the disclaimer made by the first angels we meet in Pullman's Book II, when Queen Ruta Skadi encounters angels who look like human forms to her only because she is unaware "that she saw them as human-formed only because she expected to" and that, really, they were more "like architecture than organism, huge structures composed of intelligence and feeling" (*The Subtle Knife*, p. 141). This corresponds to Milton's description of angelic nature as "All heart they live, all head, all eye, all ear / All intellect, all sense; and as they please /They limb themselves, and color, shape, or size / Assume, as likes them best, condense or rare" (VI, 350–54).

This explains why Balthamos can play the part of Will's daemon if he so chooses, and why it is humiliating for him to condense himself in a mere bird. Much of Pullman's angelology follows Milton, but both also follow certain older texts. The Jewish angelology of the time of Jesus is very similar, and descends from an older Hebrew counterpart, of course, which itself traces back to ancient Persia and Mesopotamia. St. Augustine's views are explicitly mentioned, but also there are the shared sources of the Bible and the *Pseudepigrapha*. I'll get to that in a minute, since I know you're just dying to find out all this stuff. The point is that Milton is hardly the original source.

But the idea that humans of flesh and blood can sometimes *become* angels is also in Milton, in much the way Pullman describes it. Remember that Balthamos was *always* an angel, but he helped Baruch, who had been a man, the brother of Enoch, *become* an angel; meanwhile, the Authority also made Enoch an angel, renamed "Metatron." Milton says that men and angels differ in degree but are of the same kind (V, 490), and has Raphael say to Adam: "Wonder not then, what God for you saw good / If I refuse not, but convert, as you, / To proper substance. Time may come when men / With angels may participate, and find / No inconvenient diet, nor too light fare; / Your bodies may at last turn all to spirit, /Improved by tract of time, and winged ascend / Ethereal as we, or may, at choice / Here or in heav'nly paradises dwell" (V, 491–501).

So, it looks to me like Pullman intends to stick with Milton on this relationship between angels and humans, and if you found Pullman's description of angels a bit unfamiliar, it's because you forgot how it works in *Paradise Lost* (or because you never read that far). It is really difficult to get all this exposition and explanation into the dialogue and pictures of a show, whether movie or TV series. So maybe you're finding this helpful, since it would be terribly boring to try to do much of this on a screen

That Knife

Of course I talked about this in some detail in the last chapter, but there is more to say. The subtle knife, the star of the second book and of Season Two, itself also comes from Milton, at least partly, I think. It is modeled on the sword of Michael, the Archangel who leads God's troops into battle, and who clashes with Satan himself. Milton says: ". . . the sword / Of Michael from the armory of God / Was giv'n him tempered so, that neither keen / Nor solid might resist that edge" (VI, 320–23). Michael slices Satan's sword easily with it, and then cuts right into the Fiend himself, yet "The girding sword, with discontinuous wound / Passed through him; but th' ethereal substance closed / Not long divisible," (VI, 328–331) which may have given Pullman some ideas about how to describe cutting into other worlds. Also, when we consider how Will's fingers are cut off and simply won't stop bleeding, the explanation might be that the knife has cut not only his body but also his spirit and his ghost, each of which might have some role to play in the processes of physical healing.

That Compass

Everyone knows that the phrase "His Dark Materials" came from Milton, but not as many know that the American title of Book I, *The Golden Compass* is also from Milton. The Son is creating the world we inhabit, at God's behest, and in carrying out the task, "He took the golden compasses, prepared / In God's eternal store, to circumscribe / This universe, and all created things" (VII, 225–27). This is not the alethiometer as a device, it is just the phrase that was used for the title, but it's hardly an accident that it is in Milton. Still, my point is that it's there.

The Sons of God

Enough already? Not quite. The juiciest bit of Pullman's story is drawn from a very strange passage in the Bible, from Genesis 6:1–4:

> When men began to multiply on the face of the land and daughters were born to them, the sons of God saw that the daughters of man were so fair. And they took as their wives any they chose. Then the Lord said, "My Spirit shall not abide in man forever, for he is flesh: his days shall be 120 years." The Nephilim were on the earth in those days, and also afterward, when the sons of God came into the daughters of man and they bore children to them. These were the mighty men who were of old, the men of renown.

Weird, huh? I never heard a sermon on this passage. One wonders what a preacher would convey as the moral message here. The Bible proper doesn't say much more about this little episode, but what happens next (in the Bible) is that the people turn away from God and become wicked, and then God slays them all in a flood—I think you've heard about that part.

But more than a few people have scratched their heads at this passage. What's up with the "sons of God" doing the dirty deed with the "daughters of men." If you're curious, there is a great deal more about this obscure part of world history in the Deutero-cannonical writings (I'll say more shortly on that topic), but for now what's important is that Milton takes up and explains all this stuff.

In Book XI, lines 556–715 (I know, you never made it that far in high school), the Archangel Michael has been sent to kick Adam out of the Garden of Eden, but he consoles Adam by showing him all of the future, including the salvation of humanity by the Son of God (Michael does not mention Pullman's novel to Adam, for some reason, but then, I guess it's just a sketch of the future, not the details).

Milton explains this odd passage from Genesis by expanding it. The world was pastoral and good, Michael says, but somewhere another angel was up to something naughty, deep in a cave, pounding on an iron forge, "Laboring, two massy clods of iron and brass / Had melted . . . the liquid ore he drained / Into fit molds prepared; from which he formed / First his own tools; then, what else might be wrought" (XI, 565–573).

In Greek mythology, this naughty fellow is called Hephaestus, while the Romans called him Vulcan. He has a Hebrew name too. Wait for it. This naughty angel heads down to the world of human beings with a troop of followers and teaches the humans metal craft, including how to make weapons and to adorn themselves with jewelry made of fine metals.

It's pretty much all downhill from there. The human race in intercourse with these lusty angels make war, and build their cities, and they forget about God as they fall into what Michael calls "effeminate slackness." Basically, when all is said and done, the "sons of God" and the "daughters of men" have created a whole race of giants who are violent and very difficult to feed. These are "the mighty men of old" from Genesis, and Michael describes them as "Destroyers rightlier called and plagues of men" (XI, 697).

Pullman knows this story from Milton, but he also has studied the writings on this strange episode from the *Pseudepigrapha*, which is a name given to various ancient writings in the Biblical style (often held in esteem and given some degree of authority by the Church, the Deutero-cannon, or secondary authorities). Important among these writings are three apocalyptic writings called First, Second, and Third Enoch, and also Second and Third Baruch. Pullman draws heavily from these writings for his content.

For example, the idea that Enoch, the seventh generation from Adam, became an angel renamed Metatron comes from Chapters 3–4 of Third Enoch. There's a great deal more from these writings that Pullman uses for his story, but for the moment, the important event comes when an angel with the interesting name of Azazel (which is Hebrew for "scapegoat") takes a notion to pay the Earth a visit:

> In those days, when the children of man had multiplied, it happened that there were born unto them handsome and beautiful daughters. And the angels, the children of heaven, saw them and desired them; and they said to one another, "Come, let us choose wives for ourselves from among the daughters of man and beget us children . . . And they took wives unto themselves, and everyone respectively chose one woman for himself, and they began to go unto them. And they taught them magical medicine, incantations, the cutting of roots, and taught them about plants. (First Enoch 6: 1–2, 7: 1–2)

Here we find the origin of the witches of Lyra's world, and the reason they live so long (they are the daughters of angels), and what sort of magic they can perform. But there's more. "And

Azazel taught the people the art of making swords and knives, and shields, and breastplates, and . . . decorations" (8:1). For disclosing the arts of metallurgy to the humans, Azazel is punished by God, who tells Raphael: "Bind Azazel hand and foot and throw him into the darkness!" (10:4). Enoch (Metatron) says to Azazel: "There will not be peace unto you; a grave judgment has come upon you. They will put you in bonds, and you will not have an opportunity for rest and supplication, because you have taught injustice, and because you have shown the people deeds of shame, injustice, and sin" (13:1–2). Milton also mentions Azazel by name, and designates him as the standard bearer for Lucifer's army.

So, putting two and two together, here's what you get: the model for Asriel is Azazel. Lord Asriel is not a man, he's an angel who has chosen a wife from among the daughters of men, namely Mrs. Coulter. The enmity between Enoch (Metatron) and Asriel goes back to the time when Asriel was cast down and bound. The angel of light in Pullman is not Lucifer but is Xaphania, and she and Asriel have planned this new challenge to the old order, and have done so by repeating the "sin" of Genesis 6:1–4. Outcome? Lyra. Holy cod. You wanna talk about a spoiler alert? This isn't a piece of imaginative fiction Pullman wrote, it's a freakin' *adaptation*. So the series is an adaptation of an adaptation.

The witches have a prophecy about Lyra because they are the surviving female offspring of the fallen angels who retain the wisdom they learned back in the days before the first war in Heaven. They know that the sign of the new challenge will come when one of the defeated angels has a daughter by one of the daughters of men. This hypothesis about Asriel is confirmed when the witch Queen Ruta Skadi describes her visit to Lord Asriel's Adamant Tower ("Adamant" comes from the name "Adam" which is a Hebrew word that means primal material, or . . . dust). The Tower (Of Babel? Of Cirith Ungol?), which was raised to make war with heaven:

> How has he done this? I think he must have been preparing this for a long time, for eons. He was preparing this before we were born, sisters, even though he is so much younger . . . But how can that be? I don't know I can't understand. I think he commands time, he makes it run fast or slow according to his will. (*The Amber Spyglass*, p. 270)

The queen's erotic desire is inflamed and she does with Lord Asriel what the witches did back in Genesis. The suggestion that witches are the daughters of the angels is, as far as I can tell, Pullman's invention, but it nicely draws the story together. There is a great deal of crypto-matriarchy being suggested here, which may be the reason that instead of Lucifer, the principal among the fallen angels is female. And perhaps the angel Xaphania is really in charge of all this rebellion. Her name is probably taken from the *Pseudepigrapha* also, from the Apocalypse of Zephania, which is (among other things) a study in angelology and their orders and places in the heavenly city.

The discussion of Pullman's use of sources beyond Milton could go on forever, so I bring in the *Pseudepigrapha* here more to suggest where you might look for more information. A lot of people don't know about these writings. The Church is rarely eager to promote them. The Catholics have always been hesitant to promote the general reading of the Bible itself, by the ordinary believer. Protestants do that and you see what a mess *they* make of the Bible. The Catholics are surely right in pointing out that it is a very difficult book and easily misunderstood without training, but then they have historically withheld that training from all but the few they approve. That part is bullshit. Since Vatican II things have been more open. I mention all this only to the degree that this information solves some riddles that remain from the Pullman trilogy. His quarrels with the present-day churches are not very interesting to me.

Pullman never really explains that Asriel is an angel who has succeeded in breaking his ancient bonds and condensing into a substantial form so that the re-enactment of the sin of Genesis 6 is now possible again. Pullman never tells us why Lyra is so special, or what gives her the standing to play the part of Eve again, but the key is Genesis 6. Pullman gives us enough clues to work out who Asriel is, if we're willing to follow the trail. And obviously, this tells us a bit about Mrs. Coulter too. She is irresistible to the angels, whether Asriel or Metatron. But why? She is not Eve, after all.

A hint is to be found when Milton, describing Eve as she serves supper to Adam and Raphael in paradise, says, tantalizingly: "Meanwhile at table Eve / Ministered naked, and their flowing cups / with pleasant liquors crowned. O innocence / Deserving Paradise! If ever, then, / Then had the Sons of God excuse to have been / Enamored at that sight; but in those hearts / Love unlibidinous reigned . . ."

To paraphrase a bit, here is Eve without so much as a fig leaf, pouring a righteous single malt for Adam and Raphael, and they don't even lust after her, *but Milton does.* He is sitting there thinking to himself "Those idiots, there is *womanhood itself* right in front of you, and you're just drinking and chatting!" Granted, Mrs. Coulter isn't Eve, but she's the freaking *Mother* of Eve, which might be, well, matriarchally speaking, still more of a challenge than Eve.

Hmmm. Lilith. Yes, that was the name I was looking for . . . So now you know. Mrs. Coulter is Lilith.

Übermenschen

As interesting as it is, none of this source material is "philosophy," *per se.* It is important to look at some of it so that we understand what sort of dark materials Pullman is working with, but until the materials are placed in some sort of order (whether human or divine—or daemonic), there is really nothing more here than a lot of images and ideas. But these are not your run of the mill images. They are archetypes. A dance of the archetypes, in the dust.

The more I have read his sources, the more I have become convinced that our man Pullman has intentionally modeled a number of his characters on types that are "beyond good and evil." The script writers and actors have to find a way to capture this. It is not the fact that they are angels or children, or men and women, that is crucial; it is how these characters understand morality as a set of conventions that they might or might not choose to believe (and stay within).

This is the famous idea (and book title) belonging to Friedrich Nietzsche (1844–1900). This little guy was withdrawn, very quiet, and a profoundly tortured soul. He wrote as if it was his personal calling to cast thunderbolts from the clouds at every conventional value or traditional practice.

Nietzsche has been dead for well over a hundred years, but he still makes religious people (and a lot of non-religious ones) very nervous. He was most notorious for having proclaimed that "God is dead." In Book III of the trilogy, Mrs. Coulter, confronts Father MacPhail (President of the Consistorial Court of Discipline) with the same idea, in words quite similar to a famous passage by Nietzsche. Father MacPhailsays: "There are some people who claim that God is dead already. Presumably Asriel is not one of those, if he retains the ambition to kill him."

To this, Mrs. Coulter replies; "Well, where is God, if he's alive? And why doesn't he speak anymore? . . .Where is he now? Is he still alive, at some inconceivable age, decrepit and demented, unable to think or act or speak and unable to die, a rotten hulk? And if that is his condition, wouldn't it be the most merciful thing, the truest proof of our love of God, to seek him out and give him the gift of death?" (*The Amber Spyglass*, pp. 293–94).

Thus spake Philip Pullman. I wonder if this will make it
into Season Three. It's pretty confrontational. This passage
clinches the deal. It is pure Nietzsche, and Pullman intends us
to know this. He built into Mrs. Coulter's discourse not only
words and dialectical twists exactly in the style of Nietzsche,
but also included a description of how Nietzsche spent the last
twelve years of his own short life—"decrepit and demented,
unable to think, act, speak, and unable to die." I do believe I
discern Pullman's desire to go back in time and free Nietzsche
from this suffering.

And Nietzsche famously spoke of "Free Death," the heroic
choice to die at the time of one's own choosing, just a few pages
away from his most infamous passage about the death of God
in his book *The Gay Science*. There is no question in my mind
that Pullman intends us to understand Mrs. Coulter in association with Nietzsche. He even adds, after Mrs. Coulter has
challenged Father MacPhail, that "Mrs. Coulter felt a calm
exhilaration as she spoke. She wondered if she'd ever get out
alive; but it was intoxicating, to speak like this to this man" (p.
294). Mrs. Coulter has a number of tense conversations with
Father MacPhail (and his lizard) in Seasons One and Two, and
I assume that will continue to build in Season Three.

Once it's clear that Pullman intends his readers to see an
engagement with Nietzsche's philosophy in his writing, other
things about the story fall into place. He also intends us to see
the characters of Lyra and Will, along with those of Asriel, Mrs.
Coulter, John Parry, and Metatron, as carrying out a cosmic
battle that is "beyond good and evil," which is to say, they
employ a kind of judgment that is incomprehensible from
within conventional moral standards and ideas. None of these
characters feels the least bit bound either by conventional
morals or by any kind of ordinary human emotion. They are
"overmen," or in German, *Übermenschen*.

Beyond Good and Evil

This doctrine of Nietzsche's has caused a lot of problems historically—the idea that a race of men will appear that supersedes
and replaces humankind as we now know it. To such beings as
these, we seem like insects, almost brainless slaves to everything that is weak and contemptible. Overmen don't live by
our standards, and they ought not to, since our morality is
devised by the weakest, most envious and vile among us
(the Magisterium of our own history)—in Nietzsche's word,
"Christians."

Pullman stays away from any serious critique of Jesus or Christ, but this only reinforces Nietzsche's distinction between The Church, which was the invention of St. Paul, whom Nietzsche detests, and Jesus, whom Nietzsche admires as one who was too good for this world. Pullman steers clear of anything praiseworthy in the history of conventional religion and concentrates on the aspects of religious history that Nietzsche roundly condemned. So Pullman is playing, in public, a sort of Zarathustra to his own Nietzsche.

Asriel and Metatron are neither villains nor heroes; they are contending forces more powerful than we conventional humans can understand. Their concerns are beyond our ken, and our moral judgments regarding them are of no interest to them. If you don't especially like Lord Asriel, who mercilessly murders Roger the kitchen boy so that he can re-establish his forges and smithies in an empty world, well, you aren't *supposed* to like him, and what's that to him? If Metatron seems to be a lecherous old angel, he isn't even slightly ashamed of it. Shades of Trump? Well, time is a funny eternal return, ain't it? You and your silly little moral qualms can go to blazes for all the Trumps and the Asriels and Metatrons care.

Girl Meets Boy

What about our favorite children, Will and Lyra? How does a child exist beyond conventional morality, and become stronger than all others, in spite of having conventional morality constantly thrust upon him/her? First, Pullman is careful to give the children extra-ordinary genes (and we have already noted Lyra's genealogy), but then he also devises childhood settings that deprive them of ordinary experiences. He suggests, by way of his plot choices, that the paths that lead to a girl version and a boy version of the "overman" are quite different.

On the "boy" side, Will is driven by *will*—not the will to power in the conventional sense, but the will to fulfill his fate (*amor fati*, as Nietzsche says), to take up his father's mantle of warrior and shaman, and to exist beyond the limitations of ordinary men by the strength of his will. They set this up nicely in the series. Will has to *become what he is*, to use Nietzsche's phrase, by learning to love his fate. He was born for this.

The Freudian implications of his bearing a "subtle knife" are obvious enough, I suppose, as are those of fighting with one's own father in the dark. There is nothing subtle about the positioning of Will's mother between him and his father. Apparently, such a boy doesn't automatically evade the oedipal struggle just by being beyond good and evil. As with Nietzsche's overman, Will simultaneously detests violence and uses it without a moment's hesitation. The boy rises to over-man by means of his will, it seems.

The girl rises to overwoman by more subtle and complex pathways. Pullman names her "Lyra" to emphasize the stark contrast between truth and lies. There's a difference, Nietzsche says, between "truth-and-falsehood," which is a conventional, intellectual idea (driven by a simple-minded logic and infected with conventional judgments about good and bad), and between "truth-and-lies," which is a contest of imaginations, he says. His famous essay "On Truth and Lies in the Non-moral Sense" has commanded much attention in the last fifty years, and I feel pretty certain that Pullman has studied it closely.

Lyra has to learn to lie well. By tricking a bear (and you can't trick a bear) she earns the name Lyra Silvertongue. What is this about? In all cases we try to survive by inventing simu-lations, but this is the means by which the weaker, less robust individuals preserve themselves . . . In man [not overman], this art of simulation reaches its peak: here deception, flattery, lying, and cheating, talking behind the back, living in borrowed splendor, being masked, the disguise of convention, acting a role before others and before oneself—in short, the constant fluttering around the single flame of vanity is so much the rule and the law that *almost* nothing is more incomprehensible than how an honest and pure urge for truth could make its appearance among men (*The Portable Nietzsche*, p. 43).

But Lyra will overcome this dilemma. Here, in a nutshell, is the tension Mrs. Coulter also has to face as she tries to ascend from the fetters of convention and the church to her genuine nature, which is beyond all that, Lilithly lying (say that five times fast, but not to a mirror in the dark). It's difficult, isn't it, Marisa, to be a substitute within the Magisterium for Mary? Lyra, on the other hand, is given, by her nature, a perfect com-mand of both truth and lies, once she learns from Mrs. Coulter how to escape being detected in a lie. But Lyra doesn't read that damned device, *it* reads *her*.

Both overcomings require practice, but both arts come eas-ily to Lyra: the lies come not by way of imagination (Pullman makes a point of saying she is unimaginative), but simply because Lyra feels no constraint; and truth comes to her by way of a technology of symbols, *active* symbols. As Nietzsche puts it: "What, then, is truth? A mobile army of metaphors, metonyms, and anthropomorphisms" (p. 46). In short, truth is an alethiometer. Vivid imagination is not to blame for Lyra's lies. Xaphania's later teaching about the value of imagination, and the difficulty of learning to travel by its means, is at stake here. I sure hope they include that in the HBO series.

Thus, Lyra tells the truth just as she lies: from beyond conventional morality. By analogy, Will is the true despiser of violence but finds himself continually obliged to engage in it to preserve his own unalterable purpose. His violence is not the violence of blind followers or of those who oppress others and call the situation "peace" or "order" or "law." He is beyond good and evil, but nothing like the Magisterium or Trump. Thus, one of the more peculiar passages in the trilogy is explained. When Lyra first encounters Will in Cittàgazze. Lyra asks the alethiometer *"What is he* [Will]*? A friend or an enemy?* The alethiometer answered: *He is a murderer"* (*The Subtle Knife*, p. 28).

Now, I don't know about you, but if I was in Lyra's spot, I wouldn't be inclined to think of that as good news. But Pullman says, "When she saw the answer, she relaxed at once. He could find food, and show her how to reach Oxford, and those were powers that were useful, but he might still have been untrustworthy or cowardly. A murderer was a worthy companion. She felt as safe with him as she'd felt with Iorek Byrnison, the armored bear."

Matriarchy Meets Patriarchy

That's it. That's pretty much the whole explanation we ever get from Pullman. There's a tiny bit of elaboration on it later in the story, but the bottom line is that Lyra trusts Will *because* Will is, like herself, operating outside of conventional, cowardly morality, where no one can be trusted. And as Nietzsche puts it, "Is it not better to fall into the hands of a murerer than into the dreams of a lustful woman?" (*Thus Spoke Zarathustra*, "Of Chastity," p. 81). There we pretty much have Nietzsche's version of the story of Will rescuing Lyra from the sleep into which Mrs. Coulter has delivered her.

But notice that Lyra's path to overwoman is not a fight, it is a decision about which boy to follow. When she does anything apart from following Will, she gets into terrible trouble and messes everything up. Will on the other hand always knows what to do, because he does only what he *has* to do and nothing else. Eventually, Will even begins to tell Lyra when to use the alethiometer, and she pretty much does whatever he says. I admit that I am uncomfortable with this patriarchal arrangement, but Pullman didn't ask my permission to create it this way. We will discover more about the overwoman shortly, but for now, I just want to register with you, dear reader, that this arrangement between overman and overwoman follows Nietzsche's very controversial views about women. He rather famously characterizes them as being clever liars, but the hardest pills to swallow these days are these three remarks:

1. Everthing about a woman is a riddle, and everything about a woman has one solution: pregnancy.

2. The man's happiness is: I will. The woman's happiness is: He will.

3. Are you visiting women? Don't forget your whip!

These are all from the same section of *Thus Spake Zarathustra* ("Of Old and Young Women") which would be worth your while to read in full, thinking all the while of Lyra and Mrs. Coulter.

Uncomfortable as it may be, Pullman is following this line of thinking in Nietzsche as well. He retains the ideas of active masculine virtues and passive feminine virtues. If anything, Mrs. Coulter rather than Lyra poses a challenge to this scheme of things, which is part of the reason Mrs. Coulter is more interesting than her daughter.

Pullman has written his epic trilogy on a latticework of Milton's poem and Nietzsche's philosophical ideas about the death of God, about the ideas of good and evil, truth and lies, the will to power, and overmen and overwomen. I wonder how Nietzsche and Milton would have gotten on with each other. It might have worked. It is not quite right to think of Pullman as having rewritten John Milton or the Bible or *The Chronicles of Narnia* or Tolkien's trilogy with an inverted theology. Some people have suggested these things. Those elements contribute to the content of Pullman's trilogy, but the *ideas* under consideration are pretty much Nietzsche's. Pullman has narrated what Nietzsche called the "transvaluation of all values" in the form of a fable—which is exactly what Nietzsche himself did in *Thus Spake Zarathustra*. But Pullman's story is for children, the children of the future, after the long-awaited death of God.

Romantic Manifestos?

Pullman names Nietzsche in interviews about this subject, and the evangelical Christians have been quick to exploit Nietzsche's "bad reputation" as a weapon against Pullman. I might add here that it is even less comfortable for me to contemplate the other author who attempted this, Ayn Rand. Her lead characters were beyond good and evil, and Lord Asriel bears a striking resemblance to John Galt in *Atlas Shrugged*. But in my judgment, if one has any affinity for Nietzsche at all, one does well to skip Rand and just read Nietzsche. Rand's awful writing and ideas are caricatures of Nietzschean ideas and lead only to narrow-minded selfishness, not to anything morally interesting.

Pullman, by contrast, has far greater subtlety. He is a very good writer, and an excellent audio reader as well. And I don't see Pullman endorsing Nietzsche's views or advocating them. I think he is probably offering a critique of Nietzsche, along with appropriating the ideas that are good for the story he wants to tell. Pullman probably despises romanticism as much as Nietzsche did, but that doesn't make them birds of a feather. Maybe this little journey through Nietzsche hasn't been all that much fun (as far as I can tell, Nietzsche never had fun in his life), but hold your horses for a second—Nietzsche's last act before they institutionalized him for insanity was to collapse at the sight of a horse being beaten, but I won't beat your horses, I just want them held. Pullman is not a raving Nietzschean, I promise.

In Mrs. Coulter's Cave

In Book III, Pullman has Mrs. Coulter and Lyra re-enact the mythic drama of Demeter and Persephone, in which Will, acting the part of Hades, steals Lyra (Persephone) from Mrs. Coulter (Demeter) and takes her to the underworld to be queen there. Afterwards, Mrs. Coulter is altered. She is now (and only now) at the mercy of the power of motherhood, and she provides several drippy (and to my mind over-written and over-wrought) apologies for motherhood. It is all pretty unconvincing. This is *not* Mrs. Coulter, or at least, it isn't the Mrs. Coulter I have a crush on, the one who slaps her own daemon and has utterly silenced it.

This also isn't Lilith anymore. Even Asriel expresses something like contempt for this new, simpering, shadow-of-the-woman-she-was. Yes, she still plays each side off against the other, but there is a change. Now Mrs. Coulter is bereft of all religiousness, which is the power of fear, and this had been a source of her mystery and strength.

I want to make two points about where Pullman goes with his wicked woman:

1. Pullman created a character so powerful he didn't know what to do with her. Falling back on the Demeter archetype was a cop-out. Mrs. Coulter, he says (in effect), is what happens to woman

in a world dominated by the two overmen, Metatron and Asriel. There is no way for a woman to prevail in such a world, and that leads to my second point.

2. Sending Marisa (no longer quite Lilith) Coulter into the abyss with Asriel and Metatron suggests to me a no-win situation for the Nietzschean overwoman. Pullman is not endorsing the world of Nietzsche and is suggesting that in such a world, the superior woman has no real place.

The most interesting path would have been to let Mrs. Coulter's character go where she naturally would have—which is to say, in a fearless story, Mrs. Coulter *prevails* (like Claire Underwood). Why should Lyra (and motherhood) be such a weakness for a woman who is corruption incarnate? (Of course, Claire Underwood has several abortions to avoid this kind of entanglement.)

And with a choice between a woman who is beyond good and evil and a rival man, my money is on the woman. This is the woman who can break the subtle knife, see witches when they're invisible, tortures a witch without a moment's hesitation, and has the entire Church trembling in fear. This is the woman who can even command the specters, which is to say that she even commands the abyss. And she isn't equal to the task of being Lyra's mother? Seriously?

Mrs. Coulter, if you must know, just *is* the woman Milton was lusting after when he imagined Eve, the babe so righteous looking that she could seduce an angel or a man as upright as Adam. But having created her, Pullman pulls back from the edge. Having created the *perfect* character, the one that might have won him literary infamy, he chose to cripple her with motherhood. It's interesting that, as far as we know, he spares Lyra that burden. So I'm not happy about Pullman's effort to weasel out of his dilemma by using the *Demeter-ex-machina* strategy. But this is not about me.

Thus Spake Philip Pullman

So what is Pullman's "teaching?" I think many people have misunderstood his point. There are so many characters with so many variant points of view that it might be difficult to extract the genuine moral theme from the trilogy. But with a little reflection, his point comes clear. Pullman puts his teaching into the words of Mary Malone, Serafina Pekkala,and the angel Xaphania. It's a matriarchal teaching, sort of.

Mary is the wisdom of clear-headed scientific understanding that is not the servant of dogma and also not closed to spiritual realities. She is the "sister" of the witch, since the witch's understanding of nature is intuitive rather than scientific, and the relevant witch has also reformed the traditional ways of witches with a willingness to consider innovation and to overcome dogma as it has settled in to the society of witches. Xaphania speaks for the spiritual wisdom of the ages, and for the proper use of human imagination. All of this is offered in the final chapters of Book III. It isn't very exciting.

Pullman also provides Will's and Lyra's responses to their womanly teaching. Will, the masculine principle, takes Mary as his friend and guide. Lyra takes Serafina as hers. In so doing, Lyra overcomes the lies, but also loses access to truth when she can no longer read the Alethiometer—unless she is willing to commit a lifetime of study to the task.

Pullman is saying truth isn't easy. But in the underworld Lyra learns that truth is really *narrative* in form—the way to stay within the truth involves faithfulness to one's *own* narrative, not to a piece of technology created by tiresome or Faustian scholars.

Will's peculiar challenge is that of freedom and determinism. He has struggled throughout the story with whether he is determined to be a warrior by "his nature." He declares war on his fate early in Book III when he says that even if he can't choose his nature, he *can* choose what he does. Nietzsche has counseled that the overman is able to love his fate, but Will (and Pullman) takes a different view. Xaphania suggests the same.

But in the crucial moment, when Will has asked Xaphania what his "task" in life is, he stops her from telling him, because knowing her wisdom only perpetuates the struggle between freedom and fate. Thus, Pullman isn't saying he has a solution to the issue of freedom and fate, or of truth and lies. He is saying that even for Will and Lyra, after the crash and collapse of the world of powers beyond good and evil, still the philosophical problems remain. Pullman's advice is: truth is hard to know and knowing it takes work, and we are free to choose what we do, so long as we don't trouble ourselves overmuch about questions that are beyond our ken. As Alexander Pope (who might easily have played a larger part in this chapter) said: The proper study of mankind is man. Pullman is that sort of humanist, I feel pretty sure.

It is important that Pullman places all three teachings in the viewpoints of female characters. It's very clear that Pullman regards not only wisdom, but intuition and empirical knowledge as feminine virtues. That's why the "yearly meeting" is Lyra's idea, not Will's. They live in different worlds, but for an hour, in the noonday sun, on midsummer's day, they might quietly seek to occupy the same time in complementary spaces.

Xaphania's teaching is of the goodness of dust, and it sounds like the Boy Scout pledge: we are supposed to be cheerful, kind, patient, and curious, and that's how we renew the life force. But in particular, Xaphania wants to redeem imagination, and traveling by its means:

> We [angels] have other ways of traveling . . . It uses the faculty of what you call imagination. But that does not mean *making things up.* It is a form of seeing. . . . Pretending is easy. This way is hard, but much truer. . . . It takes long practice, yes. You have to work. Did you think you could snap your fingers, and have it as a gift? What is worth having is worth working for. (*The Amber Spyglass*, p. 443)

This is Pullman's theme, and it is equally critical of church and of state, and of any and every dogma. What he praises and advocates is not an overthrow of dogma, narrow-mindedness, and fear. He teaches that it always destroys itself, falls into the abyss under its own weight. And Nietzsche's world, which is our world, allows no place for feminine wisdom. That is not a good thing. That sucks the very life out of our world civilization.

Thus, Mrs. Coulter has no choice but to re-enact all that the collective unconscious determines her to do wherever the will to power is dominant. Pullman's interest in not in what happens to the will to power, but in what alternatives there might be. That is why he doesn't need to invert Milton, doesn't need to endorse Nietzsche, doesn't need to attack scriptural or mythic traditions, or anything of the sort. His positive suggestions may not be so startlingly new or profound, but they do have the tinge of common sense.

Incidentally, Xaphania's teaching also fulfills what I promised at the outset of this chapter. Philosophy, like the travel of angels, isn't just making things up, at least not really. It requires imagination (albeit reflective imagination, which is not the novelist's domain), but also a lifetime of work. But it's worth working for, and by taking the time to read thought-provoking literature, like Pullman's books, you are well on your way to learning that way of traveling.

It is difficult to know how much of what I have been discussing will find its way into Season Three. As I said, Book III is almost a philosophy book, and that doesn't make for good movie scripting. We'll see how clever those BBC writers are, and very soon. I wonder if they need a philosophical consultant. I could make some space in my schedule. Assuming Susan Sarandon doesn't call me.

Part III

Rated R: Restricted Audiences Only

10
A Very Naughty Boy

<small>GETTING RIGHT WITH BRIAN AND
MONTY PYTHON</small>

The Church and the Deity have been taking a licking here for quite a few pages. I'm afraid it will get worse before it gets better. In fact, it won't really get better. Just worse.

And we are far from done with Nietzsche. Like Kierkegaard, he has a power of shocking the bourgeoisie that I can't resist. Let's pile on (I gave some discussion to that back in the chapters on *South Park*). As with *His Dark Materials*, the Church did not care for *Monty Python's The Life of Brian*, and as with Pullman's work, the Church probably sold more tickets than any other publicity could have. You would think that one day they'd get the message about what happens when they come out publicly against a movie. They manage to keep away people who wouldn't have seen it anyway, and attract many who would never have known about the movie but for the fuss made by the Church.

So, I have one thing to request: please, ban this book. I'll blaspheme, whatever it takes. Did my remark about God, the Holy Spirit and Mary as a threesome not get me anything toward a ban? C'mon guys, *list me*. I'm a good Methodist, you know, but I wanna be listed! List *me*! (I will go on bended knee and kiss the ring, *anything* to offend you sufficiently.)

How I Was Saved

Let's start by just facing it. We're all sinners—not me so much as you, because I've actually done pretty well, but I could stand a bit of regeneration and I can see that you are in real trouble with you-know-Who. He told me so Himself, last night, over a bottle of three-buck-chuck. He likes cheap wine because, well,

He loves a bargain. Here is the point. I have a message for you from Him, so listen up: "You are to regard the following chapter as *revealed*, on peril of your eternal soul" (and if you are still reading this, I'm sure the peril is quite real). I don't ask any more of you than would any other inspired being.

How came I to possess such particular favor with He-Who-cannot-be-named? I was a delinquent of fourteen, wandering down a street in Memphis, when a small band of renegade Baptists sidled up to me, sincerely inquiring as to the likely destination of my soul.[1] I said I was late to meet my dealer. They were undeterred. I told them he would be armed and dangerous, and that he was a Methodist. That just encouraged them.

They said that if I would pray a simple prayer with them and ask Brian into my heart, my life would be changed, Brian would take away my sins and save me a seat on that Great Greyhound to Chicago (you can't go to Hell or Heaven without a layover in Chicago). I could see these were no ordinary Baptists. These fellows had something.

That was long ago, and many things have been revealed to me since, including the actual code for the Google search, which I now know to have come directly from Satan. I stand before you today an altered man, yes, some of it was surgical, but some came by direct action of the Almighty. If you care for your soul, turn back.

God Is Dead (and I'm Not Feeling so Good Myself)

Alright, I can see your priorities. Let me play, then, Virgil to your Dante, Socrates to your Plato, Pontius Pilate to your Biggus . . . well, never mind. Let's examine the remarkable, sinless life of Brian Cohen (Maximus) in light of certain philosophical and theological worries. And regarding such worries, God is on top of the heap, so let's get right to that.

This may be objectionable to some. Perhaps I'm bound for the infernal region. Handily, my Baptist friends believed that once you're saved, you'll always be saved, and they have even been known to toss out those who disagree (although I was never clear whether that is enough to get a person "unsaved"). It seems the Baptists can send you on your way, but not pre-

---

[1] I don't want to single out Baptists for ridicule. Some of my best friends were once Baptists. And I have enough ridicule to spread among many deserving factions, each convinced that the others are bound for Hades. This special conviction is my cue that God wants me to make fun of them.

cisely to hell, so they, along with most Protestants, seem to have signed a sort of non-proliferation of damnation pact, abdicating the nuclear option for the soul. The Roman Catholics wisely retain their weapon stock, leaving them the only remaining super(natural)-power. But as I mentioned, I got saved by the Baptists and I am not going to look a gift-Deity (or badger) in the mouth.

You are quite another matter. You may need to go and find your own Baptists. Mine are probably in Heaven by now. But it is your soul I am most worried about, as you will see.

So, God. In 1882, Friedrich Nietzsche, whom we have already met, in an especially foul mood, published the following infamous words (except they were in German):

> Have you not heard of that madman who lit a lantern in the bright morning hours, ran to the market place and cried incessantly: "I seek God! I seek God!" As many of those who did not believe in God were standing around just then, he provoked much laughter. "Is God lost?" one asked. . . . "Or is he hiding?" "Is he afraid of us?" "Has he gone on a voyage? Emigrated?" [I thought God was non-migratory.] The madman jumped into their midst. . . . "Whither is God?" he cried. "I will tell you. We have killed him, you and I. All of us are his murderers. But how did we do this? How could we drink up the sea? . . . [a dozen more such questions] . . . Do we hear nothing yet of the gravediggers of God? . . . God is dead. God remains dead. And we have killed him. (*The Gay Science*, p. 181, translation slightly modified)

Nietzsche was never renowned for his lightness of heart. It is not easy to distinguish the philosophical from the theological sense in this little narrative. Until recently both theologians and philosophers were plenty occupied with the Big Guy, so how to tell the difference?

One might think, "no theologian would proclaim the death of God," but in the 1960s a bunch of theologians got a wild hair and did just that, and started wringing their hands over what becomes of theology afterwards.[2] It was a silly time. They mostly went away, some not by their own choosing.

So what is Nietzsche on about, and what makes it philosophy? In the passage, the crowd of unbelievers is laughing at the man who would be sincere. Make no mistake, this is all about laughing at God, and what perils to the soul accompany this activity. What kills God is the laughter—or at least, laughter

---

2   Altizer, *The Gospel of Christian Atheism*; Altizer and Hamilton, *Radical Theology and the Death of God*.

kills the cheerless God sought by those whose dominant religious passion is wrapped in pathos.

Few have contributed more to laughing at such a God (and His followers) than the loyal Pythons, but they begin by having God (a less austere one) laugh at such believers. In *Monty Python and The Holy Grail*, addressing the believers adopting the "correct" pathos, God says: "Oh, don't grovel . . . do get up! If there's one thing I can't stand it's people groveling!!" When Arthur apologizes, God rebukes him: "And don't apologize. Every time I try to talk to someone it's sorry this and forgive me that and I'm not worthy . . ." and "It's like those miserable psalms. They're so depressing. Now knock it off" (*Monty Python and the Holy Grail (Book)*, pp. 23–24).

This is the sort of situation into which Nietzsche's "madman" steps, as a pathetic follower (or so he is taken to be by those laughing). The laughter is the clue that whatever reverence the solemn God once commanded has lost its grip. This may be the "madman's" point, of course.

This Deity Is Bleedin' Demised

Nietzsche is quite right. If that God ever really existed, He is dead now. That so many people find the Pythons funny is Nietzsche's justification. The God of our Victorian foreparents doesn't frighten us now nearly so much as a Stephen King novel, although His followers (God's, not King's) are still numerous enough and in themselves plenty scary and increasingly desperate in an unbelieving world. Stephen King's followers are scarier when one sits near them at dinner, although they get on nicely with Nietzsche's people, since they all wear black, chew with their mouths open, and happily endure the interminable ramblings of self-indulgent writers who need editors far more than followers.

The old God has been reduced now to a weapon of mass destruction, wielded by those angry about His death. They are the same ones who think that Trump is God's chosen leader and that COVID vaccines are the Mark of the Beast. I wonder if things could get weirder. Yet, to have a personal relationship with the dead God, one must supplement the historic pathos with a peculiar narcissistic psychosis.[3] This psychosis I will call "the Comic," following a usage by Henri Bergson (1859–1943), which I will explain in a moment. For now, grant that reflection

---

[4]   Freud describes the problem in *The Future of an Illusion*.

upon the difference between the history of the pathos of Christianity and its modern transformation into a psychosis is very much a philosophical matter, not a theological one, and this is what Nietzsche was foreseeing.

Philosophy is reflection upon all experience and aims at self-knowledge, including religious experience and ideas like "God." Theology, by contrast, is reflection upon religious experience and ideas, undertaken in faith that such experiences do exist and such ideas do refer to realities beyond themselves. This makes theology a more specialized activity. If you are already offended by what I have said, you'll prefer theology. But there may still be a God never dreamed of in your theology, and He (or She, or It) may be laughing at you.

On the far side of theology, you don't know very much; even Dr. bloody Bronowski doesn't know very much.[4] That "far side" is where philosophical consideration of God finds itself after a couple of World Wars and a Cold War. Thus, where the faith can no longer be assumed, one moves past theology into philosophy. While we might be tempted to build an "alternative theology" based upon the Pythonic revelation, indeed, sorely tempted (forgive me Brian), instead we need to grasp how the Pythons enter the philosophical world precisely on the assumption that (the old) God is dead, or at least might be (I mean, maybe he's not dead yet, but will be any moment).

At the end of the infamous passage quoted above, Nietzsche's madman says "I have come too early. My time is not yet. This tremendous event is still on its way" (*The Gay Science*, p. 182). If his time was not yet in 1882, certainly by 1979 (when *Monty Python's Life of Brian* was filmed) the days had been accomplished. The Pythons speak of God and all this hilarity is not only tolerated, it drowns out the rage of those "serious" Christians.

Yet, laughing at God is dicey business any time. As I said, I'm right with Brian, and I am here to help you get right; I think it may be too late for Nietzsche. Even the Mormons, with their wise doctrine of salvation for the dead, show no interest in reclamation of the retiring little guy with the migraine that wouldn't quit. In some ways, however, Nietzsche's seriousness touches upon a characteristic of all that is comic. We can use it here.

---

[4]   Dr. Jacob Bronowski, author of *The Ascent of Man*, the text version of a BBC TV series. Bronowski, who "knows everything," was a mathematician, statistician, poet, historian, teacher, inventor and a leader in the Scientific Humanism movement.

So Brian Cohen (Maximus) stands continually before new incarnations of the same crowd as Nietzsche's madman, asking the same sorts of questions. But Brian's pathos is different from the madman's; Brian has the sincerity of the divine idiot.[5] Recall the following exchange, when Brian finds himself obliged to prophesy:

BRIAN: Don't you, eh, pass judgment on other people, or you might get judged yourself.

COLIN: What?

BRIAN: I said, 'Don't pass judgment on other people, or else you might get judged, too.'

COLIN: Who, me?

BRIAN: Yes.

COLIN: Oh. Ooh. Thank you very much.

BRIAN: Well, not just you. All of you. . . . Yes. Consider the lilies . . . in the field.

ELSIE: Consider the lilies?

BRIAN: Uh, well, the birds, then.

EDDIE: What birds?

BRIAN: Any birds.

EDDIE: Why?

BRIAN: Well, have they got jobs?

EDDIE: Who?

BRIAN: The birds.

EDDIE: Have the birds got jobs?!

FRANK: What's the matter with him?

ARTHUR: He says the birds are scrounging.

BRIAN: Oh, uhh, no, the point is the birds. They do all right. Don't they?

FRANK: Well, good luck to 'em.

EDDIE: Yeah. They're very pretty.

BRIAN: Okay, and you're much more important than they are, right? So, what are you worrying about? There you are. See?

---

[5] Nietzsche associates Jesus himself with the psychological type of the divine idiot, and means it as praise for Jesus. See *The Anti-Christ*, Section 29.

EDDIE: I'm worrying about what you have got against birds.

BRIAN: I haven't got anything against the birds. Consider the lilies.

ARTHUR: He's having a go at the flowers now.

All one needs is a literal-minded group who neither believe nor disbelieve, asking obvious questions. Religious sincerity crumbles. The same could be done to any preacher in his pulpit anywhere, but none will do it. Yet when fire-and-brimstone evangelists ply their trade on college campuses, sometimes this scene is replayed. More often the listeners are beset with the countervailing pathos, opposing the pathos of the evangelist.

Throughout *Monty Python's Life of Brian*, detachment from such pathos pushes the plot and generates the humor. The story depends not upon mocking God, Jesus, or even Brian, but upon holding oneself at a distance, not allowing the countervailing pathos of opposition to take hold—Nietzsche called this countervailing pathos *ressentiment*.[6]

And how is the latter pathos avoided? One can rise above it, as would an *Übermensch* (see the last chapter), but that isn't funny; or one can idiotically fall below this dialectic, a sort of divine *Untermensch*. That *is* funny. Brian doesn't claim to know anything. He would be glad to, but he doesn't. He is a well-meaning moral idiot, just like nearly everyone else. When questioned, he shifts ground and finally gives up, like anyone with common sense.

The Plumage Don't Enter into It

Thus, the death of God is not simply the end of a certain concept of God, nor of the power of that concept to fill us with fear. The "death of God," however it is cashed out, is the onset of a detachment from the entire *question* of God, and common sense telling us that no one actually has the answers to questions like "Is there a God?" Those who possess such detachment by native temperament find Pythonic religious humor pleasing. Meanwhile those who do *not* have detachment, who still fear God and the question of God, who are burdened with the *pathos* of the God-fearers, find it troubling, offensive, or even blasphemous.

Common-sense detachment from impossible questions (not just God, but ultimate origins and other prideful notions that somehow an infinite universe has to fit into our tiny minds and

---

6   Nietzsche, *Ecce Homo and On the Genealogy of Morals*, pp. 36–37, 40, 73f.

systems of metaphysics) leads us to tend our *mortal* souls, leaving the immortal soul, if there is one, to its own fortunes.

Today we need not be as upset about all this as Nietzsche. Seemed like bad news to him. Seems like old news to me. He thought that killing off this old God means humans would have to bear God's burden—and we would be unequal to the task. But I think we're probably up to the chore, which is part of the revelation I received when I asked Brian into my heart. Yet there really is a "moment of decision" Brian puts to his hearers: "Shall I shun this, be offended by this, condemn this?" If the still small voice in the back of your brain says, as mine did: "No, if there is a God, He's surely enjoying this too, and if not, bugger Him," then you are open to salvation of the sort Brian brings.

Of course, this is salvation from the pathos of religious authorities who would ruin your cheer that comes from wrestling with their dreary pronouncements of Hellfire, with a thinly veiled confidence in the absolute truth of their own convictions (concealing an utterly unconscious fear that they may be wrong). Their confidence is difficult to distinguish from mere pride, but it is best not to judge, since, as Brian taught, you might get judged yourself if you do it. Better to laugh. They can't do much about that—at least, not any more.

According to Henri Bergson, "the Comic" just is anything overly stiff that holds itself opposed to the flow of experience, and when its rigid bearing is noted by others, laughter results. The person who is "comic" has at least two very important characteristics. John Cleese is a master of this kind of stiffness for comic effect. So was Graham Chapman, which is why he plays "straight man" in all the movies. What is the stiffness that Bergson calls "the comic"?

First is this mechanical inelasticity, this rigidity amid what should be a flowing present. Second, a "comic" person is invisible to himself as comic, does not realize he is being rigid. As Bergson says, "the comic person is unconscious. As though wearing the ring of Gyges with reverse effect, he becomes invisible to himself while remaining visible to all the world."[7] Hence, the art of the straight man affects sincerity, rigidity, unselfconscious pathos—and the Pythons, especially Chapman and Cleese, are among the best straight men comedy has ever produced. But for the pathetic follower of the dead God, comic rigidity is no affectation, it is a mode of existence. So the issue

---

[7] *Laughter*, pp. 16–17. The ring of Gyges is a Greek legend (see Plato in *The Republic*, Book II) about a ring that turns the wearer invisible, bringing absolute power and some very naughty behavior.

is not whether religious fundamentalists are utterly comic, *they are.*

The crux (they love cruxes, so the Pythons give them dozens, but only one cross each, please) of the matter is whether anyone will point it out so that we can all laugh. But *your* soul is still in jeopardy, so don't laugh yet.

We have more to say of rigidity and the comic, but please grant that it is far more difficult to be funny about things that are already funny, like the Pythons, because funny stuff isn't rigid and comic. In such situations one needs recourse to the lower types of humor: puns, off-color jokes, ethnic slurs, or, at the very bottom rung, politics. We are not scrupulous people. Let's do politics.

Romani Ite Domum

It's hard to be the only remaining super-power. One's empire is always getting a bad rap. But there's no pleasing some people, as both Jesus and Brian taught. Bring people the aqueduct, sanitation, roads, medicine, education, order, peace, and even the public baths and good wine, and what do you get? Just complaints about little foibles that come along with it—a taste for ocelot spleens and jaguar's earlobes, or blood pudding and Branston Pickle. Yes, those silly Brits playing silly Romans.

British humor has a connection to Roman stoicism, for the humor works in inverse proportion to the degree in which the humorists' culture is repressed: the more repressed the conquerors, the greater the comic possibilities, which is one reason why British humor seems almost surreal to the American ear (one can hardly be more repressed than the British). But get one thing straight: It's *their* empire, *not* ours, even when we have temporary administrative responsibility. As in the present.

On a recent trip to Britain I discovered to my (very American) dismay that the British are unimpressed with American wine. I was poking around in a good wine store in Oxford and finding little or nothing American to drink. I affected my best West Midlands working class British accent (the secret is to speak without moving the upper lip, and through your nose for West Midlands the rest takes care of itself, with some practice), and inquired after some wine from California. The clerk (pronounced "clark") lilted back: "'Aven't got any; tried it once, can't sell the stuff."

He *had* spam, though. It's pretty clear this was about business, not quality standards. I thought about asking if he had any cheese. Managed to stop myself. I had thought they made some *pretty good* wine in California, and here it isn't even taken seriously. And if you pour what the Brits know about wine-making into a thimble, it wouldn't even be half empty. No matter. Obviously, I am a colonist. These niceties evade me.

Having worn out the bit about "taxation without representation," I'm looking now for the headquarters of the American People's Front. What have the lousy British ever done for us? And here's the lesson of *empire*. Empire takes mettle. It isn't for nancies or pleasure-loving creatures of comfort like the Australians and the Americans. Empire requires one weapon: organizational genius. And of course, an unfailing sense of what is and is not important. So the *two* weapons of empire are organizational genius and an unfailing sense of what is and is not important. And perfect confidence in one's own superiority. So, the *three* weapons of empire are: organizational genius, an unfailing sense of what is and is not important, and a perfect confidence in one's own superiority. I mean, *nobody* expects a perfect confidence in one's own superiority.

"Great race, the Romans," says Michael Palin, hanging from the ceiling in chains the Romans granted him the privilege of wearing. But the same might be said of the British. It takes an astonishingly blithe attitude toward suffering (your own and other people's) to keep hopping in your boats and invading every place you can even land, not to mention constantly having to spank (for their own good) the troublesome Dutch and French and Spanish who are without even the decency to bring British civilization to other lands.

No, the Aussies and Yanks don't have that in them.

To illustrate, it is far, far more important that Brian be made to conjugate his Latin correctly than that he be silenced from saying "Romans Go Home." The true threat to empire is people who refuse to learn the *lingua franca* correctly. Was I not, after all, asking after American wine in the Queen's own English? When in Rome. . . . You can see why I didn't want to ask the clark in an American accent, right?

History is a stubborn and harsh teacher. Right up to my own middle school years we were still learning, at the tip of a blade, to conjugate Latin. The language had been dead for five centuries. Now *that's* an impressive cultural imperialism. People will be learning the Queen's English everywhere for another two millennia, minimum. Some things come and go, some come and stay. Latin and English are of the latter sort.

The Romans and the Britons, kindred spirits and stoically convinced of the unlimited power of self-mastery, are confident that when they have imparted their cultural forms to lesser people, that's all that can be done for our betterment. Having borne the superior man's burden, a Roman or a Briton may freely stare in incomprehension at the ridiculous behavior of his empire's foreign subjects. Yes, the foreigners have silly beliefs and customs; it hardly matters. But let them misuse the mother tongue and, well, they're in for a good thrashing.

It is little known that the actual cause of the American Revolution was an intense desire on the part of the British to teach table manners to the colonists. Not the Battle of Yorktown but our utter incompetence at eating peas off the convex curve of a fork led the British to give up on civilizing us. We would just have to improve ourselves after 1783. They were bored with the chore. They went away. Mostly. They still visit sometimes. Once in a while they burn down the White House, but recently they have left even that to us.

But our superior masters, Roman or British, ask no more of us than they ask of themselves—not one of the Queen's *native* subjects can possibly fail to see his own Latin teacher in Cleese's centurion, nor fail to see himself in Brian's own cowering submission to correction. Romanes eunt domus? I think not. A hundred times on the blackboard and no blood pudding. And of course, if Americans had anything like the British confidence of civilized superiority, they wouldn't make such a fuss about being the greatest nation since 1066.

Americans go on so much about it just because they *know* it isn't true. Don't be misled by a few simplified spellings, you self-appointed purveyors of American superiority. You know you love the Queen. You *know* you do. Look at you, paying your subscription fees to watch *The Crown*, feeling all smug about stealing Harry from the Royal Family, delivering a mixed race child into the Royal Lineange, and all. Yes, I admit that feels pretty good, but only if you already give a damn about the Queen.

Praise Brian for the self-loathing Canadians. With them around at least Americans can feel truly superior to one other passel of British subjects. Now have some back bacon and return to your seat.

I 'Ate You, 'Enry 'Iggins

But there is more to it. One thing that is utterly lost on American audiences is how the Pythons use British class-consciousness as a continual source of contextual humor. Apart from the social situations themselves, the class consciousness is mainly conveyed by the various accents adopted by the

Python characters, all the way from Terry Jones's shrillest cockney up to John Cleese's Oxbridge titter. It's no accident that the individual Pythons tend to occupy roles that cast them within the same class range of British society (with some small social mobility). But a lot of their posture towards all things British has to do with the re-enactment of their own class forms, made comic. It is the very rigidity of British class consciousness that creates the comic context.

And here we draw closer to the true secret that was revealed to me by God. The British understand the Romans so well because they built an empire to rival Rome's own—not only by organizational genius, or an unfailing sense of what is and is not important, or by a perfect confidence in their own superiority, but also by sheer self-mastery and utter repression of all emotional weaknesses. So, four weapons. (Five is right out.) Stiff upper lip, never give up that ship, blood, sweat and tears, all that shit. And the unexpected gift that accompanies these repressions is, surprisingly, an ability on the part of Romans and Britains to laugh at themselves.

Americans simply don't possess this capacity, at least not *qua* American. The British, like the Romans, are fascinated with how well they can mock themselves. Americans, lacking the needed detachment, become unconscious of their own pathos. The Americans may laugh at the British, but not at themselves, and which is the greater virtue? This is why Americans could never have built the empire they now enjoy at the beneficent *noblesse oblige* of their British cousins (shame that the French got that phrase when the British own the virtue).

Americans do not want to suffer for the sake of imparting higher culture to a barbaric world. Not that we have one to impart. We have a lower culture we can sell, and do, but "impart"? Nah. There's no free lunch, buster. You'll *pay* for that music, those movies, and our porn, which is better than yours, Britain. Take that on the nose, you hoidy-toidies. (Of course, it's not as good as the French and German stuff.) Americans want to make money and B movies and live in Florida. Only their own comfort, security, and wealth moves them in any serious way. Yes, yes, democracy, freedom, things of that nature, but it's not like we will hop in our boats and go off to *create* it (not really).

The British and the Romans willingly ordered their societies in ways as repressive to themselves as to those they conquered, and all for the sake of civilizing the world, and without a moment's doubt that they were the ones to do it. But of course, this is funny, is it not, or more precisely, "comic"?

Are they able to laugh at themselves because their sense of superiority is so little threatened by seeing how comical it is? Or are they actually superior because they have always been able to laugh at themselves? This is too great a question. Neither God nor Brian has revealed this bit to me.

A Good Spanking

You may doubt that anyone, even a writer with a special revelation, could now tie together all this business about God being dead and the comic and politics and empire, but you underestimate the power of Brianic salvation. Your lack of faith is appalling. I should give you all a good spanking. Like an alien craft catching my fall from the tower of my own babbling, comes the saving stroke of an Italian pen. (You realize that Italians are just Romans who've lost the lust for empire?)

The idea of laughter as blasphemy is nicely joined to its class context near the end of Umberto Eco's *The Name of the Rose*, a historical novel set in 1327. Romans were well into the process of becoming Italians by then. An old Spanish monk named Jorge, the librarian of a remote abbey, booby-traps the very last copy of Aristotle's (now) lost treatise on comedy. Jorge is unable to bring himself to destroy the blasphemous book (he is a librarian after all), or allow anyone to read it (I always suspect librarians of secretly not trusting me with their books, and really wanting them all for themselves). Thus, Jorge poisons the pages so that anyone will die from the sin of reading it.

William of Baskerville, Eco's protagonist, a sort of medieval Sherlock Holmes (and proper Englishman), asks the old librarian in the climactic scene: "What frightened you in this discussion of laughter? You cannot eliminate laughter by eliminating the book." The old monk answers, in a speech that would make even John Calvin proud (you remember him, the Pope of Mrs. Coulter's world):

> No, to be sure. But laughter is weakness, corruption, the foolishness of our flesh. It is the peasant's entertainment, the drunkard's license. . . . laughter remains base, a defense for the simple, a mystery desecrated for the plebeians...laugh and enjoy your foul parodies of order, at the end of the meal, after you have drained jugs and flasks. Elect the king of fools, lose yourselves in the liturgy of the ass and the pig, play at performing your saturnalia head down. . . . But here, here

[indicating Aristotle's book] the function of laughter is reversed, it is elevated to art, the doors of the world of the learned are opened to it, it becomes the object of philosophy, and of perfidious theology . . . . [T]he church can deal with the heresy of the simple, who condemn themselves on their own . . . provided the act is not transformed into plan, provided this vulgar tongue does not find a Latin that translates it . . . in the feast of fools, the Devil also appears poor and foolish, and therefore controllable. But this book could teach that freeing oneself of the fear of the Devil is wisdom. . . . Look at the young monks who shamelessly read the buffoonery of the Coena Cypriani.[8] What a diabolical transfiguration of the Holy Scripture! And yet as they read it they know it is evil. . . . The prudence of our fathers made its choice: if laughter is the delight of the plebeians, the license of the plebeians must be restrained and humiliated, and intimidated by sternness. (*The Name of the Rose*, pp. 576–78)

Quite an un-British speech. This man clearly has no sense of humor. We see, now, why your soul is in such peril. You have been very naughty indeed. You shamelessly watched *Monty Python's Life of Brian* just like one of those young monks, and you *knew* it was evil, not because it was funny, but because it unfolds according to the *best* principles of the comedic art.

There's something very twisted about its being so good. So long as humor remains a mere ethnic joke of the working class told over too many beers, it can be tolerated, but raised to a standard of educated taste, even to the level of philosophy, it is more threatening to authorities, religious or political, in Jorge's view. Such humor undermines the efforts of our serious "betters" to shepherd us toward order—unless of course (and this is what Jorge misses) those "betters" are Roman or British.

If our "betters" are these psychotic Christians of the Falwell type, and who isn't laughing at Jerry Jr. the cuckold and Becky the slutwife? I mean, I'm fine with what they do, if it turns them on, but let's just say it poses a problem for the psychotic Christian. Watching your boy from Heaven, Jerry? These hypocritical assholes can't *ever* laugh at themselves. If these are our betters, then yes, the comedy becomes a palpable threat as the humor becomes more intelligent. These folks can't stand *Monty Python*, or *Rocky Horror*, or *Bull Durham*, or anything genuinely both smart and funny.

---

8   "Cyprian's Supper" is an anonymous parody from the fifth or sixth century in which many biblical characters, from Adam to St. Peter, take part in a great banquet and are satirized with brief, sharp verses.

In the case of *Monty Python's Life of Brian*, the better the movie is at depicting the times of Christ, the more diabolical is the effect to pathetic followers of the dead God. This film is, by the estimate of all the Pythons, their best film.[9] Yet the British do not worry (much).[10] How can this be sac-religious unless one has already taken the immortal soul too seriously? Now let's consider your soul. You apparently have two souls. The soul you know about is human, mortal (as far as you can tell), and inhabits this world, this life only. This is the soul which "animates" your physical existence, brings you to life, moves your body, fuels your consciousness (probably). The immortal soul, if there is one, is a sort of sojourner in this world, it doesn't much like your body (and if you look in the mirror I'm sure you'll see the reasons), and *that* soul frankly can't wait to get the hell out of Dodge (or Hampstead, in fact, especially Hampstead). If these two souls are really the same, it isn't obvious. So which soul is in peril? Must you lose one to save the other?

Getting Right with Brian (Just in Case)

There was a morose philosopher named Blaise Pascal (1623–1662) who, in spite of his dreary mood, can help you. We have seen the extent of your sin. You laughed. You may think this is not your worst sin, but if so, you just aren't listening. I almost think you must be British. Anyway, Pascal thought too much, way too much, and left behind his fragmentary putterings which were gathered together and published (Pascal, *Pensées*) by still gloomier admirers, and that takes some doing. One of these fragments received the number "233," and contains what is called "Pascal's Wager."

I won't ruin your dinner with Pascal's words, but I'll adapt his wager to your current dilemma, according my own less moribund, er, umm . . . "idiom Sir?" Yes, that's it, idiom; thank you Patsy. So you know you have a finite soul (you aren't the All-Being, even Trump cannot believe that, right?). You also know that infinite things exist, like numbers. But here is a curiosity: "Infinity" is by definition a number, yet no one knows what it is, or much about it—for instance, whether it is odd or

---

[9]   Even though *Monty Python's The Meaning of Life* won the jury prize at Cannes. Watch *The Life of Python*, BBC/A&E.

[10]   See Robert Hewison, *Monty Python: The Case Against*. Shortly after the film was released, Cleese and Palin debated Malcolm Muggeridge and the Bishop of Southwark on the BBC2 discussion program *Friday Night, Saturday Morning*. You can find it if you Google it. Cleese turns out to be a crackerjack debater. Palin, not so much. Too emotional.

even.[11] Yet, every number must be either odd or even. Don't get your knickers in a twist. You don't *need* to know, but you see it's possible for you to know that something exists without knowing *what* it is. Your immortal soul is analogous. It *may* exist even if you don't know *what* it is (and of course, the same for God, but never mind Him).

And *if* you have an immortal soul, you have already wagered it: you laughed, not once but repeatedly during *Monty Python's Life of Brian*. I firmly suspect you saw it more than once; you probably have the video saved on your hard drive, don't you? You *have* wagered, my child. Soooo (imagine a screechy cockney), what do you stand to lose and gain? *If* you have an immortal soul and the dead God isn't *quite* dead, isn't an ex-God, is only stunned or resting, you lose all. But *if* the dead God never was God, and you *do* have an immortal soul, then you don't really know if you've gained or lost, since that really depends on whether God finds Monty Python funny—in short, *if* God is British, you're okay—your laughter even counts as worship of such a God, you're among the elect, and will receive a fine German car in paradise (since it is paradise, it won't be a British car).

What I mean by "British" is that God is of the sort who not only can take a joke, but positively laugh at Himself. You have wagered your immortal soul, if you have one, on the chance that God is British. Does that make you worried or what? Well, it's not just you, it's me too, but I have Brian and I am doing my best to bring him to *you*. Now you may have *no* immortal soul (I mean others, yes, but not you), and in that case the bet is really off. Might as well enjoy yourself—where was the Castle Anthrax exactly? But let's suppose you have one, so it's down to God being British. We need some way to decide. The evidence is a bit ambiguous. I mean, the sinking of the Spanish Armada was a hell of a thing, and Trafalgar, well, these *seem* to suggest God may be British. Then there was Waterloo. But it's hard to be sure. We only know He isn't Spanish or French.

God might still be German, but here Nietzsche helps, since the "madman" was unable to find him there. If God is German, He is hiding or afraid of us or has emigrated (in which case He might still be British by naturalization—maybe their Germans

---

11   After an earlier version of this piece was published way back when, I got e-mails from a number of assholes informing me that infinity is *not* a number. Let me make this perfectly clear, in the idiom of *The Good Place*: I don't give a shirt whether infinity is a forking number, ash-hole. I am reporting what forking Pascal says. Take it up with him.

are smarter than our Germans). Since God was drinking Three-Buck-Chuck with me, He isn't Italian. If God is Russian, everyone is screwed, starting with the Russians. No point in worrying over that.

We might go on by this process of elimination that philosophers call "induction" until the salmon goes bad, but let's use a handier method. Philosophers call it "deduction," which is induction for lazy, impatient people.

1. If God is *not* British, you are screwed (since you laughed at Brian).

2. If God is British, you're saved.

3. God is either British or not British

This last proposition 3. is where the cheating occurs. It's called the Law of Excluded Middle, which is a fancy name designed to distract you from its real nature, which is The Law of "I Shall Finish this Thought by Tea Time." If 1. is true, indulge your mortal soul for whatever time it has left. I know you watched *Monty Python's Life of Brian* and you laughed—this hasn't actually been revealed to me, I'm doing induction. You're still reading this.

Only three possibilities present themselves: a. you watched the movie and laughed (like a Roman soldier); b. you are *going* to watch the movie and laugh (which amounts to the same as a.); or c. you have nefarious intentions toward me and everyone *like* me.

In case you haven't noticed, if a's and b's are screwed for watching *Monty Python's Life of Brian*, imagine how it will be for me. I'm just reminding you of how much faith I have in Brian. Soooo, if you have evil intentions toward my lot, have a little faith in your cheerless God and let Him take care of me and my ilk. Your "God" has already fed Graham Chapman and Terry Jones (he *directed* this heresy for Brian's sake) to Lucifer and the rest of us can't be so far behind. Be patient and have the courage of your convictions.

I deduce: The rest of you are A's or B's, which means either God is British or it's too late for you.

I realize you want some modicum of hope that God is not only *not* French (I mean, *obviously*), but actually is British. I know what's nagging at you. It's Cornwallis's (really unnecessary) surrender at Yorktown. I mean, the British had surrendered an expeditionary force in toto before, and after (look at Gallipoli for example, and nobody is thinking God might be

Turkish. They couldn't beat Sobieski and it took a thousand years to take Constantinople.) The British could have well afforded to sacrifice that little army trapped on the peninsula. But no. They wimped out, didn't want to spend the money on the war.

Yes, for that faithless act, God might have gone over to the Americans. You couldn't blame him. Americans can't laugh at themselves. God is a forking Baptist or cheerless Appalachian Calvinist descended from a pissed off Scots-nationalist-refugee-from-Culloden. You're forked. I'm more forked.

Here is the hope. The strongest competitor for God's nationality is, well, American, as I said. If ever a bunch of undeserving people was touched by divine favor, it's the Americans—even *luck* seems eliminated as a competitor.

Now, if God is an American, we're goners. And frankly, most of the evidence, with the exception of Vietnam and Iraq, points to an American God. But consider: isn't it right that *only* a British God could have thought up America? America is to Britain what Disneyworld is to, well, America. It's an impossible gift, beyond human imagination, to be allowed to be British and to see what your entire culture would look like if it were a cartoon.

It is true that America could never be as funny to the British as they are to themselves, but it runs a fair second. Yes, God is British and when the Britons had everything else God could give them, an Empire/Commonwealth (same thing without the expense) upon which the sun (still) never sets, and became bored with it, the Supernatural Make-a-Wish Foundation for declining empires waved a wand. Poof. Post-World-War-II- America.

And here we are: watching Monty Python, not exactly getting it, but laughing at it just as cartoon characters would laugh at us if they could see us watching them on the telly. And if you *must* know, that is why the penguin was on top of that idiot box. The penguin was an American spy, not Burmese. It also explains the bomb.

You can get off your knees now. Brian's saving work is done. You've been naughty, but God is not an American and your mortal soul is healthy. Your immortal soul, if you have one, has *my* assurance that God is not angry, and that your enemies will all die at some point. I could be wrong of course. Now go away, or I shall taunt you a second time.

11
Have You No Decency?

CLAIRE, FRANK, AND THEIR *HOUSE OF CARDS*

Many forms of Government have been tried, and will be tried in this world of sin and woe. No one pretends that democracy is perfect or all-wise. Indeed it has been said that democracy is the worst form of Government except for all those other forms that have been tried from time to time.

—WINSTON CHURCHILL, House of Commons, November 11th, 1947

We are far from done with our British cousins. You may think of *House of Cards* as such a very American series that it could not possibly be British. You would be very wrong. I saved you for nothing, apparently. When will you get it through your head? God is British. Or non-existent, but that's about the same thing *to you*. On my first visit to England, I learned some interesting things. They believe *Tide* laundry detergent is British. That and a shirtload of other Procter and Gamble products that were quietly transplanted (inception?) into the British common consciousness. I'm sorry, but when it comes to toxic chemicals, we *own* the British and everybody else (probably thanks to our Germans).

The British also believe, in their simplicity, that Americans eat corn (they call it maize) on pizza. This would be enough to turn the appetite of any respectable American. But go to Piccadilly Circus (or anywhere), and watch the Brits greedily gobbling down "American style pizza" with forking corn on it. They have a thing called "Tennessee Fried Chicken," as if that has anything to do with us. The list does go on. There is this fundamental disconnect that is, nevertheless, a connection. Patton said "one people separated by a common language." Or at least, that was in the movie. Like I have any idea what Patton really said. My reality comes from movies. Anyway . . . what was it I said a while back? Oh yeah: She's Cleopatra, Mata Hari, Madame Bovary, and Joan of Arc all rolled into one . . .

Character Studies and Studies in Character

Who is morally worse, Francis or Claire Underwood? The earlier version of this study was written when *House of Cards* was only in Season Three, and Kevin Spacey had not yet been exposed as . . . worse than Robin Wright. But now we have seen the development and conclusion. It really is possible now to compare and contrast this with the British miniseries (1990) of the same name.

Asking whether Frank or Claire is worse seems like an invented question, the sort of thing philosophers make up in order to have something to talk about? Yes, musing about such things can be a waste of energy. And I was going to let this question slide, with a private smile about the blasphemous twist on the names Francis and Claire—the saints of Assisi. But then I watched the British version of *House of Cards* and I became aware that (by the end at least) those writers exercised a good deal of calculation and thought about this question of who is worse. They indelicately name our wicked woman "Elizabeth," as though that name didn't carry some connotations for the British public. My question ceased being something for giggles.

Besides, at this point I have been discussing *femmes fatales* for quite some pages. These additions are irresistible, as is, I must say, the homoerotic aspect that comes increasingly to the fore as Frank relieves his "dynamic tension," shall we say, as a different Frank calls it in *Rocky Horror*.

A Novel Story

In the initial novel (1989), the spouse of Francis Urquhart is called "Miranda," and she had no significant role; and, indeed, Francis himself commits suicide rather than murder at the end. Michael Dobbs, the novelist (and former chief of staff of the British Conservative Party, nudge-nudge, wink-wink), had envisioned a much more limited story. When the BBC contemplated the miniseries, however, they saw a wider opportunity.

What if Lady Macbeth had married Richard III? Macbeth himself was too weak and foolish for his ambitious Lady. What a disappointing match. Besides, Lady Macbeth was haunted by her conscience, in dreams at least. We need someone strong enough to sleep well at night after doing, well, what must be done, you know? Now, what woman in English history could handle that? And she needs a more suitable mate, and who better than the last of the Plantagenets? Let's call her, oh, I don't know, what about "Elizabeth"?

Richard Plantagenet and Elizabeth Tudor

Ian Richardson, who plays our antihero in the British series, had a Shakespearean background and readily owned that he had patterned his characterization of Francis along the lines of *Richard III*. But Richardson knew that the historical Richard III, when one removes the pro-Tudor propaganda of Shakespeare, was actually a very brave soldier, a good lawgiver, and a devoted protector of the common people.

Our British Francis was also a dutiful protector of the Empire, even executing his own Cyprian spies when it became "necessary." Urquhart likewise seems to have been both a popular and effective Prime Minister. The writers did not choose to continue the myth of a physically deformed Richard III—who probably had scoliosis (although this claim is disputed by some who have examined his recently discovered remains), but the defect was minor and would have been concealed by his clothing, and he was not otherwise physically deformed.

Francis Urquhart is a fair specimen of English manhood— much more (by anticipation) than is Francis Underwood an example of American masculinity. Richardson's portrayal of Francis does mix the historical man and the Shakespearean character, and this is a mate fit for Elizabeth Tudor.

The devilish decision to rename Francis's spouse "Elizabeth" is also fitting, given that it is she who arranges for his assassination at the end of the whole story—the Tudors did, after all, displace the Plantagenets in rivers of blood. Urquhart has finally gotten himself into a tangle he can't possibly get out of, and if Elizabeth hadn't put him out of his, well, impending misery, she would go down with him. She can't have that.

As *House of Cards* fans will know, the fact is that assassination can be interpreted as an "act of kindness" (the phrase Francis himself chooses for his murder of Roger O'Neill, who is the British counterpart of Peter Russo), but also it is in Elizabeth's self-interest. She has reason to preserve his legacy of service to the people, for his own good (of course). So she has him "put down" in spectacular fashion so as to insure he will be remembered as a martyr, a servant, a soldier. This tidy ending also serves the Conservative Party. As we know, Francis Underwood doesn't get so grand an exit. But perhaps it was a mercy killing, of both the character and the actor's career.

The directors of the British series go to some trouble to close the miniseries with a shot of Francis's blood on Elizabeth's hands, and even a bit on her face, just in case we were too dense to grasp her Lady Macbethness—but without the bad dreams. She is, indeed, worse (that is, "stronger") than her Scottish forerunner. But we need both, since Elizabeth Tudor didn't have the opportunity to seek power by means of a man. So the character of Elizabeth is a composite.

Thus, Elizabeth Urquhart and, hence, Claire Underwood (by anticipation) are creations not of the page but of the screen, albeit the smaller screen (not that it makes much difference these days). Clearly the American screenwriters have studied the British series closely—the adaptation is fascinating. There are all sorts of things that just wouldn't work in the American context. For example, we don't have a monarch, and our upper house makes an actual difference to our governance. But the twists in the American version go deeper than just these obvious contrasts.

The playful variations on the British themes are highly imaginative and yet recognizable as belonging to the same general story.

St. Francis and St. Claire

Frank and Claire are not like the Old World pairing Richard III and Elizabeth Tudor/Lady Macbeth. And their implicit differences between Frank and Claire, dormant until one became President and the other, well, didn't, became the central focus of the third season, and, as we know, got more and more problematic as time wore on. Initially we were allowed to think of them as the perfect power couple. But if not the toxic Shakespeareans, who are they, really? I will take a shot at answering this at the end of the chapter. The American series followed the British series about as far as it could, but its worldwide success and longer run required the invention of entirely new plot twists and intrigue.

If it had just followed the British series (as perhaps it was projected to do), Claire would have eventually gotten Meechum to arrange for Frank's assassination, Catherine Durant (the Secretary of State) would have become President, and Jackie Sharp (the new Whip) would survive but end up very much on the outs. Doug Stamper had already outlasted his British predecessor, Tim Stamper, by Season Three, and, unlike Tim, Doug managed to weave himself in and out of all six seasons. Frank would have been elected to the presidency twice, after finishing Garrett's term, to become the longest serving President since FDR. But it was not to be.

No one would have been making the Netflix writers stay close, of course. I think they held close for as long as they could because the British story line and characters are excellent. But they also undoubtedly adapted to the strengths of their principal American actors and to the audience response and the momentum of the series itself. The "chemistry" worked all around. It was a for-profit enterprise. They were after a winner among audiences, and especially in the midst of Trump's rise to power, the audience's situation was radicalized, you might say. The "series Francis" wasn't actually Machiavellian enough. Neither was Claire. Now Trump was setting the bar at an unprecedented low. This was new territory for everybody. It was not easy to zig against such a zag.

And I don't think our dynamic duo was simply the Americanized Richard and Elizabeth, or only underwent minor adjustments. These are different characters, and Claire is much more developed, independent, and ambitious in her own way. Elizabeth never attempts to become a part of the government, and we don't ever learn quite what her game is. We have ample opportunity to learn Claire's game—one thing that comes to mind is the moment when she fires her entire cabinet and then shows up with a new one, all women, with an agenda so progressive that even AOC would approve. Hell, she belongs in Claire's cabinet. *That* was the zig to Trump's zag, for sure. Very Hollywood.

Meanwhile, our male (biologically at least) Underwood is compensating for deep-seated childhood issues, including being a closeted "bisexual" (to use the term they would have used back when he was growing up) from the South, and he is the polar opposite of a privileged elitist, like his Urquhart counterpart. Yet, most of the other characters in the two series are really very closely built on analogies to their British predecessors.

There is more than a philosopher's reasons to keep an eye on Claire (even in the future, for a sequel), and reason to ask what she is capable of. We were set up, in the course of the British version, for something that was foreshadowed but not really set out on the table, which was Elizabeth's ambitions for herself as allied with her husband's, but not to be identified with them. But Claire is no free-rider on the Francis Underwood ambition train, and she has her own destination,

farther down the line than her husband's. For about three seasons it seemed like she might be content to promote his ambition and take the coat-tails. It didn't go so well for her in those
early seasons. We saw her lose in a high-stakes game of diplo-
macy with the Russian President, but I don't think she was
ever down for the count.

If you watch those early seasons now, you can see that the
writers always had in mind something like what actually
happened in the later seasons. There were hints, looks, unfin-
ished thoughts, private shots. She was going to get her chance
to even the score, and much depended on opportunity, but also
on what she was willing to *do*. How far would she go? Could
Francis stop her?

The Past, the Present Perfect, and the Future Subjunctive

There are three ways we can think about how bad a person is.
When we were taking the measure of Westley in *The Princess
Bride* chapter, the whole argument depended on the past and
the present: what had he done and what was he doing in the
movie? But we need more nuance in this case. And we have
new questions.

We can take a conservative approach and insist that people
ought to be judged only on the basis of what they have actually
done. And maybe include why they did it. In this case, we have
a pretty clear picture of Frank and Claire. For the sake of ambition alone (this is the why), and to feel his power also, perhaps,
Frank committed murder, personally, twice (Zoe and Peter),
and perhaps ordered it directly or indirectly at least once and
maybe more than once, resulting in at least one death; and his
ambition has ruined other people less directly (Freddy, for
example) and then led to many deaths when people knew too
much or became inconvenient.

As far as we know, Claire had nothing comparable in her
past as part of her climb to power; she let Frank do the dirty
work. That changed when power was in her grasp. Before that,
she ruined a few people, a former employee here, a Marine
Corps General there, but that was hardly murder. On that
strict standard, Claire may be a detestable human being, but
Frank was quite a bit worse, when we consider their rise to
power.

Still, there is more to making a judgment like this. We have
to ask not only what a person has done, but what that person
is doing that will have consequences in the future. Francis's

dealings with Raymond Tusk are very interesting in this area, as are Claire's later dealings, which are largely the consequences of Frank's decisions. To the extent that such activities portend disaster, we have to consider them. Frank Underwood plays most foully to become President of the United States, and God only knows what will happen to this country to the extent that it depends upon his *character*. That is the guttural experience the audience is supposed to have as the series unfolds. (Hold on to that thought; it is the key to the riddle.)

In this sense, Claire has a number of ongoing "projects" that are troubling, but again, nothing to compare with the stakes Frank set up in rising to power. After all, he gets his finger on the button and a rather powerful military at his disposal. It was dangerous to cross the boy before, but now? Yes, he is worse than Claire in the present perfect, up until he has to resign the presidency. If he didn't misuse the office, it wasn't because he was unwilling. It just wasn't necessary. But note that Frank really did not (in any obvious way) abuse his power as president. It was the past catching up with him that forced his resignation.

Only at that point do we begin to see what he has been overlooking all along. And that was Claire.

Finding a way to get himself elected provided the scenario— and there is no better way to remain in that particular office than to start a splendid little war. This was suggested but, as with Trump, surprisingly didn't materialize. In a way I suppose that was a relief. So, Frank wasn't as bad as, for example, George W. Bush, who actually *did* start an unnecessary war to consolidate his power, and lacking the credibility to do this himself, managed to trade on Colin Powell's credibility to bring it about. But W. is far from the first POTUS to start a splendid little war, so we aren't breaking new ground if the writers of *House of Cards* had gone that way. So, maybe not an unnecessary war in addressing what Frank would do. Would he? Maybe, we don't know.

Still, we have to consider the subjunctive question "What *would* you do?" in assessing your full morality, and Frank's and Claire's and anyone else's.

Well, Would You . . .

In the British series, Elizabeth also doesn't initially seem like her husband's ruthless moral equivalent . . . until the very end, when we realize that perhaps she has been *subjunctively* worse all along. Our human moral character isn't determined solely by what we are doing and have done, or even by these combined with what we *actually* will do in the future. Frank didn't actually start a war, but would he have done so if he needed to? Surely. The most comprehensive judgment of character also takes into account what you would do to have what you want or what you need, or to get something for another.

There are plenty of sociopaths getting by in the world because they are able to get what they want and need without tipping anyone off to their real moral depravity. I am pretty sure we all deal with such people almost daily. This subjunctive standard thus needs to be included in an informed judgment. To be honest, I am not sure what I would do, under extreme circumstances, but we are really talking not about what we do under pressure—a test not many people can pass. Rather, the issue is, what would you do to get what you want, mainly, or need in the soft sense of needing things as means to attain desirable ends—fame, wealth, power, sex, victory? If your goal is world peace, maybe you'd wage war to get it? The relationship of means and ends is always on the table. A number of important moral theorists, such as Reinhold Niebuhr and Martin Luther King, Jr., have insisted that "the ends are immanent in the means" we employ to attain them. So, peace obtained by violence is very different from peace attained by peaceful means.

So we know Frank is capable of murder, as is Claire, we eventually learn. Both of them are willing to whack people who know too much (and thus pose a threat to future ends), and both of them are willing to do it *personally*. But they show no inclination to do so unless they feel they must. So, maybe some scruples? Wanton murder is not in their repertoire, but why? Because it isn't in their interest. They show no remorse whatsoever for having done what they did. It was "necessary"—to protect their devotion to getting what they want, which is definitely power.

And what else is each capable of?

An Indirect Route

It isn't easy to figure out what people might do, given the right circumstances. We can't even be sure about ourselves. Am I capable of killing someone, say, in self-defense, or to defend someone else? Or what about in revenge, if someone had harmed a person I love and feel responsible for protecting? I just don't know. And I'm *glad* not to know. So the question carries a problem. How do we think about what we are glad not knowing?

One way is to ask a more general question, a question about context—relevant context. Most people would probably kill, or anything short of killing, if they *believed* they had no choice. But where there is a choice, different communities and different political systems see matters differently. V.I. Lenin freely advocated the execution of his political enemies, authorized it, and believed it justified. Yet, he is not usually listed among the genocidal monsters of the twentieth century, with Stalin, Hitler, Mao, Pol Pot, and so on. Maybe he just didn't have enough time to achieve the status of "monster." But maybe he wouldn't have done what was necessary? (In spite of his book title to the contrary.)

Routinely, the French and Spanish, through the nineteenth and the first half of the twentieth centuries, took turns lining up their political enemies against walls and shooting them in great numbers. None of the colonial powers (including the United States) flinched at bringing on the deaths of millions and tens of millions of innocent people in the course of colonizing undeveloped countries and then using the colonized populous as proxies and pawns in the Cold War. W.'s Iraq War really was a colonialist war, being motivated as it was by the aim at US pre-eminence in the Middle East, with its economic benefits for the colonizer.

The death toll estimates range from 200,000 to over a million. All that blood is on the hands of the US government, not to mention the torture, oppression, profiteering, and other nasty business it brought. This is not counting Afghanistan or Syria or the other closely related human rights disasters that are closely related to the Iraq adventure, and when added up, we could say without exaggeration that the policies of the administration under George W. Bush, and continued through Obama's, is responsible for surely a couple of million human deaths and untold suffering that continues into the present. How necessary any of it was is at least a serious discussion, no matter how one understands the causes and motives.

World leaders have a hard time keeping their hands clean these days. But a number of the Western powers, and especially the US, have not even made a serious effort to minimize the use of deadly force, internally and externally, to maintain pre-eminence to the current neo-liberal and neo-fascist regimes. Compared to these actual people, who actually seem not to mind very much whether they are responsible for all this suffering, the question of personal character almost becomes ironic. Maybe there are some things they wouldn't do, but given the past and present, it beggars the imagination to try to imagine what they would do that is worse than what they have done and are doing. But let's try.

It seems to me fair to ask you, dear reader, whether you would give the orders that the US leaders have given. I believe pretty firmly that I would not. I do not believe that our vital interests have ever actually been at stake, and that if they were, the only path to "protecting them" was by the use of force. So, no, I *wouldn't*. I would rather see the US fall than make it guilty of what it has actually done. Is that an unusual view? Apparently so. From what I can tell. But does that make me morally better than those who would give those orders? That's a very hard question.

Context Matters

This generalized situation provokes a broader question, then. Aristotle says that our moral development is *limited* by our political community. One can rise above the values of one's community, but not wholly. Before I go and get all smug about my precious subjunctively clean hands, better ask whether they are already dirty. So in a democratic republic, such as the United States, our moral judgments may really depend on whether our political system *facilitates* moral development, and within what limits.

This may seem like a question that is rather distant from whether Claire is worse than Frank, but I will try to convince you otherwise. There is a lot of truth to the old saw that we have gotten the leaders we deserved. Do we deserve Frank? What about Claire (assuming that at this point, we still haven't elected her to the highest office, but we made her the Veep)? Do they really fall below the standards of our system?

We, here in the US, commonly *praise* people who, in the course of carrying out the duties of a political office, have been responsible for the deaths (and, indeed, the murder) of many thousands of human beings.

One assumes that George Washington, for example, perhaps (indeed probably) actually killed people, personally, when he was rising in the British colonial army. Any US President has to be willing to use the military and the intelligence community to protect the country, especially if it is attacked. We have had presidents who killed people long before Frank and Claire Underwood, although one assumes we have not had many actual first-degree murderers. We don't necessarily know, however.

Still, our system demands people capable of, frankly, murder. Although he doesn't admit much, even Dick Cheney might be willing to admit *this*. It is clear that at least some inspiration for Frank's character is taken from Cheney's ruthless style (House Minority Whip, 1989, before becoming dangerously close to the Presidency for eight harrowing years, although, in light of Trump's four years, one almost wonders whether Cheney is so very bad). One shudders to imagine what Cheney might be capable of, *in addition* to what he has actually done, that he is presently not incarcerated for (and for which he will apparently go to his grave unpunished—is that dude ever going to die?).

I think the writers tried to concoct the Frank Underwood character along the lines of the worst they could imagine, namely, Cheney, only a little worse, and who knew that before the series was over, someone brazenly morally worse would actually become POTUS? There are obvious analogies, of course, between Frank and Cheney. Our writers probably stole some Cheney moves, especially as the public imagines Cheney's designs on becoming President (by any means necessary), recognizing, as he surely did, that he could never be elected. Frank really almost couldn't be elected either—it really took Claire's popularity and a folding by his opponent. But there you have it. Maybe Cheney could have managed it by some similar means.

Power Couples

And indeed, Cheney has a Claire-like spouse, as well, in terms of the nonprofit path to influence. And this is not to mention an oddly controversial daughter, who is well-positioned to reform the GOP around principles that look like the now very moral-looking policies of her parents. Every evaluation requires comparison, no? But one might equally point out that Bill and Hillary Clinton bear an undeniable resemblance to Frank and Claire. I don't have to spell it out, I'm sure. I have no doubt that the Cheneys and Clintons served as touchstones for these characters.

There are numerous other political couples one might name, and not just Americans. Take a look at Justinian I and Theodora, or Antony and Cleopatra, or Odysseus and Penelope, among the other poisonous couples of history. You'll find patterns in each pair that have been used by these writers. I think the Clinton-Cheney blending is flesh on the bones, but it isn't the key or the meaning of the characters or their union. The important clues lie in the democratic context of the American republic, just as the British series investigates something quite fundamental to the disease of British parliamentary democracy.

These contexts produce different kinds of ambition, and the moral character of the *agents* of such governments is adapted to that system as surely as are the classic couples of history. What people have done, are doing, and might be willing to do flows from the system of rewards and consequences of acting one way or another within a larger system.

Learning from Our Betters

Can individual people really expect to be morally better than the political system that provides their laws, their ideals, and their heroes and villains? Can we rise above our governmental forms to become, somehow, better? We find it hard to look at ourselves with unclouded eyes, and we wince at the criticisms hurled our way from the people and the press of other nations. But we also don't want to endure fundamental *self*-assessment. If we *were* able to do that, a good portion of the most recent Bush administration would be in prison, as Richard Nixon himself would have been, also, and who knows who else. Whether Trump gets away with his abuses of power is an open question, still, but he seems to be doing so.

Reinhold Niebuhr (1892–1971), whom I mentioned above, famously said:

> Self-criticism is a kind of inner disunity, which the feeble mind of a nation finds difficulty in distinguishing from dangerous forms of inner conflict. So nations crucify their moral rebels with their criminals upon the same Golgotha, not being able to distinguish between the moral idealism which surpasses, and the anti-social conduct which falls below that moral mediocrity, on the level of which every society unifies its life. (*Moral Man and Immoral Society*, p. 89)

Here in America, our moral mediocrity casts a wide net and tacitly condones much. Americans don't like the abstract idea of anyone being morally better than anyone else—we admit it only grudgingly, on special days set aside for, well, whomever we can't find a way to destroy with sleazy tales of slumming it or the simple fictions we prefer to enduring inner criticism from someone actually morally superior to ourselves.

The full list of our moral betters turns out to be, at present, just Martin Luther King, Jr., and even in his case I think many people take a quiet satisfaction in recalling his personal failings while paying the required lip service his achievements. Nobody apart from MLK has a real holiday on account of reforming our morals, and many legislatures resisted and swerved to get rid of *his* day. My favorite example was the sixteen years during which Virginia declared the holiday "Lee-Jackson-King Day" (yes, *that* Lee, and suffice to say it isn't Jesse Jackson).

Our moral superiors get an extra two minutes in the news cycle on the anniversary of some notable death event (especially assassinations), which we morbidly love to revisit, and then we whisper about FDR's and JFK's affairs or TR's recklessness and egomaniacal personality, or RFK's petulance, or what have you. We even managed to roll the significant virtues of Washington and Lincoln into a single day that no one would remember at all if there weren't sales at the retail stores to remind us, or if February wasn't so god-awful boring. (I do love Groundhog Day . . . a holiday for the bored if ever there was one.)

The British are less squeamish about what makes a person better than just any old bloke at the pub, but they have a thousand shades of 'better', better in this way but not that way, so that no one gets to ride the high horse too long (except perhaps Lord Nelson, and one doubts whether he'd have any such notice if he hadn't had the decency to die in battle).

The Brits thus have a thousand ways to tear a person down, but they seem at home with the idea that some people are better than others. This discussion belongs in *Downton Abbey and Philosophy*, but we already visited it in the Monty Python chapter. The Brits do allow that God is better than we are. I am not clear whether evangelical Americans do allow that. But it is another reason to think that the American series really had to take a different turn from the British miniseries.

One reason Elizabeth had her Francis assassinated is to save his own good name—and Americans would rather go down in flame and shame than sacrifice anything so dear as life for the sake of a paltry bit of posthumous praise.

So Americans wear their discomfort openly when it comes to any talk of 'betters', moral or otherwise, but they are pretty much at home with the idea that some people may be genuinely *worse* than others, so long as no one is *better*. That might be one reason we have so many grades of prisons and so very many people in them. We don't know who's good, but we bloody well know who needs locking up, and we don't stop short of scrubbing the floor with "enemy combatants" (booo, hsssss, enemy combatants).

And unlike every other civilized nation, we don't mind "putting down" a few dozen fellow citizens every year in Texas and Oklahoma and Florida and other barbarous borderlands where nobody much notices what happens to poor people, especially if they are also minorities. In the more civilized places, like Minneapolis, we just have the police shoot or choke the suspicious-looking ones, if they try to sell untaxed cigarettes, or pass a bad $20 bill, or steal cigars—or shop at Walmart or play in the park, or walk down the street, or go jogging, and scare people with their hoodies and dark skin. Yes, that is the American way: People like that are bad and must die, evidently, but at least we didn't say we were *better* than them, like those British assholes, thank God.

No, the egalitarian conceit of the citizens of the United States rejects superiority only upward from wherever "we" are, our peculiar moral mediocrity, and never down, into risking a modicum of sympathy for those who "need controlling." The huddled masses yearning to breathe free look okay from *within* the mass, but from behind the picket fence of South Carolina, well, they seem more like a problem to be "handled," by Stamper or some other loyal American(s).

I remember reading the results of Hogan's Survey of Ethical Attitudes when given to prison inmates. Inmates say the same things that people on the outside say, always rating themselves just a little lower than they would prefer to be, morally, but not really bad. But then you ask them, "Who is bad?" it's always anyone who would do something "I just wouldn't do." So armed robbers think rapists are bad, and rapists think murderers are bad, and murderers think child molesters are bad, and child molesters, well, they don't live very long on the inside.

And this, for better or worse, is the moral mediocrity Niebuhr was talking about, that cannot distinguish criminals from great moral teachers. In such a political system, is it any wonder that Frank and Claire are as they are? The wonder is that Dick and Lynne and Bill and Hillary aren't worse.

Democracy behind the Eight Ball

Plato and Aristotle were pretty smart, and both of them held democracy in contempt. They believed that it appealed to what is lowest in human nature rather than to what is best. Neither of them would have expected that a mob, motivated by what is lowest and most common among us, could be a guide to good decision making. I don't think they could have imagined the British House of Commons or the US House of Representatives, but if they had, horror would surely have been their feeling, both initially and upon reflection.

Indeed, Plato and Aristotle also agreed that no one could prevent democracies from falling into tyrannies. That seems a livelier probability now in the US than at any time in living memory, I think. But many people called FDR a tyrant, and he did have a kind of hold on the US that few people have ever had. So perhaps we swing between poles in our flirtations with tyranny. But Plato and Aristotle, whether or not they could imagine us, had plenty of opportunity to watch that happen in Athens, several times. And it was, after all, a democracy that put Socrates to death. It wasn't just snooty disdain for "the common," or the morally mediocre, that motivated their acerbic prose about democracies. It was watching people with no scruples do whatever they believed "necessary" to wrest power from a changeable mob, a crowd of Athenians that was easily frightened and probably unfit to govern itself even when calm. The crowd will do anything, justify anything, kill anything, and steal anything. That was what Plato and Aristotle saw.

And, more generally, as Niebuhr points out, groups will behave in ways that we would not tolerate from individuals and will celebrate those who lead them in such behavior. The crowd is so unstable that democracy inevitably becomes tyranny, as Plato and Aristotle said. For all their disagreements, Plato and Aristotle could not see how a crowd could possibly get good leaders. There really is a thick relationship between the character of individuals and the groups they belong to.

Is it possible, just possible, that Frank and Claire are us, in the sense of US(A)? It is impossible to deny, as a fact of history, that democracies, and indeed republics generally, do eventually become tyrannies. If that has *not* yet happened in Britain or the United States—and that isn't altogether clear—then you could count a couple of very smart Greeks among the most surprised witnesses of history. If an ape looks in the mirror, no saint will be looking back—and I say this with apologies to apes, who deserve better than to be compared to the main characters in *House of Cards*. Or most of the leaders of the supposedly free world.

On the other hand, these democracies can say that they have lasted longer than anyone thought they could. Yes, there have been civil wars, and yes, we have come close to losing the American republic a few times. On yet another hand, the American republic has proven surprisingly resilient.

We the People

We might not all agree on which times in US history we came closest to losing the whole shebang. Everyone will list our Civil War first, but thereafter it's a discussion. A great number of people would probably list the various crises of the Cold War, especially the Cuban Missile Crisis, as being high on the list. Others, such as Mark Twain and William James, would say that our decision to enter the colonial gambit with the European powers cost us our national soul. If there is one thing we could not afford to do, as a nation, it was exploit other nations and peoples for our national advantage. But arguably we never had a national soul to lose, having built, as we did, the nation upon the deaths and subjection of millions of native peoples and captive Africans. We have always been part of the colonial enterprise.

I would place high on that list of moments when the American republic was almost lost, for you to consider, the panic of the early 1950s that goes by the name of "McCarthyism." The American republic was perhaps saved in the moment when Joseph N. Welch, head counsel for the US Army, in the endless hearings initiated by Senator Joseph McCarthy and his rabid anticommunists, finally found the words necessary to help the public see that McCarthy was a paranoid bully who was an enemy of freedom.

The moment went like this. Welch said:

> Until this moment, Senator, I think I have never really gauged your cruelty or your recklessness. Fred Fisher is a young man who went to the Harvard Law School and came into my firm and is starting what looks to be a brilliant career with us. Little did I dream you could be so reckless and so cruel as to do an injury to that lad. It is true he is still with Hale and Dorr. It is true that he will continue to be with Hale and Dorr. It is, I regret to say, equally true that I fear he shall always bear a scar needlessly inflicted by you. If it were in my power to forgive you for your reckless cruelty I would do so. I like to think I am a gentle man, but your forgiveness will have to come from someone other than me.

When McCarthy tried to renew his attack, Welch interrupted him:

> Senator, may we not drop this? We know he belonged to the Lawyers Guild. Let us not assassinate this lad further, Senator. You've done enough. Have you no sense of decency, sir? At long last, have you left no sense of decency?

McCarthy tried to ask Welch another question about Fisher, and Welch cut him off:

> Mr. McCarthy, I will not discuss this further with you. You have sat within six feet of me and could have asked me about Fred Fisher. You

have seen fit to bring it out. And if there is a God in Heaven it will do neither you nor your cause any good. I will not discuss it further. I will not ask Mr. Cohn any more questions. You, Mr. Chairman, may, if you will, call the next witness.[1]

This was the moment when a television audience became self-aware as citizens of what they had been allowing. Some condemned McCarthy, while most only quietly withdrew their support and he slinked away in shame. I do not mean to claim that Joe Welch saved the nation, precisely; I mean to say that a democratic republic that can long endure requires Joe Welches. Someone has to find the words (or images) that enable the ape to look in the mirror and see *an ape.* The bad news is that in our polity, we will usually do much damage before anyone finds the words. (Look at what the GOP has done to Liz Cheney for attempting to save the republic. You don't get much of a thank you for putting the republic ahead of your party mob.)

We the people move slowly when it comes to recognizing our mistakes and glacially when it comes to rectifying them. But up until now, there has always been a "Welch moment" when it was needed, even if it doesn't come in time to save those who are tortured, killed, ruined, and otherwise "crucified" as a result of our moral mediocrity. Maybe it was good fortune, but maybe not, when Joe Welch found the words.

Yet: the same society that made Joe McCarthy also made Joe Welch. The good guys are out there. It is hard, so far, to find them on *House of Cards*, but that was true in the British version too.

A Guess at a Riddle

The British trilogy of miniseries that is responsible for blazing the television trail has some interesting features that we lack on this side of the Pond (like a King and a robust, if deeply oppressive, sense of decency). One thing both governments have in common, however, is the problem of the Lower House. If any Tom, Dick, or Francis (or Marjorie Taylor Greene) can be elected to the lower house, then the cleverest boy (or girl) in that unruly free-for-all may well lay hands upon supreme power, but that is exceedingly rare in the United States.

The British bear the burden of an ineffective and nearly useless Upper House. The Prime Minister is easier to pull

---

[1]   This is taken from the Wikipedia article on Welch, but the exchange can be heard and read here: <www.americanrhetoric.com/speeches/welch-mccarthy.html>..

down, but exercises more power than anyone in the Lower House in the United States could hope to gain. But . . .

In only one case has it ever happened that a person moved from the Lower House to the Presidency entirely by appointments. It was Gerald R. Ford, whose path the writers of *House of Cards* followed in making Frank Underwood into a President. Everyone knows that Ford did not seek the Presidency under his own steam and that he was unelectable (as he discovered in 1976). Some see him as a lapdog of the corrupt Republican Party, but the truth is surely more complicated.

Ford was an able worker in the fields of the Lower House and nothing like Frank Underwood. The challenge faced by the *House of Cards* writers was to find a way to make someone like him President, and the path has to be very twisted, involving as much luck as calculation. No one man could do it, believably, by intrigue in the treacherous Lower House. In short, the writers needed Claire.

Much of what transpired in the British series was repeated here, with the creative turns you'd expect. But there was never an open conflict between Elizabeth and her Francis such as we saw beginning in Season Three of the Netflix version. The writers decided early on to create fractures and follow them. Our antihero in Britain, Urquhart, actually enjoys a long and distinguished career as Prime Minister, although we don't see most of his career depicted in the series. He ends up serving one day longer than Margaret Thatcher herself. He does some good things, but his past finally catches him. In a way, that is what happened to Frank Underwood, but it happened with a shorter 'reign'.

By degrees we have come to our answer about Frank and Claire, but we have done so by a side entrance. I suggest that the greater logic at work is this: Frank is the House of Representatives, as a symbol, and Claire is the Senate, as a symbol, morally speaking. I do not mean *only* the recent Houses and Senates, I mean the whole history of the House and Senate.

Frank's character and his moral limits are the same as those of the House. He's much more likely to go bad, and fast, and he is mercurial, changing with every circumstance and adapting to it. Claire is far more considered, elevated, from a very privileged background, deliberate.

Frank goes slumming. Claire sleeps with an artist who flatters her. (They are equally dangerous to those who sleep with them.) Frank pisses on his father's grave. It's pretty clear that he isn't exactly from the other side of the tracks, but certainly not from a situation of influence. Claire doesn't speak about her background any more than is absolutely necessary, although she occasionally does play her hand as the daughter of a prominent Republican politician. They have done different things in the past and do things that bring different consequences in the present, and in the future subjunctive they are capable of different things, as suits their peculiar powers.

Some people have been amazed at how much power the Senate exercises during recent years, but the frustration of many with the Senate's amazing range of powers has recurred in US history. The Constitutional amendment providing for the direct election of senators was a response to the Senate's misuse of its *un*representative character, but that change hasn't done much to bring it into a closer willingness to consider matters in bi-partisan ways, when push comes to shove.

The crucial moments in the early seasons occurred when Frank and Claire jogged together (that's Conference Committee) and shared a cigarette (that's backroom stuff). Yet, they always had one thing in common, this Upper and Lower House in the House of Cards: They wanted executive power. And such has always been the character of the legislative branch. Our writers posed us the hypothetical question as to what would happen if ever the House and Senate were in bed together and *succeeded* in getting executive power. It is very unlikely, but it is possible. The system has been designed carefully always to pit the three branches against one another, and to prevent the creeping tendency of each branch to usurp the authority of the others.

Still . . . In Season Three, the writers began to struggle with the answer to that question—and I confess, I think they really were struggling with what they had created. They had both Frank and Claire, separately, had a flirtation with the prospect of governing honestly and even nobly. As we see, sending Claire forth to the wider world to bring a tough but higher sense of our interests and obligations. Claire isn't good at that. And when Frank tries to govern domestically, well, he isn't very good at that either: his enemies are just too devoted to their special interests.

They are too far down the road of perdition to pull themselves up to that place that would support and ground noble governance. The lure of *holding* power is too tempting, and the stress of governing erodes their alliance. When it gets right down to it, the character of the House is different from that of the Senate because they value different things, even if power (and acquiring it) had seemed like an end in itself.

Having power means using it, and people with elevated tastes use it differently from, well, people whose *haute cuisine* is barbecued ribs. It can't work—in the sense that a split is inevitable. But these two houses, the House of Frank and the House of Claire, know too much about each other, and they have different powers. It was always going to get worse.

When we see what Frank was willing to do and use our imaginations to translate it into the rough and tumble of our Lower House, and when we see what Claire was and is willing to do (after all, she's still in power when the series ends), and imaginatively transmute it into the actions of our Senate, we see the true American House of Cards. The inverted flag waves a warning here. The truth of the matter is that what is lower in us can rule what is higher in us only with the cooperation of the higher part.

This is what Plato and Aristotle both said. Frank never realized it, until it was too late, but he was completely powerless without Claire's co-operation. She could have destroyed him in an instant, at any time, but why would she? At least until he became unmanageable.

And here we arrive at the true heart of the matter: What does Claire really want? We never really find out, but it looks like a progressive agenda at the end. Yet, I wonder how much of that writing was motivated by the fact that the country was coming under the sway of a neo-fascist. I wonder how true to her character that final zig was.

If we follow the analogy I have suggested, while the lower house wants to run the country, the upper house wants to run the world. Claire might turn out to be more ambitious than Frank was, and, indeed, the Senate wants that power to control foreign policy—has always wanted that power. Think of how Senator Lodge sank our participation in the League of Nations after the first war to end all wars. If it were possible to make one person responsible for the Second World War, that person would be Henry Cabot Lodge.

So, as we well know, our Senate isn't incorruptible, but it is difficult to twist. And yet, Joe McCarthy was a Senator. A bad Senator, like McCarthy or Lodge, or McConnell, is far, far more dangerous than a bad Congressional Representative (think of the clowns currently shaming themselves and us all, such as Marjorie Taylor Greene and Matt Gaetz, but no one party has the market cornered on idiots who get elected to the lower house).

Yet, by way of abuse and the dissimulations that pile on it over the years, a highborn calling can become a perverse pursuit. I can answer the question as to how Francis and Claire got to where they are: They wanted the same things, or, more precisely, they wanted exactly compatible things (including, apparently, Meechum, their bodyguard, poor guy). But they are not the same, and they were bound to come apart.

It may seem crude, but the shocker of the second season, the ménage à trois with their bodyguard, is the clue. If you trace in your mind what happened after the camera cut away, showing first that Claire kisses Meechum, and then the two men kiss, as the writers want you to do, you will see that they are foreshadowing the inevitable. So how does this sex go? Is Claire the object, between two men? No. Is Frank submissive to either or both of the others? No. You *know* this. Then just how *does* it go?

The answer: Frank and Claire take turns doing whatever they want to Meechum, sometimes co-operating. And who, then, is Meechum? He is the military, isn't he? Utterly loyal, utterly deadly. Prophetically, he is also the Capitol Police and the Metro police (this is all in his background). The point is that he enforces the will of these dangerous people. They bury him in Arlington, one of the only Secret Service agents to receive that honor. It's pretty clear that he represents domestic and military enforcement. What are they without this? Sitting ducks?

The toxic pairing of Lower and Upper morality with executive power leads to one and only one thing: the misuse and subsequent underestimation of the military. It did make me wonder, as the actual President, the Bonespur in Chief, mocked and repeatedly derided members of the US military, whether they would follow him in a coup attempt. I think possibly they would have if he had shown them even a modicum of respect. The Capitol Police seem pretty clearly to have sided with this despicable scumbag of a person (never mind whether you support or don't support Trump, he's a scumbag, and very good at being one, just admit it).

The warning in the series, symbolically, is that we cannot use our military for our pleasure and expect to have our republic survive. In a way, that is what this country has been doing since we went to a volunteer military. This is where the danger lies for the Americans, and the writers of *House of Cards* know it well. If the American republic is to fall into a tyranny, it will be the military that takes over. Maybe not this time, but if HoC were to have a sequel? Perhaps we are not as afraid of this as we should be.

So who is worse, Claire or Frank? The answer is that they are far worse together than either is alone. It is not the individuals but the union that has no decency, as Joe Welch might put it. But with their union very much in doubt, it may be well to

remember that Claire might be more ambitious than Frank
was. Why, after all, did she *want* the UN assignment, and why
did she *want* to be the high-stakes player at the table when
matters concern the whole world? And was Frank not stifling
her ambitions? He should have been more careful. Didn't he see
how the British series ended?

12
Vinnie's Very Bad Day

TWISTING THE TALE OF TIME IN *PULP FICTION*

We commence now upon three chapters dedicated to the problem of time. If you have been reading up to now and saying "I was promised some metaphysics, and all I get is phenomenology, existentialism, aesthetics, ethics, and politics . . ." I wager that after these next three chapters you will have had enough metaphysics and epistemology to last you a lifetime. The problem of time is my favorite problem. It has been in the background of everything you read up to now. It now takes center stage.

I am going to begin this adventure with a phenomenology of time, asking about how the order of events in our experience affects our knowledge and our "narrative understanding," our capacity to make judgments about the relative importance of events. In the two chapters following this one, I will take you into pretty much everything I know about time, and believe me, I have spent way too much, well, time thinking about it and reading about it and . . . oh, nevermind.

Faire des Singeries, or Monkey See, Monkey Do

There was nothing essentially new in Quentin Tarantino's *Pulp Fiction*, and that's part of the point, as he often says in interviews—to use every Hollywood cliché, but to present these in combinations that the audience has not seen before. It's Hollywood with a (Jack Rabbit Slim's) twist contest.

Aristotle once insisted that the whole "poetic art" was just one big imitation of life (and that includes film, although Aristotle wasn't much of a movie-goer). For about two thousand years after Aristotle said that, everybody agreed—until one day in the late eighteenth century when some Germans and a few renegade Brits got bored with watching French soldiers kill everybody, and started insisting that the poetic art is really the expression of the artist's feelings, not mainly an imitation of life.

They said it out of pure spite. That really pissed off the French army, because they liked Aristotle. The French, who were the champions of "classical aesthetics," had an especially snooty way of reading Aristotle. They said you have to follow the rules in order to make worthy art, and especially you have to have three things to make a story work, the "three unities" is what we now call them: unity of 1. time, 2. place, and 3. action. You have to tell your audience, at least vaguely, where the characters are, and keep it constant. And they also thought you should present the events in their *proper* temporal sequence, so that no one gets confused.

You can see where this is going, I'll bet. In the movie industry, even in Tarantino movies, there is a dude whose job it is to assure the "continuity" of the set and props to make sure things don't move around from one cut to the next and one scene to the next. He's sort of the master of time and space in the movie universe—or perhaps he's just Aristotle's Gallic slave boy.

But really time and place are just unities of action, which is what all the fuss is actually about. Aristotle says:

> The truth is that . . . imitation is of one thing, so in poetry the story, as an imitation of action, must represent one action, a complete whole, with its several incidents so closely connected that the transposal or withdrawal of any one of them will disjoin [that is the time requirement] or dislocate [that is the place requirement] the whole.[1]

The French were quite inflexible about this "requirement" back in those days. At first, they had long-winded arguments with the Germans and the Brits (the French even accused Shakespeare of being a bad playwright because he liked to mess around with the three unities), but eventually it just had to become a shooting war. This was called the Battle of Classicism and Romanticism.

The Germans pulled out the big guns to hold the center, like Goethe and Beethoven, and finished with a heroic charge by Wagner (commanding some Vikings and a detachment called

---

[1] Aristotle, *Poetics*, translated by Ingram Bywater [God, I love that name], in *The Basic Works of Aristotle* (New York: Random House, 1941 [a very bad year]), lines 1451a30–34.

the Light Brigade, borrowed from a poet); the Brits reinforced with Byron and Shelley and Keats (all regrettably killed in action), and deployed Coleridge and Wordsworth to protect the flanks. The French eventually moved on to Africa to kill people who didn't have quite so many guns. The three unities were in full retreat before the Germans and Brits. (My, how those pesky Brits keep coming up.) People started writing whatever they damn well pleased while the Sun King turned over in his lavish rococo grave. It's amazing the things people will fight for.[2]

Le Big Mac, or "'Garçon' means 'Boy'"

Americans don't give a shit about such things. That's why we serve (bad) beer at the McDonald's in Paris and call the sandwich "Le Big Mac." We're mocking them and they just eat it up (complaining all the while). And then they pay us good money to watch our supposedly inferior movies (and that's what they are, "movies," not "films"). We're laughing all the way to the bank.

That's our revenge on the French for their uppity ingratitude. (I mean, how many times have we saved them from the Germans?[3]) So that's our revenge. That and Michael Moore. They must know, I mean they *must*, that we set up that whole *Fahrenheit 9/11* thing just to see if they were really so far up their own asses as to honestly give that joker the Palm d'Or. Of course, he repaid them with praise for their healthcare system in *Sicko*, but I think it's pretty clear we set them up. They went for it, and for Le Big Mac. Suckers![4]

Art Imitating Art Imitating Life

Tarantino doesn't read Aristotle, and he doesn't imitate life; he imitates other art. And no one, I mean no one, is having more

---

[2] Some of you will say that I am gratuitously picking on the French in this chapter. I may be, but I'm not the one who built a cryptic critique of French cinema into *Pulp Fiction*. Watch it again, and watch for all things French, and see whether you think this was my idea or Tarantino's. Pay close attention to Fabienne's conversation with Butch about why she has not properly valued his father's watch. That's Tarantino telling you that French cinema has lost its sense of film time, and if Fabienne will ever just get on that damned chopper, she might learn a thing or two about how important time is in a movie. Otherwise she will make us all late for the train. To put it more plainly, the French have forgotten the audience, and are wasting our time. You may not believe me now, but watch it again and ask yourself "Why is Fabienne so very French?"

[3] Okay, so we didn't do it alone. The Russians might have helped. But you can't be grateful to Stalin, right? He was harder on his inner circle than his enemies.

[4] Say, you know what they call a "monkey wrench" in France? They call it "clé anglaise." "Clé" means "key," and I think you know what "anglaise" means.

fun than our boy Tarantino. It ought to be a crime. In France it is. He bats around the three unities like a *Bärenjude*. And he's no romantic either. If Tarantino were actually expressing his feelings in his movies, we would have to wonder about whether he should be locked up. Of course, Mel Gibson should be locked up regardless of whether he's imitating or expressing.[5] Maybe we should put him in a birka and send him to gay Paris. See how long he lasts.

But with Tarantino, this imitation/expression thing actually makes a real difference. He is imitating other art—well, just other movies. We talked about "quotationalism" early in the book, about how movies can roll up our whole culture, and especially other movies, into one long quotation. Part of the reason Tarantino can get away with making us cringe so often is that we know he's toying with the art form, and with us, and it is thoroughly playful. I mean this penchant lately for rewriting history so that Hitler gets assassinated or the Manson family gets taken down by Brad Pitt because they just chose the wrong house. Geez. We love it.

Yes, we wonder about him a little bit, but not too much, once we get his game. One of the techniques discussed over and over in Tarantino interviews, reviews, and criticism, is his boyish experimentation with showing us what was *not* on the screen in some classic scene he imitates, and *not* showing us what they originally showed us. He knows we will fill in the other part ourselves. It gives us something to do.

The Use and Abuse of Imagination

Tarantino is always playing this game—look at a classic movie (even a B or a C movie), ask yourself what you're not seeing that you *want* to see, reframe the scene from a new perspective, and then let everybody fill in the rest. It's great fun. Tarantino almost never shows the gore, he suggests it. He turns the dismemberment of a beautiful woman in an auto accident into slow motion *art* in *Deathproof*. It's hard to know how to experience that. It isn't gross, it's, well, forbidden, in about the way that Victorian pornography was forbidden.

By contrast, Mel Gibson thinks something like: chain the viewer to a seat like poor Alex in *A Clockwork Orange* and administer the Ludovico Technique. Leave *nothing* to the imag-

---

[5]   Here is a case where the Aussies pulled one over on us. Ask an Aussie if he or she *likes* Mel Gibson's films. See if you don't get an evasion, with just a hint of a wry grin that says "he used to be our problem, but he's your problem now."

ination, and be certain your movie-goer is no longer able to think when it's over, or to get the images out of his poor brain ever afterwards. It is *not* fun. It is abuse. So while Tarantino is about art imitating art for the delight of us all, Gibson is about art imitating the behavior of Nazi prison guards for the sake of . . . only God knows what. Certainly not the salvation of our souls (see the Monty Python chapter).

Some part of us apparently likes to be tortured (after all, we elected Bush and Cheney twice, sort of, and Donald Trump once), but not our best part. Just say no.

Odd Expressions

But that old argument the philosophers used to have over whether art is imitation or expression can help us a little bit. No matter how hard he may try, an artist can't really imitate anything without placing an original stamp on the final product. It happens, one way or another, as decisions are made about "what to leave in and what to leave out," to quote Bob Seeger.

We love Tarantino because he lets us play along, participate in the movie, place our own stamp on the film in all the places that he activates our imaginations with whatever he left out of the frame. On the other side, Gibson expresses himself, alone, and forbids us, with a cat-o'-nine-tails if necessary, to see anything but what he shows us. If Tarantino is the *enfant terrible* of contemporary directors, Gibson has surely been the *rex tyrannis*. I could be wrong about this, but I would wager a Hattori Hanz Katana that not one person who truly admires and understands Tarantino also likes Gibson's films. There is a reason. Some people like to have fun, others just want to be tortured.

Laissez les Bon Temps Rouler, or Tempus Fugit (When You're Having Fun)

Much ink has been spilt over the temporal sequencing of *Pulp Fiction*, but the critics and writers are not often familiar with the philosophy of time. The point that intrigues me most is that Tarantino points out (in an interview he did with Charlie Rose way back in 1994) that for all of its disjointed sequencing, there is nothing confusing about the movie—it's easy to follow, so long as you pay attention. Tarantino made this remark with perfect confidence, and indeed he is correct. Anyone who watches the movie can also untangle its temporal sequence with a little effort, but you don't actually have to do that to "get" the movie.

Tarantino invites us to untangle it, and most of us will go some way down that path. Not many will go the whole way. This feat of untangling is easier to accomplish intuitively than intellectually. There are really two ways of understanding time. There is "clock time" and there is "experienced time." They aren't the same at all. Sometimes an hour on the clock seems like it takes forever to pass, like when you're at the dentist or watching a Mel Gibson film. Other times, an hour just seems to fly by, like when you're watching *Kill Bill* the way it was intended to be seen—all four hours at once.

Henri Bergson (we discussed him in the Monty Python chapter on laughter and "the comic") wrote a bunch of books about the differences between "clock time" and "experienced time." I know that his name sounds French, and yes, he was born in Paris, but his early years were in London and his parents were Polish and English-Irish, and the attitudes of the French film snobs are not Bergson's fault. They regard themselves as too hip to read Bergson now, even though he wrote in French and won the Nobel Prize for literature. His coolest books are *Time and Free Will*; *Laughter: An Essay on the Meaning of the Comic*; and *Creative Evolution*. The famous part where he talks about the film projector and its relation to time is in Chapter 4 of *Creative Evolution*. Another French philosopher (who wasn't very French in my opinion, since he liked Alfred North Whitehead—see the next two chapters) named Gilles Deleuze wrote a book on Bergson called *Bergsonism*, and then applied the theory to cinema in a very cool book called *Cinema One: The Movement Image*. You should check out the Deleuze. I know Tarantino isn't an avid reader of philosophy, so I'm not saying *he* read this, but if *you* want to understand how he does what he does and why it has the effect on you that it has, it's pretty hard to beat Deleuze's theory.

People who like movies love this guy Bergson, because all the way back in 1907 he started writing about how movies do what they do—using light and the movement of machinery (the camera and then the projector) to create the illusion that real time is unfolding before our eyes.

Bergson thought that "clock time" wasn't *really* "time" at all; we just invent ways of turning time into space (that way we can artificially "even out" the dentist chair experience and the experience of the Tarantino movie). Think about it for a second. Look at the calendar on your wall. It's a bunch of little squares arranged on a rectangle. That's space, *mon ami*, not time. The calendar just sort of sits there, being the same, and only your *act of reading* the calendar, anticipating the next days and remembering the last ones, brings it to life.

It's the same with a clock, hanging there in space, being an arrangement of circles and lines. Yes, it moves, but you have to admit that it isn't very interesting to watch it move (same for watching the numbers change on a digital readout). It's just spatial arrangements *imitating* in space the experience of time.

A movie is sort of like a clock combined with a calendar: lots of little squares strung together with a motor to make them move. But it's really all just space and machinery. So Bergson says, "real time" is in our *experience* of things, not in the way we turn those experiences into spatial arrangements that imitate the experience. If that's right (and it is) then the "real" movie is not the string of celluloid running through the projector; the real movie is what's happening *to you* when you sit through it. The rest of it is just a bunch of still pictures, residue of past moments arrested and sequenced.

Tarantino gets this. How many times has he said that the key to being a good director and writer is to be a good moviegoer? Pay attention to what you are experiencing when you watch a movie. Aristotle said as much in his clear emphasis on the audience being persuaded and catharted in his *Rhetoric* and *Poetics*.

It is true that a movie is *made* by turning every single second into something like a calendar: we storyboard the script down to the level of the "shot," analyze each shot down to the last detail, and then create the illusion of continuity by setting actions into motion within the narrow limits of the shot. In this case, actors are like machines adding motion to the temporal limits of the "shot." As soon as they've gotten the shot, what was "experienced time" for the actors is now just a series of still pictures, but we can re-assemble the pictures any way we like.

Yet, a mere assemblage of pictures does not make a "movie." The movie becomes a real movie when someone sees it, experiences it in his own "real time". . . with popcorn, or KY jelly, or whatever you like to bring along to enhance your experience. A projector just running a film, no matter how well made, but with no one watching, may still be a "film," but it isn't a movie.[6]

---

[6] The days of the living projectionist are long gone, but I have sometimes wondered whether commercial movie theaters ever ran the film through the projector at the appointed clock time even if no one bought a ticket. I'll bet some did. I think it's largely automated in the digital age, so I wouldn't be surprised if it happens all the time now. But back in the day, a physical film would hold up only to so many trips through the projector. It's weird to contemplate whether anything meaningful is actually happening when the machine runs the film and no one watches. Sort of an updated version of "if a tree falls in the forest . . . ."

So we're watching *Pulp Fiction*, and that devilish director has arranged the whole thing for the editor to put "out of sequence." But not in some simple sense. Movies are almost never shot "in sequence" anyway, but in this case Tarantino went further. Tarantino's and Avary's script was already presented "out of sequence," so that even the actors never saw it "in sequence," which is perhaps why even the actors couldn't really answer the question as to what the movie was about in interviews. Each of them had digested his or her character's perspective on the events, but even the actors would have been hard pressed to identify the "main" character. So it isn't really that the film was just edited out of sequence, it's that Tarantino and Avary had already conceived of it in sequence (presumably), varied it in their imaginations for the anticipated effect (on the audience and the actors and crew) and then edited *the script* to reflect the temporal choices they settled upon.

The fact that most movies are shot out of sequence makes movie-acting an interesting challenge. The actors must thoroughly imagine what their characters do and don't know yet, often shooting the end first and the beginning last. They must capture the state of mind and emotional condition of the characters at every stage along the way and be able to produce that exact moment on command. It is an incredible act of reflective organization to have each stage fully digested, take them apart, enact them out of order, and create the illusion of a continuous development. But that is what movie actors do. It occurred to Tarantino that it wouldn't matter much to his actors if they couldn't really think out the movie as a whole, so long as they grasped their own characters' parts and perspectives and development.

But Tarantino also wanted *us*, watching in the theater, to *experience* it out of sequence. He is far from the first to try this, but he may be better at it than others. Part of the reason he wanted us to do that is that it helps us understand his world, just how free he is to play around with the art form of filmmaking. Christopher Nolan, by contrast, presents *Memento* out of sequence to convey to us the confusion of his main character, Leonard Shelby, who can't "make new memories." But where Nolan is (carefully) confusing us for an effect, he is not exactly inviting us into his world. With Tarantino, we become aware that he can put things just anywhere he wants them. He wants *us* to experience what it is like for him to have that freedom, so that we can appreciate the decisions he made and share his playful delight at the effects. We all left the movie re-narrating the events and discussing with our friends what happened before what.

Yes, he is playing with us, but he is not toying with us; he is toying with the three unities for our edification. Even Tarantino cannot tell a story without the three unities—no one can—but he can toy with them in ways that *enhance* the story, if he's good (and he is good). Aristotle's point (if those old French fuddy-duddies had read him a little more closely) was not that the three unities must be preserved at all costs; his point was don't confuse your audience, needlessly, if you want to tell a good story—the French seem to enjoy being confused by their filmmakers, but non-French audiences will put up with very little of being confused, and most importantly, the audience wants catharsis.

That means, the audience wants to give you, the playwright, the filmmaker, the screenwriter, a stretch of their time, of their experience, and they will give you their "willing suspension of disbelief" (they will pretend what you are showing them is "real"), so they can have a certain kind of experience, and when it is over, well, they want to feel better. So if you want the audience to experience catharsis, you should keep in mind that the three unities are important. It's not like Tarantino doesn't know that.

Yet, toying around with the three unities can create an enhanced experience, and can bring the audience closer to the filmmaker's art. Putting the vignettes out of sequence can (and does in the case of *Pulp Fiction*) force us to focus more of our attention on the *characters*. But we don't focus on their development, or even on their likely destinies in the story—I mean, halfway through the movie we already know that Vinnie bites the big one. Rather, we focus on who these people are, how they think, what their values are. What *kind* of person is this?

Since we don't know which characters are more important (which is usually obvious from the opening moments of a movie), we pay attention to all of them. Thus, Tarantino invites us to enjoy his characters, just for who they are, and uses time-twisting to *give* us that experience. But whereas Hitchcock, for example, likes to create a distance between the filmmaker's art and the audience, to conceal his art so that, frankly, he can toy with their psychology, and whereas Gibson wants to do experiments in mind-control, Tarantino is like a boy in his tree house. And you are invited to join the club.

Yes, it's *his* tree house, but all you need is the password, and he'll give you all the clues you need to get in. He doesn't want to control you, or toy with you for his private amusement, he just wants to play. You already know the game. It's just good (not so clean) fun, and time flies when you're having it. In my opinion, he has never let us down.

Un Ménage à Trois, or It's Three, Three, Three Plots in One

With *Pulp Fiction*, it is easy to experience the movie and "get it," intuitively. As Tarantino told Charlie Rose, it isn't confusing at all. Focus on the characters and don't worry too much about the order of events, at least not *as* you are watching. Trust Tarantino. He has a plan. But actually sitting down and graphing the "objective" sequence of events is more challenging than just sort of intuitively "understanding" what happened.

I couldn't resist taking the script and putting it in temporal sequence, just to see how it looks. There is now a sequence available on Wikipedia (which didn't exist when I was first untangling the sequence—that would have helped), and it is basically correct, but it is pretty vague. I will provide more detail.[7] This is how it happens:

The whole sequence unfolds on three different days. The movie begins around 7:00 A.M. on one day and the first event is Vincent Vega (John Travolta[8]) and Jules Winnfield (Samuel L. Jackson) driving to a "hit." The last event is Butch Coolidge (Bruce Willis) and Fabienne (Maria de Medeiros) driving off on poor dead Zed's chopper.[9] Butch has just shot Vinnie, after catching him with his pants down. All the other events in the movie happen in between.

The first day is mainly Jules's story. The second day is mainly Vinnie's story. The third day is mainly Butch's story. These days are not necessarily consecutive.

It may seem like only one continuous day, but Tarantino makes clear in a number of places that the story of Jules Winnfield's exit from the hit-man profession happens on one day, that Vinnie's date with Mia is not that same night, but the next night. An indeterminate amount of time passes between Vinnie's date with Mia and the night that Butch wins the fight he was supposed to throw; Butch's exit with Fabienne is the morning after his fight.

---

[7]   There is a much more detailed breakdown and analysis by Justin Kownacki here: <www.justinkownacki.com/the-real-hidden-genius-of-pulp-fiction>. I disagree with several points in his analysis, but overall this is a good article. He misses the crucial thing I will reveal, however.

[8]   No one calls Vincent Vega "Vinnie" in the movie. This is by design, I suspect. Tarantino knows we (who were old enough to catch this movie on its first run) will think of him as Vinnie Barbarino from *Welcome Back Kotter* in any case. I am calling him "Vinnie" because that's who John Travolta is and will always be.

[9]   I would like to point out that when you say the alphabet in French, the last letter of the alphabet is pronounced "Zed."

The coffee shop stand-off is on day one, and that day includes the visit to Jimmie's house and Monster Joe's Truck and Tow, and also the scene at the bar where Vinnie first encounters Butch. How that evening passes we are not told. The next thing that we see is day two, beginning with Vinnie's visit to Lance the drug dealer, before his date with Mia. The third day is indicated because Mia has recovered from her overdose and Marsellus is back from Florida by the time of Butch's fight, so it may be a few days later, but since Marsellus is still wearing the mysterious bandage on the back of his head, it is not long enough for a minor wound to heal. The interesting events in the back of the Pawn Shop store unfold the following morning. If you don't just love the character of The Gimp, you just aren't quite playful enough to be in this tree house. I mean was The Gimp gratuitous or what? I admit I haven't figured out why he's in the script, but I'm working on it.

The script, if it were in sequence, is written in the classic style, a main plot, "Vinnie's very bad day" (okay, three days, all bad), and two subplots, Jules and Butch. It isn't really about three characters, as so many reviewers claim; it's about Vinnie, plus two subplots. The rest of the characters support either the main story of Vinnie, or one of the subplots, or two of the subplots, or one subplot and the main story, or both subplots and the main story. The three main characters play supporting roles in each other's stories to varying degrees. Then each story includes discussion of the other stories in the dialogue. It isn't all that complicated.

McGuffins

I mentioned this back in the Hitchcock chapter, but I'll explain it a bit more here. The "McGuffin" is the term Hitchcock used to describe the object of desire that motivates the plot's action—something that has to be retrieved for some reason. *The Maltese Falcon* is the classic example. It makes no particular difference what the McGuffin is, so long as there is something the characters want, simply *must* have. There can be more than one, and the complexities multiply when they want different things. It can be a lot of fun to look for the McGuffin in a film. Tarantino uses this device in pretty much every script.[10]

The McGuffin of Butch's story is a watch handed down from Butch's father—a *time*piece of course, and Butch simply cannot

---

[7]   See Thomas E. Wartenberg, "Ethics or Film Theory."

go into the future without it; he would sooner die. The clues about *time* throughout the movie are everywhere: there is a gratuitous clock ticking in the background in scene after scene. Tarantino wants us to know what time it is, but he buries the time references like clues to a treasure in the constant banter and in the background. He *wants* us to piece the actual temporal sequence together. He dares us to do it.

Why? Because it's fun; it's a *clé anglaise* Tarantino wants us to discover for ourselves. Obviously he (and Avary) conceived of the story roughly in order, at first, and then monkeyed around with it until it made a different kind of sense, showed us different things about these characters than we could have seen in the regular sequence, and concealed things we surely would have noticed. Tarantino builds the "dare" into his subtitle: "Three Stories . . . About One Story . . ." So what's the "one story" and what are the "three stories"? It's Vinnie's Very Bad Day(s), but wait for the true subtitle; it's a doozy. Tarantino even puts in the ellipses to clue you in to the fact that you're supposed to fill in the blanks. I couldn't resist. It's too much fun.

One of the concealed things that everyone would immediately notice, if the movie unfolded in temporal sequence, everyone would see it's about Vinnie. Out of sequence it isn't obvious that Vinnie is the main character, especially since he gets killed in the middle. But in sequence the whole movie is a story about how he screws up just one time too many.

Placing the movie out of sequence leads us to pay more attention to the supporting characters than we otherwise would, as I mentioned. In our unsequenced haze, we don't know if the movie is about Vinnie, or Jules, or Butch. This is our unholy trinity: we are led to have some sympathy for each of them, in spite of their, shall we say, "flaws." When we take Vinnie as the main character, the thing that becomes undeniably clear is *the moral of the story*. Butch and Jules walk away and Vinnie dies. The question is why? What is Tarantino's point?

I may be wrong, but I think I've got it figured out. There is something about the way that Butch and Jules think, about the way they see life and face its challenges that Vinnie just doesn't get.

The Mexican Stand-off, or Three Well-Dressed, Slightly Toasted Mexican Men

It's impossible not to notice how Tarantino loves to cross-reference and inter-mix his movies, so there are clues in other movies about how to understand *Pulp Fiction*. Everyone knows that Vincent Vega is Vic Vega's brother, and Vic is the scariest of all the scary characters in *Reservoir Dogs*. And it is as plain as the nose on your face that the entire script in *Reservoir Dogs* was designed to set up a show-down" imitating the Mexican Standoff in *The Good, the Bad and the Ugly*, when Blondie, Angel Eyes, and Tuco stand almost endlessly in the Sad Hill Cemetery, while the audience sweats. (I explained that way back in Chapter 6.) By the time it's over with, we are all ready to shoot Sergio Leone for torturing us (we loved it, it's so not like Mel Gibson), and then we later find out that we were screwed—Tuco's gun wasn't even loaded, and Blondie knew it all along. We love that too.

Tarantino knows that we know the game and that we love it. So in *Reservoir Dogs* he gives us a Mexican stand-off in which we cannot see how any of the characters can back down, and then he makes us wait. We wonder whether someone's gun isn't loaded and someone else knows it. But no, everyone has bullets. And no, no one backs down. Tarantino shows us what we actually (sort of) wanted to see in *The Good, the Bad, and the Ugly*, but Sergio Leone hadn't left that option for himself— the movie would have been over and no one would have gotten the treasure (which was the McGuffin in this case).

In *Reservoir Dogs*, Tarantino saves the stand-off for the end of the movie. By the time we come to it, he can do anything he wants, and we all know it. We have absolutely no idea what he will do. That's fun. But Tarantino cannot stand to settle on just one ending for such a great scenario. Taken in sequence, the Mexican stand-off in *Pulp Fiction* would have happened in the middle of the movie—after the visit to Monster Joe's Truck and Tow, but just before Jules delivers the mysterious glowing briefcase (which is the McGuffin of Jules's story) to Marsellus Wallace at the bar.[11]

Having the Mexican stand-off in the middle would be no good at all, as anyone can plainly see (although we get it in the middle of *Inglourious Basterds* and it works fine there). Of course, by showing it out of sequence, Tarantino frames the movie with the Mexican Stand-off, and then has everyone walk away, having gotten some of what they wanted, but sacrificing something to get it.[12] That works.

---

[11] The bar is called "Sally LeRoy's." LeRoy is a French name.

[12] The original script has Jules imagining the bloody outcome and then snapping back into the present. Tarantino did *shoot* the daydream segment, but wisely left it out of the final movie—it disturbs the stand-off too much. But of course, he put it in the out-takes on the DVD (remember those?), as I'm sure he knew he would when he made the final edits, so he knew we would still get to see what we wanted to see, which is really whether anyone would do us the kindness of shooting Amanda Plummer (who is most annoying).

But Tarantino's stand-offs are all very different. In these two early movies, instead of playing off of greed, self-interest, and the survival instinct, he makes each scenario revolve around loyalty. This raises the Mexican stand-off to a much higher ethical plane. The reason no one can back down in *Reservoir Dogs* is because each is loyal to a person or a principle that he simply cannot violate.

Joe Cabot and Nice Guy Eddie know that Vic Vega has been loyal to them, because of the years he spent in prison to protect them, and that is why they know Mr. Orange, who killed Vic, is the undercover detective. They would rather die rather than let Orange live. This establishes the "loyalty of the Vegas," or the family honor, in the Tarantino universe. This is an important point to notice. But where loyalty is easy for Vic (he is simply made of loyalty), his little brother Vinnie has to struggle with the idea. Vinnie doesn't lack courage, but he is weak-willed; Aristotle calls this weakness of the will "incontinence."

Incontinent people fare poorly in Tarantino's ethical world. As Winston Wolf so memorably puts it, "Just because you are a character doesn't mean you *have* character."

Character Flaws

Aristotle makes a point about characters that is pretty hard to deny: "the agents represented must be either above our own level of goodness, or beneath it, or just such as we are." (*Poetics*, line 1448a4). Now, if you want to tell a good story, one that brings catharsis, you don't have that many choices. You can start with good men/women and teach us that they are more like us than we thought (the tragic fall), or you can start with bad men/women and show that they are more like us than we thought. We are pretty boring, which is why we go to the movies. You can't very successfully tell a story about us just as we are. It has been tried. Sometimes with success. *Ordinary People* comes to mind. But catharsis is hard to get.

You would think that the French, for all their love of Aristotle, would understand this simple point. But they are still quite peevish about the defeat of Classicism; Aristotle is now their ex-husband, and now they must pretend they never were married to him. Now the *modes du temps* is to be more *avant-garde* than Thou. Yeah, right, whatever. Anyway, French directors love to show people who are better than us becoming worse than us, people like us getting worse than bad people, and people who are worse than us getting worse than they already were. Sometimes they show people like us doing nothing at all. Anything else is a "Hollywood ending" and beneath their aesthetic dignity.

A Gratuitous Trip to Spain

I think you still doubt me about this concealed critique of French cinema. Okay, explain this: why does every important character, except Butch, have a French name: Jules, Vincent, Marsellus, Mia, Lance, and most of the minor characters, Maynard, Raquel, Roger, Brett (which means someone who is a Breton, the French invaders of 1066 included Bretons) . . . the list goes on. You will say, "Ah, but it is just a coincidence, what about Butch?" Well, Butch tells us, and I quote: "I'm an American. Our names don't mean shit."

By implication, Tarantino is trying his best tell us to pay attention to what the non-American names mean. Why, pray tell, do Butch and Esmerelda have a conversation about the meanings of names? You have to pay attention if you want into the tree house. Now, Quentin, this part of the chapter is just for you, when you read this: You're thinking that "Yes, he got the French thing, but he missed the Spanish thing." Not so. I certainly caught the Spanish names—Yolanda, Ringo, Esmerelda, and I certainly noticed when Butch says good night to Esmerelda, he says "Bon soir" and she replies "Buenas noches." And I know Sergio Leone shot *The Good, the Bad, and the Ugly* in Spain, so I do know the "true" identities of Esmerelda's three slightly toasted Mexican men. And, yes, I even watched the Spanish subtitles under the French dialogue on your DVD, back when I had a DVD player, just as you hoped some of us would. Hilarious. But someone else will have to write the essay on your Spanish subplot. I just don't have the time.

Back to Aristotle

Tarantino, without exception, starts out with people who are worse than we are and shows us how they aren't so very bad. That's how we get catharsis. Think about Jimmie's wife in *Pulp Fiction*, the vignette he calls "The Bonnie Situation."[13] Here you have two vicious killers and a dude they call "The Wolf" dashing around, like their heads are fire and their asses are

---

[13] Bonnie is a French name. And since when is "Jimmie" spelled with an "ie" at the end? Oh, wait. I think I do know of a language in which they spell "Jimmie" that way. . . .

catchin', to clean up evidence of poor Marvin's mishap,[14] and the principal thing that motivates this rush is . . . what Jimmie's wife will say when she gets home and the house is full of killers covered with blood? Now that, that would be pretty bad, if Jimmie got in trouble with his wife.

It's hard to deny that Tarantino is consciously moving these killers in our general direction (morally—we can all relate to getting a buddy in trouble with his wife). But that isn't the Moral of the Story. It's just a condition for catharsis. Nothing fancy is going on here, just a boy in a tree house playing cops and robbers, with Aristotle.

But the rules are a little different in this game. As I said, Vinnie is the main character in the movie, which isn't obvious until the script is put into sequence. When it is, it becomes very clear that Vinnie is a bumbling antihero who becomes the victim of his own carelessness. None of his character flaws—selfishness, laziness, hubris, careless inattention, even weakness of the will—is his "central flaw." And we are supposed to overlook the fact that Vinnie is a ruthless killer, because frankly, everyone he kills is at least as bad as he is. As the Wolf says, "Nobody who'll be missed," at least by us.[15] There will be no serious investigation, and you, my dear middle-American, have nothing to fear from Vincent Vega. Tarantino is not going to get preachy about character flaws in any case. The Moral of the Story does not come from some lesson about what makes a hit man a bad person.

Apart from Vinnie, it is pretty hard to miss that Butch, filled with testosterone and pride as he is, has a soft spot for his dear departed dad, and dangerous though he is, he puts up with whining from Fabienne that none of us would begin to tolerate.[16] And Jules, well, he is trying to be the shepherd. He is by far the most dangerous of these dangerous boys, but even he believes in miracles, scolds blasphemers, and reads the Bible.[17]

---

[14]   You don't want to play "Marvin" in a Tarantino movie. Marvin was the police officer who got his ear cut off by Vic Vega in *Reservoir Dogs*, and then met with a pretty bad end. By the way, "Marvin" is a French name.

[15]   They're all bad people, except maybe Marvin, and that was definitely an accident.

[16]   I don't guess I really have to point out that not only is Fabienne French, she whines *because* she is so very French. And she wants blueberry pancakes because she isn't terribly well-connected to the way things really are; she'll have to settle for buttermilk pancakes, since this is an American movie.

[17]   I know very well that you already looked it up. I mean Ezekiel 25:17. No, it does not quite say what Jules says before he "caps someone's ass," but it's not that far off. Call it *license poétique*. Here is the passage in French: "J'exercerai sur eux de grandes vengeances, En les châtiant avec fureur. Et ils sauront que je suis l'Eternel, Quand j'exercerai sur eux ma vengeance." Ha.

Le temps de me laver les mains, or Bathroom Loyalties

It is easy to miss, but Vinnie's "incontinence"—and I mean this in the ordinary sense of the word—is the master key to the movie, and the monkey wrench. That's the password to Taratino's tree house. Everything bad that happens to Vinnie is signaled by what's happening in the bathroom.

1. The "fourth man" with the hand cannon is hiding in the bathroom when Vinnie and Jules make the "hit" in the apartment, but Jules takes the hint and Vinnie doesn't get it.

2. Vinnie is in the bathroom when Honey Bunny and Pumpkin pull their guns at the coffee shop to create the Mexican stand-off.

3. Vinnie is in the bathroom when Mia Wallace mistakes his heroin for cocaine (saving them both from an impending and very disloyal tryst).

4. And Vinnie is in the bathroom when Butch returns for his beloved watch, which is the end of Vinnie.

We do see Jules in the bathroom only once, and we do see Butch there once: each is washing off the stain of a former life he intends to leave behind. And Tarantino makes it very, very clear that Vinnie *does not wash his hands*, showing him emerging from the bathroom at Butch's apartment immediately after he flushes the toilet, still fastening his belt. You think I'm making too much of it. If so, then why do Jules and Vinnie have an argument about washing their hands in Jimmie's bathroom? And I quote:

JULES: What the fuck did you just do to his towel?

VINCENT: I was just dryin' my hands.

JULES: You're supposed to wash 'em first.

VINCENT: You watched me wash 'em.

JULES: I watched you get 'em wet.

VINCENT: I washed 'em. Blood's real hard to get off. Maybe if he had some Lava,[18] I coulda done a better job.

JULES: I used the same soap you did and when I dried my hands, the towel didn't look like a fuckin' Maxipad.

---

[18] "Lava," from "laver," the French verb for "to wash." It's also a French soap.

Nothing happens by accident in a Tarantino movie. As Aristotle puts it, "That which makes no perceptible difference by its presence or absence is no real part of the whole" (*Poetics*, lines 1451a–35). Tarantino doesn't waste your time with "that which makes no perceptible difference." If Vinnie had the sense to wash his hands, thoroughly, he might still be with us—Butch would have had time to escape, and some noise to cover his exit. But no. Vinnie is lazy and careless and incontinent.

Tarantino tells us what we need to know. It comes when Vinnie has taken Mia Wallace home after their "date" at Jack Rabbit Slim's. Mia has her own issues with incontinence (as Marsellus well knows, from the infamous "foot massage" episode—he is testing Vinnie's loyalty). Having excused himself to go to the bathroom after an "uncomfortable silence" with Mia, Vinnie has the following conversation with himself in the mirror:

> "One drink and leave. Don't be rude, but drink your drink quickly, say goodbye, walk out the door, get in your car, and go down the road. . . . It's a moral test of yourself, whether or not you can maintain loyalty. Because when people are loyal to each other, that's very meaningful. So you're gonna go out there, drink your drink, say "Goodnight, I've had a very lovely evening," go home, and jack off. And that's all you're gonna do."

That's the password to Tarantino's tree house: "loyalty." It's very meaningful. I talked about that back in Chapter 1. I noted in this chapter that the McGuffin for Butch is the watch and for Jules it's the briefcase. What is the McGuffin in Vinnie's story? Let me ask it another way. What does he truly want that he cannot get? I mean he has the drugs and the cars and the money and women if he wants them (he turns down a free tryst with Trudi, so we know this isn't his weakness). He tells us what he doesn't have that he wants: self-control and true loyalty. The McGuffin evades him.

We may not be able to understand a world filled with people none of whom is morally similar to us, except that Tarantino shows us that they *do* have loyalties. Even Vic Vega. Jules *will* deliver that briefcase to Marsellus even after he has decided to leave the "business," and *will* risk his life to do so. Loyalty.

Butch is loyal to the memory of his father, yes, but why, pray tell, does he turn around and save Marsellus Wallace when he could just as easily leave him to die at the hands of Zed and Maynard and The Gimp? If they kill Marsellus, all of Butch's problems are actually over. But Butch is a man of honor, a man's man, and he knows Marsellus is another man of honor, and to put it in his own words Marsellus at that moment is "very far from okay." A loyal man just can't let another loyal man meet such an end.

Marsellus recognizes the deed for what it is when Butch saves him and also leaves him the privilege of taking care of Zed in "medieval" fashion.

We never quite learn whether Vinnie is capable of genuine loyalty or not. We know he *wants* to be loyal. We know he is *trying* to be loyal. We know he *values* loyalty. We also know that he is weak-willed, careless, and incontinent; he knows *that* too, and doesn't like it. But in the end, there is something different about Vinnie that curbs our sympathy: He doesn't wash his hands when he goes to the bathroom.

So the moral of the story? It's three morals, but they all amount to one: Be loyal. It's important. Don't be weak-willed. It will lead you to a bad end. And wash your hands when you go to the bathroom . . . thoroughly; it says more about your character than you may realize.

13
Once Upon a Time

IN *INCEPTION*

So the experience of time can seriously affect our judgments about what's important (and not just in the movies). Untangling a sequence of events is something lawyers and police investigators, and even families must do in coming to fair interpretations of someone's level of responsibility, culpability, intentions (to some extent), and yes, character. But how does objective time, if we could get at it, really order the world? That issue seems very much on the table in Christopher Nolan's mind-bender, *Inception*.

I'm well aware that the debate that has raged for years is whether we are in Cobb's head the whole time. I think there is no question that Nolan planted—no, inceived—this very debate, and I will address it. Three times he shows Mal waking up on the living room floor and Cobb still sleeping. Three times. It's a little like Robert Fischer finding the paper pinwheel. There is something a bit too tidy about the image Nolan repeated. He is mischievous for sure. He has Cobb inceive the idea in Mal's mind that she is stuck in a dream, and it won't go away. Has Nolan not done the same thing to the public, inceiving in us the idea that his whole story is in *Cobb's* dream?

Just Because We're Paranoid . . .

I admit I'm worried. Worried and suspicious. I think Christopher Nolan has been messing with my mind and maybe I have been inceived, or incepted, or whatever it is he does when he plants a doubt in my brain that won't stop nagging me. Yes, are we in Cobb's dream the whole time? It will take a while for me to formulate what I have to say about this, but I promise I will get there.

Maybe you know what that's like, to get inceived, huh? But first, before we deal with our deeper misgivings, here's an easier one, just a little riddle: Remember when Cobb tells Ariadne to make him a maze in one minute that takes two minutes to solve? Why is that a test of whether she can be a dream architect? I think maybe it's because the dream architect always needs to be a couple of (dream)-minutes ahead of the dreamers (or the defenses of the dreamers), anticipating where they're going and providing them with specific passages, twists, and turns.

And no matter how clever the dreamers are, they should never be able to catch her turning a space back on itself.

I bring this up because, well, I don't know about you, but sometimes I feel like Nolan is the Architect and I'm the hapless dreamer lost in his dreamscape. And sometimes I think I can just catch a glimpse of his shadow as he leads me on. That's surely one way to approach directing a movie—especially if you're also writing the script. If you control both the story and the images someone takes in, that's a lot of power (as we have seen in our examinations of the various *auteur* directors in this book), and that is one attraction of film as an artistic medium.

I'm convinced, as I have said, that the greatest artistic geniuses of the last hundred years have been increasingly drawn to film—the best writers are writing scripts, and the best actors establish themselves in film so as to command the attention (and salaries) they want when "returning" to the stage. Meanwhile really accomplished sculptors, painters, and even some architects are designing sets and costumes, while the best photographers are now cinematographers, and the most creative technical people are developing special effects of all kinds. Needless to say, the coolest orchestral composers are doing movie music, and so on.

All artists want an audience and they want to make a living. It's no wonder they're drawn into working together in the amazing, all-encompassing, all-consuming medium of film. There is an audience, and hence, there is a living for those who can get in on the action.

. . . Doesn't Mean They're Not After Us

Among all these artists, that "writer-director" is the arch-creator, the puppet-master of the medium. In a recent interview one of the members of Clint Eastwood's "team" (speaking of his movie *Hereafter*) made the remark that a lot of directors would love to have Eastwood's team, but the team draws its liveliness and purpose from the way Eastwood works (collaboratively and loosely).

Who would've believed, watching Eastwood's early Sergio Leone films that the grim, silent, smoking, spitting, executor of cowboy justice was really a latter day Picasso of filmmaking? But there Eastwood is, still writing scripts, composing scores, directing, still acting, and being a renaissance man in everyone's admiring estimation (with reservations about his politics). And who could resist that kind of artistic power? We love Eastwood, now, with something like the affection Florence must surely have felt for Michelangelo. In the last ten or twelve years you would think Eastwood could do no wrong (people have evidently forgotten how awful *Blood Work* was).

We're not quite ready to gush like that over Christopher Nolan, though. We don't really trust him, yet, but I notice that he rates highly with his peers. They speak of him with considerable reverence because, unlike most of us, they know how he gets us to experience whatever he wants, and they all know that it isn't so easy to cover one's own tracks as a director (especially from others who belong to the guild). I mentioned in the last chapter that Tarantino likes to share his art, but that Nolan does not.

Threads

Since no director, no matter how brilliant, can *completely* conceal his art, there has to be a thread. It's like that in life too, you know. There's always a thread (one can usually follow a money trail . . . almost no matter what one is tracing). That traceable trail is the reason it pays to be on your guard when you feel yourself being propelled toward a conclusion you didn't produce spontaneously in your own cogitations—and after all, that's what "inception" means in Nolan's world: to obscure the process by which an idea that propels us toward a course of action has been implanted. We mistake for our own, apparently, whatever viral ideas we can't trace to anyone else.

Whether this is true isn't terribly important. I think I have a lot of ideas I can't trace, and I don't think I give up my freedom to act on them or ignore them on account of their origin. But I think we all have to admit that we have plotted with others to bring certain people to the conviction that "x was his/her own idea," because we knew we were more likely to get action from said person on said idea under such conviction. So the premise of *Inception* is only something we all know and even do (and have done to us by others). If we exaggerate the importance of this bit of common sense for theatrical and narrative effects, that seems like something well within the artist's license. All we need is to make the health of the planet and billions of people depend on a certain idea, and imagine a key character powerful and stubborn enough to warrant taking amazing risks to get that idea inceived.

Claim Your Own Baggage

So I want to ask you a question. You may have thought of it already, but I think it is pretty revealing. There is a moment, near the end of *Inception*, when the dream-invaders are claiming baggage at the airport. In that scene, Cobb comes face to face with Robert Fischer, the "target" of the inception plot. Remember, they all just spent the last ten hours dreaming together, and lucidly dreaming at that.

I would interpret the look that Fischer gives Cobb in that moment to be ambiguous. Maybe it *has* to be ambiguous because this is a place where the story doesn't quite hang together. Maybe. Why doesn't Fischer seem to recognize Cobb (or Mr. Charles, as he has introduced himself)? Or maybe he does, but if so, what is Fischer thinking? Is his expression one of private recognition, perhaps even gratitude? That would make sense, but probably that's not it.

More likely: Cobb looks familiar and Fischer is trying to remember who he is, having the common difficulty we all have in recalling our dreams. But now remember, Fischer is trained to resist dream-invasion. Wouldn't this include not only the discipline of lucid dreaming but also training in remembering dreams? It seems odd that Fischer is formidable enough to require a "Mr. Charles" gambit to neutralize his defenses, but he apparently can't remember his dreams. That isn't believable, is it?

Surely he ought to recognize Cobb at baggage claim. But the situation is actually even less believable than that. Maybe it occurred to you too, but obviously Robert Fischer *must* recognize *all* these people from waking life who were with him in First Class. We have all been on flights and we do recognize in baggage claim the people we sat near on a flight, especially if it's a long one. These are also the people with whom Fischer just traveled through three dreams (or four if you count the dream in which Mal kidnapped him, although Fischer was "dead" when that happened), and the climax of the third dream was profoundly emotional for him.

Even if he can't remember them all, surely he remembers *Cobb*. And in waking life, what were these people doing on his flight, and in his head? Does he think their presence in his dream on the plane was "day residue"?

In any case, Fischer didn't call the police on them, didn't say a word. Perhaps he even believes they are all his own security people. But if so, wouldn't he recognize his own people? In a nutshell, what's the deal when they land? What does that look really mean? When the flight is over, what does Robert Fischer know and what does he not know? It's an epistemological dilemma, because if he knows these people were in his dream, then he can trace the thread and knows he was inceived by dream invasion. If he does not know who they are, that seems to falsify the claim that that he has been trained to defend himself against dream invasion.

In our present flight of fancy, feel free to think of this question as a baggage claim check. You can redeem it at the end of the chapter for an answer. But in the meantime you have to keep me out of your head because I'm dead set on re-arranging your ideas before we land. You can trust me. I promise I'm on your side. Really.

Training Day?

The reason that over a hundred generations of the human race have preserved and returned to and built upon the story of Ariadne and Theseus (in its many forms) is because there's something in that tale that plucks the taut strings of our collective being. Myths don't just inform our cultures, they well upwards anew in every generation to tell us who and what we are.

We can't really even prevent this renewal, and we wouldn't want it to stop even if we could. But that doesn't keep us from wondering whether we ever really say anything new or do anything genuinely novel. Are we not also confined by the pre-conscious "archetypes" of the human race, these fundamental narratives telling us what we must do? We fall in love, or strive to free ourselves from our parents, or try not to wound our children, but in spite of our efforts we end up being the same old warriors and kings and tricksters and eternal youths that our human race always begets from the womb of our unconscious, collective past.

I don't know about you, but I can't keep myself from re-enacting the human drama any more than I can quit puzzling over Nolan's damnable labyrinth of a movie. I don't even feel free to slow myself down as I barrel toward whatever diabolical end he may have prepared for me and my little ponderings. So

I'm wondering whether I might be able to militarize *my* unconscious, become trained to resist Nolan and his army of archetypal images and mythic plots.

Robert Fischer has somehow gotten such training, much to the surprise of our team of the dream-invaders. In the opening scene, Cobb and Arthur are offering that sort of training to Saito. So there must be some sort of possible training in *how* to dream, in the Nolan universe. What sort of training is that? Does Fischer have a Zen master who teaches him to empty his mind? That seems more like something Saito might have pursued. Fischer's defenses are of a military character, closer to Rambo's with guns blazing than to Zen masters and silent Ninjas.

This militarization of Fischer's unconscious mind is not driven by ideals of honorable combat, and even if it is about mind-control, in some sense, this militarization isn't brainwashing. The discipline Fischer has learned seems to be a kind of control over the *way* the subconscious energies *enter* the conscious mind (albeit dream consciousness), and the aim of the training appears to be the identification and total, violent elimination of "foreign" presences in one's dreams.

But how can "foreign" presences in a dream be identified? All kinds of stuff ends up in our dreams, after all. We can work this out, and maybe even get ourselves some training, but the path is a bit circuitous. I need to talk a little bit about brain chemistry (in Nolanland) and a bit about dream architecture. I wouldn't want my offerings to be mistaken for *actual* brain chemistry (about which I know very little), or *actual* architecture, (no one would want to use so much as a staircase of my design—I'm no Ariadne).

But I'm guessing that you and I know as much about this kind of brain chemistry and dream architecture as Nolan does, since he is making it up and tells us what we need to know, presumably. And besides, the "facts" reported by the characters are driven by the demands of the story, as we also know, and within the framework of what we can plausibly believe for the sake of the plot.

It isn't rocket science and it definitely isn't brain surgery. But explaining *group lucid dreaming* in *Inception* is a little bit like trying to explain how the transporter works on *Star Trek*. There is a certain sense to it, but thinking through it, using what is known about our physiology and our dream states, and filling in the rest with plausible suppositions, we can have an account of how dream architecture is possible, how it could "actually" work in a way that is consistent with the clues provided by Nolan. I'm not saying that what follows is the *only* way it could work, but the "right" story would surely be akin to the one I'll now tell.

One thing I'll never explain is how everybody among the dream invaders can fall asleep instantly. Yes, they are getting some chemical help, but it is incredible how quickly they are all able to do it. It is also interesting how they can be rolled over in a cargo van, or tied into a neat bundle without waking up. But that does bring us to the chemist, which is where this has to start.

Sharing the Dream

Yusuf is our crack chemist-for-hire in *Inception*, and from him we learn the basic facts about what happens, physically, that makes group dreaming possible. Group dreaming has to be possible before dream architecture can be done, so let's look just at group dreaming, first off.

There is the vague suggestion in the movie that the knowledge of how to dream in groups is ancient (and African), at least as it concerns the drugs to be used. We have old African men gathering in the dank cellars under the apothecaries of Mombasa (or Nairobi, or wherever) to "share the dream." Yusuf tells us that they do this because it's the only way they can still dream—together, as assisted by these chemicals.

This explanation connects the idea of group dreaming to mythic consciousness, and perhaps we're meant to think that modern life has made group dreaming impossible, and that in these unwise times, the wise yearn for the kind of attachment to each other and their dreams that existed before civilization became so much controlled by greed and technology.

We're led to imagine a world in which elders would gather around a fire in a sacred circle, take the drugs and share the dream. Here the ancestors would instruct them together in the ways of war, peace, and spirit. The ancestors wouldn't need the electrodes, the processor, and the chemicals, we assume.

The reason the old men can't dream together (anymore) without Yusuf's electro-chemical help is that the puny dreams they have *alone* are not real dreams at all. When you've shared the dream with others and explored the possibilities of *that* world, it's difficult to take seriously the impoverished dreams of a lonely dreamer. One could even see such a dreamer as "lost," and modern dreamers don't even know they are lost—and that's as lost as you can be. People ask what limbo is on Reddit and all sorts of social media. It's pretty clear to me that dreaming alone and not being able to wake up is limbo. And this does sound like the picture of Cobb suggested to us repeatedly. Mal wakes up. Cobb is still asleep.

History Is a Nightmare from which I Am Trying to Awake

James Joyce said that. Add in a little Kafka and you might substitute "modernity" for "history." Something similar might be said for our modern form of waking consciousness. We wrongly believe that our consciousness is individual in form, when in truth we are all fragments, using very little of our brain power because we don't know how to reconnect with what is real.

Waking consciousness was once collective as well. We had a group mind before we came to be fragmented, even if we have to trace our evolutionary line back to a time before we had backbones and centralized nervous systems. I don't think we have to go back that far, nothing close to that far. I think it's pretty hard to study this empirically, but in our most ancient rituals, the ecstatic (and sometimes chemically enhanced) actions can and do bring about a shared consciousness. I think it's reasonable to assume that such acts of "recollection" really tap in to something in the past that is still with us in latent accompaniment to what we now call "waking life."

But Joyce is right. Once we have history, it becomes increasingly difficult to emerge and arise from its spell. We re-experience that arising from our dismemberment into individuals in ecstatic praise and worship gathering, or rock concerts. Somehow we are all there, all together, all parts of a greater body, our consciousness raised in its combining with others, and the whole is greater than the sum of its parts. It isn't like the Borg because the parts remain distinct, but in their distinctness and perspective, they are able to instensify the whole in a way that individuality will not accomplish.

Mythic consciousness, on the other hand, is, I think (and I am far from alone), a shared consciousness, and *it* (and *not* what we call waking consciousness) is the measure of genuine reality. Individual consciousness is an evolutionary aberration, a pathology of consciousness in which the individual foolishly mistakes his tiny perspective for reality. It is a nightmare. But in every isolated individual lies the common memory of the race and the power to find the way out of the labyrinth of modern consciousness and into genuine, shared, collective consciousness. Bergson (yes, him again) defines an evolutionary "tendency" is the experience of the way the *past as a whole* presses upon and even overruns the present. The past is active, not over and gone. He then says this:

> When a tendency splits up in the course of its [evolutionary] develop-
> ment, each of the special tendencies which thus arise tries to pre-
> serve and develop everything in the primitive tendency that is not
> incompatible with the work for which it is specialized. (*Creative
> Evolution*, p. 119)

That's a mouthful, but what it means is that everything that ever happened to us in the past is still with us to the maximal degree that it *can be*. Forgetting the past is not something our bodies do, let alone our minds. Our bodies and minds are aggregations of the past acting in the present, and when you dream, more of the past is active than when you are awake, Bergson says. As a physical and mental reality, you are more open to the true action of the past (and not just your personal past) when you are dreaming.

Group Dreaming, Redux

Our group dreaming is the training for finding the path *toward* shared waking consciousness. Some kind of story like this lies behind Nolan's depiction of the old men in the basement, and Yusuf is more than an apothecary, he is more like the Medicine Man.

But anything can be commodified in the modern world, packaged, sold and enhanced with the latest technologies. In a world so misguided, people might break into one another's dreams and steal things, or worse yet, *leave things behind*. (*How* did Cobb come to be in possession of Mal's totem? He left it spinning in a safe in limbo, didn't he? We will get to this.) There is no human thing, no matter how pure, that can't be misused, and the discipline of group dreaming is no exception.

Better Living through Electro-Chemistry

So how does the science work? The suggestion I would make about the chemicals is that perhaps they have an effect on our brainwaves similar to the way that a laser beam works with light waves. A laser device takes variable light waves that would normally cancel each other out and aligns them so that they are mutually reinforcing. What if some psychotropic concoction could bring about a similar effect on our brainwaves? I take it that everyone is aware that a weak electromagnetic field surrounds the human body and overlaps with the fields of others and fields outside of our bodies. It is not absurd to imagine a process by which these fields are aligned.

And what if, to such a mixture, we add a sedative, nay, a "powerful" sedative, carefully adjusted to the aim of going down extra levels, to simpler orders within the more complex overlap of fields? We can imagine something along these lines being accomplished with drugs, and in the same way that a laser beam can be intensified by concentrating more and more energy into the same mutually reinforcing wave-pattern, what about an organizing of brainwaves that employs increasingly more of the brain's total "neural capacity"?

Such an idea is suggested by Cobb when he reminds us of how little of our brain capacity we use in waking life (another argument against privileging waking life). Perhaps the chemically controlled alignment of brainwaves can unlock something like our greater "neural capacity." So we could think of this enhancement of "neural capacity" as a measurable electrochemical ratio, where the effect of the drugs is to produce an iterated electromagnetic field within a field within a field, and with each incremental increase of neural energy, we can skip down more deeply into the dynamics of that nested field. The field is also open to electrical manipulation.

Perhaps the electromagnetic field can jump incrementally in intensity: as energy is added, at a certain point a threshold is reached and passed, the "next level down" becomes sufficiently organized to "visit."

And if that's right, then the *temporality* of each deeper level might be like the Richter scale for earthquakes (where a one-point change represents is an earthquake ten times as powerful/intense), so that when the intensity of brainwave alignment is cranked up, the effect is a leap to a frighteningly greater and greater expansion of actual time.

So, to supercharge the serum, as Yusuf does, creates the conditions for a three- or four-level expansion of the same five actual minutes, pulling those minutes apart to the point of approaching a quantum minimum of time, a smallest "time-particle" or something which would make a second seem like an eternity, if you could *experience it* (this is my best shot at saying what "limbo" is in this movie, by the way!).

And so, unlike with the Richter scale, which has no minimum, maybe there is a minimum "time burst," a set amount of required expansion when one goes to the next "level," or maybe there isn't, but to keep using chemicals to align brainwaves only really gets us access to smaller and smaller "drops of experience," as William James called them. Each deeper level is built from more rarified or subtle waves.

This is all pretty weird to contemplate, but here is an analogy that may help: If you run audio or video tape faster across a magnet, less information goes on each physical segment of the tape as it passes, and the effect is higher fidelity. Less information spread across more space, due to the faster passage of time, preserves that information more faithfully. When you run the tape slower, more information is packed into less space, and the result is a lower fidelity.

So maybe our experience of dream-time is sort of like that. The more it's expanded into nested levels of space, the slower it goes, but in this case, perhaps we should get less "lucidity" (that is, "fidelity"), because the brainwaves are so rarified and delicate. I don't quite have that difference clear in my imagination because there isn't any "space" corresponding to the tape. In a dream, it's *all* time, in terms of the physiological processes involved, and the body itself looks like a spatial constant, not getting bigger or smaller as it dreams. But, to be as clear as I can manage, maybe it becomes harder and harder to maintain the dream architecture and to *interpret* our own dream experience as we pack more and more of it into the same five (waking) minutes—or ten waking hours of the plane ride, or whatever.

The margin of error for variation in the individual wave vibrations would become increasingly thin, and the manipulation of the electromagnetic field produced by those waves becomes more and more delicate (unstable), while the experiences had by the dreamers become harder to interpret as the waves are more rarified. One result of wandering around in a dream that is three or four levels removed from waking life is the increasing loss, then, of lucidity and the onset of a kind of "psychosis of forgetting" that replaces the lucidity. One could go so far as to suppose that the wanderer in limbo is physically lost in a quantum foam.

The Ghost in the Machine

Then we have to consider that for our team of inceivers, there is the dream machine they carry around in various metal suitcases. There is such a machine in Yusuf's basement as well. Precisely what the machine is, and how people might have dreamt *en mass* without it, in ancient days, is something we don't know. I took a guess above. But I think we're supposed to infer that the drugs do something of a chemical nature to our brains and bodies, while the machine, which seems to have electrical leads that can transmit impulses of some sort from one dreamer to others allows for the manipulation of the electromagnetic field created by the sympathetic alignment of our brainwaves.

It's not important that we know exactly how this process works, but I do think that it needs to seem plausible to those who watch the movie—not because all stories need to stay within the bounds of plausibility, but because this particular story would quickly lose the kind of profoundly human interest it has *unless* we can persuade ourselves of the premise about group dreaming. Not content with the idea that this is an ancient art, Nolan adds on modern technology, and a vague illustration of old men dreaming together because they cannot (in the modern day) dream alone any more.

I think it's probably safe to infer, from what we're shown, that perhaps "group dreaming" is the only ancient part. The elders "remember" when the great grandfathers told them about sharing the dream and meeting the ancestors there, but some of the old magic is now lost, so they depend on the machine (and that is sad, as Yusuf seems to imply). But maybe even crude electrical leads from dreamer to dreamer would suffice for conducting the impulses of a shared experience, at one level down, and maybe it is the leads that enables one dreamer to produce images in a dream that belongs to another dreamer.

I can imagine ancient dreamers grasping the same living vine, or a strand of sinew taken from a totem animal. Perhaps the ancients never got that far. They weren't interested in manipulating the shared dream to their personal advantage, so a crude connection would be enough. The fancy high-tech machine is needed for the kind of highly organized invasion and theft that are practiced by our hired team, and for going two, three or even four levels into shared dreaming.

It's notable that Nolan chose to represent this technology as electrical rather than electronic. To introduce computers into the narrative would change the story greatly. It seems to have been important to him to stay away from the idea that the ways we can control dream architecture involve computer manipulation. He wanted this to be a skill you learn by controlling your thoughts (like a shaman), not by manipulating a computer (like a geek).

Part of the reason I'm certain that Nolan wants to invoke our sense of mythic consciousness (apart from the obvious clues, like laying the story out over the lattice work of the myth of Theseus) is that he so obviously avoided introducing electronic elements into the story.

Once Upon a Time

So what is mythic consciousness anyway? There are a number of theories out there, and not much agreement among anthropologists, psychologists, and other theorists (including philosophers). I will give you the brief version of one theory that meshes well with what Nolan does in this movie. I am not sure I buy this theory, overall, but I do admit that I'm convinced by the part I am going to tell you about.

The theory belongs to a philosopher named Susanne Langer. We met her back in Chapter 1, when we looked at *The Princess Bride*. That theory of fairytales was part of a larger theory. She wrote a famous book called *Philosophy in a New Key* (1942) in which she provided a theory of mythic consciousness that used narrative principles to explain what mythic consciousness is and how it works.

The basic idea is this: the difference between a dream and a myth is that dreams slip around, all over the place and myths do not. In a dream, one thing can turn into something else without warning, and that's what we expect from dreams. It surprises us sometimes, and sometimes it doesn't, when (for example), a seashell is suddenly a bird that talks to us, or our parents are suddenly our children, or our companions become trees, or some other such transmogrification. But since it's a dream, we always know this is a possibility. Note, that doesn't happen in Nolan's depiction of dreaming. That is a key point. One might fairly ask, "are any of these characters actually dreaming?" Their dreams aren't like *mine*, in any case. In my dreams, things transmogrify, especially if I have been eating catfish. (This ought to be studied—the effect of catfish on dreaming.)

In Langer's theory, the reason dreams can behave this way is because we don't have to communicate them to others. If you really must communicate something to someone else, you will have to put it in a time sequence (time t_1 to time t_n) and make it conform to the boundaries of narrative communication— there will be a beginning, middle, and end, and a sort of plot thread. But dreams don't have to behave that way. We *do* put them in that order when we tell others about our dreams, but we always know it's a bit artificial to impose narrative order on the experience.

Langer doesn't talk about lucid dreams, but they would exist in between ordinary individual dreaming and storytelling. Lucid dreams do have narrative structure, but they are still dreams, with transmogrifications and metamorphoses. It's just that the dreamer is aware that he or she is dreaming and presumably has some control over the narrative. I suppose seashells can still become birds spontaneously, but in a lucid dream we could get some control over that process: make things become other things—or prevent it—by using our minds and wills.

And here we begin to get close to the idea of "training" the dreamer. Perhaps it is possible to train people to generate images in a lucid dream that become elements of the narrative, regardless of who is in control of the narration.

Castles in the Air

It is believable that a person could be better or worse at this interposition of images, as a matter of natural aptitude (like being good at math or music). Practicing could improve the capacity to generate these images in one's own dreams. Ariadne has a gift for this sort of thing, for generating images of spaces, and she learns to do it regardless of who is narrating the dream.

For his story, Nolan needs it to be possible for more than one dreamer to be lucid at the same time, in group dreaming, but I think that idea is consistent with the story of group dreaming I already gave you. There's a sort of structural regression to group mythic consciousness made possible by the drugs and the machine, where the form of collective consciousness is mythic, but individuals still carry their modern abilities of narration with them when they "travel" this way.

It's like Mark Twain's Connecticut Yankee having a dream of an even more primitive time. (I think Hank Morgan had been eating catfish.) The same idea may explain how Robert Fischer is "trained" to generate images of a well-armed Delta Force or SWAT team that comes to rescue him if he is trapped in a dream narrative that poses a threat to his secrets.

I'll say more about that training, but the point is to recognize that whatever Ariadne is doing to get better at dream architecture is probably closely related to what Fischer is doing to "militarize" his unconscious mind. But the unconscious is a little more unruly and a little less responsive to simple habituation than is the conscious mind. So no amount of conscious practicing will perfect the militarization of the unconscious. (Hence the vulnerability of Fischer to the Mr. Charles scheme.)

No matter how much we habituate ourselves to certain patterns of conscious thinking, and no matter how hard we try to tame them, our unconscious minds still have a spontaneous tendency to supply images to our waking minds and to our dreams that we don't create with our wills. Freud's way of distinguishing the conscious from the unconscious mind is to say that there is a sort of sentinel, the "ego," who guards the threshold between consciousness and the unconscious, but sometimes (especially in dreams) unconscious desires slip past our defenses and become images.

This idea explains Cobb's limitations and failures controlling the images that show up wherever he goes in the dream world. All of this tug of war between the conscious and the unconscious seems to happen in the liminal domain of lucid dreaming, somewhere between the world of conscious storytelling and the world of dreams.

Langer goes on to say that as we attempt to communicate the crazy swirl of our inner conscious lives, we increasingly restrict what "counts" in our stream of thought, that is, what we actively pay attention to, and we select just those aspects of conscious life that we can place into narrative order. I don't know about you, but if I actually tried to communicate to you what goes on in my inner life, well, you wouldn't want to know. It's a perfect chaos, when I try to survey it as a whole.

The demands of communicating our inner lives to others, with all the organizing and censorship we impose, are severe and we eliminate most of what we think and even more of what we feel. In time we acquire the habit of ignoring things we can't easily communicate, pretending those thoughts and feelings don't really exist. These habits explain not only how we move from the rich imaginative life of childhood into a less lively adult world, but also how the human race loses its mythic childhood as it takes on the strictures of "civilization," in which science takes the place of magic, and written novels replace oral traditions, and solemn worship replaces ecstatic rites. What counts as an acceptable story for "civilized" people must be "rational," which is to say, highly regimented.

As you can see, these ideas about mythic consciousness and the narrowing of consciousness into "civilized life" have some implications for the story of inceiving the mind of Robert Fischer. As our team knows, to inceive successfully requires the use of symbols, especially ones tied to strong emotion, and those symbols have to spread through the target's unconscious mind and eventually break past the sentinel, the ego, and manifest themselves as hunches, or as notions, or even as ideas, but not as mere images.

It would do no good for Robert Fischer to suddenly have an image in his mind of the pinwheel his father gave him. He would go "humph" and dismiss it. Rather, to inceive, the symbol's meaning has to be taken up as a disposition to behave one way rather than another. I would suppose that the way a symbol spreads through the unconscious is by a series of transformations that preserves the essence or the basic energy or tendency of the original symbol. By the time the symbol has pervaded the unconscious, it is no longer traceable to its source.

What this hypothesis of mine implies, putting it all together, is that inception would actually be easy for "archaic" people (residents of traditional places/times[1]) but difficult for sophisticated, modern "civilized" people, whose defenses are always up, and whose over-active egos are so thoroughly "protected" against any genuine contact with the inner life of another, as well as from their own unconscious desires.

"Archaic" people would be open, would have no secrets to protect (in the traditional village, everyone knows everything about everybody), and would be taught to believe that the distance between waking and dreaming is not great. That's why the interpretation of dreams is received as a useful art among them. Such people would not fear inception. They might even welcome it and practice it as a kind of gift-giving or hospitality. (Although gift-giving is pretty complicated in traditional human life.) Upon encountering modern people who can't be inceived easily, perhaps they would be sad for such people. The modern person is so alone, so confused, and is forced to endure such a narrow, uninteresting world, a world in which everything must be just what it is and nothing else, a world of impoverished signs and with no living symbols, that the situation is pitiable.

To the "archaic" mind, language teems with living symbols, while to the supposedly "civilized" mind, language is a dead conveyer of abstract signs. With this small bit of Langer's philosophy of myth, we are now in a position to return to the movie itself with a better understanding of what happens and how dream architecture works, along with getting a grip on the process of inception itself.

Whose Dream Is This, Anyway?

One thing you might not have worked through is the question of who is the principal narrator of each dream. That turns out to be an important point because apparently one principle of

---

[1] I am using the term preferred by Marcel Mauss (1872–1950), who wrote a number of famous books on the topic of social practices of pre-modern people.

Nolan's dream architecture is that the architect is most effective when she/he is *not* the dreamer. So Ariadne is *in* all the dreams, but she is never the dreamer. It also appears that being the dreamer may eliminate you from descending deeper. You can appear in your own dream, but if someone else is dreaming within your dream, you can't appear in the deeper dream (apparently).

The first dream on the airplane is Yusuf's, which is why he stays in the van "awake" (in his own dream, narrating it lucidly) while everyone else dreams of a hotel. The second dream is Arthur's, which is why he stays in the hotel while everyone else dreams of a snow fortress. But whose dream is the snow fortress? There are a few clues.

First, when Ariadne has prepared her physical models for each dreamer to study, Eames walks to the model of the snow fortress. Second, remember that Fischer believes that Eames is Peter Browning (the character played by Tom Berenger), *and* in the hotel (Arthur's dream), Fischer believes he is going *into* Browning's dream, to break into Browning's dreamsafe, and *that* is in the snow fort. Of course, Eames is Browning. Third, all the other characters except Eames (Saito, Ariadne, Cobb, Fischer) appear at the deeper levels, below the snow fort.

So the snow fort is really Eames's dream, and he is maintaining that dream level as its narrator, but he is dreaming *as* Peter Browning in order to deceive Fischer. That's why they keep referring to "Browning's defenses" and "where would Browning put it?" and so on, when they're in the dream of the snow fort. And Eames is separated from Fischer in the snow fort assignments, staying awake there after Saito and Fischer "die."

All the architecture in the first three dream levels is Ariadne's (with some invasions by Cobb's projections), until they unexpectedly find themselves having to go into Cobb's dream, where Mal has taken Fischer hostage. So when Ariadne and Cobb go to sleep in the snow fortress, they go into Cobb's dream. He is the architect, but it was built a long time ago and is now falling apart.

The key to understanding the planned inception of Fischer is to look at the snow fort that Eames is dreaming about. Ariadne has built the safe there for Maurice Fischer's Last Will and Testament, but she left the safe empty, as is the rule for heavily defended secret places (we learn that early in the movie, when Cobb and Arthur are in Saito's dream, presumably—the one in which the architect screwed up the feel of the carpet and got dragged away to his demise).

So, if I've worked through this rightly, Eames is the one who puts the pinwheel in the safe—that is the inception—and he figures out *what* to do when the picture of Maurice and Robert with the pinwheel is in Robert's wallet, which Eames has lifted when he is disguised as a bodacious blonde bar patron in the bar in Arthur's hotel. Eames has a bodacious skill there, reminiscent of Ross Martin's Artemus Gordon in *The Wild, Wild West,* or the character of "The Great Paris" played by Leonard Nimoy in *Mission Impossible.*

A Pinwheel and a Picture

I think that maybe, just maybe, that picture is Robert Fischer's totem. Eames recognizes its importance. Granted, Fischer doesn't know he's going to be spending time in other people's dreams when he gets on the airplane, but he is trained in "dream defense" and a totem is something these dreamy people always keep with them. There must be some way that a person's totem crosses from waking reality into all these dreams, right?

It makes sense to believe that these people are all trained to generate the *image* of that totem in any dream, and only *they* can generate it rightly (along with the *absence* of some secret characteristic it possesses only in waking life, like its weight or tendency to fall one way or another). We already know that handling another person's totem gives one great power over that person. The reason is that if someone knows the totem in that wat way, he or she could generate an image of it that another would not be able yto distinguish from the original. Keep that in mind for the end of the next chapter, and also for the answer to how Cobb got Mal's totem.

So the picture of Robert with his father and the pinwheel shows up in Arthur's dream, and Eames is the character who keeps it and says it will be useful. Eames, then, placed the pinwheel (from the picture) in the safe (as a generated image), following the clue he picked up in the stolen picture, but the inception only works because Robert Fischer believes he has placed the pinwheel in there *himself,* unconsciously. The Will is what Browning has supposedly put there. Remember Robert is trained, his mind is "militarized," so he knows that Browning will fill the safe with something secret from his own unconscious. But in fact, Robert is the one who puts the Will in the safe. It is actually his own projection because it is what he *expected* to find. Yet, he discounts the Will because he wrongly believes Browning has put it there, unconsciously.

The switcheroo is that the pinwheel is such a powerful symbol that Robert believes he has put it there himself, and the meaning it carries is that, deep down, he knows his father always loved him and isn't disappointed. Robert drops his defenses for just that moment and connects with a feeling about his father—one that will spread: he shouldn't try to be like the man.

Do You Doubt Me?

Fischer doubts whether Peter Browning has really been kidnapped (the doubt suggested to him by Cobb), and Fischer also suspects that Browning is the one behind the attempt to invade his dreams. So Fischer is convinced by the Mr. Charles gambit to turn the tables on Browning by going where Browning didn't expect him to go, which is into Browning's own dream, to discover what Browning was trying to hide (the true contents of the Last Will and Testament of Maurice Fischer).

Part of the standard "Mr. Charles" gambit is to convince the target to reveal his secret while believing he is revealing someone else's secret. But in this case, no one is interested in Robert's *secrets*; the mission is inception, which adds a twist to the standard Mr. Charles routine. What seemed like a revelation of a secret was actually an implant.

A doubt is easier to inceive than a positive idea, but as Cobb briefly says, it's better to use positive symbols, things that evoke good feelings. Doubt tends to tear down meanings, not build them. Doubt arrests action rather than motivating it. If you want your target to do something he wouldn't otherwise do, you have to *relieve* doubt, *counteract* it. Both doubt and its opposite, the relief of doubt, will spread in the unconscious.

Doubt is what overtook Mal's unconscious (see my next chapter), and Cobb has learned from that what *not* to do in attempting inception.

Proceed to Carousel One

I promised you an answer to what Fischer does and does not know when everyone (except Saito) is at baggage claim (Saito owns the airline, so one assumes he doesn't have to go through the regular baggage claim). I think the key to it is to understand that a doubt has been *lifted* from Fischer, although he doesn't think the dreams he had are the reason it disappeared. He probably feels like his own man for the first time in his life. And here we learn something like the moral or the "theme" of the whole tale.

Modernity is an age of doubt and doubt spreads across the unconscious, manifesting in millions of ways. We are all so very afraid, so guilty, so lacking in confidence in our own judgments, in the work of our own hands, and so isolated from one another that we substitute emotional bravado for genuine healing.

The same deep structures of consciousness that make it possible for us to dream *together* are the ones that lead us to doubt each other. Doubt is easy to create in modern people and difficult to relieve. But for traditional people, the ones who live in closer proximity to the world of dreams, and to one another, it is the other way around: belief is easy to create and doubt is hard to implant. They know who and what they are and they have no deep-seated doubt in their unconscious minds. The unconscious is the place where the ancestors speak, and so long as it is approached with reverence and awe, the ancestors will be benevolent.

Robert Fischer has touched that place—his father, now the departed and revered ancestor, speaks and is in fact benevolent. Robert has recovered himself by getting below the doubt to what our collective and primitive selves have always known, which is that our ancestors desire our happiness.

So when everybody wakes up, Fischer doesn't say anything to the people he has just spent the last ten hours dreaming with. Maybe he recognizes them, from the dream, but either he believes they are his own security people, in waking life, that they helped him defeat the attempt to steal his secret and instead, perhaps they got Browning's knowledge of the Will, but it really doesn't matter. Maybe all of that was "just a dream."

Robert is confident and not suspicious and fearful now, and it doesn't matter who these people are. Otherwise I guess he would have had everyone arrested when they landed. What is relevant is that Browning is *not* among the bag-collectors. Saito has disappeared when they land, so Robert may believe Saito was Browning's co-conspirator. That would make sense. Robert surely knows who Saito is, what he looks like in waking life, and would have been naturally suspicious of him, as his father's main competitor. The fact that Saito is not at baggage claim would tend to confirm that if someone was trying to steal Robert's secrets, it was probably Saito, and the people on the plane were sent by Browning, or someone else, to protect Robert on the flight. Something like this story would supply the unstated narrative moves that finish out the "whodunit" aspect of the tale. I might be wrong, but that's the best I can do.

Day Residue

I'm not absolutely certain how "dream architecture" works, but I believe it requires the *waking* co-operation of the dreamer, in order for the architecture to "take." The dreamer has to be lucid enough to choose the architecture created by the architect, and I think they probably have to study it together. The dreamer dreams the superstructure and the architect supplies the particulars about the dream space. The architect can build in some features the dreamer doesn't know about, but the comprehensive whole has to be chosen by the dreamer, I'm pretty sure.

So the superstructure is what dream theorists call "day residue," stuff that carries over from your daily activities and experiences and shows up in your dreams without being transformed by the dream state. So if you are studying for a math test, you dream about actual math, and so on. This explains why Ariadne teaches each dreamer the general space of his dream while both are awake. It is like storyboarding a movie.

Robert Fischer believes the *first* dream is his own dream, at the very least (it is really Yusuf 's). But at the baggage claim, he has the option of believing *all* the dreams were his own, and that the people in them were day residue, just as I suggested at the outset. But I also said I would try to inceive something in you. Since you are a modern, civilized reader, it is far easier to get you to doubt something, and for that doubt to spread, than to get you to do something I want you to do. But I'm better than your average inceiver.

If you are still reading this, I managed what I set out to do, which was to keep you reading to find out what I was trying to inceive in you. You mainly doubted that I could really do it, I'm sure, and maybe now you're disappointed, but if I managed to get your suspicion of me to work as a lever to get you to the end of the chapter, I succeeded in the waking inception. Christopher Nolan did something like that to those who saw his movie. You're wondering whether all of it was Cobb's dream, or, if you are a little less suspicious, simply whether the spinning top at the end of the movie falls. Nolan did that to you. It was inception.

I also promised some training. You now know that doubt spreads more easily than does its opposite, for the people you care about. Your training is, then, an object lesson in resisting the urge to plant doubts in the unconscious depths of the people around you. If you make a habit of doing that, you may not be able to keep them from spreading. You don't want to leave anyone in the position Robert Fischer was in. Or worse yet, Mal (assuming Cobb is telling the truth about inceiving her).

On the other hand, if you want to protect yourself from being inceived by Christopher Nolan's movies, stay away from the movies altogether. To place yourself in the theater is to place yourself at his mercy, to invite him into your dreams. He knows that you go to the movies to be able to dream, with others. And after all, Nolan *is* Cobb.

14
Dream Time

In *INCEPTION*

We've talked a lot about the experience of time, but not much about time itself, the time that presumably passes whether we are aware of it or not. One assumes that time passed before there were humans, or biological life, or planet earth, or Milky Way, and so on. What is *that* time? One thing to accept at the outset: you are the one wondering about this, so the answer can't really overcome the stamp you place on it as the experiencer of what you are seeking to know about independent of your experience of it. That is a pretty standard problem and paradox in philosophy: we want to know how and what and why things are apart from the fact that it's *us* doing to wondering. We'll do the best we can with this.

Over-Confidence Is Like a Loaded Gun

At the end of *Inception*, when Cobb arrives home and finally sees his children, he spins the top and walks away. Does the totem finally tumble? We all know that's the question. Christopher Nolan has scoffed at those who expected him to answer it. People have exchanged theories *ad nauseum*, and most of you have probably decided there is no definite solution, so you might doubt it when I say this: I actually know the answer, with something like clear certainty.

The answer is pretty simple (so I claim), but getting there is a little tougher. It's sort of like the touching simplicity of Robert Fischer's believing that he planted his own pinwheel in his father's safe, and since Nolan miraculously succeeded in preventing that "Rosebud" moment from being anti-climactic, I'll aspire to the same. But don't you dare skip to the end. That's cheating, and you're only spoiling it for yourself.

Just remember the first rule of any well-written play: The gun you see in the first act always goes off in the third. You should also be forewarned that I'm attempting waking inception in this chapter (but not a doubt this time, something tastier).

Lasagna for Lunch

Our man Nolan is fascinated by the topic of time, especially the various ways we humans can experience it. And his curiosity is peculiarly drawn to what we can call the "pathologies of temporal experience"—where time goes bad on us for one reason or another, or for no reason at all. In *Memento*, Nolan explored the way time and memory become strange when a head injury to his main character breaks the link between the present and the past by destroying his ability to make new long-term memories—that is an example of a pathology of temporal experience.

I want to talk about that in a minute or two, but first a word about dreams. Time in dreams is also weird, but maybe not as weird as some other things about dreams (we talked about some of these in the last chapter). There's trouble with working our way through the layers of *Inception*. By the time we see the finished movie, Nolan and company have already analyzed all the time-stuff that interests them and have embedded their results back into the script and the images. We have to swallow everything whole, as it were. It's sort of a lasagna of ideas about time and dreams.

I don't mind ingesting someone else's intellectual main course, but if I'm curious about the ingredients and the process of preparation, I may have to ask after the recipe (and hope it wasn't a close family secret).

On the other hand (and there always seems to be another hand, doesn't there?), it's no fun just to pull apart somebody's lasagna. Even if you could get a clue from looking at the resulting mess, you still might miss the secret ingredient. Is that cottage cheese from the store or feta from the Old Country? Or maybe ricotta? That's a fair question. Can't tell much from looking at the steamy melted pile of goo on the plate. And there is something to be said for using the best ingredients, but we also don't want to walk to Umbria to see what the goats eat. We know good cheese when we taste it, but it's also wise to find out at least where we can order some of it, you know? Such is the analogy with Nolan's lasagna of a movie. All those tasty layers, with squishy dividers.

So I promise not to make you feel like you have to eat on the run, or like a pedestrian on a slow tour of goat forage in the Old

Country, but maybe we can share a table for a while and I'll just prompt you to notice some of the prominent spices and speculate with you about how the cook combined them. Anyone can see this is mainly about the pasta (time) and the cheese (dreams), and that one is soggy and the other is actually melting everywhere. But on one thing I'll tip my hand: like everything else in life, the secret's in the ingredients, but not just individually. This is about how certain kinds of ingredients blend and interact when they're baked. Christopher Nolan is quite the cook.

Part of the reason a lasagna comes to mind is that I saw an image on the web that reminds me of a Penrose lasagna (that, and I'm hungry). The image is sort of an Escher-esque staircase of the dreamers and their dreams and the kicks that catapult them from one level to another. The web address for this image is:

<thecrapbox.com/wp-content/uploads/2010/07/ZZ79EABF11small.jpg>

Very cool. The more I study this image, the more I like it.

Mementos and Totems

In *Inception,* the idea of a "totem" is an item that our professional dream-invaders keep with them, always and everywhere, especially in the dream world. It has to be something with a certain recognizable feel and weight, and uniquely identifiable, and something they don't let others touch or handle (for reasons I already gave). Its function is to provide a test that enables a dream-invader to know whether he or she is in a dream or just knocking about in the real world. You apparently make a deal with your own mind that if the totem feels and behaves in a particular, expected way, that's a sign that you're in the real world, while any deviation from that expectation indicates that you're in a dream (since no one knows how to make your token feel except you).

The idea is set up and justified early in the movie when Nash, the first (unfaithful) architect, fails to design the apartment in Saito's "test dream" with a carpet that smells right, and so Saito is tipped off that he's dreaming. The brief exchange between Nash, Cobb, and Arthur that follows is meant to show that even details as small as the smell of the carpet must be known to a dream architect (and considered in building a labyrinth).

So, the reason that our dream-invaders do not let anyone handle their totems is that such handling would allow any architect to duplicate its expected behavior in a dream and the invader could then be deceived about the dream-reality relation.

But this safeguard only works in helping you identify whether you're in someone else's architecture. It doesn't help you distinguish your own architecture as a dreamer from your waking life. You know how to recreate your totem if you serve as your own architect, and this is why architects are not the ones dreaming; they are working within other people's dreams. So the scope and limit of a totem is that it only helps you discover whether you are in a dream some other architect is creating. It is useless in helping you distinguish your own waking reality from your dream architecture.

"Totem" is a good word for such an item, sacred and untouchable as it is. It answers only the question whether I'm in someone else's dream, and not whether I am in my own dream as both dreamer and architect. Teaching Ariadne how to be an architect, they go into Cobb's dream, not Ariadne's. Remember (for later) that one character does not let another handle his or her totem—to do so would require absolute trust or, dare I say it, a leap of faith. It's also good at this point to keep in mind that the totem needs to be substantial in weight and something the dream-invader always, always has with him.

So the totem is supposed to be a sign or indicator of what is true about your external world, a point of connection between what you're experiencing within yourself (beliefs, perceptions, assumptions) and the way the world really is.

This is not the first time Christopher Nolan has dealt with the problem of connecting our inner experience with our outer world. *Memento* (written with his brother Jonathan) confronts the same problem. Both movies point to the devilish problem of temporality in experiential terms, and they pose the problem very nicely. The question is really about continuity and discontinuity in our experience, and especially the effect of discontinuity on our ability to know the truth about the world.

All of us have gaps in our experience—and by the way, how did you get to be sitting where you are right now . . . Do you remember? *Memento* teaches us the problem of discontinuity "from the inside out," or, what happens when we can't make the real world a permanent part of our on-going inner selves. We know that there is often a difference, a gap, between the way time passes in the world and the way we experience it—after all, time flies when you're having fun, and a watched pot never boils.

Memory is the ability to make the world your own, and to carry it around with you as an accumulated touchstone for grasping whatever you're experiencing now. In *Memento*, the story assumes that time is continuous and orderly in the objective world, but our central character, Leonard Shelby, has suffered a head injury and can no longer move his short-term experiences into his long-term memory. (Such injuries can and do occur, although their consequences have been slightly different than the Nolans present in their story.)

There's no problem with Shelby's *perception*, but his higher order world effectively begins anew every five minutes or so, against the background of all he learned in life before his injury. So the past world, as Leonard knew it long ago, does remain "intact," so to speak, but as he tries to live a normal life now, that past world becomes less and less relevant to making his way in the present. Eventually he doesn't know where he is or why he's there. If he had stayed home and kept everything as it was before his injury, he might have been okay, but his complex circumstances made that impossible.

In order to live life in the present, Leonard has to find ways of arranging the objective world of the recent past and immediate present so that he can compensate for that crippling discontinuity in his higher mental functioning, and most importantly, he must discern the difference between the truth and deception in order to navigate the social world.

Is there an adequate method of arranging the objective, changing world so as to compensate for a radical discontinuity in our internal experience of time? Leonard combines many methods, but the most poignant is tattooing on his body "true propositions," statements he regards as certainties. These supposed "certainties" get him into trouble, eventually, since it turns out that they may not all be true. But if we think about that too much, we will never get back to *Inception*.

My point is a small one. How Leonard remembers that the things on his body are "truths" is one of many problems the Nolans can't really solve (not without trickery), since it requires the continuity in Leonard's memory of the idea "the statements tattooed on my body are true," to hold from one radical break to the next in Leonard's experience. I assume his decision to tattoo himself with only true statements was made after his injury. The Nolans actually have to smuggle some continuity back into Leonard's inner experience. Without cheating, they have no story, no unified narrative.

And here, boys and girls, is a lesson worth remembering: Whenever an author messes with the continuity of time, said author will have to cheat eventually to get it back into the narrative, somehow. Otherwise, the story falls apart in ways that don't sell tickets and books.

So, the "totem" idea is a sort of "continuity machine." It says to its owner: "No matter what you think right now, there is a continuous self somewhere (maybe here and now), and that one is the real 'you'. So, my dear Cobb, look for *dis*continuities and let them be your clue that you are dreaming. I, your totem, am the most trustworthy guide."

Like the Corners of My Mind

Misty and water-colored (so the song goes) are our memories. Memory is the way the past "gnaws into the future," according to Bergson (yes, him again). The past isn't really dead and gone. You may not be very much aware of it but your past is quite active in your present experience, even overrunning the present and stretching into the future. When you walk into a room you've been in a thousand times before, you really don't mainly *see* it, you mainly *remember* it, and as you prepare to walk in, your memory runs ahead and tells you what to expect.

That's why you may notice if something is out of place, say the pepper grinder, or the jars of dried basil and oregano (I always like to be generous with the basil, especially, but simple spice combinations are the best). You experience the change in position of the displaced item first as a gap between memory and present perception; only then do you work to try to identify and fill the gap.

But memory also accumulates. As we get older, our memories and our past experiences become so heavy upon us that they overtake the present fill it with the past. You struggle against this as you get older, trying to stay in meaningful touch with your present experience, but it's a losing battle. In fact, there comes a point, and we've all seen it in our grandparents and other loved ones, when the past really eclipses the present, even before that person gets a fair chance to perceive the present. Our extreme elders experience very little of their genuine present and live mostly in the past.

Part of the reason it gets harder to remember what you've read when you reach middle age is that in the process of reading you are, more and more, remembering other things you've read before that were similar. It is the same with trying to see, really see new places. Mostly your perception is experienced as familiar places from the past.

Failures of short-term memory, such as we see in Alzheimer's disease, have the initial effect of invigorating the relationship of long-term memory to present perception. Thus, you can still have lively conversations about the old days with people who can't remember what they did a few minutes ago. Indeed, you certainly *should* have such conversations with your elders, with all the vigor and detail you can call up. This brightening of the more distant past continues until the expanding erasure of short-term memory begins to wipe out the awareness of where one is and who one is with in the present.

Alzheimer's spreads backwards in time, increasingly destroying the active presence of what *was*, from most recent to the increasingly remote. The patient's finally left with an uninterpretable present devoid of anything familiar. Little wonder such people ask to be taken home, even when they already are home. They are asking for something—anything—familiar.

This variable intensity and the "trade-off " of memory and perception is something Nolan has noticed. Memory has an odd and covariant relation to present perception. So if you want to become an architect for the dream-invaders, you'll want to be sure to make your mazes by thoroughly rearranging and recombining things you've seen before, and doing so in light of new possibilities. Let the novelties dominate. Don't, and I repeat, do not use your memory, *unaltered*. That is dangerous because it's too close to being continuous with your personal past experiences, and you need those experiences in order to interpret your present perceptions (whether dreaming or waking). Your totem won't help here, since you have to *remember* what it is like. That will be a memory you take with you through your own dreams as well as anyone else's you happen to invade.

Our hero Cobb cannot be an architect any more because he's overtaken by memory—it's not just because he can't forget Mal, but also because he's getting older. Part of the reason Ariadne is a promising dream architect is because she's so young, with less total memory and more intense connection to her present perception (both in dreams and in the waking world). She also has more possibilities ahead of her and so her memories, such as they are, spill over into an open swath of possible futures, and these possibilities are the sources of her novel variations for building her dreamscapes.

It would be dangerous (not to mention unprofessional) for Cobb to mix his work life and his personal life, right? But that isn't the only problem he has. The difficulty goes deeper, and it is partly in the aging process. According to Bergson, all dreaming is remembering, but it isn't necessarily the remembering of my personal past. I can also "remember" (in dreams) the collective past of my family, my species, of life itself—it's all still active in there, as we learned in the last chapter. Long before *Inception*, Bergson not only suggested the possibility of group dreaming, he showed how it occurs—memory is embodied and your body carries forward in time the traces of all the bodies that contributed material to generating your body (or even just patterns of order and processes).

The memory of the species lives in your active body. It isn't easy to get at, but it's there. You need the right kind of chemist or a hypnotist to help you tap in. But like Cobb, the older I get, the more my general, impersonal "species memory" is made inaudible and invisible to me by the vivid intervention of my personal past. Children of four dream the dreams of the species, of the collective mind. Being now fairly old, I have come to the point that I don't so much dream as re-enact, with variations, my own life. The more I do that, the fewer are the gaps between my dreamlife and my waking perception.

So the advice Cobb gives early on to Ariadne, "never use your memories," can be rephrased as such: "Introduce gaps when you create your (professional) dream spaces so that you can find your way home, by rediscovering the gaps." The gaps are Ariadne's thread to follow out of the labyrinth. If Cobb can't introduce gaps any more, and he can't, then he can't be an architect, and he can't (sort of—he's still got a few twists left in the old noggin).

But there's too much continuity between his waking and dreaming, and that gets worse as he gets older because memory fills both sides. Yet, to introduce gaps between your dream and your real world is to invite discontinuities into your experience of time. When we mess around with the idea of time's continuity, whether it's the continuity (or at least the accumulative tendency) of our internal time consciousness, or the assumed continuity of objective time in the world, things get strange in a hurry.

And now I must make an assertion: It is not actually possible to make *narrative* sense of radical temporal discontinuity.

Thus, Leonard Shelby really does accumulate experience, whether the Nolans make a point of it or not, for without this accumulation, there would be no arrow of events. Even though *Memento* is presented in reverse chronological order, to help us feel some of Leonard's confusion, still, the accumulation of experience is built into the way Leonard perceives his world. In spite of the discontinuity in his higher order experiences, he remains a living, biological being. Not only is he aging, but in fact each new physical experience is conforming to his previous experiences. And he *knows* that. Otherwise, he wouldn't bother to tattoo himself with true statements. If he gets a superficial injury on his body (like a new tattoo), the injury will still be there after he can't remember getting it, and will still heal gradually, regardless of whether he remembers where it came from.

There is plenty of continuity in Leonard's experience of time, it's just that Leonard isn't able to gain access to what his body has experienced.

A Selective Physics?

One wild thing about dreams is that they can seem so continuous with waking experience (and ordinary time). We sometimes are unsure whether we are awake, a point that comes up a lot in *Inception*. The relation is even closer in lucid dreaming. Part of the reason for the continuity is that stuff from the waking world *does* seep into our dreams. Music especially has the power to retain its own form as it pervades and accompanies sleep. That's why music is the marker for our lucid dreamers at whatever level they are dreaming, and unlike the rest of the dreamscape, the music does not undergo time-expansion as it shoots down the levels of unconsciousness. Ten seconds of Edith Piaf music is still ten seconds, even at the third dream level, where time is radically expanded. As far as I can tell, even Edith can't get all the way to limbo. I am not sure why, but my guess is that there is not enough order to support the wave structure of sound.

The outside, the waking world, definitely gets into our dreams, whether or not it undergoes temporal expansion or transmogrification. What a great scene it was when Cobb was being awakened by a bathtub-dousing in one dream while water impossibly shoots into every opening of Saito's mountain fortress in the deeper dream. But water is still water from one dream level to another.

It raises a question—perhaps even a doubt. I've heard people say that the physics in *Inception* is "selective," and they elaborate by claiming that the gravitational effects that slosh over from Yusuf 's dream (the kidnapping/van/bridge) to Arthur's dream (the hotel) ought also to have carried over into Eames's dream (the snow-fortress).

I disagree. In fact, Nolan really has this right, in my view. But to make good on this claim, I'll have to drug you and take you on an airplane flight, or at least feed you something Italian. To see why, we have to understand time better.

The More Things Stay the Same . . .

Most philosophy depends on the way things stay the same, what persists through change. If you can't count it, it doesn't count. When we count things, we insist that they stay the same at least until we finish counting. But real things in the real world don't ever stay still. That makes most philosophy not so good at dealing with time and change.

But there is a type of philosophy that specializes in the nature of time called "process philosophy." Bergson, whom I mentioned numerous times earlier, is a "process philosopher," but the real "Christopher Nolan" of process philosophy is a guy named Alfred North Whitehead (1861–1947). He specialized in trying to understand change. Of necessity, process philosophers practice their arcane arts in the midst of change, since change is one of the main ingredients of every process. Remember I was riffing on ingredients earlier—I haven't forgotten, so you don't forget either.

"Change" is an ingredient of time. Nothing on Earth is wholly exempt from change (as far as we know), and you and me least of all, so it makes sense for us to try to understand change, to discern its patterns and meanings. But it isn't easy to get a grip on such a topic when nothing consents to sit still. The best you can do is to compare the things that change slowly to those that change more quickly.

Fortunately, understanding change is aided by two basic kinds of expression. The first is "narrative," learning to tell a kind of story we make up about what's happening, and the second is visualizing a whole series of changes as if they all existed at the *same* time (this is what traditional philosophy does), in a co-ordinated "space" created just for those changes, and adapted to our ways of envisioning changes all at once. You learned how to do this in grade school, when they taught you Cartesian coordinates, except in this case there are three axes, minimum (usually x, y, and z), and the each represent a continuous type of change.

The space defined by the axes consists at a minimum of eight open, three-dimensional spaces, above and below each axis (just imagine a cube, but with no beginning and no end), and a perspective on the whole can be situated "in" any of these, and holds a position relative to every possible space. This is pretty close to the way I am imagining Nolan's idea of dream space, except that he has Cobb tell Ariadne to close the space on itself so that things don't get out of hand.

That's pretty much what Whitehead does when he hypothesizes what he calls "the extensive continuum," which is defined as "the undivided divisible." A tough notion to get your head around, but just go slow: it's everything in the universe that could be divided, but hasn't been. Then Whitehead says, and hold onto your seat, "time" is the first division of the undivided divisible, and thus, every further division presupposes and includes the way time divides things. I know this is hard to think about, but if you liked *Inception*, you already bit into this apple. Now take the fall.

Delectations

That lasagna-looking image I brought up at the beginning is an example of such a co-ordinate "space." The "space" thing may sound fancy, but this is really just common sense. If you want to make dinner, say, lasagna, you need to be able to "see" what will be on your plate when dinner is made. The plate is the "space" you imagine, where your dinner will be, all together, existing at one time (and lasagna is a pretty complete meal, by the way, especially if you pack some veggies in, like fresh baby spinach, so if you just want to imagine that lasagna on the plate alone, be my guest, and include a little spinach sticking out from the edges—I mean, do that if you want to).

But this plate in your head right now isn't an actual plate, it's the image of a plate, and that plate-image is really just a virtual space. Since you do want dinner, eventually, and since dinner has to consist of *something*, you actively fill the plate-image with whatever other images you intend to see later, all stacked on the plate image, as the real cooked ingredients you will eat. The ingredients divide the plate relationally, in their diffusion through the food, while the lasagna itself and some veggies perhaps divide the plate actually, into visible places where the lasagna is and where it isn't, along with where the asparagus is and isn't, and so on.

You hear what I'm saying? I suggest the plate here, in my chapter, and *you* fill it with what *you* really want. Is this sounding familiar to you? Are you wondering why we would ever put our deepest secrets into the secret place someone else has constructed in our dreamworld?

It's coming to that, boys and girls, because we wouldn't do that, if we could help it. But nothing is quite as hard to resist as an empty space, imagined, real, or dreamt. You might never have thought of your dinner plate as an "imaginative space" before, but it is. The image provides an opportunity to co-ordinate the ingredients you'll have for dinner, which will require a process to change each of them from wherever they are, and whatever condition they are in, to the coordinated condition they will be in on your plate.

So you also need to be able to specify in your imagination the steps you will go through to acquire and prepare each item, and this will normally proceed from the present situation you now inhabit, and arrive in the imagined future, with the plate-image serving as the stopping place for that story, a narrative, which ends with "and then I ate it."

I Ate It

That statement, "I ate it" is what Whitehead calls a "generic contrast." It's "generic" because it is more "general" than either of the contrasting terms (I and it), and this is a contrast because the food is still "the food" and I am still "myself "(in the sentence "and then I ate it"), even though the food is sating my hunger and nourishing my body—which marks the change that has occurred.

Even though I and the lasagna were covariant, I varied less than did the dinner, which gives me fair claim to the nominative spot in the grammar of the contrast. The lasagna is just the object, the "it." If the lasagna should happen to eat me (as it might in a dream, after all), I'll be obliged to alter the grammar of my contrast. The point is that both my narrative about dinner and my imagined destiny for that narrative, the plate, are taken up into a higher level of generality—it's sort of a "kick," in Nolan's terms, because moving from one level of generalization to another actually involves traversing gaps in our thinking. It can be tough to follow the thread.

These sorts of imaginative spaces and narrative tales, like the tale of the lasagna and the plate and the "then I ate it," are extremely supple and elastic. You can arrange the narratives and vary the virtual spaces (in which the narratives end) almost infinitely without destroying their intelligibility and usefulness. Recognizing the relations between the narrative and the destined space, and how these are covariant, is the whole secret to thinking clearly about change, and kicking yourself from one level of generalization to another.

And there is a rule: the space is always more stable than the story it co-ordinates. That's why you can so easily go back and imagine the same image a second time and use it as a touchstone for telling your story. You do it absolutely all the time, but to take control of what you're doing, like Cobb and the lucid dream-invaders (and their puppet-master Nolan), to think lucidly (while not being too much at the mercy of your habits and your memory), is part of the value of process philosophy. I get the distinct impression that Michael Cain's character in *Inception* is more than a psychologist; I think he's probably a specialist in what is called "the philosophy of mind," which we have been examining now for most of three chapters.

Beyond Psychology

Whitehead says that philosophy is more closely akin to poetry than to science, and that the practice of philosophy, the discipline it requires, is very much that of learning to create spaces and tell stories that follow, well, not the order and demands of pure expression, as poetry does, but those of possible patterns of order. If this discipline sounds a little like a Christopher Nolan movie to you, well, that's how it sounds to me too. And the kinds of order and stories that philosophy specializes in creating, in spite of our poetic proclivities, are basically mathematical.

Our philosophical spaces are geometric and our narratives are algebraic. We don't just make up narratives and fanciful spaces in doing philosophy. Rather, we explore highly ordered possibilities and collections and clusters of possibilities as suggested by logical and mathematical kinds of order. It's more fun than it sounds. I'll try to prove it. There are three basic ways we do this.

1. We reason from what is actual to other things that were, are, or will be actual. This is called "assertoric" thinking, mainly because it's for assholes.

2. We reason from what is, was or will be actual to what is possible. This is called "problematic" thinking, because it starts with real problems and considers possible solutions.

3. We reason from what is possible in principle back toward what is, was, or will be actual. This is called "hypothetical" thinking. It is for process philosophers and others who see what is actual as just a contingent example of what might have been or might be. Science fiction (as I will discuss in some detail in the final chapter) is an example of the style of thinking and the logic we call "hypothetical."

Nolan's *Inception* has elements of science fiction, but its closeness to actual present-day experience, to human psychology, to human limitations as we currently understand them, suggests that its logic is problematization more than hypothetical. That matters when it comes to answering questions about the movie. Not just anything goes in this story. It is supposed to feel "actualist," although we have a difficult time holding it into the actual as we understand it. But that is what he is going for: "given everything you know, isn't this a genuine problem? This inception idea is believable, no?" It is the psychology that holds us close.

Time Won't Give Me Time

You have all probably suffered though quadratic equations—if a train leaves from Boston and another from Chicago, . . . and so on—but you might never have seen them as a sort of story, or narrative, at bottom. It usually isn't a very interesting story, but that's because it's stripped down for the purposes of exhibiting some of the patterns of order implicit in all such "stories." I know this is a dated example, but if I were to add that Kanye West is on the Boston train and Taylor Swift is on the Chicago train, just to spice it up (and speaking of spices, sea salt and marjoram), and I expect you to tell me at what time he interrupts her, it might make the story a little more interesting, but it doesn't really change the mathematical aspects.

If I say that the elapsed time from Chicago is exactly the amount of time you should bake lasagna at four hundred degrees, you would curse me for adding a second variable, wouldn't you? Even if I said that is the exact time to Toledo at the speed I'm thinking of? But there's a solution, or at least a set of possible solutions, and you know that much. *Why* is there a solution?

All narratives, and I mean *all*, exhibit algebraic order, including those written and directed by Christopher Nolan, because all temporal processes possess that kind of order. That's why we use various kinds of algebra to describe the general features of covariant change. In fact, your ability to understand a story, to follow it, *depends* on this kind of order—it need not be explicit (fortunately, since you may suck at math), but the reason you know the difference between a story that makes sense and one that doesn't is because the algebraic order is already implicit in your own life processes, including your thinking (which is one of your life processes).

Narrative is about time, how it passes and what you can do with it—the way time makes available to us our possibilities (variables) for action. Nolan may press the boundaries of our ability to make sense of his stories, but he does insist, as he must, on coherence in his narratives. And that is why he can't really hide the answer to the question about whether the top tumbles, as you will see if you can stay with me a little longer. And when we have the answer to that riddle, we also will know whether this was all Cobb's dream.

But I want to point out that Nolan's physics is consistent, because with each move to a deeper dream level, the same "amount" of time, the same five minutes, is dispersed over a larger total dreamspace (the city plus the hotel, plus the fortress, and so on), and that dispersal not only dilutes the effects of gravity, it also creates a numerical progression (it isn't geometrical, but why should it be?) of time expansions: in the fan-o-sphere, the consensus is that the expansion is a ratio of 20:1, at least where the sedative is "strong." It may be 12:1 on a "normal" sedative. The exact math doesn't matter so long as Cobb knows how to calculate the "kicks" at each level, which he does several times. It's algebra, by the way; with all the variables that satisfy the equation being factors of the ratio 20:1. Fill in an amount of time at any level, and put it through the formula, and of course one must remember that the progression is not a regular progression because the ratio of seconds to minutes and minutes to hours is 60:1, and the ratio of hours to days is 24:1, and the ratio of days to years is 365.25:1. So you have to express your expansion in minutes of hours and then convert it to days and years.

If you picture those times all at once, in an image, it becomes a kind of space with its peculiar geometry, but if you want to express the time-pattern upon which the visualization of that image depends, it's algebraic. How does algebra become space?

Wide Open Spaces

You've been through geometry class, I'm sure, and you had to "describe" (mathematically) the necessary and invariant features of pure spatial forms—because that's what they make you do in geometry class. But you might never have considered those lovely "pure spatial forms" as imaginative *places* you might arrive at by telling the right kind of story, or as ways of coordinating all the elements of the story. (That's because you needed a more imaginative geometry teacher than you probably got.)

Geometry is really about space and the ways we can think about it (and remember, thinking is a kind of imagining), but space has far more richness to it than its Euclidian structure. You were being taught about very simple and totally boring spaces in geometry class. Now might be a good moment for me to suggest that you check out an old story (1884) by Edwin

Abbott called *Flatland*. You can get the full text by googling it. This is the geometry teacher you wish you'd had.

I should also mention that when you're rolling out your own pasta, the closer to absolute flatness you get it, the better, and the trick to that is to 1. keep the surface utterly dry and well sprinkled with flour and 2. use only fresh, room-temperature eggs and no water, and 3. don't be in a hurry. But unlike, say, linguine, which can be cooked without drying it, the geometry of a baked lasagna depends upon drying the (very flat) pasta on a rippled board for at least a day (in dream time, that's more than a week); that will give it a three-dimensional geometry and creates space for things like baby spinach, feta cheese, and a very lean organic ground beef, browned in a pan for just a few minutes (keep the drippings and add those to the 4.5 ounces of tomato paste and sixteen ounces of fresh chopped tomatoes).

How rich is space? Well, it's exactly as rich as time is varied, and the reason is simple, and I am going to say this twice and then pause for a moment while you consider it—to let it rise, so to speak. Imagined space is the destiny of imagined time.

Just as the plate is the destiny of your narrative about preparing dinner, any—and indeed every—space just is the destiny of some time process. Indeed, when it comes to our imaginative lives, space is frozen time. (But don't freeze your pasta, just wrap it in some Saran Wrap and let it sit for half an hour, kneading it through the wrap every five minutes or so to raise its temperature above that of the room.)

Now wait a minute. Space is frozen time? Yes, that's what I said. If you want to understand something, narrate it until you have all the elements, or all the ingredients, well described, and how they should be combined, and then consider the end result as a frozen picture in which they are all together at the same time. That last "all-together-now" is the space that was always the destiny of your narrative. The study of that space is your very own new geometry. It is also a space that could be divided into three or more axes for a coordinate analysis.

You're Waiting for a Train

Mathematical order, then, comes in those two forms, narrative and spatial. In my example above I asked: at what time does Kanye interrupt Taylor? Now that's an algebraic question about an algebraic relation. I could have asked "where are they when he interrupts her?" (It's only Toledo if you're looking for the baking time). The "where" would be a geometric question about an algebraic relation, and it coordinates as an image everything it took to get them both there.

You can sort of feel it happening—you're waiting for that train (keep your head off the tracks), and you feel those trains converging, you see the train tracks, don't you? And have you ever asked yourself why Cobb and Mal choose to commit suicide in limbo by putting their heads on the railroad tracks and summoning a train? Why not use Cobb's gun? Why not jump from a skyscraper, as Ariadne does? Why the tracks? And why do they keep repeating "You're waiting for a train"? Hold that thought.

Where are we? You know that at any place along that track, Kanye and Taylor could meet, the Cobb and Mal of pop music, depending on their individual speeds, and now you're just waiting for me to say "Cleveland, in time for dinner" and when I do, not only will you be able to calculate how fast each train had to be travelling—that's the time issue. You are also picturing a real place, say, Cleveland (even if you haven't been there), and ignoring the fact that it was a geometric "at-the-same-timeness" that enabled you to proceed with your algebraic calculation.

"At the same time" just is the meaning of space. Space comes from time and depends on time. Space is *created* by variable time. And I must tell you that it really is Cleveland where they meet because I know the best restaurant there, on Euclid Avenue, where they have an incredible lasagna (veggie version available, but not nearly as tasty), and Kanye and Taylor definitely ought to meet there, as should Leo DiCaprio and Marion Cotillard, even though they'll all need a taxi from the train station (where they arrive at about 5:30, give or take, since it's Amtrak).

If you want to understand something, incisively and accurately, you have to be able to tell the story that ends in and *is* co-ordinated by the right kind of space. One of those axes can be space, the z axis, but the x is experienced time and the y is clock time. Relations of x to y are strictly algebraic (this includes calculus, which is algebraic), and only taken together can we locate any event on z —at least if our reasoning is problematic, rather than assertoric or hypothetical. Assertoric reasoning treats everything spatially. If we want to reason hypothetically, we can put space first, which is what most science does. Science fiction does too.

When we're philosophizing, we may work in any of these three logics, but problematic reasoning keeps us close to experience, and to stable shared space, while inviting imagination to furnish images. We're looking for the more variable features of the story against the backdrop of the features that vary less, and if we have chosen the best ingredients to compare, the dinner plate is filled with a most edible meal, so to speak, the intellectual lasagna of your dreams. The generic contrast is "achieved" ("and then I ate it") because the higher level of generality in which the contrasting things can co-exist is a space of some kind. Hypothetical thinking does not place such constraints on imagination in advance. Assertoric thinking seeks to eliminate imagination.

What I am now prepared to offer is the thought you have been wanting to think all along, about the movie you liked well enough to read this far.

The Secret Ingredient

My man Whitehead has a lot of specialized vocabulary to describe this method of narrative and space in all of its subtleties, and his descriptions are, to his admirers, a perfect poetry of creative, reflective imagination. His system is hypothetical, working its way from a possible coordinate whole to the actual occasion which is a genuine perspective on the whole of reality. But we don't need all that vocabulary for now.

Yet, I have to add the disclaimer that I have already created the narrative and the space in which it ends, and my choices are filled with contingencies, and configured by imagination. This chapter is problematic in form because the actual movie poses problems that I can't just make up, and I can't just suggest answers that are not close to the narrative Nolan wrote and directed.

With different choices at any stage along the way in my problematizing of the movie, the imaginative space that can be created could be similar, but not wholly consistent with what I will conclude. My conclusion, the part that says, "And then I ate it," should seem persuasive to you, at least if I compare the best factors during the narrative, and find those that interact dynamically and fruitfully. Then my story will increase the value of your life, regardless of whether you agree with it.

That is what generic contrasts are. They are "accretions of value." We think, imagine, understand, and express our ideas all for the sake of creating value. The accretion of value is the possibility that continuously lures us into action, and *thinking* is an action. That movie lured you into thinking. I *know* you've been thinking about that damned movie ever since you first saw it. Who can resist?

Is there an end to it? I'm aiming to bring that about. You have my promise that I'm sincere about adding to the value of your world in saying what I do say about this film. I love this film and I think it's important. Some of what I say may surprise and even provoke you, but when I'm finished, you'll be thinking about the future and you'll be trying to tell a story to yourself that puts you there in an imagined space you have created yourself.

Oh, and one last thing. Use semola for your pasta, not semolina. As my Italian cooking instructor once said "semolina is just a Toyota, semola is the Cadillac." Semola is the secret ingredient. Or so I believe. Since the pasta is time, and the cheese is just a melting dream, get time right, whatever else you do.

Mind the Gap

I love the voice on the London subway that says, oh so seductively, "Mind the gap" as you step off the train onto the platform. Nolan has devilishly concealed the answer to the main riddle, but it's there, actually in plain sight—and it's there because he's a great storyteller.

His plate is full, but you have to read it backwards, as a geometry, before the algebra will make sense. You were served the story and the movie fully cooked, already garnish and all. And there's always a clue. Follow the gaps. There are lots of gaps in this story, as there are in any story—just as when Arthur is showing Ariadne the Penrose stairs, even in a dream there will be gaps that can be concealed from those who only half-consciously consumed the lasagna you serve them. But if you're smart, you can learn to see those gaps.

Three gaps will help you find your way to the truth about the spinning totem, and hence, about whether this is all Cobb's dream, so let me offer you three kicks to see if I can get you there.

First Kick

The first gap is a very obvious one, if you're paying attention. It's the conversation between Saito, Arthur, and Cobb—the "Don't think of an elephant" line, a conversation in which we're led to believe that "inception" is almost impossible. The reason we're given is that even though an idea is the most contagious virus there is, we can always trace the origin of an idea if it comes from outside ourselves. This provides the entire motive for attempting inception.

But it simply isn't true that we can always trace the origins of our ideas when they come from beyond ourselves. And when those ideas are reduced to archetypes, as suggested in this movie, we can't trace them in principle. They derive from the shared experience of the whole human race. Do they *belong* to the whole race? To life itself? We don't know. And we never will.

So why, pray tell, is Nolan so quickly passing over such a knotty contradiction: ideas are super contagious, but it's devilish hard to plant one without the subject knowing it? The truth is, as you very well know, nothing is easier to plant than an idea, and the process by which it was planted can be spread out over many experiences, and you can't always trace it, no matter how smart you are. Experience is too complex and too discontinuous.

If I wanted you to be hungry for lasagna, I could even spread a recipe for it across an essay about a movie, if I had a mind to do so. And if you should find yourself wanting lasagna a year from now, long after you've forgotten reading this chapter, who's to say whether I succeeded as an "inceiver," and whether you are my very own Robert Fischer?

If you find yourself thinking, next time you're in Cleveland, "What about Euclid Avenue? I heard of a place there." Well, you get the picture (and a "picture" is exactly what it is). I give my willing suspension of disbelief to Nolan when he sets up the story, but I remember thinking the first time I heard it that you can't say "an idea is the most viral thing we know" and then pretend it's nearly impossible to give one to somebody without their being able to trace it with perfect clarity. Yes, as I said, maybe it's more *persuasive* if you can't trace it, but that is a different matter. That's not what Arthur and Cobb say, and it wouldn't make for a compelling story if they did say it. We would use easier means of persuasion.

It's a serious gap in the story—a gap in the narrative and its believability. If we move forward with the narrative after that weird moment, it's because we accept a generic contrast: "he needs this for the story."

Second Kick

That brings us to the second gap. You know this, but you may not have seen its importance. The spinning top is not *Cobb's* totem. It belonged to Mal. It's never stated anywhere in the story that the top is Cobb's totem. That's an inference you probably made (and were encouraged to make) across a gap in the narrative. And you thought that the rule Cobb had made, privately, with himself, was that if it doesn't fall, he is dreaming.

But no one ever says this or anything like it in the movie. What you saw was the top falling and Cobb deciding not to shoot himself. That's all you saw. Why did you assume the top's falling was the *reason* Cobb took the gun down from his head? Because you were strongly encouraged to make that jump and it was reinforced a number of times later.

But that, boys and girls, is cottage cheese from the grocery store, and I am going to encourage you to hold out for feta from the Old Country, and by making it this far in my discussion, you've had time to order and receive the good stuff. Hold on, because here comes the supersecret ingredient.

A gap is a gap. We're not at all *forced* to think that Cobb decided not to kill himself because the top fell. The spinning of the top for Cobb is a way of remembering Mal, it is a kind of mourning, not a test to see whether Cobb is dreaming. He knew he wasn't dreaming. He was just pondering whether to kill himself and didn't have the nerve.

Cobb is actually a coward and he knows it, with nothing like the courage of Mal or Ariadne, or anyone else who is capable of truly trusting another human being, for that matter. The reason he didn't wake up when Mal did is that he didn't leave his head on the track when they summoned the train in limbo. He didn't have the courage to shoot himself when he found Saito as an old man. Saito shoots Cobb and then himself. We don't see it, but Saito has the gun and they both wake up on the plane.

The script makes it crystal clear that the top was Mal's totem. When Cobb and Mal took their long nap together (and notice, there is no machine connecting them when she wakes up), and when she built her safe in her childhood home, it was empty, as are all dreamsafes. There is no reason to believe she preferred the dreamworld to waking life. That is never said explicitly. We infer it. Who is the architect of the dream that landed them in limbo? We are told that they built their city "together," and of course, that is the problem. Shared architecture. Cobb says he does not want to study Ariadne's architecture. He's got a rather negative past with joint building projects.

But Mal was an able architect. Why did they end up laying their heads on the railroad tracks? Something happened to Mal to plant a doubt; she could no longer rely on her totem because Cobb created a duplicate and put it in the safe. She found it there precisely because they were co-architects, sharing everything. And she could no longer distinguish the dream from reality. She doubted whether she could wake up. The reason this happened to her is because Cobb had broken the trust and had handled her totem, and he had done it while they were awake. He wanted to control her because he didn't trust her. He betrayed her. He may even have planned to trap her in the dream, she'll never know.

In any case, he was the one who wanted (at some level) the dream to last forever (and in a way, it did). So he disabled her ability to return to the real world by memorizing her totem, and then he broke into her safe, and she was completely in his power. Or at least, that was the plan. It is an interesting kind of betrayal, and it actually poses the same uncomfortable question as *The Stepford Wives*, which is, If you could render your wife utterly subservient, would you do it?

The answer is always no, if you are an even remotely decent person, because to do that is to sacrifice all your lover's "complexities" as Cobb puts it, all her "perfections" and "imperfections." Once Cobb had trapped her, he saw it was a terrible mistake, but he couldn't undo it, and he couldn't set it right within the dream. So he confessed and she had to trust him—take a leap of faith—that they really were (or weren't) dreaming.

And being an individual, an autonomous being, she didn't want to be required to trust him in that way. That's why she's afraid and he isn't when they lay their heads on the tracks. He knows they're dreaming, and she's helpless to learn on her own whether he's telling her the truth, and he has betrayed her once already. He had already done something that rendered her completely helpless, and a man who would do that to you has already killed you.

So, to atone, he lays his head on the tracks with her. As you know, she wakes up, he doesn't. Why does Mal keep showing up in his dreams? Over-active sub-conscious? Not at all. She is coming from waking life and trying to wake him up. She knows he believes he is awake, or as awake as he wants to be. She tries numerous ploys to get him to kill himself. None works. She can't rescue him. He just isn't trusting enough to take the leap. She tells him how ridiculous his dream is, corporate raiders chasing him all over the place, and never do we find out how he got into his own labyrinth. That's a clue too.

Now you know why Cobb is so deeply haunted by the moment when he spun Mal's top in the safe. Of course, Cobb had no business in Mal's safe, any more than you have any business poking around in your lover's old letters (or secret recipes). Yes, you share life, and home, and (a key point) children, but ultimately, we must leave to our lovers their deepest autonomy. In the dreamscape they built together, Cobb says clearly that Mal recreated the house she grew up in.

So even though Mal built that house in their common dream, Cobb is the one who put the top in it—or rather, he filled the safe with the very thing he most desperately desired but (perhaps) could not admit to himself, consciously. I'm giving him the benefit of the doubt here, but when he opened the safe (he is, after all, a professional thief) he saw the top because his mind *wanted* it to be there, as he well knew, or even worse, he planned the whole thing, but either way it's very bad news. To spin it and close the safe, well, it symbolizes his desire for total power over her. Only a coward needs that kind of power over another person.

Ariadne (Cobb's true sub-conscious), by the way, immediately gets all of this, after just one shared dream (she's a quick study), and she knows exactly how damaged Cobb is and what kind of man he is. But he has no intention of trusting her, so she's no threat, but it is a clue Nolan gives us: if she is Ariadne, he must be Theseus, but the roles are reversed. He is trapped in the labyrinth and she decides she will decline the job of rescuing him.

Why? He's a man who, down deep, desires complete control over others, and especially over those who are closest to him. He is a Stepford husband. That's why Ariadne tries to walk away. That is also why Mal is so very pissed off when she visits; the superego is a harsh, harsh mistress. A question, Mal's question: would you make a safe for your lover to fill with whatever he or she most deeply desires, even knowing that the person you love probably can't know or admit what he would put in that safe, given the chance? Mal is a brave one, isn't she? Assuming she made the safe in her childhood house.

Last Kick

And that brings us to the final gap. I've kept you long enough. The biggest jump in the whole movie is when Cobb and Saito (perhaps) manage to come back from limbo all the way up to the airplane. We do not see the fifty years that pass while Saito is lost, but we assume he has built his mountain fortress and posted his guards. Cobb is searching for Saito, but note that he is still young when he finds Saito, even though they speak as if they are both old. Cobb has learned his lesson about trust, by the end, but he is still a coward. But why is he still the same age? Wait for it.

But note, the children remain the same age through the whole movie. Given what we have been told, Cobb has been on the run for at least a couple of years. They simply cannot be the same as when he left the house to avoid arrest. Arrested for what? For killing their mother. And who can fix this problem? Saito. Why? Because Saito has power? Influence? A desire for world peace? No. Because Saito cannot be deceived. He is the symbol of the truth Cobb knows but won't admit, a truth he kills and tries to hide in the center of a mountain fortress. And there the truth grows old, like the picture of Dorian Grey.

Cobb, in the words of "Old Man River," is sick of living and scared of dying, but Saito, he must know something, but don't say nothing. Being given a second chance to trust, he will not make the same mistake a second time. He chooses to take the leap of faith with Saito, because without trusting somebody, he can never be shed of the weariness of the nightmare from which he is trying to awake. Taking the measure of Saito's character, Cobb decides Saito is an ordinary man, no saint, no villain, and ordinarily self-interested, but a man who does have wisdom. Saito's wisdom comes in his willingness to trust Cobb even though he knows very well that Cobb isn't trustworthy.

Cobb's dilemma is simple. Trust Saito, absolutely, or have a life that isn't worth living. Cobb chooses to trust Saito, it appears. Saito believes Cobb is self-interested enough, but also good enough, to be trusted. Saito is right. There is a crucial moment, by the way, when Cobb drops Mal's top in front of Saito, and Saito sees it but does not touch it.

When Cobb washes up on the shore of Saito's mountain fortress-palace fifty (dream) years later, he has two and only two things on his person: his gun and Mal's top. These are placed before the ancient Saito, and Cobb asks him to choose, to take a leap of faith with him. The next thing we know, they wake up on the plane. That's the gap.

What Happened?

It's so simple it's painful. Saito didn't just spin the top. He also shot Cobb and then shot himself. (That's why Cobb woke up seconds before Saito.) This is what Cobb was asking him to do, because Cobb himself didn't have the courage to do it, but he was willing to trust Saito to *follow* him.

Here's your kick: *The gun is Cobb's totem.* He doesn't let anyone else touch it in the movie—it's heavy, unique, and so forth. Why would anyone choose a gun for a totem? It's simple. Cobb decided that if he should ever come to the point that he could not distinguish dream from reality, he would rather not go on living. *Either way*, if he puts the gun to his head and pulls the trigger, he ends the trouble. For a coward, a safer totem cannot be imagined (unless your chemist has supercharged the serum). In the crucial moment, he gives it to Saito and trusts him to do the "right thing." And Saito doesn't disappoint him. So the gun in the first act really does go off in the third, and Nolan uses sleight-of-hand to keep you from noticing.

Does the Totem Tumble?

And finally we are at the answer to the question with which we began. It *doesn't matter*. Cobb's totem is back on the airplane. Remember, Saito bought the plane to get around Australian airport security, but Cobb cannot hope to get off in LA with a gun on his person and still get through security there. He knew when he got on the plane that he would lose his totem. He left his gun on the plane, along with his desire to, or need to commit suicide. He has been suicidal for years. How long? It's hard to say, since we don't have a waking reality with which to contrast Cobb's dream.

It actually doesn't matter whether the totem falls because it's Mal's totem. The only issue is whether she will ever succeed in waking him up, and that we don't find out. If the top tumbles, she succeeds; if it keeps spinning she gives up. But Cobb has made the decision not to wake up. He prefers the dream. The top isn't a symbol of whether this is dream or reality, but rather a sign of whether Cobb has changed in the relevant way. In a way, yes. He has learned to trust and is now fit to raise those lovely dream children. In a way, no. He isn't brave enough to face waking life. He is lost to the waking world. His struggle for sanity is over.

Cobb "lives" without his own totem and walks away from Mal's. She may not come back. Probably not. He has a future, but it's in the first level of the dream. He would need one more kick, but he has relinquished the links that make it possible. He doesn't want to wake up. And he's ok with that choice.

You ponder that, I'm going to get some good feta cheese. I have a lasagna to make. I do wonder what the goats of Umbria eat, but since feta requires both sheep's and goat's milk, and since it only comes from Greece, I don't need to go to Umbria. (I'm sorry about the quadratic equation on the cooking time, but you could just turn on the oven light and eyeball it—I mean, do I have to do everything for you?)

Part IV

Director's Cut

15
To Serve Man

A Visit to *The Twilight Zone*

We've been on a long, strange trip through the movies and the various branches of philosophy. We have looked at movies and TV series from pretty much every decade and era in the history of this cultural form, the movies, broadly understood, at least since the advent of talkies. We have entered into the stories, the characters, the sources, the writers and adapters, the performers, and with greater emphasis, the principal creators (that is the directors) of this cultural movement. We have used its effects, both within the film and on us, to get inside the truths and lies we are told in moving images.

We have also covered a wide range of philosophy and philosophers, from Socrates and Plato through twentieth century icons like Heidegger and Whitehead. We have looked at the method of phenomenology in some detail. We have touched on all of the main branches of philosophy—the practical branches, ethics, aesthetics and political philosophy; and the theoretical branches, metaphysics, theory of knowledge (epistemology), and to a limited extent, logic. These last two will be on display in this chapter. Altogether a fairly broad swath.

There is no doubt, at this point, about the philosophical character of the movies. They definitely show us philosophical ideas in many ways at many levels. But what we have not really done is to discuss the cultural impact and value of the movies. That topic deserves its own book, but many others have written on it. But I think there is an aspect of this topic that nobody before me has framed quite the way I want to do it. I want to bring all of the branches of philosophy and the value of the movies under one method. One thing that is great about doing philosophy is that you are allowed to create new methods for doing it. If what you suggest works (if people find it valuable for their own thinking), hey, you won the game.

I have always been impressed by the way that the movies and television have shaped our attitudes and values. There is no question in my mind that these art forms have made us better people. They are our moral teachers, and the vast majority of the shows we watch do aim at our moral improvement, and the makers realize that entertaining us is one lure for improving us. The movies make us think and they sensitize us to important issues and they inform us about oppression, in history and in the present.

But most importantly, the movies seek both to conserve and re-interpret the past, to critique the present, and to foresee and form the future. The last of these is the most important. In fact, the very reason the movies re-tell the past and critique the present is for the sake of the future. Sometimes, however, shaping the future is pretty much the whole aim of the movie—its story, its characters, its production values. No movies do this "future-shaping" better than the science-fiction genre. Let's close our inquiry with a serious look at what science fiction does and how it does it. I was seriously tempted to choose some or one of the adaptations of stories by Philip K. Dick or Robert Heinlein that found their way to the screen, but in the end, I decided that those guys were, in essence, literary teachers, not indigenous artists of the screen.

It's also hard to imagine a more powerful series than *Black Mirror*. But the more I thought about it, the more I realized that what *Black Mirror* does so well is exactly what *The Twilight Zone* did. And we don't have much historical distance on *Black Mirror* to get a sense of whether it has succeeded in shaping the future. So I chose an *auteur* who really saw how the screen might make us better, and how we really were, and historical distance helps in seeing this thing for what it is. Did Rod Serling help us avoid a nuclear holocaust? Maybe. There is no doubt that he tried. We will never know. But I remember why his stories frightened me, and I think they made me a better person. Let's look at his remarkable work.

Science Fiction Double Feature

First a word about what science fiction is and is not. I know you know this, but humor me. Most people date the birth of the genre to Mary Shelley's *Frankenstein, or The Modern Prometheus* (1818). Heaven knows Hollywood hasn't been able to leave *that* story alone. One can see the genre grow through the American dark romantics, Hawthorne, Poe, Melville, and other post-Romantics, Jules Verne, Robert Louis Stevenson, H.G. Wells. The overlap with what we now call horror, and fantasy, along with thrillers, suspense, and adventure is ever present.

But what makes a movie (or a story) science fiction is that it begins in some actual, historical place that really happened/existed, and it uses the science and technology that existed then as a starting point for its morality tale (and it always is a morality tale in real science fiction). Very often this "actual starting point has been projected into the near or distant future from the actual present of the writer.

So, *Star Trek* is set three hundred years, give or take, in the future, but their history is *our* actual history; they just have three-hundred more years of it than we have yet lived. Sometimes we set that "actual time" backward, and re-tell the story up to what would be our present, but now it's different, as with Stephen King's *11/22/63*, or even the series of movies and shows based on the *Bill and Ted* characters, or the *Back to the Future* series.

The presupposition of the genre is that scientific and technological advances are the engines of culture, social relation, political relations, legal relations, and so forth. Knowledge is usually held in the highest regard, but it always seems to get us in trouble, a panoply of Faustian bargains we make, and then some sort of reckoning. We moderns love the form. It combines, philosophically, the philosophy of science and technology with the philosophy of history, and takes a narrative form, so philosophy of literature. These are combined in an art form, so philosophy of art and aesthetics, and ethical and political questions, sometimes even religious questions, are the plot motors.

When these all come together, we really have two subdisciplines of philosophy presiding, and these are metaphysics (especially as regards possibility), and the philosophy of culture, which absorbs all the other subdisciplines I listed *as cultural forms*. In the same way that the movies absorb all the artforms and use them, the philosophy of culture absorbs all the regions of philosophy and treats them as expressions of culture. So, for example, the philosophy of religion is an important field of study, but for the philosophy of culture, the philosophy of religion, along with religion itself and everything associated with it, belongs to religion as a cultural form. The same for science, law, art, politics, and so on.

The Future and the Past: Constellations and Clusters

Popular culture is also a vital part of the philosophy of culture. Obviously, movies are a part of popular culture as well as a fine art. But I am the sort of philosopher who exercises the popular culture muscle for the sake of its value to a larger philosophy of culture. People with the good fortune to be paid to make up philosophical stuff (people like me) should be grateful to people who read it. And we are. As with science fiction, ultimately it's about trying to *learn something* and we do *that* for the sake of becoming better people.

Anywhere there are people, philosophy comes up—just as poetry and art and the all the other things that make us human and that make *being human* a rich adventure. One might think of philosophers of culture as those who are committed to keeping philosophy in the closest possible touch with what is happening in the world of the day-to-day, the people going about the business of being human. We create all sorts of things to amuse ourselves, to serve our higher and lower desires, to heal as well as to kill each other, and to deal in exchange of all sorts.

Immersion in the world of popular culture provides an immanent understanding, and after all, some of what is merely popular culture today will be the high culture of tomorrow. The genre of science fiction (and here I do not include the genre called "fantasy," which I discussed earlier in this book) has been widely recognized as being one of the more important and durable forms of cultural and social (and even religious) criticism.

Depending upon plausible analogies that depart from a present time we recognize, these narratives guide our imaginations into the relation between the might-be and the might-have-been. Plenty has been written about this, but as far as I know, no one has used its imaginative devices to develop a *method* for doing the philosophy of culture. Such is my aim here in talking about science fiction.

The basic structure I will offer here, for your consideration, as Rod Serling might say, examines the logic, metaphysics, and modeling of *possibility*. This really isn't the philosophy of culture, it's pure metaphysics. But science fiction loves possibility, so it's hard to avoid metaphysics and logic. The central idea is that possibilities have an existence that is *intelligible* to us, independent of present actualities. A part of that structure involves a distinction between "constellated possibilities" which form a pattern dependent upon one's perspective in some actual standpoint (in the present or past), and "clustered" possibilities, which actually exist entangled within themselves and are inseparable from one another (whether present, past, or future).

In this second case, we can get predictions of the future by understanding this: in seeking and attaining one or a few of the "clustered" possibilities, we will get all the rest of that cluster in the bargain. So, if you start a war for some very good reason, you get everything that goes with war (the refugees, the civilian casualties, the snowballing costs, the reconstruction costs, the ethical and legal dilemmas, the prisoners, the intermarriage between soldier and the civilians in occupied territories, and the list is very long. The cluster of possibilities associated with war is a "hard" cluster—there are not many soft possibilities in that cluster. You start a war, you get the whole cluster.

Clustering possibilities means that we can pretty clearly prognosticate future events. This foreknowledge does not happen in the case of merely "constellated" possibilities. Obviously, I am borrowing the terms from star constellations, which form patterns from one's standpoint on Earth (or some other planet), and star "clusters," which are stars that actually exist in close proximity and hence are seen together regardless of where one stands. The opening sequence of *Twilight Zone* often passes through constellated stars, and objects. They seem randomly arranged. But there is a center, and that is always Rod Serling, the narrator. The action unfolds from his point of view, and you are invited to share it. He tells stories not of what is, was, or will be, but what might have been and might be, *only*. No claim to factuality is ever made. I am suggesting that possibilities *really* have this same structure, when they are just constellated.

But when possibilities are clustered, we start to see that some things just bring other things with them, inevitably. Science-fiction writers are not usually explicit about this distinction. But intuitively they all know that if we introduce a variation into the present in order to trace a plausible alternative storyline from that standpoint, certain other variations will have to accompany the chosen variation in order to maintain the unity of the plot.

For example, if people have numbers rather than names in our future, there must be an imagined line of narration from when they had names to the replacement of these with numbers. If they have always only had numbers, it is fantasy rather than science fiction, and the rules are looser, but there are still rules, like the unity of action. Fantasy can suppose its own worlds, which may include our actual world, but need not. Science fiction is always taking its departure from our actual world. Hence, science fiction and even fantasy writers do work with clusters as well as constellations of possibilities, and they experience the clusters with a stronger feeling of necessity.

Duty Now for the Future

I want to develop this distinction between constellations and clusters of possibilities into a method for doing philosophy in what follows. It will combine everything I did up to now in this book, and, I hope, in way that makes us all better people. One does not have to limit this kind of investigation to science fiction, of course, but the features and implications of this difference between clustered and constellated possibilities appears in science fiction in the clearest fashion. Why do we project futures that we don't really believe will happen? The main aims seem to be warn, to educate, and to affirm that imagination can be an incredibly powerful tool in making things both better and worse.

Plausible Stories

The US television series *The Twilight Zone* is one example of the move from popular to high culture, and obviously spans the whole genre of science fiction. The series both encapsulated and projected the culture of mid-century America, adding variations (often alien visitation). It is easy to recognize now that these writers and directors and actors were able to get to the beating heart of the Cold War. They showed us the soft, lily-white underbelly of our bellicose dorsal, which was a people afraid of anything and everything.

The mind of one master storyteller, Rod Serling, and a team of writers and directors, seized upon this softness and began to poke, prod, and occasionally to stab until the Americans saw themselves in the mirror. But the mirror was usually displaced in time and place in a way that protected the viewers—the increasing millions of them—from having to draw straight lines from the depictions to themselves.

The art of displacement, and, if I may coin a word, "distemporalizing," is central to the philosophy of culture, especially insofar as narration is involved. To tell the story of one group of people, at a place and time, and to see the analogies to one's own place and time is the basic gesture. It is a kind of *Wirkungsgeschiche*, or "effective history," to use Hans-Georg Gadamer's term, getting our predilection for history to do some valuable (moral) work in the present. Gadamer (1900–2002) said we had to *interpret* the past in order to understand the present. Some folks are better at that than others.

I would add to Gadamer's idea *Wirkungsschiksal*, if I may be allowed to invent a word in a second language.[1] The Germans don't have this word, but they need it. (How arrogant am I? Good luck with that.) The term *Schicksal* is usually translated as 'fate' in English, but that is not quite the sense of it. It is a participial expansion of the verb *schicken*, 'to send', and so carries the sense of 'sending from the future'. The word 'destiny' is really better. Fate is too deterministic, while destiny is merely a teleological (goal-oriented) tendency. *Wirkung* gets translated as 'real', and having to do with 'reality' usually, but the word means *wirken*, 'to work', in the sense of 'to effectuate'. So *Wirkungsschicksal* is 'effective destining'. Sounds better in German, if you want *gravitas*.

One could have, for example, a machine that works (does the job) or a *narrative* that is "real" or "effective destining," *Wirkungsschicksal*: a narrative formed in the present that bears upon our futural *protention* (future intention), individually and collectively, in the way "effective history" bears upon the *retention* of the past in the present. In effective history we tell a story about the past in order to change the future; in effective destining, we tell a story about the future in order to alter our destiny.

That is the sort of analogy I have in mind for the narrative that follows. It is also, in my view, what Rod Serling did, over and over, episode by episode. Let us displace, distemporalize, and narrate, with Serling. This is our method: *Wirkungsschiksal*. What does such a method produce? And how? I will explain, by illustration, and then by explanation.

Apéritif

Respectfully submitted for your perusal: The time is late February 1962. Soon, very soon, your Emmy-winning brainchild will come to an end. You are the creator, host, and chief writer for a weekly science-fiction television show, and frankly, you are tapped out. You need a few more story ideas to make it through to the end of your contract and then, you tell yourself, you wilteach talented college students back home in Ohio. So you

---

[1]   I thank my friend and colleague Godehard Bruüntrup for helping me understand what the German language will and will not tolerate in creating such a neologism. He is, of course, not responsible for the things I plan to do with this word.

ransack the last fifteen years' worth of obscure sci-fi pulp, and there it is. *Galaxy Science Fiction* magazine, November issue, 1950.

Morsels: Short Stories, Etc.

Mr. Poe popularized the short story in the US, but truth be told, it was never that popular. People do not buy collections of short stories (with a few Poe-like exceptions). Magazines publish them for elevated content, in the case of *Playboy*, *The New Yorker*, and so forth, or for filler in lesser magazines, but delightful as the stories are, they do not sell books (or magazines, much). Still, they are excellent exercises in imagination and tremendously demanding to write (well). In prose writing they are a sort of ultimate test, because you only have about three or four words to establish a character. That is a challenge. For example: "They called him Hoss. He sold bait." Perhaps you see Hoss in your mind's eye. But now, making him do something that comes to a satisfying conclusion in three hundred to two thousand words? That will be a trick. It is an art.

After Poe there were many masters of the short story, Twain, O. Henry, Doyle, Saki, Guy de Maupassant, Robert Louis Stevenson, Ernest Hemingway, and Stephen King spring to mind. But for the Cold War era, I think Shirley Jackson (1916–1965) claims the prize for English. Her stories continue to be read and taught, and they stand the test of time. Her influence is very clear in the work of Rod Serling and Charles Beaumont (Serling's main collaborator), as it is in so many others, such as King, Ursula K. Le Guin, and yes, Damon Knight, who wrote "To Serve Man." Her famous short story collection *The Lottery* came out in 1949, and everybody read it. She reminds me of a literary version of Rod Serling. I hope it is not indelicate to say that everyone steals food from Shirley's plate.

But Serling is something of a different dish. He was not a writer of short stories, first, and TV scripts later. From the beginning he wrote TV scripts. The opportunity for his generation was extraordinary. Plenty of radio script-writers made the transition, but TV was the microwave oven of storytelling, with its own recipes. Serling saw the possibilities right away: TV was the most powerful medium for storytelling ever invented, and it remains so today, as I have said repeatedly in this book. For a while it looked like cinema was to take back its supremacy, but then the invention of the "series arc" sets a table for writers, in time and space, that cinema could never match.

It's impossible to ignore that the high-end talent has migrated toward television, after it became clear that a seven-season series arc provided a bigger platter and more people came to the buffet for samples of one's virtual preparations. Serling's big idea, after establishing himself as a high-end writer, sort of an Arthur Miller of television, was to bring the standard tropes and forms of the short story into TV, especially as it leaned to science fiction.

It was a natural analogy, assuming you could get in and out of a script in about twenty-five pages. The way Richard Matheson described the formula: "The ideal *Twilight Zone* started with a really smashing idea that hit you in the first few seconds, then you played that out, and you had a little flip at the end" (*The Twilight Zone Companion*, p. 296). All this changed with the expansion of the series to an hour after 1962. That is a completely different kind of writing. The short story becomes the novella, and the rules are different. That's Flannery O'Connor, not Shirley Jackson.

I realize there's no disputing about taste, but I am a lover of the short story, and of the twenty-four-minute *Twilight Zone*. Serling did, later, publish short stories, but the collection was written into that form by Walter B. Gibson (1963). Although the book went through many printings, Serling's magic does not, in my opinion, survive the transition. If you put him up against the best short story writers of the second half of the twentieth century, Serling does not crack the top hundred. But as a writer of the twenty-four-minute script, he has no equals. If you want to see the perfect fifty-two-minute script, see Chris Carter, and his crew, Spotnitz, Wong, the Morgans, and especially Vince Gilligan, of *The X-Files* and *Breaking Bad*, and so forth. Such is the series arc of seven seasons, and such is the fifty-two-minute script.

But Serling's art, nay, his genius, was getting in with a smashing idea and getting out with a twist in twenty-four minutes. Yet, there is so much more to chew on there, do you not think? I do. I am taken with that first season opening speech about the pit of our fears and the summit of our knowledge. But it never made perfect sense to me. What was Serling saying? I have figured it out now. I will tell you . . . at the end, with a twist. But I have to put something in your oven first, something, ummm, appetizing?

Finger-lickin' Good

The original plot of the short story "To Serve Man" by Damon Knight might cause you to question Rod Serling's judgment.[2] You would be wrong, but you might do it anyway. At this late date, we only know who Damon Knight was *because* Rod changed his story and flipped from the magazine frying pan and on to the fiery little screen.[3] The fact that the plot made better sense in Knight's version does not matter. What caught our imaginations—you know, that dimension between the pit of our fears and the summit of our knowledge—then, as now, was the twist on *The Day the Earth Stood Still* (TDtESS).[4] "To Serve Man," as a TV show, fed our growing self-cynicism in just the right way that we felt ourselves fit for some alien's *pièce de résistance*.

Too much, too fast? Okay, let's back up. "To Serve Man" is one of the more famous episodes of the *Zone*. As with so many of its kin, it irritates some nerve ending leading back to the very brain of our twitchy Cold War nervous systems. At this extremity, the aliens rather than the bombs arrive (it was always pretty much one or the other). As with Klaatu and Gort on the big screen in 1951 in TDtESS, the aliens are here to "help" us, or so it seems. They will bring an end to our wars, supply us with food enough for everyone, create leisure for us all, and so on. But this time, unlike TDtESSS, we *believe* them, more or less. We let them solve all of our human problems with their superior technology, but this time we were wrong.

They want to eat us, brazed, broiled, bar-b-cued, baked, and deep-fried. With sauce. Gives "finger-lickin' good" a new meaning. In terms of *Wirkungsschicksal*, I interpose a question at this point: Why would we believe the aliens this time? It is barely plausible. We *never* believe the aliens, right? The effective destining of the story is embedded in this question.

The Omnivore's Dilemma

Are these omnivores here to conquer and eat us or help (or both, if you are cynical)? The idea of extraterrestrial life is as old as anything in human culture. True, anciently speaking, these beings were seen (or imagined) as divine—the stars were

---

[2]   The short story is available here: <www.digital-eel.com/blog/library/To_Serve_Man.pdf>.

[3]   A compressed version of the show is available here: <www.youtube.com/watch?v=wJjvg-Gq1LE&t=52s>. There is a very nice expanded version for radio here: <www.youtube.com/watch?v=rv1Dk5tttic>. The full script is here: <http://leethomson.myzen.co.uk/The_Twilight_Zone/The_Twilight_Zone_3x24_-_To_Serve_Man.pdf>.

[4]   To see the 1951 movie, you must subscribe or rent, but here is a free radio theater presentation of the script: <www.youtube.com/watch?v=9D53xiPF8U0>.

watchers, the planets were wanderers—but divinity alone does not bestow *full* godhood; there are many kinds of semi- and demi-divine beings. And beings from beyond may "pay us a visit." Whom do you suppose all those angels and demons are? The idea is primal for humans.

They may eat us too—the Cyclops eats us, Cronos eats his young, with one important exception; the Giant at the top of Jack's beanstalk eats Englishmen; the Witch eats children like Hansel and Gretel, Jaws eats us, Grendel's mother wants to eat Beowulf, Satan is chewing on Brutus, Cassius, and Judas at the bottom circle of Dante's hell, the wolf wants to eat Little Red Riding Hood, Zombies eat us, vampires sort of eat us, and it goes on and on. Let us just say we often get eaten.

It is surely a deep response to our own eating habits. We cannot help imagining that the table can be turned, so to speak. The idea that such hungry visitors are "divine" or "giants" is just a way of recognizing the instances when we project superior intelligence and powers that exceed our own. That such visitors may mean us harm as well as good is equally old. See Genesis 6:1 and explain to me what the "sons of God" are doing with "the daughters of men," if you are brave enough. I talked about that a few chapters back. Back then, we did not think of these beings as living on other planets. That is because we never thought (until a few hundred years ago) that the celestial lights were places. We thought they were divine beings, as I said, watchers (stars) and wanderers (planets). We never thought of them as "invading," since it was their prerogative to go wherever they would.

Of Englishmen and Microbes

I guess we all trace the alien invasion scenario to H.G. Wells's *War of the Worlds* (1897). It was among the earliest versions to be written up as an invasion from another place. But back then this novel was really classed with the hundreds of stories about British imperialism that were being published (mainly by anti-imperialists, but not exclusively). Wells, noted political radical that he was, was giving the British a taste of their own stew.

Being British himself, he certainly could not imagine a superior race *on Earth* (God is British after all, as I established some chapters ago), so in order to make the British feel like insects (since that is how they treated native populations), Wells invoked the only master race that made sense to a British mind: Martians. Some astronomers had published scientific articles about seeing strange lights on Mars from 1892 to 1894.[5] Wells had seen the primal meaning of the creepy feeling "they're coming" in those articles.[6] Such possibilities.

Bacon

On the eve of a different kind of British Invasion, one that no one foresaw, although there might have been some detectable noises emanating from Liverpool had anyone possessed the right kind of ear to hear, Rod Serling adapted Damon Knight's idea and put one of those possibilities on our plates: we are not insects, we are simply delicious. If you think it sucks to wake up as Kafka's cockroach one morning, imagine what it is like to be the bacon of the Hyperboreans.

But Knight's aliens, the "Kanamits," were pig-beings: "short" with "thick bristly brown-gray hair all over their abominably plump bodies" and "their noses were snout-like and their eyes small" with "thick hands of three fingers each" ("To Serve Man," pp. 94–95). In Serling's version, however, our galactic gourmands are the giants we always expected, ever since the days of the Titans and their kin from the North Wind. Serling's Kanamit, are "a little over nine feet" and weigh "in the neighborhood of three-hundred fifty pounds." They have no hair (visibly at least), and exaggerated cranial capacity. Instead of Knight's green lederhosen, these Kanamit wear high-collared flowing robes. They do not speak but communicate telepathically with humans.

The way aliens are depicted makes a very great difference as to which nerve ending is irritated. In this case, Serling wins the writing contest with Knight. Serling must have seen that if we were going to be lulled into trusting these aliens (and this is the pivot of the problem, as I have suggested), they needed to remind us of our higher selves, not our lower selves. Perhaps the problem Klaatu had with the humans in TDtESS was that he looked just like us, and we *do not* trust us. Even less will we trust our uninvited porcine guests. This is basic.

The principle of trust, however grudging, is necessary to the story, and depends on an imaginative projection of the higher human capacities. Where you have been is where you are going. We need giants, not swine. From Wellsian slithery multi-legged Martians through Heinlein's "bugs" in "Starship Troopers," and any number of other insect-based alien images, we move up the

---

[5]   See Dobbins, Sheehan, "Solving the Martian Flares Mystery."
[6]   The name of French Astronomer Camille Flammarion is the one to follow in this time and place. Wells was certainly reading him.

spectrum of "life-forms," imagining each form to be hyper-intelligent in turn. Note your own psychological response. We even have the occasional plant-alien, as in Audrey Jr. (*The Little Shop of Horrors*, 1960) or the pods of *Invasion of the Body Snatchers* (1956).

Is it true, as Stephen King says, that the real monster is always the one who looks just like us? Some people will rank King's Pennywise (*It*) as among the most frightening monsters in literary or filmatic history—also an alien able to appear as whatever frightens us most. As we move into the human-like range, we introduce distortions or stylizations of the human form, as the plot and setting require. But if we are to be ambrosia, only a god will whet our imaginative appetitions.

An Overcooked Nibble

Speaking of the food of the gods, Immanuel Kant was quite at home with the talk of aliens and life on other planets. Hardly anyone even thought of it back then, in the eighteenth century. True, he was an astrophysicist back when few people had a mathematical understanding of space and time. All the same, Kant's casualness about the subject still surprises us. Even today the subject is exotic, and at worst fodder for the lunatic fringe. Now Kant is pretty tough to chew on, a leathery old coot. But it is nutritious reading.

Comparing ourselves to aliens had occurred to Kant by 1755. He says:

> If the idea of the most sublime classes of sensible creatures living on Jupiter or Saturn provokes the jealousy of human beings and discourages them with the knowledge of their own humble position, a glance at the lower stages [on Venus and Mercury, perhaps] brings content and calms them again. (*Theory of the Heavens*, p. 152)

Wunderbar *Wirkungsschicksal*! I would say. Did Kant have a television? Moving beyond the recognizably human poses new and curious questions, too. If the aliens look nothing like us, how will we know whether they are friends or threats (or even whether we look like treats, if they are hungry Kanamit)? Is intelligence the key? What about language? You know, "take me to your leader." Without communication of some sort, how would we ever learn whether there is intelligence? Without it, how would we know whether they are lying? Kant thought we would have to be able to communicate in order to know, a scenario replayed in ten thousand stories of the nervous twentieth century.

We see the "language" angle working as the key to temporal displacement in the popular movie *Arrival* (2016) for example, which takes the Sapir-Whorf hypothesis to new extremes. In that movie language forms our consciousness, even down to the experience of time, and not only the experience, but the way time exists. The octopus-looking aliens teach us their language so that we can help them three thousand years in the future.

Consider also the debate on *Star Trek: The Next Generation* as to whether the "Crystalline Entity" is or is not intelligent; that being is in and of the borderland, where language cannot reach. We learn too late that the entity was intelligent, since it conspired with Lore (Lt. Commander Data's evil twin) to destroy the Enterprise-D. It is too much to swallow, but here is the doggie bag to take home. The aliens cannot be *wholly other* than we are. Kant says that intelligence ("rationality") is universal (and he means, like, the whole universe).

So communication must be possible in principle, no matter how different we are, and even if it is failing at any given moment. We may not be very impressive to those Kanamit (that word reminds me of the word "Kant," somehow, with "ami" in the middle, "friend of Kant"), but they do not just eat us; they take the trouble to communicate with us. Either these hyper-intelligent beings lack a moral compass altogether (an impossibility for Kant) or they regard our lives as at least quasi-valuable, even if only to fatten us up. Why do they not just eat us without bothering to communicate? They certainly have the power to do that. Is this similar to the way Native peoples of North America ritually thank the deer they have just hunted for contributing itself willingly to their sustenance?[7]

We treat our fellow creatures in like manner, after all, and usually factory-style and without thanks or ritual or any communication at all. Maybe if the hogs sent us an e-mail, we would reconsider. I wonder. Give up bacon? Bar-b-que? The human race? Well, I guess some religions do constrain it, at least. But how do those religions even get converts? Have you tasted Memphis bar-b-que? Before you go blaming the Kanamit for their appetites, you might first want to ask why pigs can be

---

[7]　Thanking the prey is just the beginning of what we might do and have done. Patrick Durkin gathers a number of these in his article "Post-kill Rituals: Matters of the Heart." Of particular interest to us is the quote from an authority (zoology professor) named Valerius Geist (gotta love *that* name): "You also don't sit on the animal's body after you've killed it. That dishonors the creature... you show the utmost respect by concentrating on killing the animal quickly. Hunters' conduct toward wildlife and nature should be consistent with their conduct toward other humans." I never thought of it before, but I suppose if people were hunting me, I would prefer to be killed quickly and not sat upon.

trained to obey voice commands. You have perhaps seen the film *Babe* (1995). Is our willingness to farm them based on anything nobler than poor communication (for which we hold them mortally responsible)? Do they trust us? If so, why?

What's in the Soup?

Further: Have you ever noticed how much Rod's name sounds like "sirloin"? (Sapir-Whorf is hard at work in my imagination, no?) In a noisy Kanamit restaurant, you might order him up, with some Heinz 57, without even meaning to. "Sirling on a rod, please, medium rare." So, we have traced the problem, between us and our fellow porcine earthlings, as between us and our Kanamit visitors, down to a communication breakdown.[8] That is the bread and butter of both Knight's and Serling's stories. In both versions, the humans must be satisfied that the Kanamit are telling the truth, so a polygraph is used in front of the whole United Nations, with translators busy as bees to transform the Kanamit's English telepathy into, one supposes, Spanish, and Swahili, and Polish.

An aside: Why does the Kanamit telepathize in English? One would think he might be able to do the trick in all the languages of Earth, as adjusted to the hearers' understanding. But no. Aliens always speak English, the first law of science-fiction TV and movies. But communication is still pretty hard. *Star Trek* at least had a "universal translator," and some of the plots of later versions of the series depended on failures of that device. But still, universal translation always seems to be into English. Unless of course, the movie or TV show is, say, German or Russian, in which case it is only *sometimes* English, and other times comes complete with English subtitles. After all, we all want to know what the aliens are saying.[9]

When asked about their motives, in Knight's story a (pig-like) "Kanama" (singular for "Kanamit," which is plural) says: "On my planet there is a saying: 'There are more riddles in a stone than in a philosopher's head.' The motives of intelligent beings, though they may at times seem obscure, are simple things compared to the complex workings of the natural uni-

---

[8]   The basic gesture of my sketch of communication failure is filled out by John Durham Peters's excellent, far-ranging scholarly work, *Speaking into the Air*, especially see the Introduction.

[9]   Nassim Taleb observes: "I am often amazed to hear people from neighboring countries, say, between a Turk and an Iranian, or a Lebanese and a Cypriot, communicating in bad English, moving their hands for emphasis, searching for these words that come out of their throats at the cost of great physical effort. Even members of the Swiss army use English . . ." *The Black Swan*, pp. 219–220.

verse" (Knight, "To Serve Man," p. 94). That part did not make it into the broadcast show. But this line *was* in Serling's script. I do not know why it was cut, either during the filming or by an editor. But it was not broadcast, which is, I think, a shame. It damages the *Wirkungsschicksal*.

Fortunately we can recover it. Let us consider the Kanamit (friend-of-Kant) saying: Is the complexity of matters in our minds, or are our minds radical simplifications of the natural universe? I have defended the latter. Mind is inherently simpler than existence—it is generalized, amalgamated, reduced, refined, and ready for use. Our minds are in the business of sorting what we care about from what we don't care about, and what we don't care about is a much larger constellation than what we do notice. We give ourselves too much credit in examining the supposed complexity of our minds.

The difference is important, but check out the next bit. The pig in Knight's story prefaces his promise of peace with: "Therefore, I hope that the people of Earth will understand, and believe me when I say . . . " and then pledges peace. Now, the pig-being is telling the truth. He *does* "hope" we will understand that his motives are simple, like the saying on his planet, and he *does* "hope" we will believe him about the peaceful intentions. But the hope we will understand the saying and the simplicity of his intentions (in other words, to eat us) does not extend to the part about believing their intentions are peaceful, which he hopes we do not understand.

The Kanamit have noticed that we think we are very smart, but even a stone is, in its way, far smarter. It does not deceive itself. I think Serling missed this little trick of language in Knight's story—the parsing of "hope" between understanding and believing. Since he left out the part about simple motives in the broadcast version; he also left out "therefore" in the final cut. But, the "therefore" and the word "understand" referred back to the "saying" on the Kanamit planet (and its moral) about stones and philosophers' heads (which, by the way, not the tenderest part of the philosopher—it is an acquired taste, I expect). As I said, the "hope" for understanding did not refer forward to the half-truth about our *believing* the promise of peace. The hope in that case was only that Mr. Kanama will be believed. That is another beast altogether.

Copping an Attitude

Philosophers call this sort of linguistic "condition" (to hope, to believe, to understand, to intend, and so forth), a "propositional attitude." Such language alters the truth status of whatever comes after it. This is a true sentence: "The Kanamit are lying about their peaceful intentions toward humans." But "The humans *believe* the Kanamit are lying" is false (in the opinion of most of the humans, at least) even though *part* of the sentence is true. The Russian ambassador to the UN seems not to believe the Kanamit at first, but he happily gets on their ship later, to be taken away and eaten. Ambassador borscht.

After all, the Kanamit *are* lying. We have a saying among philosophers on our planet: "propositional attitudes have a scope that ranges over whatever comes afterwards, until another attitude or some punctuation limits it." The period, full stop, is a powerful tool. Always has been, except for the ancient world which did not have it. How did they get along? Did they just believe everything? Hardly.

No magic or mindpower is required to keep the polygraph needle from moving, although in Serling's final version it probably should have moved. The needle may be smarter than the polygraph operator. There is a good reason you get only "yes" and "no" questions when you take a polygraph test. Simple answers use no propositional attitudes to exert influence on the truth or falsity of what is being said. Next time you are taking a polygraph test, answer the yes/no question with "I believe so" and watch the questioner re-ask the question with an admonishment that you keep it to yes and no.

Knight's Kanama is not lying about what he *hopes*, but if you leave out the backward reference to the Kanamit saying, you imply that the Kanama hopes we understand that he is lying. That is not what he hopes. Rod Serloin should have removed the word "understand" from the final cut (or cutlet?), since he was removing the Kanamit saying and the "therefore." But he left in "understand," which indicates to me that he had not quite seen what Knight was doing. A communication failure between sci-fi writers. So Serling's Kanama *was* lying and the polygraph didn't catch it. Knight's Kanama wasn't technically lying: he was truthfully reporting what he hoped.

A Riddle, Wrapped in a Mystery, Inside an Enigma

There's yet another big difference between Knight and Serling. In Serling's script, the Kanamit leave their "cookbook" on a table at the UN, evidently so confident it cannot be decoded that they do not care whether the humans try (although they do say we will understand their intentions eventually). Knight's story is different.

In addition to our narrator, Chambers, there is a second translator named Gregori, who is Polish—the Poles being renown mathematicians, linguists, and logicians. Gregori gets a job at the Kanamit Embassy and has this Kanamit book by means undisclosed – later we find out he stole it. Gregori says: "You know language reflects the basic assumptions of those who use it. I've got a fair command of the spoken lingo already. It's not hard, really, and there are hints in it" ("To Serve Man," p. 96). A month later our narrator meets Gregori again, who has now translated the first paragraph and knows it is a cookbook.

Serling's script, as published, does not contain the instruction that the episode is to be done in flashback, with Chambers speaking from aboard the Kanamit ship, remembering the Year of the Kanamit. That sequence must have been added later. It was added at the expense of some very interesting and needful material. This temporal shift in the story moved it from *Wirkungsschicksal* to *Wirkungsgeschichte*. We are being warned by Chambers not to believe the Kanamit. But without the flashback, it is about rectifying our way of thinking about our food, by imaginatively including ourselves on the menu. That is effective destining. It is not about whom to believe.

In particular, look at this exchange between Chambers and his Secretary Pat, who is the surrogate for Knight's character Gregori. (The name "Gregori" becomes Serling's Russian ambassador to the UN—who, like Knight's character, does not believe the Kanamit, but later ends up quite eager to be a Kanamit kolbasa.)

CHAMBERS: I'm on one of the ten-year exchange group waiting lists. What about you, Pattie?

PAT: I'm on the list, too. The trouble is their quota's filled twenty-four hours after they make the announcement of a new trip. But while I'm waiting I think I'll do the next best thing. I'm studying their language. I remember a professor of mine told me that language reflects the basic assumptions of the people who use it. [*She lights a cigarette*] I've got a fair command of their spoken lingo already. It's not hard, really. And there are hints in it. Some of the idioms are quite similar to English. I think I'll get the answer eventually.

CHAMBERS: More power! I gave up a month ago. They write in ideographs worse than Chinese, but if I can help you in any way—

[*Close shot Pat as she moves away, a strange look on her face*]

CHAMBERS: [*continued*] Did I say something?

PAT: [*shakes her head*] If you could help me that was the phrase, wasn't it? [*Chambers nods*]

PAT: The only thing you can help me with— [*She looks off*]

CHAMBERS: Is what?

PAT: Help me get rid of this strange little gnaw inside me. This very funny persistent nightmarish feeling.

This dialogue did not make it into the final version of the broadcast. I can imagine a few reasons. Knight said that he was aware the weakness in the story was that the "twist" we generally find in short stories depended on a play on English: that "to serve" has both culinary and altruistic fields of meaning. It is true, as Knight pointed out, that it has the same homonymous meaning French and the connotations and usage are almost the same in German, but why would that association show up in a completely alien language like Kanamit?

Serling, as a writer, clearly worried about this glitch of idiomatic language, but perhaps his editors, director, producers, and the whole Hollywood smorgasbord, were able to convince Rod that, well, Americans are so monolingual that it would not occur to the average Ward and June and Wally and the Beav, out on Maple Street, that languages differ in these matters. They all had a little Latin in middle school and at most a year of French in college and that was it. They are just as unsuspecting . . . as hogs. They are bacon in the making.

Short stories are written for people who read. TV programs in 1962 are for people who do not (then and now). No wonder Serloin never wrote anything but scripts. Who would read them anyway? *The Twilight Zone* crew carved the meat out of this episode because they *could*, because it was TV in 1962, because it was Americans watching from Maple Street.

The Main Course

This brings us to our own main course. I know that you, like me, have thought about those introductory speeches Rod Serling made, especially the one from the first season. Let's remind ourselves of the text:

There is fifth dimension beyond that which is known to man. It is vast and timeless. It is the middle ground between light and shadow, between science and superstition and it lies between the pit of Man's fear and the summit of his knowledge. This is the dimension of Imagination. It is an area which we call: The Twilight Zone.

Note that the Twilight Zone is beyond what is "known" by us, but it is a middle ground, not some transcendent realm. It is between light and shadow—a reference to Plato and his infamous cave, perhaps, but have you ever thought about the strange gray between the object that casts a shadow and the place, in space and time, where the shadow lands? It is hard not to think of Peter Pan chasing his shadow all over the Darling's nursery, but that one has come loose, has it not? Imagination at work again. Most shadows do not behave so—physical necessity, right?

But consider: can you make a shadow darker by putting a second object between the one casting the shadow and the shadow it casts? Depends on the density of the first object, right? Assume it is dense. Is there still an effect on the shadow by a second object? How can there not be? A real, genuine action with no effect, no equal and opposite reaction? There must be an effect, right? Looks like we will have to imagine a quality of darkness in which an indiscernible non-difference does make a difference, somehow.

That middle ground is identified as the dimension of imagination. We fear it because we cannot quite know it. But knowing it is like knowing ourselves. We now come to a point you may not have considered. But Kant did (perhaps his friends also). He imagined the following:

> It could well be that on some other planet there might be rational beings who could not think in any other way but aloud; that is, they could not have any thoughts that they did not at the same time utter, whether awake or dreaming, in the company of others or alone. What kind of behavior toward others would this produce, and how would it differ from that of our human species? (*Anthropology from a Pragmatic Point of View*, p. 237)

As you might expect, Kant thinks these beings would have certain moral advantages over us, since they could not conceal their thoughts about one another from one another. The scene would look a good bit like the Ricky Gervais movie *The Invention of Lying* (2009), I suppose.[10] Kant sure hated lying. But Kant's point is that we might never in fact be able to attain self-knowledge because we do not actually have such races of beings for comparison. We only imagine them.

---

[10] For a taste of this, if you do not know the picture, see the trailer here: <www.youtube.com/watch?v=vn71hYvyqCA>.

At bottom, when we seek to understand our kind of being:

> We shall not be able to name its character because we have no knowledge of the non-terrestrial beings that would enable us to indicate their characteristic property and so to characterize this terrestrial being [humanity] among rational beings in general. It seems, therefore, that the problem of indicating the character of the human species is insoluble. (p. 225)

To make it plain, we imagine all these aliens because we are seeking a billion varieties of tiny contrasts with ourselves, and while each illuminates a corner, it casts a shadow in doing so. That shadow is us. And we do not know how delicious or bland we are. We imagine the beings and they only ask us questions we cannot answer.

The more beings we imagine, the more questions. It's not just aliens; it's all the other monsters too. We try to know ourselves and learn nothing about us, except what we put there to warn ourselves about, well, ourselves. *We* are the Kanamit. Stephen King was right. If that is not the point, there is not a point. Which is my point. *Wirkungsschicksal*. We warn ourselves about what we might become.

Yet, some of these imagined beings register with us, strike a nerve, as it were, and others do not. What Rod Serling was uncannily good at was seeing which ones would imprint themselves on our memories, which is almost the same thing as scaring us, but better, far better. If I am right, the most effective destining stories are the ones that tap into clustered possibilities, not just constellations. You *feel* a cluster. You merely ponder a constellation.

I think the getting-eaten group must be a cluster of possibilities, not just a constellation. When a pattern shows up over and over, chances are we are worried about something we definitely ought to be worried about. These clusters are normative. We are not eating right on this planet. Serling and Knight were ahead. That was their job, right? These *Wirkungschicksalhaft* writers. The factory farms were not advanced in 1950 or 1962, but they were being developed, in the shadow of Auschwitz. Same shit, different day; not your species or race today, but tomorrow?

For Dessert: Hyper-reality

Umberto Eco (and others) called this same dimension between light and shadow "hyper-reality." He saw it as the entire virtual world of meanings (and their relations) that we have to pass through every time we want to *do* something —we must move from the swirl of meanings and ideas we use to think into acting on just a few and in some particular order. We move through a shadow-land of interpretation in order to do that, None of us wants to do anything unless we are fairly sure of how it will be interpreted *by others*, and that is part of our concern for what each act means. This is a tasty idea. I feel certain that Rod Serling would gobble this up.

But for us, in this day and age, meaning is a sea of possible interpretations, with lots of fish in it. But many are just too salty and nothing to drink, you know? Every act has a multiplicity of meanings and, as Kant-a-mit indicates, no one is really in a position to say with finality what any single piece of the pie means, in relation to the whole or the other slices. You just do not know what you are eating; interpretation is mystery meat (see the chapters on *South Park*). Eco has a lot of fun with this in his novels, especially *Foucault's Pendulum*. I hope they make *that* into a TV series —it would never fit in a movie.

The failure of contrast Kant described has become, for us today, a psychosis of the middle ground, of shadows within shadows, of the middle ground between the shadows. Eco says that "semiotics," the science and superstition of hyper-reality, is the study of anything that can be used *to lie*. There is no possibility of telling the truth unless there is the prior possibility of lying, he says. Science fiction is a feast of lies in this sense. We rearrange all the ideas and words such that they remind us of ourselves, but somehow altered. We tell the lies as a means of seeing the truth about ourselves.

Eco would not be surprised by the Kanamit, and he certainly would have caught that propositional attitude, dividing "hope" between "understand" and "believe." I do not think he would be booking any space on the Kanamit Exchange Express. It was hard to get anything past him, inveterate skeptic that he was.

This semiotic domain, this hyper-reality, is the contrast that duplicates, in language and signs of all sorts, our inability to know ourselves. This duplication of lies is the basic motive behind *Wirkungsschicksal*, effective destining, which requires a willingness to lie about the future for cautionary and corrective purposes. If we cannot know who we are now, how can we evade a future that includes who we are now in what we do not want to become? That requires the contrast that Kant says we lack. I wonder what he would have thought of science fiction.

The key desire of hyper-reality is reality. One thinks of every story from *Pinocchio* to *The Velveteen Rabbit*, to the mannequins in "The After Hours" episode of *Twilight Zone*.[11] These all involve some object that strives to become "real." All our imagined objects want to be real or die in the attempt. We compare and contrast ourselves with pigs and giants, but they are really just us, exaggerated, distorted, turned, twisted, and they become not part of reality, but more vestiges of hyper-reality. The more of these creations we foist into the middle ground, the less we know about ourselves, and the more ardently we desire that knowledge.

So there is a self-defeating act behind science fiction. In attempting to find a suitable contrast to ourselves, we also lose ourselves by pushing the dimension of ourselves we used to create the contrast away, as "not us." But it is "not us" only to the extent that we *made* it so. The hope of the effective destiner, the science-fiction writer, is that we will come around from the distancing to find that the monster was us all along. Serling uses his narrator spots to suggest this over and over, to help us see ourselves in the other. Effective destining must overcome the hyper-real distancing it employs to create an unreal contrast, a projected cluster from which we might see ourselves if we inhabit the role of the other we created.

What to do in the welter of hyper-reality? Binge-watch our *Twilight Zone* and our more recent *Wirkungsschiksalkunst* like *Black Mirror*? It would be educative for sure. The shadows dancing on the walls of Plato's cave have never been better, never more "realistic." Yet, it seems to me that the Kanamit (Kan't-name-it) really have a point. We await other rational beings for contrast, so that we can know ourselves. Yet, I would add, we dismiss every candidate right here, in experience, that presents itself for real comparison and contrast. Are there not other such beings on Earth itself? When was the last time you communicated with your dog or cat? Why will you not eat them? What stops you?

Given the clear choice of whether to think of other (early) hominid species as being our equals, or brothers, we narcissistically treated them as stages on the way to ourselves, in our fairytales about how the "lower" species evolve into the "higher." Some people continue to do this fantasizing even against the clear evidence that beings like us co-existed with both Neanderthals and Homo erectus. In all likelihood, we killed them all, just as we are now wiping out the other Great Apes, and anything else that reminds us too much of ourselves

---

[11] The essence of the episode is here: <www.youtube.com/watch?v=xeB0SpWUySM>.

(including members of other nations, religions, races, gender-variations, and neighborhoods).

We do not like company, especially our own. Kant called us "sociably unsociable."

Digestif

Respectfully submitted for your perusal: a being who does not want self-knowledge . . . except through the filter of hyper-reality, that is, the products of its own imagination. This beast thrusts its own apish figure into its self-created fifth-dimensional mirror, that growing realm of ever-not-quite, and then finds no angels looking back at him.

That was Rod's true gift: toss that beast into that shadow and see what looks back. So watch. Or don't. After all, we have warned us already.

Bibliography

Agee, James. 1958 [1944]. Review of movie The Lifeboat. In James Agee, *Agee on Film*, Volume I. New York: Wideview/ Perigree.

Allen, Richard, and S. Ishii-Gonzalès, eds. 1999. *Alfred Hitchcock: Centenary Essays*. London: British Film Institute Publishing.

Altizer, Thomas J.J. 1966. *The Gospel of Christian Atheism*. Philadelphia: Westminster.

Altizer, Thomas J.J. and William Hamilton. 1966. *Radical Theology and the Death of God*. Indianapolis: Bobbs-Merrill.

Auxier, Randall E. 2013. *Time, Will, and Purpose: Living Ideas from the Philosophy of Josiah Royce*. Chicago: Open Court.

———. 2017. *Metaphysical Graffiti: Deep Cuts in the Philosophy of Rock*. Chicago: Open Court.

Auxier, Randall E., and Gary L. Herstein. 2017. *The Quantum of Explanation: Whitehead's Radical Empiricism*. New York: Routledge.

Auxier, Randall E., and Phil Seng, eds. 2008. *The Wizard of Oz and Philosophy: Wicked Wisdom of the West*. Chicago: Open Court.

Bacevich, Andrew. 2008. *The Limits of Power: The End of American Exceptionalism*. New York: Macmillan.

Beardsworth, Sara G., and Randall E. Auxier, eds. 2017. *The Philosophy of Umberto Eco*. Chicago: Open Court.

Aristotle. 1941. Poetics. In *The Basic Works of Aristotle*. New York: Random House.

Aristotle. 2019. Nicomachean Ethics. Indianapolis: Hackett.

Baum, L. Frank. 1900. *The Wonderful Wizard of Oz*. Chicago: Hill.

Bergson, Henri. 1910 [1889] *Time and Free Will*. London: Allen and Unwin.

———. 1913. *Laughter: An Essay on the Meaning of the Comic*. New York: Macmillan.

———. 1911 [1907]. *Creative Evolution*. New York: Holt.

Brickhouse Thomas C., and Nicholas D. Smith. 2000. *The Philosophy of Socrates*. Boulder: Westview.

Bronowski, Jacob. 1973. *The Ascent of Man*. Boston: Little, Brown.

Chapman, Graham, et al. 1980. *Monty Python and the Holy Grail*. New York: Methuen.

Cyprian [attrib.]. 2020. *Feast of Cyprian: The Coena Cypriani Translated to English*. Kindle.

Deleuze, Gilles. 1986. *Cinema 1: The Movement Image*. Minneapolis: University of Minnesota Press.

———. 1991 [1988]. *Bergsonism*. New York: Zone

Dobbins, Thomas, and William Sheehan. 2001. Solving the Martian Flares Mystery" *Sky and Telescope* <http://alpo-astronomy.org/mars/articles/MartianFlaresALPO.pdf>.

Durkin, Patrick. 2016. Post-kill Rituals: Matters of the Heart. *American Hunter* (August).

Eco, Umberto. 1984. *The Name of the Rose*. New York: Warner.

Farías, Victor. 1989. *Heidegger and Nazism*. Philadelphia: Temple University Press.

Freud, Sigmund. 1927. *The Future of an Illusion*. New York: Norton.

Gracia, Jorge J.E., ed. 2004. *Mel Gibson's Passion and Philosophy: The Cross, the Questions, the Controversy*. Chicago: Open Court.

Greene, Richard, and Rachel Robison-Greene. 2009. *The Golden Compass and Philosophy: God Bites the Dust*. Chicago: Open Court.

———. 2020. *His Dark Materials and Philosophy: Paradox Lost*. Chicago: Open Court.

Hardin, Garrett. 1968. The Tragedy of the Commons. *Science* 162.

———. 1974. Lifeboat Ethics: The Case against Helping the Poor. *Psychology Today* 8.

Held, Jacob, ed. 2016. *Stephen King and Philosophy*. Rowman and Littlefield.

Hewison, Robert. 1981. *Monty Python: The Case Against*. New York: Grove Press.

Husserl, Edmund. 2001. *Analyses Concerning Passive and Active Synthesis*. Kluwer.

Jung, Carl G. 1976. The Transcendent Function. In Joseph Campbell, ed., *The Portable Jung*. New York: Penguin.

Kant, Immanuel. 1987. *Critique of Judgment*. Indianapolis: Hackett.

———. 2006. *Anthropology from a Pragmatic Point of View*. Cambridge University Press.

———. 2019. *Kant's Cosmogony: As in His Essay on the Retardation of the Rotation of the Earth and His Natural History and Theory of the Heavens*. Glasgow: Maclehose.

Kierkegaard, Søren. 1938. *Purity of Heart Is to Will One Thing*. New York: Harper and Row.

————. 1981. *The Concept of Anxiety: A Simple, Psychologically Oriented Deliberation on the Dogmatic Issue of Hereditary Sin.* Princeton: Princeton University Press.

Knight, Damon. 1950. To Serve Man. *Galaxy Science Fiction* (November).

Langer, Susanne. 1996 [1942]. *Philosophy in a New Key: A Study in the Symbolism of Reason, Rite, and Art.* Harvard University Press.

Matheson, Carl. 2001. The Simpsons, Hyper-Irony, and the Meaning of Life. In William Irwin, Mark T. Conard, and Aeon J. Skoble, eds., *The Simpsons and Philosophy: The D'oh! of Homer.* Chicago: Open Court.

Mauss, Marcel. 2000 [1950]. *The Gift: The Form and Reason for Exchange in Archaic Societies.* Norton.

Merleau-Ponty, Maurice. 2013 [1945]. *The Phenomenology of Perception.* Routledge.

Niebuhr, Reinhold. 2013. *Moral Man and Immoral Society.* Louisville: Westminster John Knox Press.

Nietzsche, Friedrich. 1967. *Ecce Homo and On the Genealogy of Morals.* New York: Vintage.

————. 1969. *The Anti-Christ.* Harmondsworth: Penguin.

————. 1974. *The Gay Science.* New York: Vintage.

————. 1977 [1954]. *The Portable Nietzsche.* New York: Penguin.

————. 1997. *Thus Spake Zarathustra.* Wordsworth.

Pascal, Blaise. 1941. *Pensées.* New York: Modern Library.

Patton, Michael. 2005. Game Preserve Ethics: The Case for Hunting the Poor. *Southwest Philosophy Review* 21:1.

Peters, John Durham. 2001 [1999]. *Speaking into the Air: A History of the Idea of Communication.* University of Chicago Press.

Pink Floyd, et al. 1995. Dark Side of the Rainbow. <https://www.youtube.com/watch?v=9Dpo0IfNP44>.

Plato. 1961. Symposium. In *Plato: The Collected Dialogues.* Princeton: Princeton University Press, 1961.

Pullman, Philip. 1995. *The Golden Compass.* Knopf

————. 1997. *The Subtle Knife.* Knopf.

————. 2000. *The Amber Spyglass.* Knopf.

————. 2003. *Lyra's Oxford.* Knopf.

————. 2008. *Once Upon a Time in the North.* Knopf.

————. 2017. *Daemon Voices: On Stories and Story Telling,*

————. 2019a. *The Book of Dust: La Belle Sauvage.* Knopf

————. 2019b. *The Secret Commonwealth: The Book of Dust, Volume Two.* Knopf.

————. 2020. *His Dark Materials: Serpentine.* Knopf.

Rousseau, Jean-Jacques. 1969. *The First and Second Discourses.* New York: St. Martin's Press.

Royce, Josiah. 1908. *The Philosophy of Loyalty.* New York: Macmillan.

————. 1969. *The Basic Writings of Josiah Royce, Volume I: Culture, Philosophy, and Religion*. University of Chicago Press.

————. 2005 [1969]. *The Basic Writings of Josiah Royce, Volume II: Logic, Loyalty, and Community*. Fordham University Press.

Scheler, Max. 1970. *The Nature of Sympathy*. New York: Archon.

Shepherd, Elaine, and Amy Briamonte, executive producers. 2000. *The Life of Python*. BBC/A&E.

Spoto, Donald. 1983. *The Dark Side of Genius: The Life of Alfred Hitchcock*. New York: Ballantine.

Edith Stein. 1989. On the Problem of Empathy. In *The Collected Works of Edith Stein*. Volume 3. Washington: Institute of Carmelite Studies.

Taleb, Nassim Nicholas. 2010 [2007]. *The Black Swan: The Impact of the Highly Improbable*. Random House.

Truffaut, François. 1985. *Hitchcock*. New York: Simon and Schuster.

Twain, Mark. 1897 The Awful German Language. <https://drive.google.com/file/d/0B4xHZbr3vgOmYm5teGlsSzQ4a28/view>.

Wartenberg, Thomas E. 2007. Ethics or Film Theory: The Real McGuffin in *North by Northwest*. In David Baggett and William A. Drumin, eds., *Hitchcock and Philosophy: Dial M for Metaphysics*. Chicago: Open Court.

Zicree, Marc Scott. 2018. *The Twilight Zone Companion*. Third edition. Silman-James.

Suggestions for Reading

The book in your hands is good for introductory courses in philosophy, as a stand-alone text, using the movies as the medium for teaching philosophy. The Frampton book (see below) really is about the philosophy of film, whereas this book is really the movies *and* philosophy. Below are the readings (by chapter) you will want to associate with this book, since these are explicitly mentioned in the chapters. Together these cover all the major branches of philosophy.

If you liked this book and wonder what a whole philosophy based on such an approach to movies would look like, I recommend *Filmosophy: A Manifesto for a Radically New Way of Understanding Cinema*, by Daniel Frampton (London: Wallflower Press, 2006). It would make a good companion volume with this one for upper-level courses.

Chapter 1: The *Princess Bride*

Susanne Langer, *Philosophy in a New Key*, third edition (Cambridge: Harvard University Press, 1957), pp. 171–203 (Chapter VII).
<https://monoskop.org/images/6/6c/Langer_Susanne_K_Philosophy_in_a_New_Key.pdf>.

Josiah Royce, *The Philosophy of Loyalty* (New York: Macmillan, 1908), pp. 99–146 (Chapter III: Loyalty to Loyalty).
<https://royce-edition.iupui.edu/wp-content/uploads/2016/08/Philosophy-of-Loyalty.pdf>.

Chapter 2: *The Wizard of Oz*

Søren Kierkegaard, *The Concept of Anxiety*, edited and translated by Reidar Thomte (Princeton: Princeton University Press, 1980), pp. 41–46 (Chapter 1, Section 5).
<http://lib.stikes-mw.id/wp-content/uploads/2020/06/The-Concept-of-Anxiety_-A-Simple-Psychologically-Orienting-Deliberation-on-the-Dogmatic-Issue-of-Hereditary-Sin-PDFDr ive.com-.pdf>.

Maurice Merleau-Ponty, *The Phenomenology of Perception*, translated by D. Landes (London: Routledge, 2014), pp. 149–155 (Part 1, Section 4, "The Synthesis of One's Own Body").
<https://doubleoperative.files.wordpress.com/2012/09/merleau-ponty-synthesis006.pdf>.

Chapter 3: *Super 8*

Aristotle, *Nicomachean Ethics*, Books VIII–IX (On Friendship), translated by W.D. Ross.
<http://classics.mit.edu/Aristotle/nicomachaen.8.viii.html>.
<http://classics.mit.edu/Aristotle/nicomachaen.9.ix.html>.

Immanuel Kant, *The Critique of Judgment*, translated by W. Pluhar (Indianapolis: Hackett, 1987), pp. 89–90 (Section 22).
<https://monoskop.org/images/7/77/Kant_Immanuel_Critique_of_Judgment_1987.pdf>.

Jean-Jacques Rousseau, from "Discourse on the Origin of Inequality," in *The First and Second Discourses*, translated by RH.D. and J.R. Masters (New York: St. Martin's Press, 1964), pp. 130–134.
<http://johnstoniatexts.x10host.com/rousseau/seconddiscourse-htm.htm#firstpart> (the passage beginning near note 16).

Max Scheler, *The Nature of Sympathy*, edited by W. Stark (New Brunswick: Transaction, 2008), pp. 5–7 ("The Ethics of Sympathy," Part I, chapter 1).
<https://books.google.com/books?id=34Fl6qrpdb0C&pg=PR58&source=gbs_toc_r&cad=4#v=onepage&q&f=false>.

Edith Stein, *On the Problem of Empathy*, translated by Waltraut Stein, in *The Collected Works of Edith Stein*, Volume 3 (Washington, D.C.: ICS Publications, 1989), pp. 3–11 (Chapter II, Sections 1–2).
<https://empathyinthecontextofphilosophy.files.wordpress.com /2016/07/edithsteinon-the-problem-of-empathy-stein-st-edith_4199-copy.pdf>.

Chapter 4: *South Park* and Love

Plato, *Symposium*, "Diotima's Teaching," translated by Michael Joyce, lines 201c–212b.
<http://www.perseus.tufts.edu/hopper/text?doc=Perseus%3Ate xt%3A1999.01.0174%3Atext%3DSym.%3Asection%3D201d>.

Plato, *Phaedrus*, "The Great Myth," translated by H.N. Fowler (1966); lines 246b–257b.
<http://www.perseus.tufts.edu/hopper/text?doc=Perseus%3Ate xt%3A1999.01.0174%3Atext%3DPhaedrus%3Apage%3D246>.

Chapter 5: *South Park* and Death

Martin Heidegger, *Being and Time*, translated by J. Maquarrie and E. Robinson (London: Blackwell, 1962), pp. 279–311 (Sections 46-53).
<http://pdf-objects.com/files/Heidegger-Martin-Being-and-Time-trans.-Macquarrie-Robinson-Blackwell-1962.pdf>.

Carl G. Jung, "The Transcendent Function," in *The Portable Jung*, edited by J. Campbell, (New York: Viking, 1971), pp. 273–300 (Chapter 9); from *Collected Works*, Volume 8. There does not seem to be an available English version of this text, but here is a complete audio reading of the piece:
<https://www.youtube.com/watch?v=bpk60CdAQ2A>.

Chapter 6: *The Good, the Bad, and the Ugly*

Immanuel Kant, *The Critique of Judgment*, translated by W. Pluhar (Indianapolis: Hackett, 1987), pp. 103–126 (Sections 25–29).
<https://monoskop.org/images/7/77/Kant_Immanuel_Critique_of_Judgment_1987.pdf>.

Søren Kierkegaard, "Purity of Heart Is to Will One Thing," Chapter 3, translated by Douglas V. Steere, in *A Kierkegaard Anthology*, edited by R. Bretall (Princeton: Princeton University Press, 1946), pp. 271–281.
<https://www.religion-online.org/book-chapter/chapter-3-barriers-to-willing-one-thing-variety-and-great-moments-are-not-one-thing>.

Chapter 7: *Lifeboat*

Garrett Hardin, "Lifeboat Ethics: The Case against Helping the Poor," in *Psychology Today* Volume 8 (September 1974), pp. 38–43. <https://rintintin.colorado.edu/~vancecd/phil1100/Hardin.pdf>.

Garrett Hardin, "Living in a Lifeboat," in *BioScience*, 24:10 (1974), pp. 561–668. <https://www.garretthardinsociety.org/articles_pdf/living_on_a _lifeboat.pdf>.

Abraham Maslow, "A Theory of Human Motivation," *Psychological Review*, 50 (1943), pp. 350–376. <http://psychclassics.yorku.ca/Maslow/motivation.htm>.

Chapter 8: *His Dark Materials Part 1*

David K. Lewis, *On the Plurality of Worlds* (Oxford: Blackwell, 1986), pp. 1–5 (Chapter 1, "A Philosopher's Paradise," Section 1.1). <http://daalv.free.fr/Master-2011-2012/LMPHI%20155%20- %20Anglais%20philo/Lewis-David-(1986)-On-the-Plurality-of- Worlds.pdf>.

Charles Sanders Peirce, "The Law of Mind," in *The Monist*, 2:2 (July, 1892), pp. 533–559. <https://www.depts.ttu.edu/pragmaticism/collections/works/cs p_ms/P00477.pdf>.

Charles Sanders Peirce, "Evolutionary Love," in *The Monist*, 3:1 (January, 1893), pp. 176–200. <https://www.depts.ttu.edu/pragmaticism/collections/works/cs p_ms/P00521.pdf>.

Chapter 9: *His Dark Materials, Part 2*

Macrina, "On the Soul and Resurrection," in *In Her Words: Women's Writings in the History of Christian Thought*, edited by Amy Oden (Nashville: Abingdon Press, 1994), pp. 48–66. <https://www.ccel.org/ccel/schaff/npnf205.x.iii.ii.html>.

Friedrich Nietzsche, *Beyond Good and Evil*, translated by Walter Kaufmann (New York: Vintage, 1989), Chapter 5 "The Natural History of Morals," paragraphs186–203. The Zimmern translation is here: <https://gutenberg.org/files/4363/4363-h/4363-h.htm#link 2HCH0005>.

Friedrich Nietzsche, *The Gay Science*, translated by Walter Kaufmann (New York: Vintage, 1979), Sections 21, 23, 29, 60, 64–75. The Oscar Levy translation is here: <https://ia800300.us.archive.org/9/items/completenietasch10ni etuoft/completenietasch10nietuoft.pdf>.

Chapter 10: *The Life of Brian*

Henri Bergson, *Laughter*, translated by C. Brereton and F. Rothwell (New York: Macmillan, 1911), pp. 36–66 (Chapter 1, Section V).
<https://www.gutenberg.org/files/4352/4352-h/4352-h.htm>.

Friedrich Nietzsche, *The Gay Science*, translated by Walter Kaufmann (New York: Vintage, 1979), Sections 108, 125, 129–132. The Oscar Levy translation is here:
<https://ia800300.us.archive.org/9/items/completenietasch10ni etuoft/completenietasch10nietuoft.pdf>.

Blaise Pascal, "The Wager," in *Pensées*, translated John Warrington (London: Dent, 1932), Section 343.
<https://www.york.ac.uk/depts/maths/histstat/pascal_wager.pdf>.

Chapter 11: *House of Cards*

Aristotle, *Politics* Book III, Chapters 1–11 (lines 1274b30–1282b12), translated by H. Rackham (Cambridge: Harvard University Press, 1944).
<http://www.perseus.tufts.edu/hopper/text?doc=Perseus:abo:tl g,0086,035:3&lang=original>.

Reinhold Niebuhr, *Moral Man and Immoral Society* (New York: Scribner's, 1931), "Introduction."
<http://media.sabda.org/alkitab-2/Religion-Online .org%20 Books/ Niebuhr,%20Reinhold%20-%20Moral %20Man%20and %20Immor %20Society%20-%20Study% 20in.pdf>.

Plato, *Republic*, Book VIII (555b–562a), translated by Paul Shorey (Cambridge: Harvard University Press, 1935).
<http://www.perseus.tufts.edu/hopper/text?doc=Perseus%3Ate xt%3A1999.01.0168%3Abook%3D8>.

Chapter 12: *Pulp Fiction*

Aristotle, *Poetics*, translated by W. Rhys Roberts (London: Heinemann, 1927), Chapters 7–12 (lines 1450b20–1453 b27).
<http://www.perseus.tufts.edu/hopper/text?doc=Perseus%3Ate xt%3A1999.01.0056%3Asection%3D1450b>.

Henri Bergson, *Creative Evolution*, translated Arthur Mitchell (New York: Holt, 1911), pp. 304–329.
<https://www.gutenberg.org/files/26163/26163-h/26163-h.htm>.

Gilles Deleuze, *Cinema 1*, translated by H. Tomlinson and B. Habberjam (Minneapolis: University of Minnesota Press, 1986), pp. 1–11.
<https://monoskop.org/images/8/80/Deleuze_Gilles_Cinema_1_Movement-Image.pdf>.

Chapter 13: *Inception 1*

Henri Bergson, *Creative Evolution*, translated by Arthur Mitchell (New York: Holt, 1911), pp. 114–19.
<https://www.gutenberg.org/files/26163/26163-h/26163-h.htm>.

Henri Bergson, *Dreams*, translated by E.E. Slosson (New York: Huebsch, 1914), pp. 15–57.
<https://www.gutenberg.org/files/20842/20842-h/20842-h.htm>.

Susanne Langer, *Philosophy in a New Key*, third edition (Cambridge: Harvard University Press, 1957), pp. 144–170 (Chapter VI).
<https://monoskop.org/images/6/6c/Langer_Susanne_K_Philos ophy_in_a_New_Key.pdf>.

Chapter 14: *Inception 2*

Henri Bergson, *An Introduction to Metaphysics*, translated by T.E. Hulme (New York: Putnam, 1911).
<https://ia902703.us.archive.org/19/items/anintroductiont00be rggoog/anintroductiont00berggoog.pdf>.

Chapter 15: *The Twilight Zone*

Umberto Eco, "Untruths, Lies, Falsifications," in *On the Shoulders of Giants*, translated by Alastair McEwen (Cambridge: Harvard University Press, 2019), pp. 170–195 (Chapter 8).

Hans-Georg Gadamer, "The Principle of History of Effect (*Wirkungsgeschichte*)," in *Truth and Method*, second edition, translated by J. Weinsheimer and D.G. Marshall (New York: Crossroad, 1989), pp. 299–306.
<https://mvlindsey.files.wordpress.com/2015/08/truth-and-method-gadamer-2004.pdf>.

Immanuel Kant, *Anthropology from a Pragmatic Point of View*, translated by R.B. Louden (Cambridge: Cambridge University Press, 2006), pp. 225–232.
<https://fdocuments.in/reader/full/immanuel-kant-anthropology-from-a-pragmatic-point-of-view>.

Index

NOTE. I have not listed the occurrence of character names from the principal movies I discuss. The main characters of these movies come in for much discussion in the chapters devoted to their respective movies. Occasionally a character from my principal movies will be mentioned in a chapter not devoted to his/her movie, and in a few cases there is substantive discussion about that character. However, Frank and Claire Underwood from *House of Cards* come up so often in other chapters that I made an exception for them. Otherwise I decided to set this aside and let readers find it on their own. Otherwise, all proper names that occur in the book are here in the index, including the names of characters that come from movies other than my principal movies. I set aside articles (a, as, the, this) and alphabetize from the first major word in the titles of movies and books. There are three rather analytical entries in the index for "me," and "you," and "us." Study of these entries will give you the tone of the book and is a guide to some of the more interesting thoughts that inhabit this volume. For words that have both a philosophical and ordinary sense to them, such as "possibility," "time," "truth," or "understanding," I have erred on the side of inclusion so that readers will be able to survey the occurrence of philosophical ideas throughout the volume by reading the index. For that same reason, there are some unusual entries here, such as me, you, us, and people, which provide an overview of the generalizations made through the volume.